SANTA MONICA PUBLIC LIBRARY

I SMP 00 2463968 N

W9-BDM-211

SANTA MONICA PUBLIC LIBRARY

NOV − − 2015

RECONSTRUCTING STRATEGY

· · · · · · · ·

Dancing with the God of Objectivity

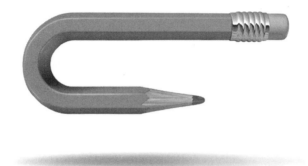

Redefining strategy for the
individual, organisation and country

DR. SAQIB QURESHI

Two Harbors Press
Minneapolis, MN

Copyright © 2015 by Dr. Saqib Qureshi

Two Harbors Press
322 First Avenue N, 5th floor
Minneapolis, MN 55401
612.455.2293
www.TwoHarborsPress.com

All rights reserved. No part of this publication may be reproduced, stored in a retrieval system, or transmitted, in any form or by any means, electronic, mechanical, photocopying, recording, or otherwise, without the prior written permission of the author.

ISBN-13: 978-1-63413-372-2
LCCN: 2015906812

42-15314261 "The earliest strategic frameworks were religions, including Christianity." © Angelo Cavalli/Corbis, reprinted with permission
42-37156228 „Many people consider Rene Descartes's Discours de la méthode of 1637 the first text of modern philosophy." © adoc-photos/Corbis, reprinted with permission
42-25954858 "Immanuel Kant was one of the most important figures in Western philosophy, even if he thought that black people ‚learned like parrots'." © The Print Collector/dpa/Corbis, reprinted with permission
PG9101 "Ibn Sina was amongst many Islamic philosophers who shaped Western philosophy." © Bettmann/CORBIS, reprinted with permission
DWF15-286801 "Phil McGraw, probably the most influential life strategist of our time and a firm advocate of facts and objectivity." © Ted Soqui/Corbis, reprinted with permission
42-24937075 "Steve Jobs: ‚I didn't want to be a father, so I wasn't.'" © ROBERT GALBRAITH/Reuters/Corbis, reprinted with permission
42-28452285 "Ed Husain was briefly attracted to Hizb ut Tahrir, who were amongst the most abusive and active religious groups in Britain in the 1990s." © Peter Marshall / Demotix/Demotix/Corbis, reprinted with permission
42-19418248 "Jan Morris had the courage to change her gender . . . and then later write about the transformation." © Colin McPherson/Corbis, reprinted with permission
U1088169 "Disneyland never saw itself as an amusement park. Its self-identity has always been as a provider of happiness." © Bettmann/CORBIS, reprinted with permission
U87027008 "Homelessness in the 1980s challenged the Port Authority of New York and New Jersey's self-identity." © Bettmann/CORBIS, reprinted with permission
42-23648727 "Gulf-based businesses often embrace two self-identities, each with powerful meanings as a private-sector firm and as a Gulf organization." © Shuli Hallak/Corbis, reprinted with permission
BE044668 "Nehru's rejection of America's self-identity was key to Truman's tilt to Pakistan." © Bettmann/CORBIS, reprinted with permission
HU050369 "The Israeli, British and French attack at Suez was a watershed in Britain's ‚great' self-identity." © Hulton-Deutsch Collection/CORBIS, reprinted with permission
BE069217 "Ayatollah Khomeini's view on Iran's true self-identity dramatically impacted Iranian foreign strategy." © Bettmann/CORBIS, reprinted with permission

Distributed by Itasca Books

Book Design by Sophie Chi

Printed in the United States of America

In memory of Razia Sultana, Wasim Ahmed Sheikh, Adeeba Manzoor and Ghazanfar Adil, amongst the many others whose wonderful, beautiful lives ended far, far too early.

ABOUT THE AUTHOR

———————————————

I'd like to introduce myself in two ways: the first is your normal "this is what I've done and this is what qualifies me to write this book" approach; the second is unconventional but an approach that a) expresses a bit about who I think I am and b) might give you a sense of my take on the "accepted" way of doing things.

So, the mundane stuff first off: I worked at HSBC Investment Bank, McKinsey & Co. and a few entrepreneurial ventures. I also worked on "strategy" for more than a decade in both the public and private sectors and completed my undergraduate degree in International Relations and my PhD in Epistemology, International Relations and Strategy, both at the London School of Economics. Besides that, I once wrote articles for the *Financial Times*.

And here's the less conventional approach: I'm a fan of dunking Rich Tea biscuits in my tea and once in a while I do enjoy a McDonald's Quarter Pounder without cheese. Occasionally, my request to hold back the cheese is ignored, which can annoy me. I also like spicy food, which clearly isn't something you'd get from McDonalds (except in India). Finally, I also think that we know a lot less than we'd like to believe we know . . . a touch of skepticism is not a bad thing. Those are the important and real things.

So that's me, the author. This book, I hope, reflects me in that it is a useful contribution to a fascinating subject but approached with an unconventionally straightforward attitude.

PREFACE

This is a book about strategy—the path that a person or group of people (such as an organisation or country) take to get from where they are today to where they want to be in the future. It's a bit different from most other strategy books. Unlike that largely stale collection, this book isn't filled with pretentious, intoxicating self-certainty. It's not accompanied by some baloney claim to objectivity or truth. This book is also a bit different because it focuses on several strategic genres. It explores strategy in the context of the individual person, organization and country. The book's final distinction is that it rattles off at a sort of Mary Poppins pace. It's punchy, brisk and opinionated. We are all opinionated. We all have opinions. Objectivity is always subjective. But this book doesn't shy away from acknowledging any of that.

It's the combination of being a little unorthodox yet dealing with strategic and intellectual issues which underlies some of the ideas in this book. In essence, I believe a lot of thinking and writing about strategy in all areas of life but specifically in the foreign policy, business and personal arenas is both pedestrian and prosaic. This realisation inspired me to put finger to keyboard. The problem is that so many modern "strategists" in these fields (and we'll touch upon what I mean by the "modern" in the second chapter) have ignored—often through inexcusable ignorance—important advances in other disciplines; more specifically, they have excluded from their theories any reference to the way our self-identity plays a fundamental part in the way we effect strategy.

These ways are powerful, unconventional, motivating and original. Having mulled over strategy during my moderately abstract PhD and then having shaped it while working on daily strategic issues for individual people, organisations and countries, I thought about the absence of a book that placed self-identity at the heart of our understanding of strategy. This book is the outcome.

I would like to thank several people who helped me with this book. First, I thank my wonderful wife, Alia, who supported me as I wrote this book and, more broadly, in the journey of my life. I thank Jonny Ward, Madeeha Zahidi and Wendy Ly for their invaluable research. I also thank Martin Toseland and Jennifer Gehlhar, who helped edit the manuscript, and Brad Sniderman, Lauri Donahue and Matthew Welker, who provided valuable advice on specific parts of the book. I thank several people who reviewed portions of the book and shared their feedback. Those people include Osvaldo Pereira, Masood Razzaq, Darcy Glyn Williams, Ishtiaq Ali Khan, Robert Hine, Farheen Qureshi and Nadia Manzoor. I suppose I ought to mention a sort of thanks to Starbucks because I wrote much of this book while perched in their stores in Unionville and Box Grove, both in Markham. Without their collective help, this book would have come out as real junk.

CHAPTER 1

THE STRATEGIC
PIZZA TOPPING

Strategy

My editor suggested that it'd be breaking the rules if I, as a first-time author, started my first chapter with a long, boring quote, even if that quote directly related to my book's argument. She advised me to start with a paragraph which had some hooks to draw the reader in, to make the reader want to read more. Life, as we all recognize, would be really quite stale if all we did was conform:

> "'Modernity' is an ambiguous, multivalent characterisation of the human condition, indicating structural and ideological transformations of the social setting. Although there is no consensus as to its referent, an adequate specification would have to include both inter-subjective aspects and objective ones. In terms of the commonly accepted historical process, 'modernity' might be used to designate the inter-subjective and objective, structural features, past, present and anticipated future conditions which have heightened the reflexivity of actors in the past two hundred years. The course of modernity is not fixed or determined, for collective decisions of various orders of collectivity do influence the direction, towards or away from some desired states."[1]

One of the reasons modern strategic thinking has stagnated into an outwardly obsessed exercise, one which focuses on everything but the strategist, is that modern thinkers of strategy engage the subject with very ambiguous terms and concepts. It's a bit disturbing because it makes you wonder if when they use those terms they really understand what they're saying or even what's being understood. It's also a good way of confusing ordinary folk, throwing at them concepts that they cannot clearly grasp because . . . in fact, no one can. Equally, using lots of high-powered technical language which collectively means nothing seems to be a great way of impressing experts. Bullshitting, for want of a tidier expression, can get some people surprisingly far in life.

Academics in particular, and not just of strategy, do a pretty good job of dishing out highly ambiguous words. This is a bit counterintuitive, because you'd expect them to know more about whatever it is they're talking about and therefore be a little clearer in their communication. Apparently, the notion that there's genius in simplicity hasn't yet nestled into many parts of modern scholarship. Indeed, if there's one thing that many academics tend to struggle with it is the entire listening-communicating symbiosis. Allowing for exceptions, the senior echelons of the academic circuit are a great place to get confused by jargon.

One term that modern strategists use ambiguously is "strategy." If the term had been used clearly and consistently, the strategy industry might actually have realised that strategy depends on the strategist as much as it does on whatever is being strategized. The industry might have recognised that we need to better understand our self-identity, because strategy is as much about how we *see ourselves* as it is about a world out there, beyond ourselves. That is indeed the essence of my message: one's self-identity as an individual, organisation or country significantly influences one's strategy. Strategy is much more about you than what you've been led to believe thus far by conventional strategists.

So let's explore the clutter of definitions of strategy. While strategy has cerebral and big picture connotations, strategists use "strategy" in sharply different ways. Life strategists, corporate strategists (really should be called organisational strategists since "corporate" is a specific legal entity) and foreign policy strategists not only fail to agree amongst themselves on what strategy is, but they can't agree even within their own smaller silos as to what it means. If that isn't a recipe for pandemonium, I don't know what is. How can one advance, refine or even think about a subject if its practitioners use the core term in dozens of conflicting ways? You can't . . . which is partly the reason why modern strategy is a pretty stagnant space. Lots of micro silos bickering amongst themselves and getting not far in the process.

And that chaos has opened the door to plenty of charlatans who love to abuse the word to puff up their personal credentials. People flock to add "strategy" or "strategic" to their job title just as kids flock to a toy store. "Strategy" is sexy. Consultants suddenly become "strategy consultants," MBA students suddenly become "strategy MBAs," and departments of "odd jobs" suddenly become "Strategy Departments." It's interesting that you'll never come across "tactics consultants," a "tactics MBA student," or a "Tactics Department"— "tactics" doesn't confer a cachet. "Tactics" is not sexy. This fluffing-up of credentials will no doubt continue given the élan that the word "strategy" confers. People use it to make themselves seem much more important than they are, meanwhile strutting around wearing the smart, tailored "strategist" suit.

If I'm going to demonstrate that the self-identity of individuals, organisations and countries influences how each respectively sees the world, their vision for themselves and ultimately their strategy, I need to first get a handle on what the heck strategy means—a point, would you believe, which is lost in most strategy books. Note how organisational strategist Michael Porter's seminal work *Competitive Strategy* altogether skirts around a definition of strategy.[2] The book simply doesn't even try to define the term. Most strategy books, in fact, resist explaining their book's pivotal term, which is a bit convenient because it's much harder to challenge concrete than fluff. However, I need to define strategy in order to show that strategy is as much about oneself as it is about the world beyond the self. Otherwise, we could end up with another exercise in fluff, fluff, fluffety fluff.

One way to get a flavour of strategy's meaning, but not much more, is to revert to its origins. It should come as no surprise that its origin, as is the case of a good chunk of the English language, is Greek. I suppose the origin could have been Latin, which is another big contributor to the English language, but not in this particular case. The Greek word *Strategos* means "general" or "leader," and the term meant "governor general" in the Hellenistic and Byzantine eras.[3] As is self-evident, this really gives us a context but not an explanation of strategy. It doesn't really help us because we don't use "strategy" as a job in itself; but it's nevertheless nice to pick that piece of trivia. You should, though, feel quite free to air that if you need to impress somebody at a party or something. Perhaps use it as a chat-up line to break the ice if nothing else comes to mind?

One person to turn to in our quest for understanding what strategy means is Henry Mintzberg, a rare, thoughtful business academic who outlined no fewer than five definitions of strategy.[4] He's Canadian, so let me just plug that for my Canadian wife and friends. Business academia has perhaps tried to delve into the strategy exercise or function more than have academics of either foreign policy or personal individual strategy, so it's no surprise that we go to a business academic. Mintzberg offers several definitions of strategy. The first and perhaps the most popular is as a plan, guide or course of action to get from points A to B. This definition answers the question,

How will we get from where we are, to where we want to be? In this sense, strategy is a path or route to success. This is possibly the most preferred interpretation amongst strategy professionals, whether in life, organisational or foreign policy strategy. It's also simple, aligns with how people often use the word and works for all three genres of strategy which I explore.[5]

McKinsey & Co, the management consultants who are often misnamed "strategy consultants," nuance this approach. They define strategy as an "integrated set of actions" to achieve pre-defined objectives. It's a spin that I don't actually agree with. Strategy doesn't need to be a *set* of actions. There's no reason why a single action in itself couldn't also be a strategy—an action to achieve an objective—even if it may lack a few grandiose bells, whistles and slick presentations. In any case, a single action can itself be reinterpreted as many mini actions and vice versa, which renders the "integrated set" embellishment somewhat meaningless. To cut them some slack, all consultants have this bad habit of dressing things up just a touch, so let's not be miserable and nasty . . . for now.

A second interpretation of strategy highlighted by Mintzberg is: a deliberate set of actions which are not specified at the outset but from which retrospectively one can detect a pattern or arrangement.[6] In this approach, strategy isn't planned—it merely explains what and how key decisions were made and how a country, organisation or individual tried to achieve its objectives. Despite Mintzberg distinguishing this definition, which he called "unrealised" strategy, from the first interpretation, which he called "realised" strategy, the difference between the two doesn't matter much to me.[7] The first sees strategy as a planned exercise getting from a starting point today to an end game in the future, whereas the second isn't officially laid out or acknowledged but still gets an individual, organisation or country from the start to end points. Both definitions involve getting from a start today to an end in the future; and most living strategies are really a hybrid of realised and unrealised strategies.

A third interpretation of strategy which Mintzberg offered is: a position in the market—how a product compares against a competitor product.[8] It's hard to reject meanings because words are social constructs which aren't enshrined in a linguistic version of the Ten Commandments. There simply is no final authority on what a word means. That said, I don't like this "position in the market" take on strategy for three reasons. First, it bears no relationship to the word's etymology, which is a small point, but still. Second, I doubt most people understand strategy in this way. I'm only guesstimating because I've not interviewed *most* people, in case you're wondering. Finally, I can't make sense of strategy as a "position in the market" in life or foreign policy strategy. So, this meaning goes out the window.

A fourth definition proposed by Mintzberg is: strategy as a way of doing things—a series of tactical and cultural nuances that come together to give an advantage which rivals would struggle to copy and paste even if they understood the details of what was happening.[9] The advantages of clever ways of doing things are documented in several organisations—such as Dell, Google and Apple—and it is plausible that clever ways of doing things can be part of a strategy. To illustrate my point, Dell revolutionised the PC industry by offering to customers an online sales platform which allowed them to cut out the retailer, configure their PC needs and then allow Dell to build on specification and order, as opposed to the "sitting on shelves" preconfigured units by competitors.[10] Dell's way of doing things was a success.

This, though, doesn't feel like strategy. It feels like something very different. In fact, this fourth definition feels like a hybrid of business marketing, operations and organisation. It answers the question, How do you design, build, deliver and sell your product most effectively?

Dell nailed that in the late 1980s and 1990s. Clearly, a strategy can include smart ways of doing things, but I think that strategy extends further than that. For a start, the way I think of strategy engages the question of the organisation's long-term direction and health. It's a bigger picture piece with broader horizons. Besides, this fourth definition, again, doesn't really work in the foreign policy or personal life strategy spaces. It's alien in those genres of strategy. So again, I am throwing this meaning overboard.

Finally, Mintzberg offers a fifth definition for strategy: a plan to get the better of the competition or even to defeat it.[11] The idea being that strategy is all about beating the rival, as might be between Coca-Cola and Pepsi. This, however, is uncomfortably close to the first interpretation of strategy, only that the first interpretation has broader goals: The first asked the question, How will we get from where we are to where we want to be? This, the fifth definition, merely nuances that to: How will we get from where we are *with respect to the competitor* to where we want to be *with respect to the competitor*? In the very, very big world of subtle distinctions there is very, very little between the first and fifth definitions. Indeed, I think the fifth definition is merely a subset of the first. And what if we had a universe in which there was no competition? Many state-owned monopolies have strategies even though they have no meaningful competition for customers, talent or much else.

In our journey to understand strategy, Olaf Rughase, a business academic and consultant (a hybrid group which generally seems remarkably able to advise, yet ironically unable to itself do) offered an acrobatic twist worthy of any Olympic gymnast. Rughase wasn't a gymnast. I was using a metaphor. Anyhow, he suggested that strategy is "the way in which an organization will achieve deliberately chosen competitive advantages."[12] I don't like his stress on "organisation" or "competitive advantages" as being inherent aspects of all strategy for three reasons. (All management consultants get schooled on the importance of lists of three; and a decade on from my consulting days, I'm still struggling to shake off that part of my past, so please bear with me. It's a really tough habit to kick. Perhaps somebody could think about an Alcoholics Anonymous equivalent for it?)

The first is that strategy isn't just for organisations. Strategy is also an exercise for countries and individuals. Countries have foreign policy strategies, some of them vague while others disciplined. Entrepreneurs have strategies, as do individual ordinary folk. That said, I accept that Rughase was writing in a business context, so let's not make a song and dance about this point. Second, it's possible to have a strategy in essentially a noncompetitive environment. As I've touched upon, many countries offer electricity or water through monopolies which have organisational strategies, though I don't need at this point to go into how bad the service levels of many monopolies are. By that I mean that often the electricity supply is sporadic and the water is undrinkable. Finally, I don't think a strategy is about delivering "competitive advantages," a point which deserves elaboration.

A strategy, I think, is about getting from where you are today to where you want to get to sometime in the future. For an organisation, this might be higher shareholder returns (the fundamental reason why Anglo-American businesses exist) or expanding into new countries. These objectives are *irrespective* of any secured competitive advantages. In fact, many organisations have historically sought *not* to secure competitive advantages but have instead preferred to maintain a status quo with competitors; OPEC is as good an example as any. In such instances organisations have elected not to seek competitive advantages. British Airways, Sainsbury's and Apple have all in recent years confronted allegations of price-fixing, which leans in that same uncompetitive direction.

Having gone over some of the options to answer the question "What is strategy?", the option I feel most comfortable with happens to be the simplest. There's a lot to be said for keeping things simple in life. There's also that acronym KISS, which stands for "Keep It Simple, Stupid." Strategy is the path that a person or group of people take to get from where they are today to where they want to be in the future. This includes both top-down, consciously planned approaches as well as approaches which emerged without any deliberate detailing or thought, because, in reality, I think that most strategy is a blend of the two. And because of that, I don't see a huge difference between planned and unplanned strategy. I somehow straddle the first and second definitions which Mintzberg offered.

The Strategic Process

Within this definition of strategy, I see three critical steps to the process. That list of three strikes again. It's important to surface the steps now because they have a substantial impact later in the book. The first step in strategy is making sense of how things are today, understanding what is going on and where things stand. The second step is creating a vision or objective for the future, however vague or intangible. Finally, the third step of the strategic process is getting from where one is today to that vision or objective, which really shouldn't be a surprise. Each of these three steps, being what I collectively call the strategic process, is influenced as much by the world out there as it is by how the individual, organisation or country sees itself, meaning its self-identity.

And now it might be easier to see why it was important for me to earlier flesh out what I mean by "strategy." The point that emerged from my clarifying strategy is the importance of the start and end points which a strategy should bridge. A strategy has a start. A strategy also has an end. Modern strategists neglect these two locations because too often they don't get a handle on what strategy is in the first place. I suppose that being brutally pedantic, while understanding where one is today and where one wants to get to are both critical to strategy, I accept that neither is itself the strategy. If it's helpful, think about strategy as a bridge between the start and end of a journey. Yes, the start and end points are important, but strictly speaking they're not the bridge, they're not the strategy. Nevertheless, once these start and end points are set and detailed, the strategic options or paths become highly restricted. This is why I think that the start and end points are so important in a strategy.

Clarifying strategy in the way that I have then allows me to stress the importance of how we—as individuals, organisations or countries—*see* and *make sense of* both the start and end points of a strategic journey. Having stressed the start and end points of strategy, I now stress the importance of how we cognate those points. It's a theme I will hammer home, again and annoyingly again, through this book. Cognition influences the entire strategic process and that cognition is in turn influenced by our self-identities. I'll be hammering home that too! Besides depending on an external world out there, our strategies therefore depend on how we make sense of things. And our making sense of the world, or our cognition, itself depends on our self-identities. I don't want to sound predictable as early as this, but yes, I hammer that point too. Lots of hammering in this paragraph, hammer, hammer, hammer. Yawn if you need to. I won't take offence.

A fundamental mistake of modern strategy is its failure to recognise the influence of the strategist himself on the strategy. Modern strategy insists that strategy is an exercise wholly "out there" and has nothing to do with how the strategist sees or makes sense of things. In contrast, if we integrate the view that self-identity is an inescapable lens which helps make sense of our current situation, influences our portrayal of what kind of future we are aspiring to and also sways how we get to the Promised Land, we bring strategy back to a more meaningful place in our lives. We tie our strategy to ourselves. And we detach it from some foreign, abstract set of rules and procedures drummed up by an ivory tower academician or smartly suited consultant living thousands of miles away who has no understanding of who we are let alone the local social, cultural or epistemological framework of where we operate. Our strategy can suddenly mean something. It's suddenly coming from within.

The Different Types of Strategic Thought

Having explained what I think strategy is, I now want to give a flavour of three big modern strategic genres, each of which ignore the role of human cognition and self-identity's influence on the strategic process. Most people, again not that I've interviewed them all, might think of strategy in a business context. After I've engaged the seven or so billion people on our planet through their seven or so thousand languages, I'll be in a better position to confirm this—but for now, let's accept my assertion that strategy today has strong business and organisation connotations. If you need a "fact" to hang my assertion on, the vast majority of books on strategy that are for sale on Amazon.com sit in the business, management, investment or economics sections. They are not to be found on either the personal life strategy or foreign policy strategy "shelves."

1. Life Strategy

One thing that surprised me in my researching this book was learning that organisational strategy is the new strategy kid on the block with a history which goes back only five decades. If I brought back memories of the American boy band from the 1980s, I apologise because that wasn't my intention. Despite being the dominant genre of strategy, organisational strategy is also the most recent of the three which I look at. In contrast, the histories of life and foreign policy strategies extend to millennia.[i] When I started my research, I'd assumed that life strategy was the most recent of three genres—something that perhaps began alongside the MTV revolution. Life strategy, including life mentoring and coaching under its supporting canopy, certainly feels like it is one of those fad concepts dreamt up for American TV.[ii] However, life strategy has formally been around since at least 1937. At the very least, it's older than organisational strategy, which is very much a post-World War II product.[13]

A second surprise in my research was realizing that many of the world's great religions are themselves, in fact, life strategies. This extends life strategy's origins by thousands of years. All religions provide answers to life's key questions: "How do I make sense of the world?" "Where should my life go?" "How should I get there?"[14] These are the core questions which any individual's strategic process must engage. That all great religions have, at a high level, similar sets of answers is somewhat interesting. The packaging might not be similar but the contents often are. Now I've said that, I only hope that I'm not confronted by legions of religious mandarins sternly shaking their heads at my suggestion that their outwardly different religions are actually inwardly quite similar. My opinion on this is just the sort of thing that knocks out their social authority and destabilises their self-identity.

Even if it sounds pretty obvious, religion wasn't the first thing that

---

i   Military strategy, a genre which this book does not cover, extends at least to around the sixth century BC in the work of Sun Tzu (otherwise known as Sun Wu).

ii   Jennifer Wright's distinction that mentoring involves a hierarchical expert-novice relationship while coaching is about capacity building ("Workplace coaching: What's it all about?" in *WORK: A Journal for Prevention, Assessment and Rehabilitation*) is an insightful push-back to the conventional use of "life strategy."

went through my mind when I started brainstorming life strategy. Certainly, it's rarely featured in any strategy-type conversation that I've come across. In fact, I think the only discussions I've had which have included the words "religion" and "strategy" are very specifically military and often in the context of war. I am thinking of the Middle East with its myriad of religious militants, both state and nonstate actors, who are pursuing whatever daft agenda they have. I suppose I had also come across religions as sources of identity which in turn influence human cognition and then the strategic process. However, I hadn't till recently seen religions as strategic frameworks in themselves. Call me a plod if you must, but I'd like to see it as one of those "learn a new thing every day" moments. Religions, with some rare exceptions, are strategies to engage life.

Let's take a random example—as random, perhaps, as the "random" interview of travelling Muslims at American airports. Islam offers to its 1.6 billion followers a life strategy which is enshrined in the Qur'an, revealed by God to the prophet Mohammed over twenty-three years, starting in 610. The Qur'an is supported by several sources of guidance, interpretations and edicts which were crystallised after the Qur'an asserts that the religion was completed. The sum of all these parts is now known as the Sharia ("the way," Islam's code of conduct). For now, I will ignore the door that I have just opened up . . . after I make one last point on it. If the Qur'an asserts in 632 that the religion was complete, what exactly is the legitimacy of the stuff that came afterwards? What's all that then, an example of "double complete"? Or simply a bunch of stuff driven by another less than pious agenda?

Putting that prickly bucket of issues aside, it is the Sharia which acts as a Muslim's strategic framework, encapsulating the three key steps of the strategic process. The Sharia explains to Muslims how to make sense of the world of today, the starting point of the strategic journey. How does it do that? What are the implications of "speaking as a Muslim" on how one sees the world? One cognitive filter through which Muslims make sense of the world is the distinction between God and mankind. The Sharia demands a very tight distinction between the two. Another filter is between good and evil, which permeates the Muslim's cognitive framework. That's the ideal scenario anyhow. There's also the distinction between Muslim and non-Muslim people and lands, a division which arguably became more pronounced after the death of Mohammed.

The Sharia also, indeed, sets mankind's objective, the strategic end point or vision. One great irony of our times is that Islam translates from Arabic as "peace" (not "craziness," which is how it's sometimes portrayed as and occasionally practised). I don't want to go there, back into the parenthesis any further than I have even if I've left the door a little open yet again. Except, I want to stress one last thing, that craziness isn't part of Islam's end vision. There's nothing in the faith about being a nutcase. The Sharia does speak to the second piece of the strategic process, by repeatedly reminding its followers that their objective or vision is to reach heaven in the afterlife. The blunt aim, according to Sharia, is to get into heaven by worshipping God and being a nice dude during one's more mundane, earthly existence.

As a side note, I still remember asking my Islamic studies teacher when I was six years old if there'd be a McDonald's in the afterlife and was quite pleased when he said there would be. He then tried selling me on burgers made of partridges, which I had no interest in despite their apparent prevalence in heaven. Who the heck eats partridge burgers? And another thing, I've yet to find how he knew what kind of burgers were floating around in heaven; I clearly wasn't interested in them. I only cared for my two regular hamburgers (without pickle), french fries and chocolate shake and—like he had said—I could get them in heaven; so it was all good. All grown up now, I'm at peace with the pickle, sometimes pinching it from my children's burgers. Just so you know for reference and I have already mentioned this before, I now eat Quarter Pounders . . . without cheese, repeat: without.

With a framework in place to understand both the world and a vision ahead, the Sharia then lays out a strategy, being a set of rules and principles to follow, in order to succeed. The Qur'an outlines some foods which Muslims can and can't consume, some rules of family life and relationships (including marriage, divorce and inheritance) and some rules of society, the economy and military conduct. The folk at the Islamic State clearly need a massive refresher, especially in the latter. These principles then get a practical coating amongst other things from the other sources of the Sharia, specifically the Hadith; a source that I happen to think isn't as essential as orthodoxy suggests. Still, the idea being that if you tick these boxes in the conduct of your life and you believe in one and only one God, you get a good report card for the Day of Judgement, which allows you into heaven.

Islam's life strategy or how you go about getting to a heaven (with or without the Golden Arches) touches on much of life but it doesn't cover every aspect of it, which is what many Muslims love to claim. For instance, it doesn't cover my gym workout or how to teach my kids—important aspects of my monotone existence. More seriously, it doesn't give specific tactics to teach children or how to deal with the boss. Some Muslim clergymen and some parts of the Muslim world live in self-denial on this issue because Islam not only has a clergy but it's powerful and swampy, gets carried away with overly detailed and restrictive interpretations of Islam and pretends that Islam has a direct intervention point on absolutely everything. It's good to just flag that it doesn't. And how could it, given that the Sharia was essentially codified in the eleventh century, a pre-Facebook era which is increasingly alien to us today?

Another religion which offers a life strategy is Christianity, which with about 2.2 billion followers is the world's most popular religion.

Beginning as a Jewish sect, Christianity now has several hundred denominations, of which the Roman (Latin) Catholic Church remains the largest with 1.15 billion followers. Of these a fifth live in Brazil and Mexico alone; and, surprisingly, more than 600,000 live in Saudi Arabia of all places, representing more than 2 percent of the country's population! This, I can tell you, was news to me. Christianity relies on the Bible, which is divided into the Old and New Testaments, to guide the Christian life strategy. This geared to the goal of eternal salvation in the afterlife—a whole lot better place than its alternative, being eternal damnation. You don't need to be a genius to prioritise one over the other.

Whereas I think Islam's scriptures are boggy because they run into triple digits and many of them emerged oddly enough after the religion was completed, Christianity's core text has its own problems. For a start, it has many competing versions—including the Septuagint, Peshitta and King James—in hundreds of different languages, with varying filters of political correctness. And then we have issues around Biblical claims such as the universe consisting of a flat earth with planets revolving around it—not the sort of mistake you'd expect from God's Revelation. Another problem is that the oldest known Bible dates to three centuries *after* Jesus's life. That's like the first book on the Great Northern War of 1700–1721 between Russia and Sweden being assembled today! There's a lot of scope to forget, ignore or even to invent during that kind of timeframe. And that doesn't even speak to the point that the third century didn't have our access to information in the IT age.

All that, though, doesn't detract from Christianity being a life strategy; these points about the Bible are just interesting froth, again lest you want to impress people at parties. Christianity's cognition of the world today, the framework through which Christians are taught to make sense of the world, is both similar and different to the framework deployed by Islam. Using the forty-six books of the Old Testament and twenty-seven books of the New Testament, Christianity's sacred Scripture asks its followers to make sense of the world through multiple filters, one of which is good and evil. Christianity also employs a gender filter. It's no coincidence that Jesus was the *Son* of God and that we've never seen a female Pope. Despite those similarities with Islam, Christianity does differ from Islam in understanding the world as it is. Catholicism sees a world of original sin, the idea that we are all born sinful as we enter the world. There's also the Trinity, the notion that one God consists of three entities, a division that Islam does not see.

Interestingly, neither women nor Jews come out especially well from the Roman Catholic Church. The first group is intermittently blamed for tempting mankind out of Eden, while the second group is also intermittently blamed for helping to kill the Son of God. Mind you, there's the full-bodied argument made by today's women and Jews that neither Eve nor the Jews who brought Jesus to Pontius Pilate represent all women or all Jews, that these ancestors were acting independently and unrepresentative of their descendants, that collective guilt is simply wrong. That they even have to make this case is pretty damning. Mind you, there's lots of collective guilt floating around in Palestine and Israel today—each side loves to allocate collective guilt to the other. All of this is an inflamed war zone which I don't feel especially compelled to enter even if, again, I left the door slightly ajar, which seems to be an emerging but annoying pattern of mine.

Christianity's good life, the strategy for a Christian to get from how he sees the world today to getting into heaven in the future, involves distinguishing between venial sins, being those sins which are forgivable, and mortal sins, which are harmful to the soul and unforgivable.[15] As you'd expect, the seriousness of the sin and one's intentions go some way to classify sins. So there's a sensible catch in Christianity: don't expect to embrace Jesus and his suffering as a means to getting away with murder, adultery or blowing up innocent civilians through drone attacks in the name of "collateral damage," "shock and awe" or whatever else. It doesn't quite work that way. Catholicism also stresses the importance of being good and kind through seven "corporal works of mercy" (such as feeding the hungry) and seven "spiritual works of mercy" (such as praying for the living and dead).[16]

However, unlike strategy in Islam, strategy in Christianity demands embracing Christ's suffering at his crucifixion and thereby earning the opportunity for forgiveness. In contrast, Islam doesn't demand the same worship of Jesus or for that matter Mohammed, both highly venerated and respected prophets. In fact, Islam deeply frowns upon any associations with God. The Catholic Church simply does not allow for a strategy to heaven which does not also embrace Christ's suffering, a hurdle which makes the crucifixion and resurrection so important to Catholic Christians. That said, embracing the suffering of Jesus is necessary but by itself insufficient as a strategy for the good life—you've also got to do the right things while you're living in flesh and bones.

Fast-forwarding to more contemporary times, today's trendy life strategy industry is merely a resurrection (no pun intended of course) of an industry which has been around for thousands of years. The industry has sharply evolved though. Back in the day, imams and priests pushed life strategies. Today, these guys are often so frightening that they effortlessly scare little children. Some religious folk look as if they are all-year Halloween participants. The last imam who came to our doorstep, with deep, heavy eyes, stained teeth and a wild, unkempt, all-over-the-face beard freaked out my little two-year-old so much that he clutched onto me out of fear, digging his nails right into my skin. The poor kid practically froze. Only God knows how these same guys (and they seem to always be guys and not gals) influence people in the modern world.

Today, many modern life strategists are armed with far superior social and emotional intelligence skills as well as more sophisticated listening and communication techniques than any clergy. Life coaches are often slick and clean-shaven and can have delightful conversations over tea and scones. Legions of them know their Starbucks nuances and can blog away on their iPads for hours on end. Their clothes actually fit and they don't sell on the basis of otherwise eternal damnation which is a really unattractive way to market a philosophy or way of life. The "do this or you'll suffer in hell" doesn't do much to inspire. It's frankly a little off-putting. Most importantly, modern life strategists can empathise and relate to other folk. They can help strategise without being judgemental. Little wonder that they've blossomed since Carl Rogers's landmark book *Client Centered Therapy* in 1951.[17]

In fact, the life strategy industry has grown sharply in recent years. To illustrate my point, in the academic literature, there were only twenty-six citations of life coaching or life strategy between 1935 and 1984, one every couple of years. Clearly life strategy was then very marginalised. In contrast, between 2005 and 2008 there were no less than 214 citations, which represents a massive explosion![18] Today, thousands of life strategists and coaches operate from New York to Hong Kong, from Istanbul to São Paulo, helping people to make sense of their lives, become better employees or simply refocus on the important things in life.[19] Some estimates put the contemporary life strategy industry's value at more than a billion dollars, which feels a bit conservative.[20]

2. Foreign Policy Strategy

Just as is the case for life strategy, strategy in foreign policy, by which I mean the decisions in running a government's or a state's foreign affairs, also has a history which extends millennia.[iii] In the spirit of disclosure, I'll let you in on a secret. I do so on condition that you don't share it, if you can believe that. Despite having studied politics for more than two decades and having worked on different facets of strategy for more than a decade, I'd like to confess that I struggled with clarifying the meaning of "foreign policy strategy." I'm big enough to admit I simply couldn't get my head around what it meant, which felt a tad surreal. I have the shoulders to admit it. Compounding my problem, I daren't ask anybody out of embarrassment. Part of my difficulty was that a sound meaning of foreign policy strategy needed to work for historic as well as current governments and not just one type of government in one era.

Troubled, I rushed for the cover of first principles. I want you to now imagine a small deer running to the forest when it starts to thunder. That's how I felt. I'm a big guy at more than six feet but that's not how I felt. Anyhow, if politics is about running a government or a state, then foreign policy strategy must be about how to run a government or a state to achieve some vision or objectives in the context of foreign affairs. Within this universe, foreign policy strategy must include public policy as well as politicking; it must include the substantive, colourless and cerebral task of managing and delivering on state or government objectives as well as the sniping, communication, miscommunication, positioning, selective amnesia and propaganda which we expect from politicians. I was going to

---

iii The word "politics" comes from the Greek word *politika*, based on Aristotle's *Affairs of the City*, the name of his book on governing and governments, which was translated into English in the fifteenth century as the Latinised *Polettiques*.

be harsher but don't see the point in reminding everybody of what we think of politicians in general. I could go on to argue that the declining voter turnout (as a proportion of population) in practically every major Western country for the past few decades reflects our lack of trust in politicians, but what's the point?

I find it strangely easy at this juncture to meander into Peter Mandelson, the British former cabinet minister who was key to the creation of New Labour. Despite his success as a master of spin in the Labour cabinet, I thought his autobiography was surprisingly unconvincing and unimpressive.[21] For somebody who spun Labour into government, I had expected a bit more from his autobiography. Odd how the human mind can jump around . . . at least how my mind does. Anyhow, some people will differ with my approach to foreign policy strategy, but given my earlier interpretations of both strategy and politics, I'm comfortable with interpreting foreign policy strategy as the public policies and politicking by a government to get it from where it is today to achieve a set of objectives or a vision, again however vaguely or opaquely defined, in its foreign affairs.[iv]

One of the earliest political strategy books was the *Arthashastra*, written between the fourth and second centuries BCE in what is today India (with that title, where else could it have been written?).[22] Not only is the century of publication unclear but scholars can't work out if it was written by one, two or three people—the candidates being Kautilya, Vishnugupta and Chanakya. That said, the uncertainty surrounding the book's origins takes nothing away from its groundbreaking nature. Detailing what it takes to be a *rajarshi* (a wise king), the book covers a range of government activities including economic policy, military strategy, social welfare

---

iv   I don't buy the argument that political strategy is merely the title of Martin Wight's famous book in 1979, *Power Politics*. Power politics is simply one perspective, amongst many, on the *nature* of politics.

and social policy (including social ethics), the law and bureaucracy. The book was influential till the twelfth century before resurfacing in the West in the early twentieth century.[23] It's no longer influential today, lest you think that G8 leaders have it at their bedsides. It's resurfaced as something of a political relic.

I had a few takeaways from the book. First, that it gets a bit carried away when it dictates to the king how to spend each ninety-minute period of the day. It's a bit too micromanaged. For instance, the book recommends that the king should receive reports on revenues, costs and defence during the day's first ninety minutes, without fail. Another thought was that parts of the book are plain nasty—the use of children as assassins, when to kill one's son and how to protect oneself from one's wife are all engaged as if referring to some mundane matter such as cracking an egg, which I can do without letting a piece of shell drop. My final thought and to amplify Max Weber's point, was that the *Arthashastra* was an earlier, "bigger and badder" version of Niccolò Machiavelli's *Il Principe* ("The Prince").[24] As such, it's one of the first clear expositions of the dominant school of political strategy known as political realism . . . which as it happens rarely invokes the book.

From political strategy's earliest days, political realism has dominated foreign policy strategy, including recently through the works of Reinhold Niebuhr (*Moral Man and Immoral Society*) and Hans Morgenthau (*Politics Among Nations*). Such has been realism's command that it now permeates most media and political discussion through its proxy terms, national interest and self-interest. The starting point for realists is to see the world through power—essentially countries with or without power as well as actions to maximise or protect power. For centuries, realists have insisted that all other objectives are either means to more power, factors of production of power or mere cosmetics. Moral considerations are irrelevant to the realist, an argument which Machiavelli advocated in public policy and became infamous for.

However, beyond sharing the "do whatever it takes" and "the ends justifies the means" approach to government, the actual strategies offered by each political realist don't have that much in common. Over the centuries, the "how" to get from where you are to where you want to be has not been consistent. That's not startling because while the way to make sense of the world and the objective of maximising power have both been consistent for realists, the landscape, tools and dynamics have changed with the times. Morgenthau wrote his book in the Cold War during an era of rapid globalisation and nuclear weapons. In contrast, Machiavelli's work was written in the early sixteenth century in the context of early modern Italian city-states. You'd thus expect the strategies to change.

3. Organisational Strategy

The last strategic genre that I delve into is organisational strategy, which has also broadly failed to recognise strategy is as much about how we see ourselves as it is about an external world. Organisational strategy's origin is tightly focused, specifically on the American East Coast in the 1960s. The world beyond North America has continued to be broadly mute in this space, which makes me wonder if the seriousness that Americans gave to studying their businesses and organisations actually helped the phenomenal success of corporate America. Even to this day some fifty years on, organisational strategy is dominated by Americans . . . though curiously a fair chunk of top organisational strategy academics floating around on American business school campuses seem to have long, multi-syllable Indian-sounding names.

Organisational strategy has itself been dominated by business academics, a group category which seems in itself slightly tongue-in-cheek given that businesses are about getting things done without thinking too much while academics are about thinking a lot while getting not very much done. Mind you, only a very limited spectrum of the business community gives business academia any importance whatsoever . . . after all, why learn to drive from somebody who has himself never driven or probably can't even drive? Back to cue . . . organisational strategy began life in business schools when academics became more outwardly focused, looking beyond the internal aspects of an organisation and more at the long-term organisation-wide perspective.[25]

Pioneers of organisational strategy such as Kenneth Andrews, Alfred Chandler and Igor Ansoff began analysing the management of a firm as a single, whole entity, from the perspective of top management. It might surprise you but this had never happened before despite businesses, being groups of people working together for commercial purposes and economic gain, having been around at least since ancient Roman times. No worries if it surprised you, because it definitely surprised me. We've even had the corporate legal structure for some seven centuries. To their credit, it took Chandler, who wrote *Strategy and Structure* in 1962, Andrews, who wrote *The Concept of Corporate Strategy* in 1971, and several of their American peers to pioneer and kick-start organisational strategy.[26]

A historian, Chandler saw strategy's purpose as the long-term health of the organisation and not the analysis of the latest monthly management accounts. Most people in management consulting and in strategic planning departments will appreciate the breadth and simplicity of his definition of strategy:

> Determination of the basic long-term goals and objectives of an enterprise and the adoption of courses of action and the allocation of resources necessary for carrying out those goals.[27]

Andrews and Chandler came from the most influential organisational strategy approach, referred by Mintzberg, Bruce

Ahlstrand and Joseph Lampel, who categorised no less than ten business strategy schools as the Design School.[28] Though this approach reached its popularity amongst academics in the late 1970s and early 1980s, given its later use by business schools, management consultants and strategic planners, it's still the most influential organisational strategy school of the lot.[29] The school argues that the strategist must first understand the organisation's external threats and opportunities, as well as its internal strengths and weaknesses. With this understanding in place, the organization then needs to create and implement strategic options. Of course, the academics don't discuss how to do that last piece.

Another approach, the so-called Planning School, embraces Igor Ansoff as its founder. In 1965, his book *Corporate Strategy* defined strategy as the decisions which relate to a firm's engagement of its big picture environment including its product and market, in contrast to more menial and recurring policy, programmes and procedures. Ansoff emphasised numbers, cascading objectives, analysis and process. While this school influenced management thinking considerably in the late 1970s, it's since had only limited influence because it was considered too academic . . . by the academic community.[30] If you pause and think about that for just a moment, that sounds like a really heavy punch in the gut to take . . . it's a double whammy . . . too academic for academics!

A final influential approach, the Positioning School, comes from Michael Porter, whose *Competitive Strategy*, published in 1980, remains a popular book for management consultants.[v] He in fact used to be one such consultant. Porter distinguished himself from the Planning and Design Schools on two fronts. First, he crafted a laundry

---

v   Henry Mintzberg, et al., discuss seven other schools of corporate strategy. I have not included them here because the three reviewed schools remain the most dominant approaches to business strategy.

list to be checked off to help the strategist navigate the organisation. In other words, he simplified and broke down the conceptual strategic take-aways into simple, actionable steps. So lengthy is the laundry list that, I think, it practically transforms the strategist into a glorified numbskull bean counter. The second distinction was, Porter argued, that the right strategy was one which could be defended against competitors. Competition thus became central to his treatment of strategy. With this focus, he developed the famous "5 Forces" model which helps assess an industry's competitiveness. This school is tailor-made for consultants:

> They can arrive cold, with no particular knowledge of a business, analyze the data, juggle a set of generic strategies (building blocks) on a chart, write a report, drop an invoice and leave.[31]

Modern Strategy—Differences and Similarities

Having rummaged briefly through the three genres of life, foreign policy and organisational strategy, you might think they have little or, in fact, nothing in common. In some respects, I'd agree with that. Organisational strategy developed in a narrow American geography from the 1960s to 1980s, before being exported with MBA graduates and the emergence of business schools to Europe and beyond. This contrasts with both life and foreign policy strategy, which developed over a much longer time period across multiple countries. Islam's life strategy, for example, developed over four centuries across many empires. And while organisational strategy quickly splintered into schools and camps, both life and foreign policy strategy branched out more slowly. In short, the three genres developed at different rates and in diverse geographies.

Another difference amongst the three genres is that the pioneers of foreign policy and organisational strategy had little experience of owning and executing their strategies. The author(s) of Arthashastra wrote as an adviser(s), as did Machiavelli. Neither implemented strategy. Andrews, Chandler and Ansoff were principally academics, a community that is not known for implementation. To this day, academic consultants, most of whom have skeletal experience of executing strategy but plenty of expertise in advising others how to do it, dominate the organisational strategy industry. It's a pretty cool party trick, I think, to tell others what to do without having a track record in doing it yourself. Anyhow, Andrews, Chandler and Ansoff— and most of the platoon of strategy academics since—have had very little experience of driving strategy.

In contrast, many life strategists lived and owned their strategies. Jesus and Mohammed lived the strategies which they preached, as did Krishna, Guru Nanak and Moses. They didn't prance about advising people what to do for an exorbitant consulting fee plus ridiculous "out of pocket" expenses. Their impressive followerships, moreover, partly stem from the alignment between what they preached and how they lived. They didn't just talk the talk; they walked the walk—even if that "talk" and "walk" are today often twisted by the lunatic fringe elements of their religions. When one lady regularly dumped filth and rubbish on Mohammed, he equally regularly ignored her. He didn't declare war on her. He didn't accuse her of blasphemy. And when she was ill, he actually visited her to wish her a good recovery.[32] He didn't see her situation as an opportunity to kill her, her entire family and the dogs and cats in the vicinity.

Though the three genres of strategy do have differences, a deeper dive into the development of life, foreign policy and organisational strategies reveals at least one critical commonality. Each genre of strategy either evolved in or was fundamentally reshaped by the modern philosophical era. And that era was marked by the ascendency of certain methodological and epistemological assumptions which emerged in Europe. Modern philosophy's assumptions have, in fact, influenced most human learning in the West since the seventeenth century. Given the West's subsequent imperialism over much of the world, modern philosophy has thus influenced most human learning in the past few centuries—full stop. And it is modern philosophy's assumptions that are common now to all three genres of strategy. The failure of modern strategy, which I will seek to demonstrate, is in fact a failure of modern philosophy's assumptions . . . which I will also seek to demonstrate.

It is this common piece that opens modern strategy, across all its genres, to the allegation that its intellectual foundations are anaemic and wishy-washy. Modern strategy uncritically and unconsciously embraced modern philosophy's epistemological and methodological assumptions. As a result, modern strategy today ignores the impact of how we see ourselves or how each of us see the world today, how we craft our vision or objectives for the future and how we get from where we are to where we want to be. Modern strategy is now largely oblivious to the role of human cognition in each step of the strategic process. And that means that modern strategists are just as oblivious to recognising that our strategy, whether we stand from the vantage point of an individual, organisation or country, is deeply integrated with how we see ourselves, meaning our self-identity.

You might mull that around and even push back that organisational strategy began not in Europe but America, and thus it wasn't impacted by modern philosophical assumptions or the modern era. But in this tussle, I would push back still further and for now, unfortunately, I get to have the final say. If you reviewed this book online, you could then of course have the final, final say. While Americans love to view themselves, as do many other people, as unique, there has been nothing unique about their reliance on Europe's modernist methodological and epistemological assumptions. Notwithstanding the subtle differences between continental and analytical philosophy, modern American philosophy is principally an extension of European philosophy, especially with respect to its philosophical assumptions.[33] Empiricism, modern philosophy's dominant epistemology, is as welcome in North America as it is in Europe. It's not subject to any obtrusive "random" airport security measures.

American society has embraced, in much the same way as has European society, modern philosophical assumptions. Empiricism, including empirical evidence, facts and objectivity, is worshipped in America. So though organisational strategy emerged in America, it did so in the modern philosophical framework which Europe developed and exported.[34] In fact, right from the get go, since the arrival of the Puritans in the seventeenth century, American philosophy has been dominated by modern philosophical assumptions. Samuel Johnson and Jonathan Edwards, considered by some as the first major American philosophers, held deeply to Europe's modern philosophical assumptions. And they were followed by countless others, including Henry David Thoreau and Charles Peirce, both of whom maintained a commitment to empiricism.[35]

Going beyond organisational strategy and with one eye on old religions, it's important to stress that personal life strategy has also been reshaped by modern philosophy's assumptions. Modern philosophy has had a huge impact on today's religious thinking. Examples of this impact include the notion of a religious state, the alignment between science and a religion, and the roles and rights of women (interestingly, there's scant debate on the roles and rights of men). All these debates reflect modern philosophy's impact on traditional religions. Modern philosophy's assumptions are now the basis of extensive swathes of religious knowledge. The assumptions are the basis of our claim to know. And that basis is now overwhelmingly and uncritically retained by all religions, traditional or not. I'm not saying that religions that began outside of Europe merely engaged with modern Europe. I'm saying that all major religions have been intensely influenced by Europe's modern philosophical charter.

And lest you're wondering, the slick, contemporary version of personal life strategy didn't get a bill of clean health or an immunity from modern philosophy's assumptions. Like organisational strategy, it developed in America, a society that was embedded with assumptions from modern philosophy. Modern life strategists fully embrace modern philosophy's epistemological and methodological assumptions. It's interesting that modern life strategists blossomed in America probably as a response to the social and cultural erosion caused by the post-modern era. The randomness, defragmentation and seeming chaos of post-modernity have ebbed away at modernism's stable, structured, single narratives faster in America than perhaps in any other country. And it is contemporary life strategists who have assumed the role of architects and renovators of people's narratives, to help individuals make sense of the world and their lives. Viewed in this light, contemporary life strategists are simply repairing what the post-modern onslaught is destroying.

Can all this be true? The "truth" may be a bit beyond us, so let's re-ask the question. Can modern strategic thought be so bound up with modern philosophical assumptions and assertions that it neglects newer and more useful ways of thinking and understanding? Can we lay the blame for the failure of modern strategy at the door of modern philosophy? To tackle one of the central premises of the book, we need first to understand and elucidate precisely the issues I think modern philosophy has dumped on strategy or, more cynically, the assumptions that modern thinkers about strategy—in whichever field—have lazily adopted in constructing their theories. I will thus in the next couple of chapters outline much of the canon of modern philosophy where it relates to and has influenced modern strategic thought. By the end of these chapters I hope you'll see how shaky the foundations of modern strategy are and, once we understand this, how we can analyse the problems that lie at the very heart of so much modern strategic thought.

1   VH Schmidt, "Into the Second Millennium: Modernity at the Beginning of the 21st Century" in *Modernity at the Beginning of the 21ˢᵗ Century,*" edited by VH Schmidt, Cambridge Scholars Publishing, 2007

2   M Porter, *Competitive Strategy*, The Free Press, New York, 1998

3   http://en.wikipedia.org/wiki/Strategos

4   H Mintzberg, "The Strategy Concept 1: Five Ps for Strategy" in *California Management Review*, June 1987

5   H Mintzberg, B Ahltsrand and J Lampel, *Strategy Safari*, Prentice Hall, Harlow, 2009

6   *Ibid.*

7   *Ibid.*

8   *Ibid.*

9   *Ibid.*

10 M Dell and C Fredman, *Direct from Dell*, HarperBusiness, New York, 1999

11 H Mintzberg, B Ahltsrand and J Lampel, *Strategy Safari*, Prentice Hall, Harlow, 2009

12 OG Rughase, *Identity and Strategy*, Edward Elgar Publishing, Cheltenham, 2006

13 AM Grant, "Workplace, Executive and Life Coaching: An Annotated Bibliography from the Behavioural Science Literature," Coaching Psychology Unit, University of Sydney, Sydney, 2008

14 AM Grant, "The Impact of Life Coaching on Goal Attainment, Metacognition and Mental Health" in *Social Behaviour and Personality*, 2003

15 A McCoy, *An Intelligent Person's Guide to Catholicism*, Continuum International Publishing, New York, 2008

16 R Barron, *Catholicism*, Image Books, New York, 2011

17 AM Grant, "The Impact of Life Coaching on Goal Attainment, Metacognition and Mental Health" in *Social Behaviour and Personality*, 2003

18 AM Grant, "Workplace, Executive and Life Coaching: An Annotated Bibliography from the Behavioural Science Literature," Coaching Psychology Unit, University of Sydney, Sydney, 2008

19 AD Toit, "Making Sense through Coaching" in *Journal of Management Development*, 2007

[20]   http://www.cbsnews.com/8301-505125_162-57345386/top-10-professional-life-coaching-myths/

[21]   PB Mandelson, *The Third Man*, HarperPress, London, 2010

[22]   Kautilya, *The Arthashastra*, Penguin Books, New Delhi, 1992

[23]   R Boesche, *The First Great Political Realist: Kautilya and His Arthashatra*, Lexington Books, Lanham, 2002

[24]   KEM Weber, *Politics as a Vocation*, Facet Books, London, 1972

[25]   JI Moore, *Writers on Strategy and Strategic Management*, Penguin Books, London, 1992

[26]   KR Andrews cited in JI Moore, *Writers on Strategy and Strategic Management*, Penguin Books, London, 1992

[27]   AD Chandler cited in JI Moore, *Writers on Strategy and Strategic Management*, Penguin Books, London, 1992

[28]   H Mintzberg, B Ahltsrand and J Lampel, *Strategy Safari*, Prentice Hall, Harlow, 2009

[29]   *Ibid.*

[30]   JF Welch cited in H Mintzberg, B Ahltsrand and J Lampel, *Strategy Safari*, Prentice Hall, Harlow, 2009

[31]   H Mintzberg, B Ahltsrand and J Lampel, *Strategy Safari*, Prentice Hall, Harlow, 2009

[32]   M Lings, *Muhammad: His Life Based on the Earliest Sources*, Islamic Texts Society, Cambridge, 1983

[33]   N Stanlick, *American Philosophy: The Basics*, Routledge, Abingdon, 2013

[34]   *Ibid.*

[35]   *Ibid.*

**The earliest strategic frameworks were religions,
including Christianity.**

**Many people consider Rene Descartes's *Discours de la méthode*
of 1637 the first text of modern philosophy.**

CHAPTER 2

THE PHILOSOPHICAL BASE

Exploration and Criticism

The first time I remember coming across the term "modern" it was used pejoratively. My aunt was sneering at the attire of a Pakistani teenager whose skimpy clothing looked like something from Gap, befitting more London's Piccadilly Circus than Lahore's Anarkali. In a tone I've heard a few times amongst Pakistanis, "She's a *wery modern* girl; she thinks she's *wery* something." Anyhow, "modern," at least the way my aunt used it, was a bad word. Not as bad as some other bad, bad words, but still bad . . . even if the word could do with some clarity given it has a diversity of meanings across subjects. I am sure somebody out there is thinking that I misspelled part of her quote . . . but I did not, ha ha! Practically everybody I know who was educated in Pakistan pronounces Vs for Ws and vice versa. It's just one of those peculiar linguistic birthmarks that very rarely erodes.

In the previous chapter, I had noted that life, organisational and foreign policy strategy rests on modern philosophy's assumptions. I also noted that modern philosophy's shortcomings have left modern strategy blind to the idea that our strategy depends on how we see ourselves, our self-identities, as much as our strategy depends on a world out there. Before I explain modern philosophy's flaws, I want to first shed some light on modern philosophy. To do that, I need to briefly touch upon pre-modern philosophy given that modern philosophy developed as a reaction to its pre-modern sister. You didn't expect a strategy book to dive into pre-modern philosophy. Mind you, you don't expect a lot of things that you read every morning in the newspaper, and it's sometimes a good thing to be presented with the unexpected.

The trick for me, I acknowledge, is to get the philosophy piece across without boring you. I suspect that most people who've tried reading any philosophy face a grim hurdle. Most philosophers express themselves in the most incoherent fashion, clamouring to out-jargon each other, with no end in the race to gobbledegook. I empathise with some historians, economists and political scientists whose inclination is often to dismiss philosophy as futile word-games. Yes, the language is often inaccessible. Further, in my humble opinion, some philosophers who use such language do so because they don't know what they're talking about. But no, a lot of philosophy isn't claptrap. In fact, the post-modern stuff opens a bag of a super-charged set of ideas which crash into the social sciences and sciences. I will avoid the typical unintelligibility of a dusty, three-kilogram, font-five philosophy textbook and try to present the material at a rather jolly pace.

The pre-modern or medieval philosophical period dates from the fifth century slow-motion fall of the Roman Empire to the fifteenth century early Renaissance period. There is, surprise, surprise, a lack of consensus around the start and end dates of the pre-modern period, a point not lost on Fred Robinson, an expert on medieval literature:

> It ends . . . with the fall of Constantinople or with the invention of printing or with the discovery of America or with the beginning of the Italian wars (1494) or with the Lutheran Reformation (1517) or with the election of Charles V (1519). Several reference works I

have consulted simply assert that the Middle Ages ended in 1500, presumably on New Year's Eve.[1]

Connoisseurs split the millennium-long pre-modern period into two smaller, bite-sized periods—a bit like what Shredded Wheat did to their cumbersome full-sized biscuit.[i] That was a smart move because those biscuits are pretty tough work first thing in the morning. Personally, I recommend soaking them in milk for a while before eating them. Anyhow, the first pre-modern period extends to about the end of the eleventh century, followed by a "golden age" or "high medieval" era, which was marked by the revived interest in ancient philosophers, especially in Aristotle, as well as the injection of Arab thinking from Ibn Sina and Ibn Rushd amongst others.[2] One encyclopaedia packaged the pre-modern period quite poetically:

> Combine classical pagan philosophy, mainly Greek but also in its Roman versions, with the new Christian religion. Season with a variety of flavorings from the Jewish and Islamic intellectual heritages. Stir and simmer for 1300 years or more, until done.[3]

Amongst their shared characteristics, pre-modern philosophers embraced supernaturalism and mysticism. They placed mankind's nature as second in importance to either original sin or God's will. Pre-modern philosophy also emphasised tradition and faith. In doing so, pre-modern philosophers stressed either man-centric or earth-centric spiritual laws. They also stressed the tribe, clan or feudal hierarchy above the individual. Implicit in that, they regarded the group as more important than the individual. In the debate between reason and faith, the same philosophers tilted towards faith.[4] They didn't give reason and rational thinking half

---

i   This reminds me of a joke by the British comedian Bernard Manning: "Why does Arthur Scargill take three Shredded Wheat? He eats two and puts the third on his head" (in reference to Scargill's interesting hairstyle).

the importance as it's given today in the West.

In contrast, modern philosophers share a belief in reason and objectivity. They're rather smug about it too, but we'll touch upon that a bit later. I write in the present tense because they still exist. In fact, they dominate the world's epistemological landscape. Mind you, we still have large pockets of the world, especially in Africa and Asia, which subscribe to pre-modern philosophical frameworks even if they're not as popular as they used to be. Modern philosophers claim that mankind, with his objective mind, can know things about life, the universe and everything else through reason and sense-perception.[5] Objectivity is important to modern philosophy, as important as booze is to an Irish party. And my using "his" is pretty deliberate because most modern philosophers to date have been male.

Modern philosophy has tremendous confidence in reason, individualism and scientific truth, emphasising the secular and natural as intellectual starting points.[6] It stresses that not only do laws of nature exist but that they're *knowable*. At the heart of modern philosophy is the distinction between fact and theory, a point especially stressed by Émile Durkheim, the sociologist, and as relevant to the sciences as it is to the social sciences.[7] The modern philosophy bandwagon argues that facts are independent of theory. This ties nicely to their belief in objectivism, the notion that the world exists independently of the mind, and let me stress this: that the mind has no role in making sense of the world. The same philosophers brand religion, spirituality and the supernatural as airy-fairy, mumbo-jumbo and voodoo.

Three connected currents of air are essential to appreciating the massive impact which modern philosophy had in its heyday—the Renaissance, the Reformation and the scientific revolution. These currents carried the seeds of modern philosophy, including its claims of objectivity, across the world and across different intellectual subjects.

During the twentieth century, modern philosophy's influence eroded only in trivial intellectual circles (count me in that group) with the onslaught of post-modern philosophy. As one might expect of any movement, especially one which spanned centuries, there was variety, evolution and debate within modern philosophy. This diversity has not, however, hindered modern philosophy and its claims of objectivity, for its assumptions still dominate our way of understanding.

To be more specific, modern philosophy's epistemological assumptions have dominated the evolution of almost every major intellectual discipline in the West. These in turn—underpinned by the West's political and economic dominance over the past few centuries—now dominate the thinking landscape of the globe. The populations of most major metropolises, most people in the West and a whole lot more think in a modern philosophical framework. It is thus today's accepted wisdom that we can use our senses such as touch and sight to everyday happenings, from the mundane to the spectacular, then apply logic and reason to objectively understand whatever we're engaging. The notion that we use our senses and brain to *impartially* understand the world sits at ease with almost every intellectual discipline in the world.[8]

I accept that it is hard and hazardous to define the consequences of any philosophy into neatly delineated cause and effect. The real world doesn't work to laboratory rules, and I think that any such exercise has definite limitations. Even then, I appreciate the effort by Stephen Hicks, a philosopher, to give a flavour of modern philosophy's impact.[9] It's worth sharing his take because it gives a sense of what modern philosophy has done for us. That impact has been nothing short of seismic, and Hicks did a great job in fleshing out the impact. For instance, Hicks argued that modern philosophy enabled the environment for science to take off, including the specific examples of the respective contributions of Isaac Newton to modern physics,

Gottfried Leibniz to calculus and Carl Linnaeus to biology.[10]

Hicks also argued that modern philosophy's individualism permeated politics, which ultimately led to the formation of liberal democracy, with its accent on individual rights and freedoms.[11] He added that this drove the political revolutions of the seventeenth and eighteenth centuries in Europe and America and the liberations of slaves and women. Meanwhile, that same individualism flooded into economics and nurtured free markets and capitalism. Without modern philosophy, it's hard to see how modern science, social science or indeed strategy could have emerged, in no small part because they all rely on modern philosophy's dominant epistemology: empiricism.

While Hicks focused on some of the positive consequences, it's fair to say that some of modern philosophy's consequences weren't so stellar. Modern philosophy has been integral to the development of racism in the West. Immanuel Kant, the philosopher, approvingly cited the insight of David Hume, another philosopher, that "negroes" learned like parrots.[12] Both philosophers, who are part of Western philosophy's core arsenal, insisted black people were stupid.[13] That's not a very nice thing to say, is it? Hume went on to add that Jews were "fraudulent," Arabs "uncouth and disagreeable," while "negroes" (his term) achieved absolutely nothing.[14] And that's really not very nice either. Going one better, Kant noted:

> So fundamental is the difference between these two races (Black and White) of man and it appears to be as great in regard to mental capacities as in colour.[15]

Noam Chomsky, a semiotician, philosopher and political activist, overlooked modern philosophy's problem by arguing that modern philosophy failed to resist racism.[16] Modern philosophy's assumptions actually *secured* racism. Classification, the Enlightenment's categorisation project that was grounded in modern philosophy's empiricism, was essential to scientific development.[17] Classifying the human race merely followed. Darwin's theory of evolution spun into social Darwinism with black people placed between ape and man. American leaders supported this hierarchy. I am thinking of John Rockefeller and Andrew Carnegie—who as it happens funded institutes which decades later poetically hired black people—in a country which even more poetically a century later elected a black president.[18] That all this happened in Rockefeller and Carnegie's own country is way too much poetry for a nonfiction paragraph. It's poetry overdose and a *chatpatta* point if ever there was one.[ii]

The Crux of Modern Philosophy: Empiricism

Modern philosophy's origins are attributed to Descartes, whose portraits make him look a lot like the image I have of Cardinal Richelieu, the bad guy in Alexandre Dumas's *The Three Musketeers*. Don't ask me where my image of Richelieu comes from. Anyhow, back on track, those origins lie in Descartes's reaction to pre-modern philosophy's reliance on spirituality and metaphysics.[iii] To be really finicky, many treat his *Discours de la méthode* (Discourse on the method) of 1637 as the start of modern philosophy even if most commentators consider *Meditationes de prima philosophia* (Meditations on first philosophy) of 1641 as his masterpiece. It's almost as if we can put a start date to modern philosophy, which feels a bit weird given we are talking about philosophical eras and not

---

ii   *Chatpatta* is an Urdu and Hindi word which means something between "spicy" and "delicious," and is often communicated with a particularly rapid South Asian head wobble. It's typically used to describe terrific, punchy food. You may want to get used to it because I throw it about occasionally in this book.

iii   A minority of experts suggest modern philosophy starts with Socrates as the founding father of rationalism.

something as definitive as somebody's birth or death.

Wanting to connect and cement all knowledge through reason, Descartes argued that while he could doubt the existence of almost anything, he couldn't doubt his act of doubting—and thus his famous, "I think, therefore I am." Interestingly, Ibn Sina, the eleventh-century Arab philosopher and physician, noted practically the same thing. He argued that a person could have thoughts without any input to their senses simply because such a person would at least be aware of his own existence.[19] However, Ibn Sina wasn't European so nobody wanted to put him on a pedestal. Moving on, Descartes claimed that knowledge depended more on reason than on the senses, and posthumously he was made the champion of the smaller of the two main branches of modern philosophy, the rationalist school. It is from Descartes's *Je pense, donc je suis* (I think, therefore I am) that the rationalists, including Francis Bacon and Baruch Spinoza, later argued that knowledge begins from ideas in the mind as opposed to reason alone.[20]

Modern philosophy's really big epistemological school is empiricism, which has impacted the development of practically every social science and science and has had a far greater impact than rationalism has had. And it is because modern strategy assumes an empiricist epistemology that it fails to appreciate that strategy is as dependent on how we self-identify as it is on something outside or external to us. That said, even though empiricism was adopted by modern philosophy, it's fair to say that forms of empiricism in fact pre-date modern philosophy. Ancient Greek physicians first used the term "empirical" when insisting on observing phenomena as they sensed it through *experientia* (experience). Arab intellectuals in the eleventh and twelfth centuries, too played around with empiricism.

Empiricism emphasises sense-perception and has as its champion John Locke, who influenced many leading thinkers, including

François-Marie Arouet de Voltaire, Thomas Jefferson and Jean-Jacques Rousseau, amongst others.[21] In simplest form, empiricists believe that knowledge begins from the senses and the subsequent experiences which those senses generate. Our senses give knowledge to us. Empiricists reject the rationalist claim that we can have knowledge without experience, arguing that knowledge is acquired exclusively from evidentiary sensory experience. The House of Locke does not doubt either the integrity or the neutrality of our senses, which suggests its members have not seen the David Copperfield show of 1983 in which he made the Statue of Liberty seemingly disappear. They argue that our senses are robust and neutral.

What does that mean? What does it mean when empiricists argue that all of our knowledge comes exclusively from our sense experience?[iv] Basically, we see, hear, smell, taste and touch the physical world—and from those interactions, we acquire knowledge. Given this, empiricists believe that human nature is a *tabula rasa* (blank slate). This means that individuals are born without mental content, all of which they acquire during later life from experience and reason. While the idea of *tabula rasa* goes back to Aristotle in the fourth century BC, it was really developed by Ibn Sina in the eleventh century. He suggested the "human intellect at birth is rather like a tabula rasa, a pure potentiality that is actualized through education and comes to know."[22] Incongruously, experts accredit the blank slate to Locke, even if he only referred to the concept as the "white paper."[23] There is another pattern emerging here. I don't want to come across as an Arab PR machine, but in fairness Arab thinkers had a huge and unrecognised hand in modern philosophy.

---

iv   Empiricism is the dominant school of foundationalism, an epistemological theory which assumes the integrity and neutrality of the human senses and insists in mankind's infallible knowledge of certain first principles, which can then be used to build (secondary) knowledge.

One challenge for all empiricists is to list or define the senses. Aristotle talked of five external senses of sight (ophthalmoception), hearing (audioception), taste (gustaoception), smell (olfacoception) and touch (tactioception).[24] A millennium ago, Ibn Sina referred to five external senses and five internal senses, and that, ladies and gentlemen, boys and girls, is the model adopted in principle today by modern neurologists. They refer to senses that are stimulated external to the body, such as temperature (thermoception), kinesthetic sense (proprioception) and pain (nociception), as well as internal senses (interoceptors), being those that are stimulated from within the body. These include stretch, cutaneous receptors and other sensory receptors such as those that are in the mucous membrane of the digestive and respiratory tracts.

With that overview of empiricism, we've arrived at a basic understanding of modern philosophy and its dominant epistemology (empiricism), which cradles modern strategy. This was an important piece because the rest of the chapter demonstrates the weaknesses of modern philosophy and empiricism and the impact of those weaknesses on modern strategy. Having set up modern philosophy, I can now shoot it down—a bit like what the tabloids do so well. I suppose I could be empathetic, because tabloid journalists after all need to make a living somehow. In the next chapter, I then identify those same weaknesses of modern philosophy in the works of leading modern strategists. Demonstrating the failure of modern philosophy opens the door to demonstrating the failure of modern strategy, which then allows me to introduce the role of self-identity in strategy.

Challenges to Modern Philosophy

Matei Calinescu, a literary critic, once referred to modernism's "fifth face," the "philosophical, including problems of epistemology, the history and philosophy of science and hermeneutics."[25] It is this fifth dimension of modernism that ultimately punctures modern philosophy's tyres. It is also this dimension which ultimately opens the intellectual space to introduce and explore self-identity's impact on each of the three steps of the strategic process. These three steps, which I will drum away ad nauseam so you might as well get used to them, consist of making sense of the world as it is right now; developing some kind of vision or objective, however vague, for the future; and then, finally, taking the steps to get from the world of today to the world of the future.

Though there's a fashionable feel today to the criticisms of modern philosophy, the origins of the attacks lie in eighteenth-century Germany. In fact, the first critics of modern philosophy were religious thinkers who wanted to defend orthodox religion. While Anglo-French thinkers embraced the Enlightenment, their German counterparts feared that science and modern philosophy were undermining religion. Science challenged the Church, even on supposedly Church issues such as determining the age of the universe and the orbital structure of our solar system (both of which the Church got wrong). Modern philosophy's earliest critics were thus folk worried by "the spectre of a godless, spiritless, passionless and amoral future," which would destroy society.[26]

The genesis of the attack on modern philosophy and empiricism came from Kant, the same chap who thought that black people learned like parrots yet is about as important to philosophy as Isaac Newton is to physics. Born in 1724 in what is now Kaliningrad, Russia, a country with ironically enough very nasty racial problems, Kant wrote *Kritik der reinen Vernunft* (Critique of pure Reason), one of the most important texts in Western philosophy, the foundation of German idealism and a turning point in modern philosophy.[27] In case you're wondering, it was another of those swampy unreadable texts so incredibly useful for chronic hyper-insomniacs. How could the text be anything else? How could a philosopher deliver otherwise?

It was Hume who had inspired Kant by arguing that cause and effect could not be based on reason. Cause and effect had to be based on sentiment and precedent (or what Bertrand Russell would later call superstition).[28] Before Hume, rationalists had believed that the effect of an action could be objectively deduced from a cause. Hume argued against this—that the cause and effect of an event could never itself be sensed or perceived. This meant there was no place for causality in empiricism. Causality was no more than invariably sequential events. When we repeatedly see a cause and effect, we give them a relationship when in fact there might not be one. We learn a virus causes an illness only through experience. How do we know that this will always be the case? We assume that the past will not change. This, however, can't be rationally justified, because we can't *prove* the past will be repeated in the future. We can *imagine* cause and effect but cannot *experience the causation*.[29] I can't resist mentioning that Hume merely rehashed Al Ghazali's same point from the eleventh century.[30]

Kant grasped that Hume's conclusions were based on the assumption that knowledge was empirical. If principles like cause and effect can't be *empirically* derived, a pure empiricist position was therefore inadequate to completely and cleanly understand reality. Empiricism couldn't deliver a perfect platform to develop knowledge. From this, Kant concluded that there must be "synthetic a priori knowledge," meaning knowledge that exists *independent* of experience. This kind of knowledge must be acquired without any sensory input. He thought that it must be acquired from reason, in the shape perhaps of pure maths. Kant thought empiricism, the foundation of modern science, was not a sound enough basis to *know* reality.[31] He thus found himself in the odd position of being a supporter in principle of science, while undermining its epistemology.

On top of this, Kant also realised that our sense perception was limited. Within empiricism, knowledge depends on two pillars: experience of the world through our senses and the concepts we use in our mind to filter that experience.[32] And Kant realised neither was especially robust. On the first, whereas empiricists had argued that all knowledge had to be experienced, Kant noted that we never directly *experience* reality. We, in fact, mediate reality through sense-perception, which only gives us internal, mental representations of the external world. We are therefore always working with internal sensory representations of reality and not reality itself. Counterintuitively, our senses actually impede knowing reality:

> All objects of an experience possible to us, are nothing but appearances; i.e., that is, mere representations—that in the way in which they are represented, viz., as extended beings or as series of changes—have no existence within an intrinsic basis; i.e., outside our thoughts.[33]

On the second, Kant argued that concepts, which are mere artifices used by our minds, are also tainted. Concepts have no objective or clean basis. There is no logic to justify the concepts that we use to understand the world. Speed, height, colour and other concepts merely developed in a particular sociocultural context. And by sociocultural historical accidence, we now use them. It is those concepts that we drill into everybody from childhood and that our minds now work with. On this basis, Kant suggested that reality partly *conforms* to our understanding of that reality; the mind thus was "not a response mechanism but a constitutive mechanism."[34] Put another way, the mind structures the world as it digests it; "In the act of human cognition, the mind doesn't conform to things; rather, things conform to the mind."[35] Without this mechanism, Kant proposed that the world would be too chaotic for mankind to deal with.

In trying to save the empiricist-inspired Enlightenment and its *Sapere aude* (Dare to know or Dare to be wise) motto from Hume's criticisms, Kant unintentionally undermined the Enlightenment by tearing its pseudo-objectivity. While he thought there was something right about science, being a fan of Newton's laws, Kant still thought mankind's observations were neither neutral nor clean. We can only know things as they appear to us. And *appearing to us* isn't a passive act. Appearance is *partly constructed* by whoever is making sense of reality. Kant's contribution was critical because he epistemologically and ontologically undermined objectivity on modern philosophy's own terms. This was a contrast to the metaphysical, esoteric "pissing outside in" attack of his contemporaries.[36] It is on this basis that the strategist then *constructs* the start and end points of the strategic process, a construction which modern strategists simply don't recognise.

Though Kant was central to the attack on modern philosophy, other thinkers chimed in on the act.[v] One was Georg Hegel, an extraordinarily difficult philosopher to understand.[37] If Hegel were alive today and if he applied to work at a communications firm (admittedly, two mighty ifs), he'd be rejected immediately because nobody would understand his cover letter. Reading Hegel's work can sometimes feel like punishment. Having got that out of my system, whereas Kant held there was a reality which our minds shape, Hegel insisted reality is created by the observer, analyst or what philosophers call "the subject." In a not-so-smart bit of cheeky acrobatics, he then used God as his subject—hence he argued that reality always exists independent of human cognition, which I don't like because God is such a hard component to get our heads around or put into a model.

Another key thinker who cut deep into modern philosophy's assumptions was Friedrich Nietzsche, who looked like Mark Twain,

---

v   Two thinkers who I have excluded because I don't want slow things down but are worth reading for their impact and following amongst philosophers and social theorists are Friedrich Schleiermacher and Søren Kierkegaard.

only with slicker hair. Nietzsche was a champion marshy writer, which backfired on him after his death, not that he could care less, I suppose.[38] His mischievous sister integrated his slushy writing with some clever forgery to hang his coat to the Nazis as she ingratiated herself in the 1930s with the emerging Third Reich. Nietzsche has since been unfairly tarnished with the Nazi brush despite his antipathy to anti-Jewish discrimination and his support for early Zionists such as Martin Buber.[39] Big take-away? Philosophers who worry about their intellectual legacy should avoid swampy writing and remember KISS. It is not a take-away to eliminate mischievous siblings. That's a bit much, really.

Born in 1844 in today's Germany, Nietzsche is famous for writing the *der Wille zur Macht* (Will to Power), which was published in 1901, a year after his death. He became popular after World War II when Michel Foucault, a social theorist and philosopher, embraced him for developing the relationship between the subject, the person who is seeing and making sense of something, and the object, whatever that person is seeing and making sense of. Foucault especially valued Nietzsche for bringing focus to the existence of the subject, which had historically hitherto been neglected. Nietzsche fundamentally challenged Western philosophy not because he critiqued reason but because he used the subject to illuminate his case. He asked some pretty insightful questions, such as how can subjects be objective if they have linguistic, ontological and epistemological warts? Or how can subjects be truthful if their conceptual tools are imperfect?[40]

Perhaps the most famous voice in the anti-modern movement is Foucault, who looked a lot like John Malkovich, the actor. Foucault remains divisive, not least because many of his critics can't make sense of his works.[41] Economists, historians and political scientists in particular tend to struggle with his obscure writing style. That's the constituency that slams Foucault because it often lacks the conceptual flexibility to cut through his style. He admonished modern philosophy and modernism for producing institutions and practices that legitimised control and domination of human behaviour—from when we wake up to when we sleep.[vi] He felt that objectivity and facts were used to reinforce existing structures of power and control. And that's why he saw modernism as the great oppressor, arguing that its regressive domination began during the Renaissance's classical era and continued into the twentieth century.[42]

Foucault's conclusions drew upon psychiatry, medicine, the humanities, prisons and sexuality and stressed the impersonal domination that came from social institutions and practices, which saturate every aspect of our lives. I like his multidisciplinary approach. For example, he noted in the eighteenth century that "madness" stigmatised not just the mentally ill but also the poor and homeless. This reminds me a bit like how "terrorism" is today used in America and parts of Europe to stigmatise Muslims.[43] Practices, discourses and institutions are adopted, imitated and gradually become accepted as knowledge and common sense. It was, after all, a very warped "common sense" that informed the Nazi atrocities. Foucault argued that knowledge and common sense thus become expressions of power, which control and administer human behaviour.[vii]

A final thinker for his impact on a generation of post-modern

---

vi   Several theorists, including Max Horkheimer and Theodor Adorno, supported Foucault's view. They suggested that reason and modernity's liberation had both come to mean the opposite of what they were meant to mean. All three viewed modernity as a coercive and destructive force, though Adorno and Horkheimer focused instead on the colonisation of nature and repression of social and psychic existence.

vii   One key criticism of Foucault is he ignored modernity's positive features such as medicine. In contrast, Karl Marx, Max Weber and Jürgen Habermas focused both on modernity's positive and repressive dimensions.

thinkers including Foucault, Ahmad Fardid, Jean-Paul Sartre and Jacques Derrida was Martin Heidegger. Some think he is the twentieth century's greatest philosopher, even though I think he makes no sense. Heidegger believed that words and concepts are obstacles to the truth. That much I get—but only that, because the rest of his core thesis feels like gobbledegook. He then went on that Western philosophy since Plato had misunderstood the nature of "Being," treating it as a being as opposed to the notion of Being itself. Previous studies of Being had focused on entities and their properties. Even though Being is common to all things, he pointed out, we only vaguely understand it.[44] This misunderstanding had polluted all Western thought from our beliefs to common sense. Everything we know is thus vulnerable to error.

A smarter way, Heidegger claimed, was to investigate whatever underlies all entities and allows them to be entities. To reverse the ways of previous generations, we must first retrace philosophy's history and replace the observer with *Da-sein* (an experience, being projected into nothing). He claimed this mechanism bypassed the problem of value-laden observation.[45] He then asked, "Why is there even Being at all?"[46] If there's no reason for Being, Being becomes absurd. If Being is for a reason, then what's the reason? If we treat reason separate from Being, reason becomes nothing. Having concluded any attempt by reason to engage metaphysics fails, Heidegger then asserted that all is nothing and nothing is all, a metaphysical nihilism![47] Very frankly, I think that sounds like complete nonsense, which is compounded by Heidegger being a proud Nazi from 1933 to 1945.

To bring the discussion down to a crunchier level, what do modern strategists fail to comprehend about these challenges to modern philosophy? How do modern strategists ignore the role of human cognition in how we see our world, the future vision that we develop and the paths we take to get there? What do we specifically want to extract from Kant & Company in order to understand the failure of modern strategy? We've now covered a chunk of philosophical material from which I now want to hone in on the specific failures of modern philosophy that become the failures of modern strategy. Not only do I want to tie those failures into modern strategy, being the remainder of this chapter, but I also want to demonstrate those failures through the works of leading modern strategists, which is the next chapter.

Hitting head on, modern philosophy has three failures that are especially relevant to modern strategy. The first is that modern philosophy thought it could provide a platform for objectivity, when it could not. Second, modern philosophy ignored the role of the subject in seeing and making sense of his object reality. Finally, modern philosophy cultivated an intellectual hubris that contaminated modern strategy's ability to learn and grow. These three weaknesses are now wired into modern strategy. These criticisms are therefore as much criticisms of modern philosophy as they are of modern strategy. They help explain why modern strategy is blind to the impact of cognition and self-identity in each of the three steps of the strategic process. Let's look more carefully at these weaknesses by taking each criticism at a time.

The Subjectivity of Objectivity

Despite its claims, modern philosophy and its dominant epistemology simply can't provide a platform for objectivity or the truth. It is because modern philosophers and strategists believe in their objectivity that they can't meaningfully embrace a role for human *cognition* in the strategic process. It makes no sense to explore and engage issues of cognition, of how we as people make sense of the world, if one believes one can be objective. Nor does it make sense to acknowledge self-identity's impact on that cognition. Because it's so important, I want to strip away the above history of some of the criticism of modern philosophy and explain without the luggage of historical context why it and empiricism can't provide a platform to be objective. Why can't modern philosophy and empiricism provide a podium for people to be objective?

At the highest level, the claim of objectivity is neatly criticised by Jim George, whose study on international relations theory is one of the genre's most under-recognised works:

> How do we know that our sense expressions are, in fact, derived from the physical world of reality, external to us?[48]

Put another way, how do we know that the world around us is directly responsible for the experiences we have? The answer cannot be experience, because our minds only work with perceptions and images. Our minds are unable to *directly experience* the external world.[49] Our minds experience the perceptions and images that have been generated of that external world from our senses and minds using language and concepts that we use to interface with that external world. The important point to stress is that our minds never directly experience that world, which in turn foils our ability to be objective or provide the truth.

Another challenge is that our observations are always value-laden by theoretical frameworks. The objective facts partly depend on the theory or some kind of theoretical framework or bias that we use.[50] Our cognition of the world reflects theoretical assumptions that have no objective basis.[51] On glancing at a restaurant menu, a Jew might focus on kosher options, a graphic designer on the layout, while a student on the best value for money. Each of the three will *see* different realities because each diner will be sensitive to different aspects of the menu. They will each have different "objective" realities. Antonio Gramsci, the philosopher, put the same point more eloquently than I ever could:

> An enquiry into a series of facts to discover the relations between them presupposes a 'concept' that permits one to distinguish that series from other possible series of facts. How can there take place a choice of facts to be adduced as proof of the truth of one's own assumption if one does not have a pre-existing criterion of choice?[52]

Students of philosophers such as Karl Popper, Norwood Hanson, Thomas Kuhn and Willard Quine will appreciate as bread and butter the notion that our theories dictate what we *choose* to see. Stephen Hicks succinctly writes:

> Our perceptual intuitions do not conform to objects but rather our intuition conforms to what our faculty of knowledge supplies from itself.[53]

I think it is impossible to isolate pure, objective knowledge, unsoiled by assumptions, since perception is influenced by our theories. Indeed, our experience says about as much about our mind, with its unique cultural, social, psychological, genetic and other nuances, as it does about whatever we're experiencing. Data is always, I argue, inherently theory-laden and contaminated.[54]

It's not just theoretical frameworks that determine how we see the world, but there's the challenge of language that mediates our understanding of reality. Language changes on an ongoing basis and impacts human behaviour, often in the subtlest manner. Language is arbitrary and ethno- and cultural-centric. It doesn't have a divine, sterile or objective basis yet it profoundly impacts human cognition and behaviour. The Punjabi language has no word for "sorry." Punjabis face a choice: they either never apologise or they borrow from Urdu or Hindi. Given many rural Punjabis don't know Urdu or Hindi, this has an interesting impact on their relationships and subsequent behaviour.

Dropping down one last level, language is merely a collection and sequencing of concepts. Even our most basic concepts, such as "on," "off," "speed" and "time," carry cultural debris given their evolution in specific social, geographic and intellectual eras.[55] Concepts thwart us from being objective. One powerful illustration of how concepts can make a difference can be found in 2001. George W. Bush (henceforth affectionately referred to as "Dubya") shoved into everybody's face the "with us or against us" concept.[viii] As a result, Pakistan agreed in a single day to realign almost its entire foreign policy to avoid finding itself in the "against us" camp, nudged by US Deputy Secretary of State Richard Armitage's polite side note that if Pakistan, an American ally since 1951, didn't align, it would be bombed back to "the stone age."[56] Pakistan transformed most of its foreign policy to conform to Dubya's concept.

You might expect scientists to aggressively challenge the criticisms of empiricism which I've outlined in this chapter. After all, empiricism and objectivity form the soul of the scientific enterprise. Science positions itself as rational, independent and objective. Its foundation is empiricism. You might think that science is going to put up a fight from the modern philosophical corner. Alas, no. Refreshingly, many scientists don't guard or shield modern philosophy's assumptions. In fact, within science there's ample criticism of empiricism and positivism, its close sister and the inability of either to offer objectivity. If you're looking for a defence from the scientific community, it's not particularly strong. At best, their response can be best surmised as "yes, our epistemology has flaws but we don't have a superior alternative." Stephen Hawking, the physicist, noted that:

---

viii "Either you are with us or you are with the terrorists" —Dubya to Congress on 20th September 2001.

> If one takes the positivist position, as I do, one cannot say what time actually is. All one can do is describe what has been found to be a very good mathematical model for time and say what predictions it makes.[57]

In similar vein, Werner Heisenberg, another physicist, hit the nail right on the head: "The science of nature does not deal with nature itself but in fact with the science of nature as man thinks and describes it."[58]

Where, then, does that leave us? If even the scientific community recognises the limits of objectivity, if objectivity is always subjective, where do we then go? How do we get over this hump? We probably do still need "truths" to give us stability from which we can then do. That's maybe why great doers tend to have simplistic minds, which can't see shades of grey. Great doers don't obsess over decisions based on objectivity. Action often requires the illusion of certainty.[59] Take, for instance, Dubya, who did many big things but wasn't entirely revered for his intellect. In eight years, he launched three wars (on Afghanistan, Iraq and "Terror"—whatever that means), took America into its biggest recession in eighty years and ripped up civil rights in the Patriot Act. America under Bush probably killed more innocent people in the world than under any other US president since the Vietnam War.[60] He did a lot of big things.

In contrast, Bill Clinton is regarded as one of the most cerebral American presidents in a long time. If any recent American president could see shades of grey, it was him, even to the extent of differentiating between "smoking" and "inhaling." At one level, technically there's a difference. Clinton, however, didn't do anything as big as Dubya did. The magnitude of Clinton's growth of the economy, budget surplus, NAFTA and some social welfare reforms pales when contrasted with the magnitude of moves by his successor. Under Clinton, the US military actions in Sudan, ex-Yugoslavia and Iraq were chicken feed compared to Bush's "shock and awe."[61] Three minor military conflicts is simply no comparison to three full-scale wars. Clinton was able to see uncertainty, subtlety and ambiguity, which in turn eroded his ability to get big things done.

Objectivity, facts and truths provide the certainty that we need to engage and do. They enable us to move and get things done. Are they a necessary evil? Probably not, because I don't see them as inherently evil. That said, they're probably necessary. Imagine a universe in which you knew nothing and were acutely aware of that. It'd be very difficult to get anything done. Even the preparation of a cup of tea would be a serious challenge. I say that having never experienced a good cup of tea in the United States except when served in a couple of homes. I don't know what American restaurants do in serving tea that tastes as if it has come from recycled tea bags. Maybe that's it, the entire restaurant industry in America recycles tea bags to produce tasteless tea?

The need for objectivity and truths then leaves the question of, What is the truth? I can think of at least two ways of re-assessing truth. Richard Rorty, a literary theorist and philosopher, neatly captured one way by describing the truth as:

> What you can defend against all corners . . . what our peers will (all things considered) let us get away with saying.[62]

In essence, this position is that the truth depends on other people's acceptance of it. And not just any ordinary people but specifically those in authority, those who have some kind of power to effect and influence, which is a view that Nietzsche tilted to a long time ago:

> What, then, is truth? A mobile army of metaphors, metonyms and anthropomorphisms—in short, a sum of human relations, which have been enhanced, transposed and embellished poetically and rhetorically and which after long use seem firm, canonical and obligatory to all people.[63]

Many post-modern philosophers buy this interpretation of truth and knowledge. They see knowledge as something that is validated by power while truth is produced. For this community and to rebut Francis Bacon's famous quote, knowledge is not power. Knowledge is a function of power. By power, we don't mean physical force or military action, but more frequently we're talking of a dispersed power, the sort that dictates that we can't call a spoon a collection of atoms or that we can't call a pen a weapon. This is for the most part a societal and cultural power.

A second way to reassess the truth is to use noumenal reality to distinguish between reality as we see and make sense of it and reality independent of our cognition or understanding of it. This idea recognises that we can only know what our minds make of the real world and not know the world itself. Derived from the Greek *noumenon* (the object of an act of thought), this approach is draped in epistemological modesty (a refreshing approach which suggests we don't know much).[64] Parenthetically, Jain philosophy used a similar tool for two and a half millennia. *Anekantavada* (not of solitary attribute) is one of Jainism's most important concepts and divides knowledge into two categories between the Absolute (the underlying reality) and the Relative (the perceived reality).[65] Jainism has it that no human can know the Absolute, which I think is a wonderful position to adopt.

Irrespective, though, of how we deal with the truth, the point remains that modern philosophy and empiricism can't provide a platform for objectivity or the truth, which pulls the rug from under the feet of modern strategists. The modern strategist advocates a particular strategic assessment or analysis on the basis of some pseudo-objectivity or truth. The delicious point is that unfortunately for the strategist, he simply can't be objective. Reality, or at least our seeing and making sense of it, is always a personal and subjective process. So when the modern strategist goes about lecturing all and sundry about the facts, truths or objectivity of his assessment, the foundations of that sermon really need to be treated on its their merits. They're simply dung.

The Subject–Object Relationship

Modern philosophy's first problem which holds back modern strategists from recognising that cognition impacts all steps in the strategic process is, as we've just discussed, the failure to appreciate that objectivity is always subjective. The second problem is the failure to engage the subject, the person making sense of things, in his seeing and understanding the object, whatever is being understood. There is a failure to recognise the subject-object relationship. This is something of a natural follow-up to the first problem. One premise of modern philosophy is that since a person can be objective, there's little point in thinking about him, the subject, when he conducts his analysis of whatever, whether it's some literature, a rock or an idea.

In fact, modern philosophy, and therefore modern strategy, completely ignores the subject, the person conducting the research, analysis or assessment. It's almost as if the subject is invisible, neutral and colourless. There's no sense that the person brings himself, his frameworks and language in order to make sense of reality. The problem with this, and as should have become evident by now, is that understanding reflects the mind of a person (the subject) trying to understand the something which is being understood (the object).[66] Any cognition or analysis is a product of subject and object, a relationship which impacts all three steps of the strategic process because all three steps are based on seeing or making sense of something. Philosophers, partly for convenience and partly to be flash, sometimes call this the subject-object interdependence.

The biologist sees a flower as petals, stamens with pollens, stigma, eggs and sepal. In contrast, the chemist sees that same flower as hydrogen, oxygen, carbon, iron, calcium and nitrogen. The two *see* different realities. Continuing the contrast, biologists classify plants and organisms by the Linnean system—species, genus, order, phylum and kingdom; chemists classify by atomic number. [ix] Neither approach is more *objective*. The two scientific communities merely have their own theoretical frameworks which they apply to see the world in resultantly different ways. The differences in the analyses does not reflect differences in the objects of their attention. The flower doesn't mysteriously change for them. It remains what it is irrespective of who is studying it. The differences of perspectives and analyses emerge from alternating the subject, being the mind which is making sense of the flower, which in turn serves to highlight the subject-object interdependence.

Bizarrely, modern strategists don't believe people have a role in seeing the world in which people engage, since the world is self-evident. In their universe, the can of cold Coke tells everybody that "I'm a cold Coke can." That is, of course, until it warms up, which is when it starts moaning, "I'm a room-temperature Coke can" in all the languages of those people who drink Coke. That's a lot of yapping by a can of Coke given we have about 7,000 languages to communicate in. Maybe the Coke can is really a vestige of C-3PO who in *Star Wars* was familiar with over six million forms of communication? Everything in the world, according to the modern strategist, self-identifies itself . . . well that's the idea, anyway. This is indeed the consistent assumption amongst modern strategists and a point that I will illustrate a bit later through the works of some of the most important strategists of modern times.

---

ix   The 1970s witnessed a conflict between two groups of biologists. One suggested classification should reflect evolutionary relationships of species; the other said classification should be independent of evolution.

Well, on that point of self-identification, I beg to differ. People, strategists included, have a role in their cognition of their world. And what's more, there's probably no single, all-inclusive explanation on how we see the world. It's a muddle that straightjackets all human behaviour, including how we craft strategy. We do not have a single, all-encompassing theory of how heterogeneous mankind—with its multiple languages, cultures and theoretical frameworks—sees and makes sense of the world. That ignorance, though, does not take away from the notion that how we see and make sense of things profoundly affects how we then engage the world. Our cognition directly impacts our understanding of reality and our vision ahead. It also influences how we get from where we think we are to where we want to be.

Constructivism, which was kick-started in the 1960s, is all about the subject-object interdependence; its core argument is that we actively construct knowledge (or whatever else we want to call our understanding of reality). While social constructivists emphasise the social act of construction and cultural constructivists emphasise culture's role on the constructing, their staple argument remains the same: knowledge is constructed.[67] We make knowledge. It is created by human minds and with all the biases and limitations thereof. Given this take on knowledge construction, neither school would be especially surprised by stuff such as the Tobacco Industry Research Committee funding research which constructed knowledge that actually exonerated smoking from lung cancer.[68] After all, if knowledge is constructed, it's not too difficult to create knowledge to support practically any argument.

Recognising that we're each unique, we subjects see our object reality in different ways. This is a big deal. I'm not playing philosophical mind games or running on a fancy intellectual treadmill. In the mid-1990s, Apple Computers had a dozen different Macintoshes—a range which was too chaotic for Steve Jobs: "I couldn't figure out. . . . Which ones do I tell my friends to buy?"[69] At a strategy session in 1997 he forced his team to think within a two-by-two grid consisting of Consumer and Pro, and Desktop and Portable. He forced everybody in that meeting room to see and make sense of (in other words, construct) the world through a different lens. With this grid, Jobs then demanded a single great product in each quadrant. Everything else would have to go. Simple yet brilliant, and thus began the Apple revolution and the genesis of one of the world's most transformative and wealthiest companies.[70]

In the modern period, some folk have tried to explore the subject's seeing of the object. In other words, they've tried to understand how people see and make sense of the world. One of the earliest attempts was by sociologists and philosophers, namely Max Weber and Georg Simmel, who pioneered the *verstehen* (interpretative) approach towards the social sciences. This is a systematic process in which an outside observer attempts to relate to a particular cultural group on the latter's own terms.[71] It's not especially easy if you pause for a moment to think it over, because one has to get to grips with the meaning-making framework of whomever one is trying to make sense of and understand. You have to really get inside the mind of who you're studying, including the cultural, psychological and emotional factors that make them who they are.

Recently there has been work on cognition in the context of decision-making. One emerging over-arching conclusion from this work is that reason, whatever the heck that is, has less influence on our cognition and decisions than we'd like to believe. We as a species don't make decisions largely on the basis of reason or rationality. David Brooks, a cultural journalist, was onto something, I think, when he suggested that we don't make decisions primarily from our "conscious thinking":

> Reason is nestled upon emotion and dependent upon it. Emotion

assigns value to things and reason can only make choices on the basis of those valuations.[72]

In fact, some argue that the subconscious dominates the mind. For example, António Damásio, a neurologist, believed it was the emotional part of the mind which measures the value of something and guides key decisions.[73] Dan Ariely, an unusual economist because he can think laterally and has a conceptually flexible mind, made a similar point:

> We usually think of ourselves as sitting in the driver's seat, with ultimate control over the decisions we make and the direction our life takes; but, alas, this perception has more to do with our desires—with how we want to view ourselves—than with reality.[74]

We've become increasingly aware of the complexity and impact of the subject-object interdependence, of the role of our cognition on the world, even within (behavioural) economics. For example, Brooks suggested that human action consists of three steps. He may well have been infected with that consultant's "list of three" disease. We perceive and make sense of a situation, use reason and rationality to calculate our actions and then deploy the willpower and drive to follow through. He added that in the nineteenth century, we generally focused on the third stage in the context of human behaviour and improving micro and macro human situations; in the twentieth century we focused on the second stage, using logic and analysis to overcome human challenges; while in the twenty-first century, we're focusing on the first stage—the perceiving of a situation as we engage problems ranging from national security to domestic household.[75] We now think that how we make sense of a situation is critical to any social and political development or improvement. I thought that was a pretty neat framework.

Brooks continued that the reason we've failed in so many social human endeavours in the past—from persisting with food diets to dealing with alcoholism—is that we've focused on reason and willpower, which aren't effective agents of change, at the expense of cognition, which is way more effective.[76] I'm not entirely convinced about his pretty framework. For instance, I don't buy his second suggestion that we use reason to calculate our behaviour. I doubt we use reason in calculating what to do; nor am I convinced that all mankind is today focusing on the first stage. A big chunk of mankind barely gets to eat properly let alone worry about this stuff. However, I agree that cognition is a big piece in how we make decisions, and in his emphasising this stage, I'm a supporter. I would go further: cognition is critical to unlocking the strategic puzzle.

In making sense of the relationship between subject and object, especially in the context of strategy, I do want to give some texture and cement some ground. There is, I think, one critical factor that influences our cognition: self-identity. How we see ourselves is a much-neglected factor in personal, organisational and foreign policy strategy. Issues of self-identity feed into how we as the subject make sense of the world, a theme which we'll explore in detail in subsequent chapters. Specifically, how we see ourselves impacts our cognition or sense-making of our strategic present, our strategic future and the strategy itself to get from how we see things today to where we want to get. Strategy, therefore, is as much about how we see ourselves—i.e., how we self-identify (whether it be as individuals, organisations or countries)—as it is about a world beyond us which we are navigating, conquering or doing whatever with.

The subject-object relationship shines a light on the importance of the strategist's making sense of his world today and vision ahead. This is a relationship which modern strategy has overlooked. As a result, modern strategy has also overlooked self-identity's impact on all aspects of the strategic process. Even so, three arguments are made to support the case that the act of cognition is self-evident and that there is no such thing as a constructed reality. The first comes from the movement known as objectivism, which is often associated with an American twentieth-century thinker, Ayn Rand.[77] This movement argues that all reality is objective and is the classic empiricist position, which I've already extensively discredited in this chapter. And I really don't want this book to be like one of those fluff-intensive books that ingratiate so many bookstore business sections, so let's not repeat my earlier argument.

Somewhat at the outskirts of objectivism, the second argument reminds me of Geoffrey Stern, an international relations don who had a penchant for wearing short maroon suits, telling tales of KGB conspiracies and lecturing heads of state. I vividly recall one incident which was so typical of Stern from decades ago. In 1993, during the Bosnian War, he was standing in front of me at a London conference on the ugly conflict. He turned to Haris Silajdžić, Bosnia's foreign minister (who at that moment was holding two cigarettes), and told him he was "stark mad." Silajdžić didn't know what to say. That was typical of Stern. Anyhow, he talked about Pepsi-cology and Coca-Cola-ism as a subtle, elusive cultural imperialism. He felt this force was as powerful as any classical, territorial imperialism.[78] His argument, simply put, was that the spread of Western icons, ideas and thinking across the world was a sort of cultural imperialism. Edward Said, a literary theorist, later wrote a stunning account of the same concept.[79]

Stern's point has been extended by some. They argue that given the dominant Western thinking, we now *all* see the world in the same way. They suggest that given globalisation, the penetration of conventional and internet media, as well as the increasing traffic of trade and people, we all pretty much see the same reality. I don't agree with this; surprise, surprise. There are limits to cultural imperialism.

Most people in developing world cities, including the Western-educated privileged elite, do not view the world through an identical Western lens (as if this was homogeneous). The perceived reality of ethnicity, religion, sect, caste, tribe and family are some of the lenses which feature much more powerfully in Asia than, if at all, in North America. Try employing an Untouchable, the people at the bottom end of India's caste system, for a senior management job in India and you'll understand my point.

The third argument made in support of the idea that we all see the world identically comes from many psychologists, including Steven Pinker, who pushed a computational theory of the mind. As far as he was concerned, the human mind absorbed inputs, followed an algorithm and then produced outputs.[80] As do many other psychologists, he argued that we all have a common set of "emotions, drives and faculties for reasoning and communicating . . . a common logic across cultures."[81] My alarm bells are ringing. Apparently we also all have ten intuitions.[82] And now my bells are ringing louder. Other psychologists, such as Daniel Kahneman, supported Pinker. Kahneman argued, "We are born to perceive the world around us, recognise objects orient attention, avoid losses and fear spiders."[83] This camp's theme is the mind (which is not the same thing as the brain) at a core level works identically, across eras and cultures. My alarm bell's gong cover just exploded because the internal hammer hit it so hard.

I thought their arguments, as I've found in the works of too many other psychologists, were pretty lame, to be honest. And that's not mainly because I thought the idea that we're all born afraid of spiders is plain silly, notwithstanding that Spider-Man, the last I heard, was still a good guy. There's little support for the assertion that all babies are arachnophobic and plenty to contradict it.[84] On the question of, How does the mind make sense of things? Pinker offered scant evidence; and he did not back his assertion that we all have common emotions, drivers or ten intuitions. If we don't have an identical language, how then can we have identical emotions? And with that, he ended up with odd convolutions. For instance, Pinker asserted that some things are socially constructed, such as money, but others are not, such as a duck. However, Pinker doesn't acknowledge (or even realise?) that a duck is *constructed* because the same duck can be seen as atoms, food or waterfowl—each of which is a *construction*; each of which relies on how we choose to see what someone else for a moment in his social and cultural environment calls a duck.[85]

Pinker, as many other psychologists, argues the case of a common, ahistoric and universal human mind which, and this is important, we can *know*.[86] To which my riposte is that we don't have a *Gray's Anatomy* of the mind and will probably never have one. We don't have one because we don't have the tools to be objective. We don't have those tools because we don't have pure, untarnished language or concepts to objectively know anything let alone something as complex and fluid as our minds. And even if we did, our minds deal with representations of reality and not reality itself . . . and those representations are socioculturally influenced. A whole lot influences our understanding of reality, all of which, as it happens, makes it impossible to fit our minds and their meaning-making mechanisms into a neat model.

Neither the cultural imperialist nor psychological-based arguments seriously challenge the idea that analysis is a product of a relationship between subject and object. If you call somebody "an absolute moron," that says as much about that person as it does about you. Nor do their arguments advance the assertion that all mankind sees reality identically. Modern philosophy's failure to see the subject-object interdependence has left modern strategy oblivious to the cognitive role which the strategist implicitly plays. That role is in seeing and making sense of the world as-is, seeing a vision ahead and determining or effecting a strategy to bridge the two. Instead, modern strategy has dedicated itself to focusing exclusively on a world external to the strategist when, in fact, cognition (and any strategy based on it) reflects the mind of the strategist as much as it does the external world. Strategy is as much about us as it is about what's outside of us, a point which modern strategy utterly fails to comprehend.

Hubris

Stemming from the first two criticisms, being the failure to appreciate both the subjectivity of objectivity and the subject's role in making sense of his reality, there is a third criticism of modern philosophy and thus all modern strategists. That third criticism is of hubris. This isn't the hubris of the personal character of modern strategists. It is the hubris of an intellectual movement. Modern strategy is based on modern philosophy and specifically the notion that smart people, such as good strategists, can objectively know certain truths about aspects of the world. These guys are the "know-it-alls." This is exactly what holds back philosopher and strategist alike from exploring new ways of thinking about engaging mankind and the world it occupies. It thwarts the sort of healthy intellectual questioning which is, in fact, necessary for growth. How can we learn or even unlearn, if we already *know*? What's the point in listening to other viewpoints if one is already objective? And how can we retain credibility without asserting the claim to know? That helps explain why the modern strategist hasn't sufficiently engaged the plethora of learning, especially in the last couple of centuries, around what mankind is about, how it knows the world or what mankind's needs are.

This is, indeed, the intellectual cemetery where modern strategy lies. It lacks the intellectual humility to doubt its own cookie-cutter frameworks and paradigms. In modern strategy, I feel that there's a profound lack of curiosity to learn from other intellectual disciplines, especially those that deal with human beings. This is weird because strategy is fundamentally an exercise about people. Far too often modern strategists have been and remain too smug to consider engaging the broad spectrum of learning about mankind in so many other disciplines. This includes, but is not limited to, learning about the challenges around objectivity, truth and facts. I could just as easily include into that bucket the role of cognition, which despite being one of the most important strategic pieces, most modern strategists don't give two hoots to.

There is irony in this last point. Any person engaged in strategy will know that once information around the starting and ending points is gathered and stabilised, the strategy—or the answers to "what should we do?" or "how do we get to our end goal?"—may not be entirely inevitable, but it does at least become highly demarcated. It might need a bit of refinement, some self-reflection, but the core strategic path is thus set. In other words, strategy's critical pivot is in understanding what is happening now, in making sense of today's infinite pieces, as well as in framing a target reality, the future ahead. That really is the meat and potatoes. The labour of strategy, counter-intuitively, is not really about working out how to get there.[x] The real effort goes into seeing and making sense of today and the future.

The first steps in strategy are assessments of both where I am and where I want to be. These are personal, subjective processes. And my highlighting those processes doesn't deserve a prize, so "Keep Calm And Carry On."[xi] The case study method at business schools,

---

x   Of course, the other hard part of strategy is implementation, especially in making the continuous, ongoing tactical modifications to manoeuvre against our understanding of the continually changing world . . . all of which needs the folk who are crafting the strategy to be the same folk who are implementing it.

xi   The British government created the slogan in 1939 for posters during World War II in the event that Germany invaded Britain. Given no invasion took place,

a strong bastion of the know-it-alls, thus is really a bit flaky because the supposedly relevant information is presented on a plate. Students are spoon-fed the most important and hardest piece of the strategic process. Once the data and "relevant" facts are given, the analysis and sequencing of actions is a comparative doddle. The hard stuff, the stuff that takes time and intellectual horsepower in the real world, is in working out what the relevant stuff is and then getting it. That's where the strategist needs to earn his living. And that's why strategy by case study isn't particularly useful.

Given that modern strategists don't engage the issue of cognition, how then can they consider the next stage? How can they engage self-identity's impact on cognition and thus on how individuals, organisations and countries see the world, see their future (however vague) and get from where they think they are to where they want to be? In essence, modern strategists have consistently ignored one of the most significant factors of strategy. And that's not because cognition isn't talked about or researched in the wider academic universe. It is engaged and studied across a wide spectrum of learning about human beings. However, the vast majority of modern strategists simply don't feel compelled to learn from the disciplines that explore the human being, which isn't surprising since they also assume that somehow they're objective, that they are, after all, the know-it-alls.

Such modern strategists very rarely attend conferences on psychology, semiotics or anthropology. Ask any such strategist to advance his skills by reading some social theory or a book on hermeneutics and you'll get an odd look. In conversation with a strategist, if you raise the implications of a psychology theory, you'll get another odd look. The paradox that the supposedly thoughtful strategy guys have been living off primitive ideas is seldom surfaced.

---

only a very limited number of the 2.5 million posters were distributed and used.

I suppose I could sympathise if strategists had ignored research on the Cambrian era, which ended 488 million years ago, because the relationship between strategy and the Cambrian era isn't especially obvious, if there is indeed one. I am sure somebody out there is going to push back on this point but, please, let's be real.

So much of strategy is about people that it's creepy that modern strategy has gotten away with ignoring centuries of research, thinking and reflection about mankind. It'd be no different to modern chemists ignoring changes in our understanding of physics over the past century or a fund manager ignoring the changes in our understanding of economics since Keynes. For people who have a reputation of being intellectually up there, it's amazing not just that modern strategy has scarcely learned from sister disciplines, but that it has barely even tried! Modern strategy has traditionally shown no interest in anthropology or the philosophy of the mind. Yet this is exactly what modern philosophy has done for modern strategy—made it so sure of its ability to *know objectively* that it's inculcated a deep hubris to the point of blindness.

Despite its cerebral branding, modern strategy is thus intellectually lifeless. It has not only broadly failed to use more than a century of learning about people, it has almost completely ignored that learning. Personal, organisational and foreign policy strategists have gone about their business oblivious to our growing awareness of mankind. Only a tiny minority have, for instance, recently questioned our ability to be objective, something that a dozen other branches of academia have been playing around with for centuries.[87] In treading an intellectually bankrupt path, modern strategy feels like a biscuit-dry skeleton. Some biscuits are moist, so I clarify: I'm thinking of McVitie's Rich Tea biscuits—firm, dry and ideal for dunking. This contrasts with a Hob Nob, which is of course far more crumbly and moist. It's completely unsuitable for dunking because it spoils the tea with a chocolate residue and small crumbly fragments.

It's no bombshell then that life and foreign policy strategies have intellectually stagnated for centuries, while organisational strategy, which is quite new, sits to this day largely where it was at its birth. None of the great religions, the original strategic frameworks, have at mainstream worked with our greater insights of human beings. They should have, because there's an immense human component in assembling, interpreting, analysing, communicating and effecting those religions, as well as in the (perceived) realities which those religions engage. In parallel, national foreign policy strategy has for centuries beaten the drum of power and interest—an assumption that's so weary that even its eyelids aren't opening. We have been aware for way more than a century that human behaviour (expressed in a country's foreign policy) is governed by more than simplistic, arithmetic calculations of power, a revelation which goes over the heads of most foreign policy strategists.

One of the things that modern strategists need to get snug with is that we don't *know* in the way we like to think we *know*. We simplify the world to give us certainty, and in doing so we mediate reality with our mental tools. As a result, we become more certain more often than can be justified, if only to give us a sense of greater control of whatever's around us. I get the need for certainty. We also communicate with certainty to influence others, recognising that communicating uncertainty will struggle to effect influence or action. I don't need an advanced education on the potential benefits of communicating with confidence. However, in this cyclical process, we begin to believe our own certainty. This, in turn, can drive more simplification, more certainty and more action—even when we might embrace a modicum of self-doubt, even when it's best to step back and reassess.

While self-doubt inhibits action, I remind all and sundry that self-certainty has led to some very, very nasty adventures. If Mao Zedong had been less certain about his analysis of and vision for China, he wouldn't have killed sixty million people through starvation, execution and forced labour, making him the biggest murderer of all time.[88] Sixty million people on the back of one person's certainty . . . the numbers might desensitise the horror, but Mao killed *several times* the number of victims who incurred Adolf Hitler's equal self-certainty. Sixty million is a whisker below the total population of the UK. There's much to be said for the perspective of Allan Bloom, a philosopher who looks a lot like the elderly Charles de Gaulle:

> The study of history and of culture teaches that all the world was mad in the past; men always thought they were right and that led to wars, persecutions, slavery, xenophobia, racism and chauvinism. The point is not to correct the mistakes and really be right; rather it is not to think you are right at all.[89]

My final point on hubris is that self-doubt or intellectual humility isn't necessarily a recipe for confusion. There's enough intellectual space to believe that one doesn't know much and that therefore one is rarely going to be right, yet at the same time accept that one has to live, make concrete assessments and make decisions in order to move on. There's enough space to live sensibly on a platform of less certainty. I suspect that one of the consequences of this co-existence is the need to be more sensitive to actions that might impact other people, as well as the need to carefully manage those actions. Put another way, it's important to recognise that we each have viewpoints that are only that, and they're never the objective truth. So when we engage other people, we've got to be a bit more mindful not to infringe upon them.

That leads me to me, myself and I. If I don't *know* what I'm writing about, why bother? If I can't be objective or independent about my research and analysis, what am I doing? It's a sensible set of questions and one that I had to mull around when starting this project. My response, which took some time to settle in my mind, boiled down to three points. First, I thought it was important to convey the problems surrounding objectivity to generate a modicum of self-doubt and intellectual humility. Each of us has a role in creating the reality we engage and we just need to get comfy with that. None of us is a truth guru, which is why I'm relaxed about not knowing. Epistemologically speaking, we all need to take a big chill pill, put our feet up and not get so stressed…because we don't really, truly *know*.

Second, even if one can't be objective, one can still influence people. Did Pablo Picasso not have a huge impact with perspectives which were hardly objective? He didn't even claim objectivity in his work, the most expensive of which (*La Reve*) was sold in March 2013 for $155.9 million. I'm clearly no Picasso, not even close, but the underlying principle remains that objectivity and truths aren't prerequisites to influence. I can think of quite a few American media sources which pummel rubbish all day long, yet they influence a lot of people too. And in any case, I think there's something to be said in not knowing and communicating that. It does require a certain strength or confidence to say, "I don't know."

Third, I felt that self-identity has a profound but overlooked impact on strategy. I'd stumbled during my PhD into a different way of seeing strategy that made a bit of sense to me. It accommodated people seeing the world in different ways, while providing a framework that seemed to offer something across personal, organisational and foreign policy strategies. That doesn't mean that I've put this matter to bed and somebody else won't later improve, refine or simply trash my thinking. Nor does it mean that I've overcome the challenges in mankind's quest for objectivity. I simply can't see that happening. What it does mean is that there's something about self-identity's impact on strategy that I think is worth considering, and for those who have the time and inclination, to explore further.

Before sailing into the next chapter, I do want to capture this chapter's essence because I know it's a lot to take in, and it's critical to grasp in order to make sense of the subsequent chapters. At modern philosophy's heart is the claim that mankind can be objective and independent about an external world. This claim is enshrined in empiricism, which emphasises the acquisition of knowledge from our senses. However, since at least the time of Kant and without plugging Arab thinkers yet again, we've been aware of modern philosophy and empiricism's intellectual failures that directly correspond to the three failures of modern strategy. That's no surprise, since the latter is wholly reliant on modern philosophy and empiricism.

The first failure is that modern strategy assumes that we can be objective and provide analysis on an objective basis, when in fact we can't. Integral to this, the second failure is the inability to recognise that any analysis is as dependent on the subject as it is on the object. Cognition and analysis reflect reality out there as much as they reflect the mind of the person who is seeing and making sense of things. Third and final, modern strategy's know-it-all-ism makes it simply too haughty to learn from intellectual disciplines which seek to understand people or the individual person, the centrepiece of life, organisational and foreign policy strategy. Collectively, these failures disable the modern strategist from exploring the influence of cognition, let alone that of self-identity, on the strategic process.

Illustrating these three weaknesses in modern strategy is important. It will help bring to life the recurring challenges of modern strategic work. It will help explain and illustrate what I am trying to convey. Finding examples of these issues is, fortunately, not very hard. One can take the work of almost any modern strategist and demonstrate the three shortcomings. Life, organisation and foreign policy strategy is littered with innocent victims—or, perhaps, lazy adopters—of modern philosophy's assumptions. What better way, then, to elucidate the failure of modern strategy than by dissecting the key work of some of the most influential and famous modern strategists? It's always fun to be a bit counter-establishment, a bit anti-authoritarian. That's exactly what we'll do in chapter 3.

1   FC Robinson, "Medieval: the Middle Ages," *Speculum*, 59, pp. 745–56. (Presidential address to the annual meeting of the Medieval Academy of America), 1984

2   T Irwin, *Classical Philosophy*, Oxford University Press, Oxford, 1999

3   http://plato.stanford.edu/entries/medieval-philosophy/-2009

4   T Irwin, *Classical Philosophy*, Oxford University Press, Oxford, 1999

5   J George, *Discourses of Global Politics*, Lynee Rienner, Boulder, 1994

6   SRC Hicks, *Explaining Postmodernism: Skepticism and Socialism from Rousseau to Foucault*, Scholargy Publishing, Tempe, 2004

7   M Fournier, *Émile Durkheim: A Biography*, Polity Press, Cambridge, 2013

8   SRC Hicks, *Explaining Postmodernism: Skepticism and Socialism from Rousseau to Foucault*, Scholargy Publishing, Tempe, 2004

9   *Ibid.*

10   *Ibid.*

11   *Ibid.*

12   P Strathern, *Kant in 90 Minutes*, Constable, London, 1996

13   *Ibid.*

14   DT Goldberg, *Racist Culture: Philosophy and the Politics of Meaning*, Blackwell Publishers, Oxford, 1993

15   I Kant, *Observations on the Feeling of the Beautiful and the Sublime*, translated by JT Goldthwait, University of California Press, Berkeley, 1960

16   N Chomsky, *Language and Responsibility*, Pantheon Books, New York, 1977

17   DT Goldberg, *Racist Culture: Philosophy and the Politics of Meaning*, Blackwell Publishers, Oxford, 1993

18   *Ibid.*

19   MH Morgan, "Lost History," *National Geographic*, Washington, DC, 2007

20   J Cottingham, *The Rationalists*, Oxford University Press, Oxford, 1988

21   SRC Hicks, *Explaining Postmodernism: Skepticism and Socialism from Rousseau to Foucault*, Scholargy Publishing, Tempe, 2004

22   SH Rizvi, "Avicenna," *Internet Encyclopaedia of Philosophy*, 2006, http://www.iep.utm.edu/avicenna/

23 J Locke, *An Essay Concerning Human Understanding*, EP Dutton, New York, 1947

24 http://en.wikipedia.org/wiki/Sense

25 M Calinescu, *The Five Faces of Modernity*, Duke University Press, Durham, 1999

26 SRC Hicks, *Explaining Postmodernism: Skepticism and Socialism from Rousseau to Foucault*, Scholargy Publishing, Tempe, 2004

27 *Ibid.*

28 B Russell, *History of Western Philosophy*, George Allen & Unwin, Ltd, London, 1946

29 AJ Ayer, *Hume: A Very Short Introduction*, Oxford University Press, Oxford, 2000

30 F Griffel, *Al-Ghazali's Philosophical Theology*, Oxford University Press, Oxford, 2009

31 K Hutchings, *Kant, Critique and Politics*, Routledge, London, 1995

32 *Ibid.*

33 I Kant, "Critique of Pure Reason," translated by WS Pluhar, Hackett Publishing, Indianapolis, 1996

34 SRC Hicks, *Explaining Postmodernism: Skepticism and Socialism from Rousseau to Foucault*, Scholargy Publishing, Tempe, 2004

35 R Tarnas, *The Passion of the Western Mind*, Ballantine, New York, 1991

36 K Hutchings, *Kant, Critique and Politics*, Routledge, London, 1995

37 B Russell, *History of Western Philosophy*, Simon & Schuster, New York, 1945

38 K Ansell-Pearson, *An Introduction to Nietzsche as Political Thinker*, Press Syndicate of the University of Cambridge, Cambridge, 1997

39 *Ibid.*

40 *Ibid.*

41 PE Gordon, "What Is Intellectual History?" http://history.fas.harvard.edu/people/faculty/documents/pgordon-whatisintellhist.pdf

42 J Rajchman, *Michel Foucault: The Freedom of Philosophy*, Columbia University Press, New York, 1986

43 *Ibid.*

44 J Reé, *Heidegger*, Phoenix, London, 1998

45 SRC Hicks, *Explaining Postmodernism: Skepticism and Socialism from Rousseau to Foucault*, Scholargy Publishing, Tempe, 2004

46 *Ibid.*

47 M Inwood, *Heidegger: A Very Short Introduction*, Oxford University Press, 1997

48 J George, *Discourses of Global Politics*, Lynee Rienner, Boulder, 1994

49 D Hume cited in B Aune, *Rationalism, Empiricism and Pragmatism*, Random House, New York, 1970

50 D Brooks, *The Social Animal*, Random House, New York, 2011

51 C List and F Dietrich, "The Impossibility of Unbiased Judgement Aggregation," *Theory and Decision*, Springer, London, 2010

52 A Gramsci quoted in, *Gramsci and the Italian State*, R Bellamy and D Schecter, Manchester University Press, Manchester, 1993

53 SRC Hicks, *Explaining Postmodernism: Skepticism and Socialism from Rousseau to Foucault*, Scholargy Publishing, Tempe, 2004

54 E Montuschi, "Rethinking Objectivity in Social Science," *Social Epistemology*, Routledge, London, April–Sept. 2004

55 P Strathern, *Kant in 90 Minutes*, Constable, London, 1996

56 P Musharraf, *In the Line of Fire*, Simon & Schuster, London, 2006

57 S Hawking, *The Universe in a Nutshell*, Bantam Press, London, 2001

58 W Heisenberg, "Planck's Discovery and the Philosophical Problems of Atomic Physics," *On Modern Physics*, Clarkson Potter, New York, 1961

59 F Nietzsche, *The Birth of Tragedy*, translated by D Smith, Oxford University Press, Oxford, 2000

60 IH Daalder and JM Lindsay, *America Unbound: The Bush Revolution in Foreign Policy*, John Wiley and Sons, Hoboken, 2003

61 N Hamilton, "Bill Clinton: Mastering the Presidency," *Public Affairs*, New York, 2007

62 R Rorty quoted in *The Theory of Knowledge*, Wadsworth Publishing Company, Belmont, 1999

[63] F Nietzsche quoted in W Kaufmann, *The Portable Nietzsche*, Penguin Classics, London, 1994

[64] D Brooks, *The Social Animal*, Random House, New York, 2011

[65] MC Jaini, *Life of Mahavira*, Kessinger Publishing, Whitefish, 2007

[66] D Brooks, *The Social Animal*, Random House, New York, 2011

[67] J Lenman and Y Shemmar, *Constructivism in Practical Philosophy*, Oxford University Press, Oxford, 2012

[68] "Smoking and Health 1964–1979: The Continuing Controversy," The Tobacco Institute, Washington, DC, 1979

[69] W Isaacson, *Steve Jobs*, Simon & Schuster, New York, 2011

[70] *Ibid.*

[71] M Martin, *Verstehen: The Use of Understanding in Social Science*, Transaction Publishers, Piscataway, 2000

[72] D Brooks, *The Social Animal*, Random House, New York, 2011

[73] A Damásio, *Descartes' Error: Emotion, Reason and the Human Brain*, HarperCollins, New York, 1994

[74] D Ariely, *Predictably Irrational*, HarperCollins, New York, 2009

[75] D Brooks, *The Social Animal*, Random House, New York, 2011

[76] *Ibid.*

[77] L Peikoff, *Understanding Objectivism: A Guide to Learning Ayn Rand's Philosophy*, New American Library, New York, 2012

[78] G Stern, *The Structure of International Society*, London, Continuum International Publishing, 1995

[79] EW Said, *Culture and Imperialism*, Vintage, London, 2007

[80] S Pinker, *The Blank Slate*, Penguin Books, London, 2002

[81] *Ibid.*

[82] *Ibid.*

[83] D Kahneman, *Thinking, Fast and Slow*, Farrar, Straus and Giroux, New York, 2011

[84] V LoBue, DH Rakison and JS DeLoache, "Threat Perception across the Life Span: Evidence for Multiple Converging Pathways," *Current Directions in Psychological Science*, 2011

85   S Pinker, *The Blank Slate*, Penguin Books, London, 2002

86   *Ibid.*

87   DF Abell, *Defining the Business*, Prentice Hall, New Jersey, 1980

88   J Chang and J Halliday, *The Unknown Story: Mao*, Anchor Books, New York, 2005

89   A Bloom, *The Closing of the American Mind*, Touchstone Books, New York, 1988

CHAPTER 3

THREE OFFERINGS TO
THE OBJECTIVITY GOD

So we now move from the more abstract, foundational stuff to the more tangible, crunchy stuff. In this chapter, I'll illustrate the failures of modern strategy by focusing on the works of three seminal, modern strategists: Hans Morgenthau, Michael Porter and Phillip McGraw. This should help land some of the material from the previous chapter. It should demonstrate with real examples the common failures of the modern strategist kingdom. My selecting these strategists might in itself raise eyebrows. I'm sure somebody out there is going to ask why I chose three white men. After all, white men seem increasingly to be on the wrong side of so many things politically correct. Indeed, global warming, slavery and nuclear weapons are just a few of the bad things that are dished out as the white man's responsibility. As it happens, the white man dominates the orthodox strategy space, and that is why I ended up dealing with three of its kind.

Second, Morgenthau and Porter are respected scholars whose names have an academic gravitas and whose works graduates don't hesitate to refer to in writing their exams. The pair are, in fact, icons and legends of academia in modern foreign policy and business organisation. So that explains their selection. The work of McGraw, in contrast, neither aspires to nor achieves an academic standard. Nor do scholars frequently cite his work. I suspect that some will even unfairly chuckle at my having placed his work at the same table as Morgenthau's and Porter's. Despite McGraw's potentially more questionable academic pedigree, he remains one of the world's leading life strategists. And that's an industry that, to its actual credit, may value conventional academic bona fides a little less than it values emotional and social intelligence, which I suspect McGraw has in abundance.

In exploring a key work of each of these three strategists, I'll show that their strategic frameworks suffer from the same issues which I've critiqued modern philosophy and modern strategy for: 1. their works are presented as if to be objective, when they can't be; 2. their works ignore the notion that we as subjects see and make sense of the object world in a subjective way, which influences all of our interpretations; 3. and, finally, their works suffer from modern philosophy's hubris, which makes it harder for them to learn from other intellectual disciplines, and reflects and reinforces the first two critiques. It is these three road bumps that collectively prevent modern strategists from recognising self-identity's influence on the strategic process—on how we see the world of today, develop the vision or objectives for the future and, finally, in how we will get from today to the future.

Politics Among Nations: Hans Morgenthau

Hans Morgenthau, a German immigrant to America, wrote *Politics Among Nations: The Struggle for Power and Peace* in 1948, when the Cold War was beginning and American policymakers were desperately searching for frameworks to address the growing international political tensions.[1] One of the best examples of a foreign policy strategy book, *Politics Among Nations* is also one of the key texts of political realism, the dominant school of international relations theory. The book had a powerful impact on US foreign policy practitioners in the emerging Cold War. Political realism believes that politics is explained by the theory of power politics.[i] Instead of offering a theory, however, the book simply reiterates the principles of the realist school (which wasn't founded by Morgenthau) and reads as a manual for navigating a world supposedly driven by power politics.

The book covers the ingredients, uses and limitations of power and touches upon morality, law, peace and security in the context of power. Morgenthau's portrayal of the world and how it works emphasises power, self-interest and a nuanced version of Hobbes's supposed depiction of life in the state of nature (that is, without a leviathan) as "solitary, poor, nasty, brutish and short."[2] I personally doubt Hobbes believed what he's often quoted on but we'll not go there now, in no small measure because he's centuries dead so he can't exactly correct misperceptions from his Derbyshire grave. I just want to add that a world without a leviathan in the first place and a world in which a leviathan is actually pulled out are very different. That said, Morgenthau was very much a believer in the certified Hobbesian school of thought:

> The struggle for power is universal in time and space and is an undeniable fact of experience. It cannot be denied that throughout historic time, regardless of social, economic and political conditions, states have met each other in contests for power. . . . International politics, like all politics, is a struggle for power. Whatever the ultimate aims of international politics, power is always the immediate aim.[3]

---

i   *Scientific Man Versus Power Politics*, Morgenthau's most comprehensive discussion of realism, was published in 1946, but it never generated the same interest as later books.

Given its impact on American policymakers and its succinct capturing of the power politics framework of the realist school, *Politics Among Nations* is widely read by first-year international relations students. For equally good reason, second-year students often strongly critique it just before they get into their third year. Many third-year students, or at least the ones who attended class and read anything in their first couple of years, treat it as intellectually highly challenged. You can definitely count me in that group.

With a message that appeals to the layman and meets the needs of the press for simplistic, sound-bite assessments of international politics, the book has little forecasting value; and true to form within the modern philosophical paradigm, the book also happens to be deeply lacking epistemologically and ontologically. The simplest illustration of that is the first test that the book fails on. Following the mantra of modern philosophy to the dotted i, *Politics Among Nations* fully embraces the idea of a world in which we can be objective and know the truth. And of course, lest there be any ambiguity, Morgenthau was on the right side of that world, in contrast to lesser minds who couldn't see the world for what it truly was.

Morgenthau's book is littered with sermons on "the objectivity of the laws of politics" and being able to distinguish between "truth and opinion."[4] The book repeatedly finger-wags those misty-eyed folk who fail to assess situations objectively. If only, so Morgenthau argues, foreign policy practitioners saw the world as it is and not what it should be, life would be so much easier. We would all live happily ever after because we would navigate the world efficiently. Instead, he claims, the idealists keep on seeing reality through biased blinkers. They let their guard down and create chaos. So energised is his posturing and relentless pursuit of facts, objectivity and truth that Morgenthau doesn't leave much space for redemption. He, indeed, drank modern philosophy's Kool-Aid and that, too, in concentrated form.

Following that, the book then completely fails to recognize the role that the foreign policy practitioner has in seeing and giving meaning to the world, a prerequisite to the strategist doing anything in it. Then again, it would have made no sense for Morgenthau to suggest we have a role in seeing our world, since he believed that some smart people (without specifying his full name, address and headshot) can be objective and can know the truth because they use the pseudo-superior scientific empiricist epistemology. It would seem that the man from Bavaria hadn't taken note of the hundreds of critiques that had discredited empiricism before he was born. Maybe the swampy language in those critiques was just too much for him? In empathy, I'm here reminded of some words of wisdom from Winnie the Pooh: "It is more fun to talk with someone who doesn't use long, difficult words but rather short, easy words like 'What about lunch?'"[5] That though is no justification for his ignoring the critiques.

The closest the book comes to recognising the impact of a foreign policy strategist's cognition or making sense of the world is in acknowledging a relationship between ideology and politics. I believe that ideology, for those who have one, can influence cognition. It often affects one's understanding of the world. However, lest Morgenthau drift far in that direction and break from modern philosophy and empiricism's ranks, he insists that ideologies merely *hide* the true nature of policymaking, which is to gain power: "ideologies render involvement in that contest for power psychologically and morally acceptable to the actors and their audience."[6] In short, the book treats ideologies as mere cosmetic camouflage; that, there, is the closest that *Politics Among Nations* gets to acknowledging the subject-object interdependence. It really isn't very close.

Morgenthau thus fails to answer the question, How do foreign policy practitioners see and give meaning to their respective worlds?

Let's be honest, he fails to recognise the question in the first place, admonishing those who can't see the obvious reality of the world as "naïve." What better way to overcome challenges than to ignore them? Politicians do a lot of this—ignoring a question that they don't like and answering a question that wasn't even posed. Be an ostrich all you want, but how we make sense of something fundamentally influences how we deal with it. Cognition is the first step, a key platform upon which any subsequent strategy is built. See a knife as that and you use it for butter; see it as a weapon and you use it for flesh. How you, the strategist, see things is accordingly very important.

Morgenthau's claim that all nation-states see the world exclusively through the identical power lens is way off. Leaving aside that most states aren't and have never been nation-states, people from different ethno-cultural backgrounds often see the same world in different ways. Compare the view of Israel in America with the view held in Africa, Europe, Asia and South America. Most of America sees Israel as a democracy of a white, biblically chosen people who survived a holocaust and were settled in their ancestral homeland, only to be surrounded by some crazy brown-skinned Arabs. That's how Americans make sense of Israel. In contrast, most of the rest of the world sees Israel as a vicious, racist bully that is itself perpetrating something in between a holocaust and apartheid against the Palestinians.

Likewise, Pakistan sees and makes sense of India differently than does the UK. Pakistan, at least its military, which has traditionally controlled its foreign policy, sees India as an imperialistic Hindu state that wants to reabsorb Pakistan into a single greater India.[ii] I

---

ii   This isn't surprising since Pakistan was created out of fear of *Hindu domination* of a post-independence India. Gandhi fanned the fear by using Hindu concepts including *ahimsa* (nonviolence), *swaraj* (self-rule) and *satyagraha* (insistence on truth) to win independence. If he had talked about *jihad* (exertion),

kid you not, that's the mind-set at army headquarters in Rawalpindi. The UK, in contrast, sees India as a former "jewel in the crown" and as a regional superpower glittered with economic opportunity. India invokes nostalgia in The Foreign and Commonwealth Office. In a similar vein, Sierra Leone and Japan see Guinea in different ways. Sierra Leone sees Guinea as a powerful neighbour, a trading partner and a sanctuary for the victims of civil war. Japan, for its part, barely sees Guinea. I suspect many of its policymakers wouldn't even be able to locate it to the nearest thousand miles on a map.

So America sees an Israel that differs from what most of the world sees, Pakistan sees an India that differs from what the UK sees and Sierra Leone sees a Guinea that differs from what Japan sees. Lest you're wondering, Canada under the Conservative party pretty much blindly sees whatever the American neo-conservative right-wing sees. None of these interpretations are make-believe, positioning claptrap. America and the rest of the world, Pakistan and the UK, and Sierra Leone and Japan really do see the same world, including specific countries, in very different ways. They aren't just making the stuff up for the heck of it. They really do see things in very different ways.

It's partly because there are divergent ways of seeing the same world that countries have different foreign policies. If all countries saw the world in the same way, their policies would be much more similar to each other's. Morgenthau, like other modern strategists, failed to appreciate that different people do see and make sense of the same world in different ways. If he'd read up on what was going on around him in the broader humanities and social sciences, he might not have ended up in a dead end. But as a committed follower

---

tawhid (oneness of God) and *mujahid* (one who exerts), Pakistan might not have come into being. That said, it's hard now to see why India would want to conquer a nuclear state flooded with firearms, religious crackpots, poverty and corruption. If anything, New Delhi is probably praying everyday that Pakistan gets a grip.

of the objectivity god, he felt no pressure to explore the several disciplines that study human beings, an exercise which might challenge his basic assumptions.

In contrast, since the 1990s a small handful of foreign policy scholars have focused on how belief and cognitive systems impact foreign policy. For instance, Margot Light successfully demonstrated that psychological lenses, cognitive maps and images of the self have a key role in shaping foreign policy.[7] Thanks to opened archival records, particularly in the former USSR, academics now have a better grasp of the role of cognition in foreign policy. They can see how cognitive systems impacted foreign policy strategy. Using such records, historians such as John Gaddis have crisply demonstrated sharp differences amongst policymakers who saw the same events.[8] In fact, in some instances where some policymakers saw a single event, other policymakers saw several, independent events.

The final hurdle that *Politics Among Nations* falls foul of is its hubris, inspired as it is by modern philosophy and empiricism. The book neither refers to nor makes use of the vibrant intellectual developments that had emerged in our understanding of human beings, including what a human is, how a human knows and what a human needs. Each of these had been energetically engaged across a broad spectrum of human learning before and during the time of Morgenthau's writing. And why should *Politics Among Nations* entertain any such notions given we obviously, objectively know human nature? Why should we bother to reassess basic assumptions given we truthfully know the laws of politics? Sarcasm aside, this is annoying given the early and mid-twentieth century was an extraordinarily rich period in our understanding of mankind and human behaviour.

If Morgenthau had been meandering in a remote African village in the thirteenth century, drinking egusi juice (there is apparently such a drink, but I've never tried it) while watching lions hunt zebras, I might understand why he would have been unaware of what was happening elsewhere in the world. He'd have been captivated by savannah issues, which would be a far cry from the cerebral, intellectual developments of the early twentieth-century humanities and social sciences across some of the world's metropolises. And communications in the thirteenth century were such that it wouldn't have been easy to keep track of what was cooking in other parts of the world. There was no radio, television or telephone to exchange information through. We didn't even have Facebook then!

However, Morgenthau wrote *Politics Among Nations* in Chicago in 1948, during a time of vigorous growth in the theories and understandings of human behaviour. Furthermore, Chicago offered no lions-eating-zebras distractions to dilute his attention: Lincoln Park Zoo never supported this class of authentic animal behaviour. Perhaps the zoo's management thought it'd be too authentic for families; or, perhaps, they didn't have enough zebras to go around? Frankly, I have no idea what the underlying rationale was. Chicago was a big city, well connected with other big cities. The point is Morgenthau was exposed to some exciting learning that could have had a substantial impact on his thinking on strategy and specifically on the subjectivity of objectivity and the interdependence of subject and object.

To give you a sense of the era's intellectual richness in the context of understanding people and individual human beings, the Frankfurt School of critical theory (including Theodor Adorno) challenged the epistemological assumptions of modernism in full swing.[9] Social theory felt the impact of Weber and Durkheim, who challenged positivism in favour of personal cognition, assessed society in a post-traditional world and, it's fair to say, established sociology as an independent academic discipline.[10] That in itself was a significant breakthrough which *Politics Among Nations* could have drawn from. Through "action theory," the sociologist Talcott Parsons advanced our understanding of individual actions and reactions while trying to gel positivism with a more subjective, motivational appreciation of mankind's behaviour.[11]

Staying within Morgenthau's continent, Franz Boas pioneered anthropology in America by changing the nature-versus-nurture debate, moving the pendulum distinctly towards nurture.[12] He also saw the world as a conglomerate of cultures that cannot easily be understood by any single anchor culture, with profound implications for all strategy. This insight punctured the illusion that any cultural community could easily generalise about other communities or establish universal human laws, with stark consequences for Morgenthau's assumption about human nature and foreign policy strategy, per se. If our vantage point is itself limited, biased or polluted by virtue of the prevailing culture, then what does that say about our objectivity? How can we understand the mental framework of another if we only use our own mental framework?

In philosophy, Edmund Husserl established phenomenology, which reached beyond positivism and empiricism in a bid to attain knowledge; Alfred Jules (AJ) Ayer and Popper were deeply engaged with the Vienna Circle, which fine-tuned positivism into logical positivism; and Heidegger (irrespective of what I think of his work), Sartre and Russell were the source of forceful, lively ideas. Russell, with George Edward Moore and Ludwig Wittgenstein, developed analytical philosophy, which emphasised conceptual clarity, formal logic and semiotics. Sartre's work on existentialism and consciousness made him a public intellectual. I could go on with Simone de Beauvoir, Albert Camus and Claude Lévi-Strauss. The point is that Morgenthau was working at a time of intellectual vibrancy in the humanities and social sciences. Yet *Politics Among*

Nations reflects none of this. It has no evidence of that vibrancy. It has no evidence of those ideas.

How silly of me. Why should it have borrowed from the other social sciences and humanities? Why should *Politics Among Nations* have looked into other nonpolitical disciplines in its quest to understand and engage foreign policy strategy? I'm asking rhetorical questions. In its simplest form, the study of foreign policy strategy is an attempt to understand how one group of people (often, but not always, congregated as a country) pursue their objectives principally but not exclusively by working with, around or through other groups of people (often, but not necessarily, other countries). It's not all that complicated. And since foreign policy is a people-to-people activity, one would think it important to be aware of the work of disciplines that study human behaviour, including how humans think and see and also what they want to achieve. That's sensible simply because foreign policy is all about people.

It doesn't mean that one need study everything, all the latest intellectual happenings about people or mankind. That would be an overwhelmingly paralysing exercise. In the modern era the humanities and social sciences produce more work in a day than can be read in a year. It does mean that the study of foreign policy strategy should entertain a flow of ideas and insights from disciplines which study the individual person or groups of people. What seems weird is to ignore all studies on human beings. It'd be different if one could see evidence that *Politics Among Nations* had used some of those insights without referring to the sources. Even if we cut Morgenthau this huge slack, I really struggled to find anything. That know-it-all hubris of modern philosophy was in full swing. What's more, Morgenthau's peers praised him for it: they made him into a guru. Other intellectual disciplines could do whatever they wanted to understand people, but modern foreign policy strategists would keep their heads buried in the savannah dirt.

Having failed to recognize both that we can't be objective and that we have a role in seeing and giving meaning to our reality, as well as demonstrating modern philosophy's know-it-all hubris, what then did Morgenthau offer to us? What was his alternative approach? Within his "objective" framework, he defined the starting point for each country, irrespective of how they saw things or what their prevailing culture was. And why not? After all, if there's an objective way to see everything and he knows it, surely he can cram it down everybody's windpipe with wild abandon. Thus, *Politics Among Nations* places each country on a power grid according to many factors. These include: population, military and industrial strength, geography, quality of government (including diplomacy), natural resources, national morale and character.[13] That is each country's starting point.

A country that scores an A on most of these criteria might stack up as a superpower, as the US so clearly did from the mid-twentieth century and especially in the 1950s and 1960s. And a country that generally scores E grades might be similar to modern-day Zimbabwe, which according to UNDP has the worst quality of life in the world.[14] Put in other words and using McDonald's French fries terminology to help communicate my point, all countries start as kid-sized (introduced in 2011), small, medium or large. If countries, meaning their senior decision-makers, have other ways of seeing the world, they're wrong and they'll make poor decisions, because Morgenthau's way is apparently the objective way. According to Morgenthau, the power grid is the only correct or objective way to understand the world.

According to Morgenthau, the starting point for all countries, irrespective of their contrasting ways of seeing the world, depends on their position on the power grid—that is, what size of French fries they are. *Politics Among Nations* offers no explanation as to why all mankind needs to see the world in the same way that the book supposedly sees it and with the same focus on power (which the book used in at least half a dozen different and sometimes conflicting ways). Nor does the book offer any consequences for those countries that want to see the world through their own lens (and thus outside of the book's framework). If a country rejects the power grid, does it have a future? Does it still exist? Does it get flicked off the edge of the universe? Could it still sell authentic French fries in its territory?

Having straitjacketed the starting point of foreign policy, *Politics Among Nations* then straitjackets the end point by locking down human nature, one of mankind's most important and complex intellectual challenges. Without the slightest gesture towards the many disciplines that explore human nature and aspiration, Morgenthau places power acquisition as the sole objective of individuals and countries alike. In his universe, mono-dimensional, computational power-obsessed practitioners, devoid of any emotion, govern countries. I am now thinking of some kind of hybrid between a calculating maths geek and a power fanatic. Further, *Politics Among Nations* claims this power goal is rooted in human nature—without, of course, backing it up. I'm being polite—it's a massive assertion which is supported by bugger all. The power goal thus anchors every Tom, Dick and Hassan's strategic end game.

The book treats all considerations of morality, law, religion, culture, relationships and domestic politics as merely cosmetic.[15] These, it argues, are all irrelevant fluff. The human species, which the book refuses to explore in any depth, is so simple, self-evident and homogeneous that everybody wants the same thing in life. That a Tibetan Buddhist monk who spends days in meditation might have different goals to a London-based investment banker counting his ethically questionable bonus didn't strike Morgenthau as problematic. That is simply flabbergasting. Call me a simpleton, but it feels a bit obvious that our needs and aspirations are more complex and varied than simply becoming "more powerful." You don't even have to read very far to be able to self-reflect that your own personal needs (assuming you're not a complete psycho or something) extend beyond merely becoming more powerful.

So what do we have then from *Politics Among Nations*? The book not only establishes each country's foreign policy starting point by placing it on a simple power grid but also claims that all countries share the same goal. If there's space left for strategic flexibility or thought, it's not much. A vegan would have more options at an American McDonald's. I had to clarify because an Indian McDonald's has quite a few veggie options, such as the McSpicy Paneer and the Veg McMuffin.[16] This isn't surprising given that Indians treat as sacrosanct that which Americans gobble up: the cow.[iii] The journey's start and end points, as laid out by *Politics Among Nations*, are thus locked down. The book offers to conceptual flexibility what Dubya offered to world peace and security: a thoroughly worn out South Asian village *chadi*.[iv]

By defining a starting point and a goal, most of the important strategic work is done. How you then get from point A to point B is the easy part. The hardest part is in first stabilising the journey's two points. That's where the strategist has to think, mull and reflect; that's where there's real graft and work to be had. And that's because

---

iii   I don't want people to think that I'm a covert public relations hack for McDonald's but practically everyone who reads this book, in every continent in the world, will be able to relate to McDonald's, so it's a useful communication device.

iv   A *chadi* is an indigenous South Asian underwear. While it lacks the finish of competing Marks & Spencer products, the chadi is well known in South Asia. A village chadi, I presume, would be one that has been worn by the entire village or perhaps its leaders. Maybe the village top guns were granted wearing rights to that chadi? I don't know, I'm just speculating. If my speculation is accurate, a village chadi is well worth staying clear of.

amongst the multitude of ways of seeing reality (whatever "realty" is), some ways might destroy a country while others might enable it to thrive and others still will deliver something in between. In fact, management consultants, who sometimes give advice to governments, often add a lot of their value precisely by stabilising and getting buy-in to just those subjective bookends of the strategic process. They run around the key stakeholders to syndicate what's going on now and where everybody wants to get to. And they take a handsome cheque for that, for developing a consensus on what the world of today and of tomorrow look like.

It's specifically because *Politics Among Nations* eradicated the opportunity for thinking by locking down start and end points that American foreign policy strategists, practitioners and academics loved it. They no longer had to . . . think! They no longer needed to exert their minds, wrack their brains or stand on their own feet. In creating simplistic cubbyholes that merely needed populating, Morgenthau's book met the need for structure and sense-making that had risen in the dramatic transition from World War II to the Cold War. It also met the need for simplicity from pedestrian academics and lazy practitioners who wanted to go to work . . . but didn't want to work. As long as everybody was populating cubbyholes, they were fine.

The grand theory of *Politics Among Nations* confines all humankind—past, present and future—to tight, suffocating frameworks that determine where they start and where they want to go. It doesn't matter how a country sees the world or what it wants. Nor does it matter that not all people and countries are power-obsessed psychopaths. The important thing is that they neatly fit into late-20th-century, power-centric, American cubbyholes that may (or, more likely, may not) mean very much to most countries. That this way of seeing reality has virtually no intellectual underpinnings should come as no surprise: it was contrived out of thin air, it was contrived out of Morgenthau's own imagination. To use an expression which I've not forgotten from Mark Hoffman's lectures at the London School of Economics on "Concepts and Methods in International Relations," Morgenthau's way of seeing things is "epistemologically bankrupt."

That's an important point to hone in. It's not that Morgenthau's strategic framework has no value . . . it does have value. It's a useful reference point, it's worth thinking about and it sheds light on *aspects* of how *some* groups of human beings might from *time to time* engage each other. However, that's about all it has to offer. *Politics Among Nations* has very brittle epistemological underpinnings. It's not a panacea for how countries do or should see the world. Its subsequent advice or guidance isn't based on an objective or comprehensive assessment of international relations. It has no authoritative basis to answer the question, How do you know that the world is the way that you see it? And as a result of all of that, it's as bad at predicting the future as it is in explaining the past.

That then leaves *Politics Among Nations* guilty of not only all three charges laid at modern philosophy but also of developing a subsequently stifling framework. The book prizes the false idea that people can be objective. It does not appreciate that analysis is dependent on both the practitioner as much as the world which is being engaged, that analysis is an interdependent outcome. Finally, it shows no desire to engage the range of disciplines that study and think about human beings. Instead, its framework forces all countries to start their journey on a cramping grid, irrespective of how they see the world. It then bludgeons them to have the same aim, irrespective of what they themselves want. You've got to wonder how a country's strategy can be effective if it completely ignores that country's perspective and aspirations.

Competitive Strategy: Michael Porter

Michael Porter is another strategist, this time from the business academic world. He also illustrates the same three failings of modern philosophy and thus modern strategy. Porter, an engineer, economist and management consultant by background, burst onto the scene in 1980 with the publication of *Competitive Strategy*, a book intended to help businesses best locate themselves in the marketplace either by defending their positions or by influencing competitive factors in their favour (a summary which I've unashamedly paraphrased from his book because I still don't totally grasp what it means).[17] The book is just a bit too consultanty for my liking, but that's just my take…and it's also possibly reflective of Porter's consulting background.

Even though I thought the book was more of a laundry list for profit-maximizing business strategies than a book about strategy per se, its impact in the business world has been at least as great as that of Morgenthau's book in the foreign policy world. Porter is perhaps his generation's most influential business academic. He is a living legend. Generations of MBA students, consultants and academics around the world are familiar with his name and the book's core content; though I doubt whether most successful business strategists have ever read it. That's not saying very much, since the vast majority of business strategists are entrepreneurs, and only a small proportion of them have had any formal academic training. The sort of folk who study for MBAs, or for that matter qualify as accountants, tend to be risk averse, which is precisely what entrepreneurs are not.

As was the case with *Politics Among Nations*, my first criticism of *Competitive Strategy* in line with its modern philosophical underpinnings is its worship of the objectivity god, the same one who sits esoterically on Mount Empiricism. Porter and his followers believed they could be objective and that they knew the truth. They believed in a world that is self-evident and knowable. They believed in the basic premise of modern philosophy, being that they could *know*. In fact, they may well have believed one step more—that in the business world *they* were the ones who really did know, that they held a privileged place on Mount Empiricism, that they were, indeed, the true disciples of the objectivity god. I suppose it's easier to fall into that trap if you're a top professor, as is Porter, at one of the world's top universities.

This failure of modern philosophy doesn't just creep into the book's outskirts. It percolates deep into its bedrock and forms an essential part of its finger-wagging sermons. *Competitive Strategy* specifically and repeatedly lauds objectivity, berating firms for filtering the events of the present through the lens of the past and thereby failing to be objective. It criticises firms for failing "to look objectively at the prospects of decline."[18] It stresses that firms need to be objective in their industry analysis, notwithstanding that I found the way the book uses the term "industry" to be confusing.[19] In a similar vein, specific research approaches are praised for their ability to provide "an unbiased overview of the industry."[20] Continuing that flow, the book then red-flags some types of research tools, such as interviews, which the book claims might compromise "objectivity."[21] Clearly, the idea that objectivity is not attainable hadn't registered with Porter.

Failure number two: Porter was writing at a time when many in the humanities and social sciences recognized cognition and analysis as a partial reflection of the mind which is making sense of, which is analysing. In contrast, *Competitive Strategy* fails to recognize that analysis is always a value-laden exercise, that analysis reflects an interdependence between a subject (which is seeing and making sense) and an object reality (which is being understood). At no point in the book's almost four hundred pages could I find a hint in this direction, making the same mistake which *Politics Among*

Nations had made some three decades before. There's nothing on this in the core argument. There's nothing in the peripheral arguments. And there's nothing in the notes. To answer the question asked by my editor, "Can you demonstrate that?" No, I can't demonstrate a nothing. It just doesn't exist!

The book ignores the role of the strategist in making sense of his reality, so it's no surprise that the book assumes everybody sees the world in the same way. The two go hand in hand: if you think the world is self-evident, it's easy to then think that everybody sees the world the same way. I don't get why Porter couldn't simply have met with a social theorist at a café and asked, "Hey dude, what's kicking in your academic universe?" For the cost of a large mocha with the trimmings, he might have been exposed to the view that reality isn't self-evident. Cognition is a process that involves both the person trying to understand and the thing being understood. The arguments, if they are made, that it was too hard for Porter to get to a coffee shop because he had to cross the Charles River to get to Peet's Coffee and Tea or that mochas weren't vogue in the late 1970s are simply bogus.

Finally, in *Competitive Strategy* there's that same hubris which is symptomatic and characteristic of modern philosophy. The book ignores a significant breadth of work in the humanities and social sciences. Like the study of foreign policy strategy, the study of business strategy is about how one group of people (grouped as a business) tries to achieve its objectives. A big part of a business achieving its objectives or vision typically requires dealing with people, whether they are customers, suppliers, managers, owners, competitors, financiers or regulators. Does that have a familiar feel to it? They're all human beings who have lives just like you and me (broadly speaking, of course, since some lives are very unorthodox. Let's not get into unorthodox lives right now because everybody has their own interpretation of unorthodoxy).

Thus, like foreign policy strategy, business strategy is a people-centric activity. And, as in the case of foreign policy strategy, and call me an idiot if you must, I think it's reasonable for a business strategist to keep abreast of our many efforts to understand people, either as individuals or groups. How do people see the world? How do they engage with it? What do people do under different conditions? How do they respond to specific actions? What behaviour is culture-specific and what is universal? How do we know? How do any of these insights impact the strategist or his situation? These are critical questions in any strategic thinking because any such thinking gravitates around people or the person, strategy's centrepiece. I don't think this point should take much convincing.

In what must now feel a bit like déjà vu, *Competitive Strategy* seems to ignore the abundant efforts, across a plethora of disciplines, to understand mankind. At least, I fail to find any evidence. That's not surprising, I guess, because true to the form of modern philosophy, why should Porter bother engaging other intellectual disciplines if he already *knows* and he's objective on whatever is relevant to business strategy? Why bother if he *knows* the right way of seeing things (at least in the context of the business) and objectively *knows* man's needs, behaviours and goals? This is not the hubris of an individual. It's important to stress that. It's definitely not about the personality of a person. This is the hubris of an entire intellectual underpinning, a whole way of understanding, crafted by modern philosophy and permeated deep into modern business strategy. But hubris, I think, it indeed is.

Like Morgenthau, Porter was surrounded by intense intellectual activity in an even more interconnected world (still admittedly pre-Facebook but more interconnected than Morgenthau's world). In sociology, the post-war domination of Marxism and functionalism rapidly eroded, giving way to a range of exciting "third generation" approaches, including phenomenological approaches, critical theory, ethnomethodology and symbolic interactionism.[22] Post-structuralists Jacques Derrida and Foucault, two of the most cited humanities scholars of the century, produced their most important works during this period. Along with Julia Kristeva and Roland Barthes, they redefined knowledge as a function of power and bonded meaning with culture. Derrida was especially influential on philosophical and literary methods, while Foucault was on social and political thought. They rewrote so many of the rules of understanding.

Even a first-year social theorist might have questioned *Competitive Strategy*'s ontology of potential entrants, buyers, substitutes and suppliers to make sense of industries. Where do these conceptual categories come from? What legitimates them? On whose authority? How do they progress our understanding of the business world? What alternative buckets might be used to engage reality? What is the effect of using one set of buckets over another? *Competitive Strategy* seems to have ignored decades of thought-provoking work in the humanities and social sciences.[23] In fact, I found nothing from these universes, explicitly or implicitly, in the book.[v] That's no different to a construction firm today ignoring everything learned about building design and materials over the past few decades.

In *Competitive Strategy* there is the implicit notion that we can guide a group of human beings (who come together as a business) to deal with other groups of human beings (other businesses and individual human beings) with the goal of achieving a set of human objectives without ever trying to meaningfully understand any aspect of . . . human beings. Let's try to navigate a people against other people by paying scant, if any, attention to what we are learning about people! It's hard to understand how Porter

---

v   Economics was granted lip service, but Porter went no further.

contemplated doing that. Moreover, how did he get away with that? If there ever was a *chatpatta* point, this is it; which is just as well, since it's been a while since I shot the last one out. It's good to spice things up, adds to a multicultural and lively feel.

What's even more *chatpatta*, as if we had starved ourselves into a double dose, is that all this "stood the test of peer review" and "survived the scrutiny" of Porter's MBA students.[24] It's got to make you wonder why those peers and students couldn't recognise that a book that purports to help one group of human beings navigate their relations with other human beings must at some level investigate and understand human beings. Did Porter's reputation stifle independent thinking from the lecture hall? Who knows, but I want to stress that it's not just *Competitive Strategy* that I'm putting in the dock. This is not a problem specific to this book or its author. Practically the entire modern business strategy sector suffers from the same issues, which somewhat reflects and explains the drought of critical thinking and conceptual latitude in business academia.

Competitive Strategy fails on the same three issues as does *Politics Among Nations*. It believes in and worships a world of objectivity, ignores the subject-object interdependence and demonstrates modern philosophy's hubris. In doing so, *Competitive Strategy* does exactly what *Politics Among Nations* had done a few decades before. It takes away from strategists the demanding and creative task of working out where things stand. It also makes life easy for the cookie cutters, pedestrians and simpletons. It's thus not difficult to see why MBA students and management consultants still love the book: it fillets away the difficult and taxing task of making sense of the world, of determining what is important and what the various components mean. In other words, its fans love the book for providing them a framework which they can mindlessly deploy.

And what is that framework? Just as Morgenthau had located

countries in a power hierarchy, Porter's starting point for a firm is how it measures on his famous five forces.[25] A firm in an industry with low barriers to entry, high threat of substitute products, strong bargaining powers on the part of both buyers and suppliers and fierce rivalry amongst industry firms is a kid-sized French fries. For some odd reason, I'm now thinking of San Francisco's futile attempt at banning kids' toys from McDonald's Happy Meals. My youngest would have been really disappointed with that. Anyhow, any such firm is up the creek: it might even need a new size, perhaps for infants (though this will precipitate a backlash from the baby nutrition lobby). I can't think of any industry that's in such an awful predicament, but you get the point.

In contrast, a firm in an industry with high barriers to entry, low threat of substitute products, weak bargaining powers on the part of both buyers and suppliers and a sense of camaraderie amongst industry firms is obviously a large French fries; and easily could have been a super size, if only the size was still around. Apparently, we shouldn't blame its withdrawal on Morgan Spurlock. Nor we should blame it on the realisation that a single pack of French fries constituted more than a third of the recommended calorific intake for women. In 2010, Apple might have been one such firm, but I doubt there was much love lost between Apple and its competitors. I can't imagine that Apple's leadership regularly sent jars of Oreo cookies to their Samsung counterparts. Refocusing away from the corporate animosity, many firms start their journey somewhere near the middle of the industry grid.

Having defined a narrow exogenous and alien framework to determine a firm's starting point, *Competitive Strategy* asserts that all firms, everywhere on this planet (past, present and future), have two goals, like it or lump it.[26] Noah's Ark had two of every animal. Porter's Ark had two goals for every business. Coincidence? Perhaps not to the hard-core Porter fans. In defining two goals, the book set in stone the end point of an organisation's strategic journey. Apart from the obvious problem in generalising for such a vast heterogeneous range of humankind, the book's suggested two goals for all organisations are confusing and potentially contradictory. The book defines the goal of strategy as follows:

> The goal of a competitive strategy for a business unit in an industry is to find a position in the industry where the company can best defend itself against . . . competitive forces or can influence them in its favor.[27]

In other words, a firm's goal is to better position itself in relation to competitive forces. I'll kick this goal completely into touch because I can't see how the goal of a business strategy is anything other than delivering on the business's objectives—irrespective of how the business deals with competitive forces. I take this position based on how I defined strategy in the first chapter, an exercise that *Competitive Strategy* didn't, strangely enough, feel compelled to do. Dealing with competitive forces is one of many *means*. It is not an end. It's not necessarily a goal. Strategies often address competitive forces, but that's not their purpose, which is to deliver on some objectives or a vision. I guess it's the sort of pickle you'd expect to be in if you don't clarify key terms such as "strategy" up front.

In any case, some organisational strategies don't engage with competitive forces at all because there aren't any such forces to engage. The British Home Office, for example, is an organisation that doesn't compete to offer British passports. There are no "competitive forces" in this sector. Nobody else can legally provide British passports, but the Home Office nevertheless has a *strategy* in place to make and distribute them efficiently (which, in my experience, I think it does well). In other words, the Porter goal of dealing with competitive forces doesn't feel like a goal at all because in some instances, there is no competition. Dealing with competitive forces is, in my humble opinion, only a strategy and not the purpose of strategy, it is not the goal.

The second goal that *Competitive Strategy* mandates for all firms has three parts, "profitability, market share and social responsiveness."[28] The book doesn't elaborate much on these, but a couple of bits come to mind. First, social responsiveness is ignored in the book. The social dimension, including social responsibility, the environment, responsibilities to employees, sensitivity to local communities and all that type of tree hugging, barely gets a mention in the book. This starkly contrasts with the book's gazillion references to profitability and market share. When *Competitive Strategy* discusses strategy in a maturing industry, the recommendations focus on revenue and costs, without mentioning "social responsiveness." When the book discusses strategy in a fragmented industry, it stresses market share, costs and niche focus, without citing a social dimension. In fact, its three generic strategies of cost leadership, product differentiation and niche focus lean only to economic goals. I'm not sure why the book mentions social responsiveness as a goal and then ignores it, but there you go.

A more substantial point is that *Competitive Strategy*'s use of profitability and market share as a firm's objective is rigid and blatantly Anglo-American. Even confining to the Anglo-American universe, which is a limited universe, many firms have goals that they prioritise above making a profit or expanding market share. For instance, many business owners who've built a firm want their children to take it over—that organisation's succession is itself a goal, and sometimes it's more important than the incremental increase in return on equity. When the owner's objective is to keep the firm in the family or for his children to lead, he's often implicitly de-prioritising earnings and prioritising family ownership and control. And that goal is by no means unique or unheard of even in London, New York and Toronto. I mention Toronto because I live in the Greater Toronto Area and it's a good chance for me to give it a plug.

Keeping the firm in the family isn't the only goal that can trump profits and market share. Sometimes one of the goals of a firm can be quite egotistic: note how wanting to be famous or showing off often drives the ownership of landmark real estate. I could mention that the Dubai real estate crash of 2009 partly came about because many developers had built super-bling real estate to show off without ever thinking about the demand for such product. I could also add that when liquidity ran dry, there simply weren't enough buyers who could afford the super-bling. But then again, I could choose not to mention all that. Wanting to be famous is fine, too, if that's what the stakeholders want. Anglo-American firms pursue other goals beyond Porter's suggested two, such as reducing the stress of running a business, ensuring income stability and protecting jobs. It's not, contrary to Porter's suggestion, all about making a buck.

Not only does *Competitive Strategy* set rigid goals for Anglo-American firms, but it also ignores the diversity of goals set by firms in other regions, which host 95 percent of the world's population. For instance, many firms in the Gulf (especially state-owned firms) prioritise employing local citizens over and above maximising profit or revenues.[29] More often than seems comfortable, local citizens are unqualified for the job positions that they're in. Indeed, too frequently they also end up managing staff whose skills, experience and work ethic are vastly superior. It's normal to see expats in the Gulf reporting to Gulf citizens who, in an ordinary universe, would be a couple of tiers below those who report to them.[30] What does nothing for profits or market share sometimes serves other political and national development purposes. And these choices are for those that own the businesses.

The Gulf's businesses aren't alone in having their own sets of goals. In Japan, a firm's manager doesn't have a fiduciary responsibility to shareholders. The objectives of a Japanese firm reflect the needs of several stakeholders, including suppliers, customers and staff—a point which Porter knew about as a supporter of Japanese corporate governance (a supporter, that is, until the Japanese economy tanked, and then he stopped being a supporter of Japanese corporate governance. In football terms, this could be interpreted as fair-weather support).[31] German firms also give significant importance to staff. In larger German companies, employees have the same number of seats on the supervisory board as shareholders. German firms don't exist for shareholders alone. Corporate Germany's objectives extend beyond meeting shareholder needs.[32]

Having straitjacketed a firm's starting point and also its objective, *Competitive Strategy* smothers the final space for breathing by presenting what are apparently the only three strategies for any firm anywhere on this planet (note that infectious list of three reflecting Porter's management consulting background). Firms of the world sit up and take note: there are only three paths to the Promised Land. To get from a restricted starting point to an even more restricted end destination, all firms must stick to three paths. I suppose that restriction is not so striking given that the journey's start and end are already so constrained. *Competitive Strategy* acknowledges some exceptions for industries that are fragmented, emerging, maturing, declining or global (whatever that means), but the three strategies are the book's Yellow Brick Road.

The first route is cost leadership, meaning that a firm provides its goods and services at the lowest cost, though not necessarily at the lowest price.[33] The second is differentiation, which means a firm distinguishes its product even if that distinction is only in the minds of potential customers. Most people say they prefer Coke to

Pepsi, even if blind taste tests suggest otherwise.[34] To pre-empt any wild speculation, especially being hounded by trailing paparazzi on this point, let me get it out there: I prefer Pepsi. The final strategy is to focus on a niche. For instance, instead of supplying pencils to all politicians, supply them to all honest politicians—that would really condense the numbers. I suppose you could collapse the numbers further if you insisted on supplying pencils only to honest politicians in Africa, possibly the most politically corrupt continent on the planet.

The pedestrian end of the strategy industry, including that silent majority of MBA whiz-kids and commercially innocent management consultants, venerate *Competitive Strategy* for having taken this one last step to simplify their lives. By restricting a business's starting point and objective and legalising only three routes to the Promised Land, *Competitive Strategy* lays out the strategic function for prosaic strategists—lock, stock and barrel. It transforms work from something which should be tilted towards a thinking and cerebral exercise into one which looks like an accumulated series of "copy and paste," vacuous—but slick—PowerPoint presentations. It takes the hard work out of a strategist's day and replaces it with dreary work akin to one of those awful mass-produced "sandwiches" which seem to linger away in every gas station's retail section.

And as I did with Morgenthau's work, the point here isn't that Porter's work is all wrong or there's nothing to be learned from it. If I were advising students of business, I'd recommend they at least get a familiarity with *Competitive Strategy* and its key concepts, because not only has it influenced so many people in business, but it can also inform their own thinking. Getting to grips with how others think is no bad thing. The point that I would stress, though, as I did with *Politics Among Nations*, is that its prescriptions and solutions aren't unbiased, objective or truthful. The book is subjective and conjured.

It says as much about Porter as it does about the world around him. Further, the book's portrayal of organisational or human objectives is pretty anaemic and ignores so much that we've learned (and are still learning) about human behaviour.

Competitive Strategy fully embraces, with robe and rosary, the objectivity god of modern philosophy that less adroit folk drifted away from with perilous consequences. *Competitive Strategy* also ignores, almost as a logical adjunct, the idea that we as subjects have a role in seeing and making sense of our object world. Finally, as a further tribute to the objectivity god, I think that the book refuses to meaningfully engage the several disciplines that explored the human being, the epicentre of strategy. It wasn't as if nothing interesting and relevant was being thought about and researched at the time the book was written. In its place, *Competitive Strategy* expounded a gagging framework in which an organisation's starting point, its goals and its strategic paths are all defined, irrespective of how the organization itself saw any of those things.

Self Matters: Phil McGraw

Having touched upon foreign policy and organizational strategy, I'd like to move to life strategy. Unlike its more academically shaped sisters, which stress the pomp and show of intellectual horsepower, life strategy generally lacks cerebral aspirations. I first came across life strategy in the 1990s and saw it then as the wishy-washy side of strategy. Actually, at that time I thought that personal coaches were little more than con artists, providing advice qualitatively similar to that found in astrology columns. As for the life strategy books, they seemed to be densely packed with silly, anecdotal and illustrative stories, without any substance or rigour. The writers seemed obsessed with emotional, right-brain thinking and lacked the capacity for hard, clear-headed thinking.

Over the years, I've changed my opinion on many things and even made full reversals. I once thought boxing was cool and now think that it's barbaric. The idea of hitting a brain until it's partially incapacitated no longer appeals to me. I once thought that people could be objective, which clearly I don't anymore. I once thought that Canadians were merely Scottish-accented Americans and now that I live in Toronto, I don't. For a start, thousands of Torontonians can only speak an Asian language, and that too not in a Scottish accent. Finally, I used to detest Dr Pepper, having no tolerance for the drink. However, I've grown into an occasional drinker, enjoying that peculiar, marzipan taste that is so socially divisive. I just want to caveat that a bit; I seldom drink a full can, given it has 40 grams of sugar, so we can ease any anxiety about my sugar levels.

My life strategy friends will be hoping, in the spirit of reversals, that I'll now cuddle them. Sadly not: if I'm ever to be fully on board, it's not today. In any case, I'm really not a big cuddler. It's not the sort of thing that we did during my decade in an English private school. However, I offer one (not three) olive branch to the life strategist community. A few years ago, I began to take a liking to life strategists in part because of my growing discontent with foreign policy and business strategists who claimed objectivity and superior knowledge while being epistemologically bankrupt. Life strategists, in contrast, rarely invoke that superiority. I found it quite refreshing to deal with humbler folk than with the ivory tower academics who, if I'm being pedantic, don't *know* even a small fraction of what they think they know.

Despite its less hubristic approach, personal strategy nevertheless carries the same modern philosophical baggage that weighs down its foreign policy and business sisters. I will elucidate this baggage through the work of Philip McGraw. Some of you'll recall his playing reverse rugby for the University of Tulsa in 1968 (when it was thrashed 100–6 by Houston University).[vi] McGraw isn't especially famous for that, though losers can sometimes make it big for losing. Nor is he famous for being Dr McGraw, which is how he's referred to on his website. To most folk, he's simply Dr Phil (which rolls off with a softer, more personal feel) and one of the most influential personal strategists in the world. Of course, life strategists from previous eras have had greater influence, but let's stay away from the hornets' nest of religious founders. McGraw is today at the very top of the personal, life strategy industry.

McGraw was a psychologist before becoming a personal strategist. As part of his practice, he advised lawyers. He got a break by helping Oprah Winfrey in her legal battle against cattlemen who claimed her remarks in 1995 about beef had an effect on their livelihoods. Oprah then brought McGraw onto her show as a life strategy expert for what seemed to me a very successful act of "she sees everybody as victims; he sees everybody as irresponsible." In 2002, he launched his own TV show, *Dr Phil*, which led to the sorts of spin-offs you'd expect from American celebrity. I'm sure there's a Dr Phil mug and T-shirt out there somewhere. Actually, I just checked on eBay and, yes, at the time of my writing, you could have bid for both there. Clearly, there's at least this distinction between the life strategy community and the business and foreign policy communities. You can't buy a mug with Porter's face.

McGraw's most important life strategy book, *Self Matters*, was published in 2001.[35] The book is about finding your "authentic self . . . the no-kidding, real you that existed before the world started crowding

---

vi   Reverse rugby is a far more appropriate name for American football. I've got no idea why Americans allowed this game to be so poorly named. Football is intuitively, as 95 percent of the world seems to understand, a game fundamentally about foot and ball. And there is practically no foot and ball contact in American football.

you out."[36] The book's core argument is that we should live lives that reflect our authentic selves. We should, so it goes on, do things which we have a genuine passion for and remove the clutter in our lives. That all sounds like good stuff. In principle, I like McGraw's idea because encouraging people to be themselves innately feels emancipating, whereas preventing people from living out who or what they sincerely are seems intuitively like a recipe for an unhappy and frustrated life. Not that McGraw could care less, but he has a thumbs-up so far. If you read this and perchance bump into him, I'd be grateful if you could please communicate that thumbs-up on my behalf. It might even be a good conversation icebreaker.

Apparently, according to McGraw, we each have one true authentic self, which is as unique as our DNA. "Authentic" is a big deal to the man who ironically enough lives in the surreal bubble of Beverly Hills. California has so many locales that feel more authentic than the Bev Hills (as it's often known), so I'm not sure what happened on that front. In contrast to McGraw's choice of residence, *Self Matters* has so many references to "authentic," it would win the "Book with the Most References to 'Authentic' Prize," if such an award existed (and, perhaps, we could create one?). I doubt McGraw would care much for such an award, but I suppose it couldn't hurt having another to put there on what is no doubt a very crowded trophy shelf. McGraw hits hard for the "authentic" movement, there's no doubt about it. So, why is it important to find this authentic self?

> Too many people in this day and time have gotten so busy "getting by," so busy being busy, that they have let the colors fade from their lives. ...If you are ignoring who you really are, your entire "system" is so distressed that it will wear out and you will be old beyond years.[37]

So given this overall advice, which I happen to think can be nourishing, where does *Self Matters* commit the same mistakes as its modern strategy siblings? It's one thing to like parts of a message or some advice and quite another to exonerate it from its failures. First, the book maintains the same position as its siblings on objectivity. Despite being written in the twenty-first century, the book is obsessed, as again I stress are nearly all modern strategy books, with objectivity and facts. *Self Matters* repeatedly refers to facts as if they are sacrosanct relics to be placed on a pedestal. Just like *Politics Among Nations* and *Competitive Strategy* and the rest of the cohort of both modern philosophy and modern strategy books, *Self Matters* worships the objectivity god and the facts that that god showered to us mere mortals.

Oblivious to the notion that clean, unbiased facts don't exist, *Self Matters* doesn't hesitate to ask, "Is it a true fact?" It lectures readers to "get in touch with the facts about yourself" and reminds all and sundry that, "Fact: Your authentic self is there."[38] The book goes on to slate people for not being "objective" about themselves. It then berates people for their "distorted perception," without realising that perception is inherently and always distorted, that objectivity is subjective and that we don't have the conceptual, linguistic or epistemological tool kits to provide *undistorted* perception.[39] Such is the fervour about objectivity and facts, it's as if *Self Matters* appoints itself as the objectivity god's pope, a grand ayatollah of objectivity if you will. Certainly, *Self Matters* pushes a tad harder on this point than do either of *Politics Among Nations* and *Competitive Strategy*.

And as you might expect with such devotion, the pontificating goes on and on. *Self Matters* deploys a "well known medical fact," before challenging readers that they "must absolutely deal with nothing but hard, objective *fact*."[40] Euphemisms aside, the book makes an absolute mountain of truth and objectivity, finger-wagging all and sundry to "stop dealing in opinions and assumptions and start dealing in facts."[41] Some readers, it argues, are stuck in their misery because "it may have been years since you dealt only in facts."[42] All that misery "would never happen if you only required yourself to deal with only the facts."[43] In short, "you have to know the facts or you're dead meat," a penalty which, I assume, is the ultimate retribution in the objectivity god's universe.[44] Embracing the "fact" world might very well be the distinction between happiness and misery.

As I've repeated as persistently as the most annoying of parrots, I don't think that mankind can be objective. I simply don't think it is possible. Analysis is inherently value-laden. The truth, irrespective of what Agents Mulder and Scully might like to think while searching for aliens (especially those who kidnapped Mulder's sister), is beyond the reach of our methodological, epistemological and ontological toolkits, a realization which I doubt, though, contributed to shutting down *The X-Files* TV series. As I argued in earlier chapters, facts arise from theory or at least some kind of theoretical framework. You can't have facts without having some kind of theory, however vague, unstructured or unsubstantiated it might be. Ask a communist, a democrat and a religious lunatic about any political crisis and you'll get three conflicting sets of "relevant" facts or truths because they will each use different theories or theoretical frameworks to determine what are and what are not "the facts".[vii] They will each have different criteria for relevant facts and the truth.

The second gaffe that *Self Matters* makes, borrowing from modern philosophy, is in not recognising the subject-object interdependence.

---

vii Although tiny minorities in the Muslim world in conjunction with a few dishonest journalists in the West do a terrific job of branding Islam as the world's leading source of religious lunatics, they don't monopolise that arena. Lunatics are spread across all the world's great religions. They share several characteristics: a belief they have direct contact with God (via a holy book, dreams, BBM, Twitter or whatever), that they know what is right and that they must force it down everybody's throat. They also reject notions of common sense or human equality, except within nonsensically narrow definitions. Finally, they reject all fun because fun is bad, bad and very bad.

Any analysis says as much about whatever is being analysed as it does about whoever is analysing. Shakira, a singer and songwriter, sort of misses the point when she suggests "Hips Don't Lie." Hips don't actually say anything. How then can they lie? That said and to its partial credit, *Self Matters* does give a person a little more breathing space in seeing his own reality than did *Politics Among Nations* and *Competitive Strategy*. The core approach in *Self Matters* hints at giving us a little flexibility in seeing our reality today and our future vision. However, the book doesn't go as far as to accept that we're partly responsible for creating our own reality. How could it, given that the book fully embraces the notion of objectivity and facts? That would contradict the idea that we're partly responsible for seeing our own reality. It'd be no different than being a vegetarian meat-eater.

Allow me to explain. The book's first of three steps has the reader rate herself on several defined statements, and here's one for illustrative purposes: "I am motivated by a need to please authority and win approval from others."[45] The book lists out several such statements and presumably the reader self-evaluates himself, notwithstanding that self-evaluations aren't "objective" in the base rubric of modern philosophy's assumptions. This test, nevertheless, stabilises the world of today. Confining a person's today to a predetermined selection of statements isn't perfect; however, at least it gives us some space to express how we see our current situation. It's not entirely exogenously imposed in the fashion of the more academic *Politics Among Nations* and *Competitive Strategy*.

The second step has the reader compare his world today with his ideal future, by comparing his life today with "what your experience would be if you were living an ideal, fully authentic" life.[46] I like the divergence between life today and the authentic life. It defines and sheds light on what is wrong or missing. It crystallises the motivation to act. Also, comparing an ideal future with the world today is better than the nonexistent choice offered by *Politics Among Nations* and *Competitive Strategy*. *Self Matters* offers a set of choices—at least it's something of a set of choices, but only on McGraw's terms and within his ontological framework. It's certainly not a set of indigenous choices from within the reader.

In the third and final step, *Self Matters* invites the reader to determine what he thinks his authentic self is, again using a pre-packaged selection of statements. The sequencing here feels a bit off because the book asks the reader to think about an ideal state *after* comparing that ideal state to the current state. *Self Matters* then suggests several exercises, all of which rely on the reader selecting from predetermined statements to access an authentic self. I must confess that all this "true self" stuff reminds me of Luke Skywalker tugging on Darth Vader in *The Return of the Jedi*.[47] If ever there was a consequential memory lapse about the self, Vader's forgetting about Anakin Skywalker was it. It led to serious problems. Anyhow, while *Self Matters* gives the reader some choice in selecting their starting point and end game, it never accepts the reader's role in seeing and making sense of his own reality. It doesn't offer a blank page for the reader to express his vision of herself. Reality today and in the future depend on the book's predefined statements.[48] And in many socio-cultures, especially those outside of North America, those statements are simply alien. They don't resonate.

The third issue, which I've critiqued modern philosophy and thus modern strategy for, its hubris, is also evident in *Self Matters*. Again, this is not a point specific to this book or its author, but the hubris of modern philosophy clearly manifests itself in *Self Matters*. Did the book fail to draw upon much of the work of the humanities and social sciences, especially over the past fifty years? Was Viv Richards a destructive batsman? My North American friends might scratch their heads a little. Of the four times as many Indian heads as there are North American heads, most will remember the most destructive batsman in cricket history. Kapil Dev, a former Indian bowler, might still have nightmares about him. Richards was cricket's "Shock and Awe." He was the ultimate master blaster. Yes, of course he was destructive. Yes, of course I think *Self Matters* fails to draw upon a lot of what we have learned and are still learning about mankind.

At the outset of its first chapter, *Self Matters* quotes Plato: "The life which is unexamined is not worth living."[49] Actually, it's a quote of Socrates, but that's not important right now.[50] The book later quotes singer-celebrities Cher and Kevin Welch; writers Ralph Waldo Emerson, Mark Twain and Oliver Goldsmith; civil rights activist and social worker Eleanor Roosevelt (whose prominence I think has much more to do with her husband than her fans seem to accept); poet, philosopher and historian Friedrich Von Schiller; philosopher and anthropologist Carlos Castaneda; and philosopher and historian Will Durant. That's the entire list of quoted people.

In glancing at this list, I'm struck by two things. First, and it's a bit irrelevant, only white folk are quoted. Isn't it a bit odd that *Self Matters* couldn't draw upon a single quote from all the nonwhite people who've graced the planet?[viii] Would it have hurt the book to quote Martin Luther King or Nelson Mandela? From a sales perspective, a quote perhaps from Confucius, Laozi or Feng Youlan might have helped with sales in China. Quoting Gandhi might have raised the book's profile with the same "four times as many Indian heads." Even the Republican Party, that enlightened bastion of tolerance and racial heterogeneity, gets that not including nonwhite people has costs— such as the most expensive election battle in history. In contrast, including them might enhance book sales and spread the word.

---

viii The US Census Bureau, under the direction of the Office of Management and Budget, classifies Hispanics as an ethnic group, not a race.

My second thought was more pertinent and around modern strategy's hubris. The book's evidentiary engagement with the broader developments in our learning about people and mankind seems to stop with those few quotes. Its entire embrace of the rich vein of learning across the planet and over the past five decades—if not more about what is man, how he operates, what he's about—seems to be limited to those quotes. I could find *nothing* else, not even in the non-existent endnotes, to suggest an awareness of what was cooking in our research and thinking on what people are about, what they need and how they think. I suppose I'm being rash. If the author is objective and he already has the facts, possibly beamed down by the objectivity god, then the book really doesn't need to bother with anybody else's learning—how silly of me!

If by now you suspect there's a conspiracy by modern strategists to shun material from disciplines that study people, as individuals or groups, that suspicion isn't entirely without foundation. You're not necessarily the next Sherlock, so don't feel compelled to inject yourself with heroin, find a Dr Watson or set up an office on Baker Street. Our understandings of human beings, as well as our intellectual self-awareness, pose livelihood-threatening problems for most modern strategists. Some parts of the academic community are increasingly posing tough, complex questions around what we know and how we know it, with many answers leading to even tougher and more complex questions. In response, most modern strategists can offer only sheepish, nervous grins to this serious intellectual probing. The modern strategy space, stuck in its cocooned tower, doesn't really know how to engage what's being thrown about.

As I did with *Politics Among Nations* and *Competitive Strategy*, let me sprinkle a flavour of what was cooking in the humanities and social sciences alone, just before *Self Matters* was published. This was so not an era of intellectual darkness. Anthony Giddens's work on modernity and the theory of structuration caused tremors in sociology.[51] His debate on the relative weight of the individual and social forces in creating society permeated every sociological crevice. Economist Amartya Sen (an Indian dude, so take note, my lovely billion Indian friends who won't easily forget Viv) reconfigured our understanding of *Development as Freedom*, to use the title of the lucid and legible book he wrote after he won the Nobel Prize in economics.[52] I'm sure my Pakistani friends are going to be irked because I like something which an Indian wrote, but this really is a good read, because it redefines in simple terms how we should see human development in an indigenous way.

Further afield, Douglas Kellner, a critical theorist, refined the thinking of the Frankfurt School, especially in his study of countercultural movements.[53] And in psychology, one of the main nesting grounds of the personal strategist, David Rumelhart, advanced our insight into human cognition. In fact, by 1980, he and Jay McClelland had built software that sort of simulated perception.[54] As it happens, I don't necessarily agree with their thinking on perception, but that's not the point. At the very least, they made some inroads in that direction. I could go on in elucidating the vibrancy and colour of what we were learning just before 2001, but I'd just be repeating the same point I've made with respect to *Politics Among Nations* and *Competitive Strategy*. To be honest, I'm right now done being a parrot.

I don't think one can seriously engage the "authentic" self, a worthy and powerful concept, without at least exploring some of psychology, semiotics, epistemology, social theory, anthropology and culture. You might even throw religion into that bucket. Getting to grips with who we are is no joke. And the argument that including insights from those fields would have "confused" the reader is a poor one. Complexity can be communicated simply. *Self Matters* advises people on how to navigate their lives while showing scant evidence of engaging the decades of studies on and thinking about people and their motives, behaviour and modus operandi. At least I struggled to find any evidence. How exactly is that different to my advising somebody how to eat and drink better while ignoring research and thinking on human physiology, the digestive system and nutrition from decades, if not centuries, past? And that's why given the stagnation under modern philosophy's epistemological principles, *Self Matters* and practically every other modern strategy book may as well have been written in or before the nineteenth century.

To illustrate modern philosophy's hubris, let's take McGraw's comments on human nature, a subject that has perplexed mankind for millennia. Human nature generates perhaps as much curiosity as do the existence of God and of aliens in outer space and has implications for so much of what we do. The nature versus nurture debate and the existence of a core human nature rather than a fluid one are two aspects of this, both of which have consequences for so much of our everyday life, from the crafting of laws and policies to cultural expectations. If (a massive "if") we ever understood human nature, we would have unlocked one of our greatest ever intellectual mysteries. It is just such a huge, huge deal. I personally don't think that's ever happening, but let's park that for a moment.

Enter into this debate one of the leading life strategists of the modern era. His position, underpinned by modern philosophy, is captured neatly in his quote, "Knowing human nature as I do."[55] McGraw may as well have said he knew the names and addresses of each alien in our universe. This is exactly what I'd expect from modern philosophy. It's not just a claim to *know*, but the carefree flamboyance to know one of the most contentious and debated issues since mankind put two and two together. My take is that we don't have a robust theory of knowledge that enables us to know very much let alone something as complex, fluid and challenging as human nature. Yet one of the world's leading strategists has no problems in asserting not only that we can know human nature but also that he, in fact, does indeed know it.

And again this hubris isn't about McGraw himself, that somehow he's smugger than the rest of the modern strategy community. Nor is it about personal life strategists who might ironically be a little less self-assured than their strategy counterparts in business and foreign policy. My criticism is aimed at the entire modern strategy space and its uncritical acceptance of the epistemological assumptions of modern philosophy and its know-it-all objectivity affliction. It's not just about *Self Matters* or even just about *Politics Among Nations* and *Competitive Strategy*. My point extends to practically the entire spectrum of modern strategy. This is interesting because despite the strategy industry's cerebral flavour, there are few better ways to arrest one's intellectual growth cold turkey than to think that one *knows*.

On that note and needing to move on, what can we conclude about *Self Matters*? It makes the same three mistakes that I've nailed on modern philosophy. That can't have surprised you. First, it assumes an ayatollah role with respect to the objectivity god, blessing the fortunate fact-lovers and damning the unfortunate fact-less ones or fact-deniers. The book's embracing of objectivity is relentless. Further, *Self Matters* demonstrates little appreciation that we each have a role in seeing and understanding the reality that we engage, that we are partly responsible for how we see our situation today. Finally, we have here the same persistent know-it-all posture, which is reflected in the book's unwillingness to engage the ongoing learning about people. The only partial redemption I could offer to *Self Matters* is that it gives its reader more breathing space than did *Politics Among Nations* and *Competitive Strategy* by letting the reader choose from predetermined lists of start and end points—at least it's something.

Concluding Remarks

That very minor optimistic note concludes my demonstration of the influence of modern philosophy's assumptions on modern strategy through three of the most influential strategic works of our time. It also concludes my demonstration of the failure of those assumptions and the strategic framework that was built on it. It's interesting to note that the leading foreign policy, organization and life strategists all succumbed to the same disease. All three strategists lived in a universe of objectivity, truths and facts, which they berated others, lesser minds, for not getting a handle on. If only people would accept and embrace the facts, the hard truths, then everything would be hunky-dory. We'd all be slurping large soft-serve ice cream. For some strange reason, the lesser minds keep ignoring the facts and in doing so make catastrophic errors that jeopardise their countries, organisations and individuals.

The works of all three modern strategists fail to appreciate the centrality of the role that people have in making sense of where a country, organisation or person stands and where it wants to go. *Politics Among Nations* and *Competitive Strategy*, indeed, straitjacketed the constructing of both starting points and goals so tight in the modern male Anglo-American cling film that they suffocate most participants. Participants are dictated to with respect to *their understanding* of where they stand and where they want to go. Even though *Self Matters* fails to demonstrate our role in assembling our reality, at least it doesn't suffocate individuals as they establish their journey's start and end points. In fact and again to its credit, it lists (predetermined) options from which the reader chooses how to cognize the worlds of today and tomorrow.

Finally, all three works of modern strategy show little interest in the rich learning about human beings that other disciplines by that time had either already garnered or were engaging. There is anaemic if any immigration or crossover from other intellectual disciplines. I really struggled to find anything that they had borrowed from other academic genres. I could detect no attempt to comprehend the implications of the latest insights about people or mankind. Forget the latest stuff, I could find no evidence of understanding or exploring what we've learned from other disciplines for several *decades*. It's hard to grasp how the three strategy texts attempted to guide groups of people (as in countries, organisations and individuals) through a journey that involved extensive people engagement without trying to understand people. But they tried it and were applauded for it and hats off to them.

Given modern strategists assume that they can be objective and that they show no appreciation for the role that people have in seeing and giving meaning to their reality, it's no real surprise that they've got no time for self-identity's impact on strategy. What's more, their intellectual certainty deters them from paying attention to the vast spectrum of continual learning in other disciplines about what mankind is, how he knows and what he wants. The modern strategist thus has no appreciation or awareness of how self-identity (or specifically how we see ourselves) influences how we see and make sense of the world today or how we see our vision ahead. Further, the modern strategist has no clue that self-identity also influences how we effect and implement the strategy that takes us from today to our vision.

In the next chapter, I'll explore self-identity and its influence on how we cognize or how we see and make sense of things. From there, I'll give an overview of self-identity's impact on strategy, meaning all three steps of the strategic process. This is important because it's the first time I share an overview of my framework. The central thesis of this is that self-identity significantly influences how we see the world as-is, our vision for the future and the steps we take to get us from today to that vision. Once I've put some foundations in place, it should be easier to convey, and more apparent to you, how strategy is as much about how you see yourself, your self-identity, as it is about external stuff in a world out there.

[1] HJ Morgenthau, *Politics Among Nations*, McGraw-Hill Higher Education, London, 2005

[2] T Hobbes, *Leviathan*, Oxford Paperbacks, Oxford, 2008

[3] HJ Morgenthau, *Politics Among Nations*, McGraw-Hill Higher Education, London, 2005

[4] *Ibid.*

[5] AA Milne, *Pooh's Little Instruction Book*, Dutton Books, New York, 1995

[6] HJ Morgenthau, *Politics Among Nations,* McGraw-Hill Higher Education, London, 2005

[7] M Light and S Wight, *Identity and Foreign Policy Perceptions in the Other Europe*, Palgrave Macmillan, Basingstoke, 2011

[8] JL Gaddis, *We Now Know*, Oxford University Press, Oxford, 1997

[9] B O'Connor, *Adorno*, Routledge, Abingdon, 2013

[10] J Hughes, W Sharrock, PJ Martin, *Understanding Classical Sociology*, Sage, London, 2003

[11] BS Turner, *The Talcott Parsons Reader*, Blackwell, Oxford, 1999

[12] A Barnard, *History and Theory in Anthropology*, Cambridge University Press, Cambridge, 2000

[13] HJ Morgenthau, *Politics Among Nations*, McGraw-Hill Higher Education, London, 2005

[14] http://www.english.rfi.fr/africa/20101104-zimbabwe-comes-last-human-development-ranking

[15] HJ Morgenthau, *Politics Among Nations*, McGraw-Hill Higher Education, London, 2005

[16] http://www.mcdonaldsindia.com/menu.html

[17] ME Porter, *Competitive Strategy*, The Free Press, New York, 1998

[18] *Ibid.*

[19] *Ibid.*

[20] *Ibid.*

[21] *Ibid.*

22   S Best and D Kellner, *Postmodern Theory*, Guilford Press, New York, 1991

23   ME Porter, *Competitive Strategy*, The Free Press, New York, 1998

24   *Ibid.*

25   *Ibid.*

26   *Ibid.*

27   *Ibid.*

28   *Ibid.*

29   http://www.bbc.com/news/world-middle-east-17485422

30   http://www.ilo.org/global/about-the-ilo/mission-and-objectives/lang--en/index.htm

31   ME Porter, "Capital Disadvantage: America's Failing Capital Investment System," *Harvard Business Review*, Cambridge, 1992; MH Miller, "Is American Corporate Governance Fatally Flawed," Second Mitsui Life Symposium on Global Financial Markets, 11 May 1993

32   M O'Sullivan, *Contests for Corporate Control*, Oxford University Press, Oxford, 2001

33   ME Porter, *Competitive Strategy*, The Free Press, New York, 1998

34   http://cokevspepsi.net/

35   PC McGraw, *Self Matters*, Simon & Schuster, London, 2001

36   *Ibid.*

37   *Ibid.*

38   *Ibid.*

39   *Ibid.*

40   *Ibid.*

41   *Ibid.*

42   *Ibid.*

43   *Ibid.*

44   *Ibid.*

45   *Ibid.*

46   *Ibid.*

47   *Star Wars*, Episode Six, "The Return of the Jedi," Lucasfilm, Ltd, San Francisco, 1983

48   PC McGraw, *Self Matters*, Simon & Schuster, London, 2001

49   *Ibid.*

50   P Johnson, *Socrates: A Man for Our Times*, Penguin, London, 2011

51   A Giddens, *The Constitution of Society*, Polity Press, Cambridge, 2004

52   A Sen, *Development as Freedom*, First Anchor Books, New York, 2000

53   S Best and D Kellner, *Postmodern Theory: Critical Investigations*, The Guilford Press, New York, 1991

54   MA Gluck and DE Rumelhart, *Neuroscience and Connectionist Theory*, Lawrence Erlbaum Associates, Hillsdale, 1990

55   PC McGraw, *Self Matters*, Simon & Schuster, London, 2001

Immanuel Kant was one of the most important figures in Western philosophy, even if he thought that black people "learned like parrots."

**Ibn Sina was amongst many Islamic philosophers
who shaped Western philosophy.**

Phil McGraw, probably the most influential life strategist of our time and a firm advocate of facts and objectivity.

Steve Jobs: "I didn't want to be a father, so I wasn't."

Ed Husain was briefly attracted to Hizb ut Tahrir, who were amongst the most abusive and active religious groups in Britain in the 1990s.

Jan Morris had the courage to change her gender . . . and then later write about the transformation.

CHAPTER 4

SELF-IDENTITY

Cognition

More than a century ago, Albert Einstein articulated what's probably the most famous equation in the world: $E = mc^2$. What this means is that the energy of an object equals its mass (in a vacuum, of course) times the speed of light squared.[1] I don't know about you, but I don't think the simple explanation of the relationship between mass and energy is especially intuitive or obvious. And I would guess that most people feel the same way. Even with some effort, it's not easy to get one's head around the notion that if you take the speed of light (in a vacuum), then multiply that speed by itself and multiply *that* by the mass of an object, you get the energy of the object. Apologies to all physicists out there, but that's not intuitive to us ordinary folk. In fact, quite a bit of our current understanding of physics doesn't fit with common sense or intuition.

Take something different such as Facebook. It wasn't obvious in 2004 that a social networking website with a few dozen members would have a billion members a decade later. Or that the same website would facilitate a series of revolts across the Middle East and North Africa, leading to the overthrow of several longstanding, corrupt, inept dictators, who just so happened to be friends of the

US.[2] We know Facebook has been a huge success, but was its success intuitive in 2004? Anybody who thinks its success was intuitive today stands accused by me of smoking some funny stuff, even if they don't care much for that. That said, David Fincher's movie *The Social Network* gave the impression that some folk involved in Facebook's start might, indeed, have *been* smoking some funny stuff.[3] I really don't want to make a huff and puff out of it (pause for some canned laughter, please).

Finally, it's no less obvious why the country that has the world's greatest number of Nobel Prize winners (39 percent across all subjects) would elect Dubya not just once but *twice*. That the same country would then give serious consideration to a presidential ticket that included Sarah Palin as vice-president is also not very instinctive. It's a reasonable argument that Nobel Prizes are probably not the best way of measuring a country's intellectual capability. It's also possible that one might understand Dubya's first election (notwithstanding Al Gore getting half a million more votes) as a reaction to two terms of an impeachment-tarnished Clinton. That said, most of the world, including billions in Asia, struggles to understand Dubya's re-election and Palin's nomination. And lest we forget, there was some fine entertainment during which Palin declared her foreign policy credentials:

> As Putin rears his head and comes into the air space of the United States of America, where—where do they go? It's Alaska. It's just right over the border.[4]

Such is the global diversity of husband-wife relationships that in America Palin's husband supported her wholeheartedly. He was always at her side and always smiling. He was like a rock of support. In contrast, if Sarah Palin had been British and had wanted to be deputy prime minister, her husband might well have instead advised her to drink a good cup of tea to calm down. If she'd been in Pakistan, her husband might have asked his mother, sisters and aunts to rid his wife of evil spirits. Hypothetically, he might also have threatened to marry a second wife, then bribe a judge and mullah to prevent his wife from getting a divorce.[i] Finally, if she'd been in the UAE as an Emirati, her husband would have driven her in his oversized SUV to prison, at twice the speed limit, lest the extended family be accused of treason.

Many things, from Einstein's equation to America's political choices, aren't intuitive. My thesis, that self-identity has a big impact on strategy, is one of them. Specifically, self-identity influences how we as individuals or groups see our world, craft our vision for the future and craft the bridge between the two. In this statement, short enough to print on a T-shirt, if one's desperate for fashion statements, I've captured this book's thrust. I know the assertion doesn't feel intuitive. That's not to say it feels ridiculous, but it just doesn't gel with how we experience life. Yet, many things that don't seem obvious form part of our everyday lives: they happen and we live with them. The impact of self-identity on strategy falls into that eclectic, nonintuitive group of $E = mc^2$, Facebook and Palin. In a flash, I have managed to place my argument in the company of some serious fame. Impressive party trick, eh?

One obvious issue that's important to engage upfront is the underlying reason to focus on self-identity in the context of strategy in the first place. Where did the link between self-identity and strategy come from given it's not intuitive? This is significant because it sheds light on a few things. In the last couple of chapters,

---

i   From the outside, the title of Pakistan's chief executive officer might not be clear. Mohammed Zia-ul Haq and Benazir Bhutto were both chief executives, the former as president and the latter as prime minister. Those within Pakistan, however, will point to the chief of army staff as the real (albeit arm's-length) chief executive.

I've demonstrated that we can't be objective and that we, as people subjects have a role in understanding our object world. Obvious questions that arise from this are then, How do we cognate? How do we see and make sense of the world? I've already suggested there is no single reductionist theory that unlocks the Holy Grail. I don't think we will *ever* have a precise, universal, all-encompassing explanation of how we cognate, which parallels my other assertion that I think we will never really *know* very much.

That said, I have a caveat that intellectually pins down my argument. The cognitive framework for self-identification must also be the framework for identification of everything beyond the self. Think about that for just a moment, because it's simple and powerful. I hope it is because it's one of my base assumptions. How one sees oneself must reflect how one sees others. The framework, core terms of reference or scaffold must be the same. The idea first occurred to me when I read a book by David Campbell, an international relations academic. He argued that foreign policy is simultaneously effected outside of a country as it is *inside* of a country, because he saw "foreign" as referring to foreign *identities* and not foreign *countries*.[5] Similarly, the grid or framework that you use to see yourself must also reflect or be similar to the grid or framework that you use to see everything beyond yourself. It makes no sense to have different meaning-making frameworks for the self and other because the mind, I don't think, works that way.

A woman who acutely sees herself as wealthy in the financial sense, who strongly self-identifies as wealthy, will see the world around her through the lens of wealth. Within that, I grant that it's one thing to be wealthy and quite another to self-identify, to see oneself, as "wealthy," partly because wealth is relative. I am focused on the self-identification and not the actual reality. A man who acutely sees himself as fat will see fat (or a lack of it) when seeing others.

Again, it's one thing to be fat and quite another to see yourself as fat. The point isn't whether you are or are not wealthy, fat or whatever else. The point is whether you identify yourself as such. And those stronger self-identities, the ones which resonate with each of us, which surface and resurface, which we are acutely attached to, will reflect the same cognitive framework which we use to identify beyond the self.

Turn the tables around. A person whose self-identity is exclusively Turkish, female and a Bayern Munich supporter (possibly because half of her family migrated into a neighbouring street or possibly because they've got a great döner kebab business next to Allianz Arena) will probably not see and attach meaning to the world through the lens of the green movement, jurisprudence or modern architecture. My example is extreme because people tend not to have only three exclusive self-identities, but it does serve to illustrate my point. I'm not suggesting that the self-identities dominate all cognition. I'm occupying a shade of grey by suggesting that our self-identities and the meanings and scaffolding that we give to them have a significant impact on cognition, on how we see the world. Again, don't ask me for percentages.

From that theoretical stand, it's easier and more practical to develop or explore a framework to self-identify than it is to develop one that demands that we identify absolutely *everything* else. It's easier to explore our self-identities—how we see ourselves and who we think we are—than it is to work out the identity of everything beyond the self, because exploring the self is so much more contained. Besides starting with self-identity, I'm at complete a loss on how we develop a framework to identify everything else. In contrast, with self-identity, all we need is a bit of honesty and self-reflection, to get to a good start. Anchoring a framework around self-identity is also much easier to grasp because it's based not on how we should see the world but how each of us, including individuals, organisations and countries, authentically see and make sense of the world. It allows for our socio-cultural, religious and any other filters that help craft each of our universes. It is indigenous and not exogenous.

That in essence is the intellectual premise for self-identity's impact on cognition and by extension the strategies of individuals, organisations and countries. In fact, it may in any case be misleading to ontologically differentiate amongst the three categories, since the relationship between self-identity and strategy exists in the mind and that same mind is common to all three buckets. Even though our behaviour subtly changes across those buckets, the act of cognition and making sense of the world consistently remains an exercise of the mind. And that cognition of the world around us in turn reflects the same sense-making framework that we use to see and make sense of ourselves. In other words, the framework for our self-identity is also that of identifying the world around the self.

Self-Identity and Strategy: The Sixty-Second Overview

In my experience, sixty-second overviews are rarely that short, extending typically to three or four minutes, and this one is no exception (but I didn't want to admit that in the subtitle). In similar fashion, it always seems to take more than sixty minutes to read a book which claims to be a sixty-minute book. Having touched upon self-identity's role in cognition, I'll now summarise self-identity's impact on strategy. I'll share a more thorough detailing of the relationship in the next chapter, but I think it's important to get the brief high-level out now; an appetizer, if you will. Something to wet the palette. Doing so should give some context to my explaining and elucidating self-identity later in this chapter. After all, there'd be no point in explaining self-identity if you don't understand why it's important in the first place or what to look for. I'd be asking you to understand something that you have no reason to.

As a first step, self-identity—including the frameworks, stories and meanings that flesh out our self-identities—helps us see and understand our reality today, as-is. Take somebody who strongly self-identifies as Orthodox Jewish. In fact, let's make that his only and thus dominant identity. People are more complex than a mono-identity, but let's put that aside for now. Irrespective of his theological religiosity, his universe, including his views on politics, parenting and justice, will by definition be filtered through the prism of his Jewish identity. He'll distinguish Jews from Gentiles, be more perceptive of the relationships between men and women and focus on the Arab–Israeli dispute. Chances are that he won't filter the world through the prism of the Kentucky Derby or pear harvesting in China, filters which are potentially equally important to other folk.

Then there's the second step. Self-identity influences our visions and goals for the future, however indistinct they might be. I keep issuing that qualification because I really think that most people, organisations and countries don't have anything like an atomic definition of where they are going. That point made, yet again, how we see ourselves impacts what we see as our vision of ourselves in the future. Consider then how terrifying multiculturalism is to old, white, male American foreign-policy guardians. A big chunk of the old school are really quite worried that embracing non-European narratives as part of America's evolving self-identity not only risks Balkanizing their country by eroding a common language, "historical traditions and political values," but might transform America's goals and objectives.[6] I agree, though I don't lose sleep over it. Reconstructing America's self-identity will probably reshape Washington's vision and objectives. In fact, I suspect it already is. To illustrate my point, I doubt hyphenated Americans give Europe the importance that nonhyphenated Americans have thus far given it.

Finally, the third step is that self-identity influences how we get from how we see the world today to where we'd like to be in the future. Self-identity influences the effecting and implementing of strategy. Besides influencing the start and end points that a strategy should bridge, any meaningful self-identity generates expectations. These, in turn, influence behaviour, which in turn influences how we implement strategy. Take somebody who is acutely aware of his or her self-identity as an athlete. Irrespective of any sports-related assessment, the self-identity as an athlete in itself generates expectations of diet, timetable and training. These, in turn, translate into behaviour—such as refraining from sugary soft drinks in favour of protein shakes—because those are *the sorts of things* an athlete does, that's what expected from an athlete. It is those behaviours that affect how the athlete goes about his strategy.

Before getting too carried away about self-identity's impact on strategy, I want to draw some boundaries. Self-identity is not the great panacea to strategic problems, nor does it guard the fountain of truth. I'd be making a big mistake if I gave the impression that self-identity is the mother of all strategy, because it's not. In any case, the re-introduction in 1990 by the right honourable insane dictator from Al-Awja, Saddam Hussein, of the term "mother of all" (referring to the Battle of Al Qādisiyyah in 637 AD) months before the brief American attack, did the term no favours.[7] Referring to my approach as "the mother of all strategy" wouldn't be smart, at least from a branding perspective. More importantly, no book can deliver that grand solution, even if some authors claim otherwise to sell a few more copies or get a job at business school. I'm sure that my warning will be lost on some people who will try to simplify my view into something like "self-identity is strategy."

So, if self-identity isn't the great solution to the puzzle of strategy, what is it? Why is it worth knowing more about? Why bother? In going to the heart of who we think and believe we are, focusing on self-identity helps us to better grasp the framework we as individuals, organisations and countries use to see ourselves and our respective worlds. Self-identity shifts the strategic debate from exclusively pointing the finger at an external world to one that initially points to inside, within ourselves, before pointing back outside of ourselves. Self-identity reemphasises the first-person (singular and plural) in strategy. It refocuses on the individual, organisation or country in the context of their strategies. By exploring the relationship between self-identity and strategy, we gain powerful insights that orthodox approaches to strategy overlook. We don't get to the objective truth of strategy. We just develop useful ways of seeing things.

Moreover, I think that self-identity helps place strategy on a firmer intellectual footing than modern strategy's shoddy intellectual underpinnings because it engages the broad question of human cognition and specifically epistemology. Is the use of self-identity a better way to *craft* strategy? It's difficult to say. And I would invite further research on precisely this. What is more accurate to say is that it's more robust than modern strategic approaches, because this self-identity framework engages the question of how we see the world and our aims in it. Neither of these processes is passive or neutral. And neither is even acknowledged let alone engaged by modern strategy. Because modern strategy has been built on modern philosophy's epistemological and methodological assumptions, it has the unfortunate problem of some very gaping holes.

I'd go one step further by arguing that a self-identity based approach is probably a more authentic and meaningful way to engage strategy because it gives us as much focus on the strategist as it does on whatever he's engaged with. In doing so, the strategic process isn't alien. Strategy need not be something imported from a foreign person living in a foreign country with a foreign culture and framework. It need not remind all and sundry of the US's appetite to tell others what to do. The works of Morgenthau, Porter and McGraw, all Americans, lead modern strategy. Coincidentally or not, this is an industry that is only too keen to force people into alien, extraneous cookie-cutter frameworks from which they must then dedicate significant resource and willpower to make life-altering decisions. Isn't that a familiar trait of US foreign policy? A self-identity approach, in contrast, speaks to how each of us sees our universe and then from that viewpoint crafts our vision or objectives ahead.

That might well underlie not only the intellectual robustness of a self-identity framework but also its explanatory power with respect to the strategies of individuals, organisations and countries. In chapters 6, 7 and 8, I explore at a high level the self-identities and strategic processes of three individuals, three organisations and three countries to bring to life self-identity's impact on the strategic processes. That the range of examples is as broad as Great Britain and the Suez Crisis to Disneyland to Ed Husain, a former Islamist, should reinforce self-identity's importance to strategy. Self-identity significantly impacts strategy. Having already discussed and explained strategy in the opening chapter, now would be a good time to explain the other big chunk of cheese resting on my plate—let's understand self-identity.

Defining Self-Identity

So much is lost through the use of vague or unclear language. Given the difficulty of obtaining consensus on definitions even in the same academic discipline, it's a big expectation to ask scholars to have a meaningful dialogue. That might explain why they're often so good at talking past each other. The pervasiveness of vague, meaningless, claptrap language also helps explain how so many inept scholars and experts have kept their academic and think-tank jobs. Note, for instance, how Islamic terrorism scholarship in America is dominated by people who are supremely illiterate on both terrorism and Islam, let alone the oxymoron of "Islamic terrorism."[8] Islam means "peace," which raises a question: What exactly is "peaceful terrorism"? And why isn't the targeting of civilians and instilling of terror by a tiny proportion of US forces in Afghanistan or Iraq called "Christian terrorism"? Who knows, but hey, there's always demand for rubbish. And that's a comment I make even before I touch upon that "expert" group's third-grade understanding of Islam.

Anyhow, now we have another concept, self-identity, which has several meanings. You might have thought that identity would have been easy to define and stabilise and that experts would have had little room to mess it up. Then again, you might have thought Palin's vice-presidential candidacy was a piece from the satirical newspaper *The Onion*. You would have been wrong both times. Palin really was a candidate against Barack Obama and Joe Biden. Trust me—you can Google that. Experts always have room to mess up simple terms and definitions. It's important that a book that engages the relationship between strategy and self-identity explains both terms. Let's get everybody onto the same page with respect to our key concepts. We've explained strategy and now, as I say, is the right time to explain self-identity.

In the past three decades, much has been written on the definition of identity, especially in philosophy, sociology and psychoanalysis.[9] Self-identity is an increasingly prominent part of the humanities and social sciences. James Fearon, a political scientist, summarised some of the work around self-identity and offered no less than fourteen definitions of identity, though many of his definitions were too similar to qualify as distinct.[10] Even so, his work demonstrated the lack of consensus on what identity means (I know this evokes that eerie sense of déjà vu). He pointed out that identity has many conflicting meanings: as a person's nature, as a person's collective commitments, as a source of behaviour, as how one sees oneself and as one's relationships with the broader world.

Etymologically, identity comes from the Latin *identitas*, which roughly translates as "sameness." Hence, we shouldn't be surprised that one dictionary defined identity as the "state of being of the same."[11] This isn't much use, partly because the definition is just a touch too abstract and partly because it's removed from our use of the word in daily life. Who really uses "identity" as a synonym for "state of being of the same"? Imagine learning from a psychiatrist that you're suffering from a "state of being of the same" crisis. That'd be disconcerting and would probably make absolutely no sense. You might actually think that it's the psychiatrist who is the one who needs help. We simply don't use identity this way in everyday language, and I can't see a good reason to use a word that is central to this book in a way that confuses everybody.

Another meaning captures a more conventional understanding of identity as "who or what a person or thing is."[12] This is more in line with how we normally use the word, in that it answers the question, Who are you? While some folk don't like departing far from a word's etymology, I think doing so is justified here. As is the case for many other words, our use of identity has come a long way since its Latin inception. That being said, even this last meaning presents one final potential challenge. Who or what a person or thing is can include not only their own understanding of who they are but also other people's understanding of who they are. An accountant will see himself differently to the way he's seen by his clients. He might see himself as a dashing business guru. Indeed, British accounting regulators bafflingly portray their members as glamorous, entrepreneurial and dynamic. In contrast, the accountant's client might see him as Mr Prudent, grey and risk-averse.

It's because of this subtle ambiguity in identity—the identity we assign ourselves differs from that which others assign to us—that I focus not on identity, per se, but specifically on self-identity. Some people, such as psychologists Michael Hogg and Dominic Abrams, don't see the difference. They think identity *excludes* how others see us and refers only to "people's concepts of who they are, of what sort of people they are."[13] I don't think their understanding is so common, but I am not sure. Given the importance of self-identity to the impact on strategy and to swat any flying confusion or ambiguity, I think it's important to distinguish self-identity from identity. It is the former, meaning how we see ourselves, which I think has a big impact on strategy.

To help distil self-identity, I want to contrast it with what it's not. That's always a good way to explain something. At least five other concepts can easily be mistaken for self-identity. The first is self-image. While self-identity answers the question, Who am I?, self-image answers the question, What do I believe people think about me? At the unfortunate moment when a person makes a fool of himself at a social gathering, he's less interested in his self-identity than in his self-image, meaning how folk see him. (It could just as easily be a woman as a man, so let's not read too much into that.) I don't deny there's a relationship between self-image and self-identity: a bad self-image can lead to a bad self-identity. But the two are distinct. It's a bit like the relationship, I suppose, between anti-Israeli and anti-Semitic. Actually, it's not—most Semites are Arab Muslims and many Jews are not Semites.

Second, self-identity isn't self-awareness. The latter answers the questions, How well do I know myself? and What do I know about myself? A businesswoman's self-identity might be that she's a brilliant businesswoman. Yet that same woman may actually be a bad businesswoman, having merely inherited a brilliant business. Again, the distinction between self-awareness and self-identity doesn't preclude a relationship between the two. For example, if a country's leadership or broader society becomes aware of its extraordinarily high corruption levels (without mentioning Somalia, Sudan and Afghanistan because there's no reason whatsoever to do so in this context), that awareness may shape the country's self-identity and policies. The two though, self-identity and self-awareness, are not the same.

The idea that we can understand who we *truly* are on the inside, that we can achieve complete self-awareness, may in any case be a bit of wishful thinking. I suspect some people have better self-awareness than others. I can buy that. Nevertheless, knowing oneself is tough for good reason. Erving Goffman, a sociologist, talked about the mask upon mask behind which we hide ourselves, pointing to the intimacy of our true inner self.[14] There are other challenges with respect to self-awareness, including, for instance, the snag that we've not tested ourselves in many situations, we change with time, we confuse who we are with who we want to be and that our sense of who we are is filtered through a sociocultural, including linguistic, context and framework. All of these make it hard to get a handle on our "true" selves.

Third, personality, being the characteristics and qualities that make up someone's character, isn't self-identity. Personality is similar to self-awareness in that both presume the possibility of a deeper, more authentic existence and understanding of the self. Self-identity, in contrast, isn't about a genuine understanding but about how people see themselves. The personality of a business, specifically of its senior management team, might be erratic, undisciplined and ineffective. But the team might view themselves as the most exciting team since Bill Gates partnered with Paul Allen to create Microsoft. Gates and Allen might well have been erratic, but undisciplined and ineffective they were most certainly not. The same distinction between personality and self-identity can, of course, be extended to individuals and organisations.

Fourth, self-identity isn't brand. A brand is made up of the perceptions and images that people have of something, from first contact to post-interaction. While a brand sits in the minds of third parties, self-identity sits within one's own mind. It's worth stressing that besides organisations, individuals have brands too. Richard Branson actually uses his personal brand effectively for the Virgin Group. He brings a refreshing anti-establishment feel to whatever the Virgin Group gets involved with. Countries also have brands. Peter van Ham, an international relations academic, noted that "the unbranded state has a difficult time attracting economic and political attention" and then rubbed salt into Belgium's wounds by reminding everybody that in the 1990s Belgium rebuilt its brand to recover from scandals in government corruption, child pornography and poisoned chicken.[15] Nice one, Peter. Clearly, Brussels isn't in a rush to courier to him a box of Godiva chocolates...partly because a Turkish firm now owns Godiva. Lest you're wondering, I love their dark chocolate pretzels.

Fifth, when I use self-identity, I'm talking about *as-is*, not as communicated or idealised.[16] Self-identity is intimate because it comes from a place of vulnerability. It asks us to consider who or what we really think we are. Our tendency to embellish our history and achievements often stands in sharp contrast to our self-identity, to how we see ourselves when we're not putting on a show.[ii] In fact, I doubt most people consciously engage their self-identity, preferring instead to let it sit, undisturbed, in their gut. People don't easily advertise their self-identity, even if they think they do. In fact, we might not even regularly surface our real self-identity. We don't

---

ii   I recall one situation where the senior management of a government agency conducted an in-house survey which suggested the agency saw itself as practically useless. Imagine if they'd posted that on their website!

readily communicate to others how we really see ourselves; and when we do, that communication is often contaminated by how we want to be seen or how we wish we were seen.

Even so, an organisation or country's communicated self-identity is interestingly often close to its actual self-identity. The act of communicating self-identity by a few for the many can often powerfully impact the self-identity of the many. International relations academics Benedict Anderson and Fred Halliday, as well as anthropologist Ernst Gellner, all stressed that national self-identity is often maintained by many social, cultural and political leaders, including but not limited to intellectuals, novelists, politicians, historians and filmmakers.[17] They are the identity guardians who repeatedly remind their communities in both subtle and overt ways "who we are" and "what we're about." This act of reminding everybody actually communicates, grounds and reinforces the group's self-identity.

What Is Self-Identity

Having clarified what self-identity is not, what can we say about what it is, beyond obviously that it's about how a person or people identify themselves? After all, there's a limit to understanding something by defining what it's not. Self-identity is neither seventeen squared nor is it Kermit the Frog, but that hardly helps.[iii] First, a point picked up by business academics John Balmer and Stephen Greyser is that self-identity is constantly evolving.[18] A significant body of work, including some by French philosopher Jean-Paul Gustave Ricoeur, supports this

---

iii   Social scientists typically refer to two types of self-identity: role-based identity (for example, parent, son or teacher) and social identity (for example, tall, dark, male and Jewish). The vast majority of social science research, as it happens, focuses on social identity.

view. He argued that the answer to, Who am I? isn't something to be discovered but it's rather a "work in progress."[19] Psychologists Hazel Markus and Ziva Kunda used the phrase "working self" to refer to the same phenomenon.[20] I like it when different genres of human learning independently row down the same river. It adds to the credibility and sense of robustness.

The self-identity of a ten-year-old American kid will not be the same after twenty years, when he's got a wife, 1.9 kids and 0.25 dogs.[21] His self-identity will change. If he were living in India, he'd probably have at least four kids but no dog. If he were in Saudi, he might very well have four wives and ten kids, but definitely no dog because the religious police, who love to suffocate fun, see dogs as dirty and make dog ownership very difficult.[22] Cats, though, aren't dirty, apparently, and they're quite welcome in a Saudi home. They're even more welcome, I suppose, in homes in southeast China, where older people in particular eat cats for lunch and dinner. It's a strange world. What is affectionately cared for in one part of the world is eaten in another.

Part of the reason our self-identity isn't static is that our circumstances and our perceptions of them aren't static either. The world, including us, changes. Margaret Thatcher saw herself as the British prime minister in 1989 but not in 1991, by which time she had been booted out of office to become an MP. That was a transition of self-identity based on a transition of her job. In 1999, Enron saw itself as a successful firm. In 2001, under a cloud of accounting fraud, it filed for bankruptcy, after which it no longer saw itself as a successful firm.[23] In 2009, the Spanish national football team saw itself as a group of talented athletes who played at some of the world's biggest clubs, including Manchester United and Real Madrid. After winning the World Cup in 2010 for the first time, the team saw itself as the best team in the world.[24] Our self-identities aren't set in stone.

Our awareness of our self-identity can actually change as fast as a flash. When I'm in the UK and about to travel from Heathrow Airport, I don't see myself as very British. A few hours later when I arrive in Canada, I feel a lot more British. It isn't that my self-identity has fundamentally changed, but that I'm just more aware of a part of my self-identity which I was less aware of before. OK, that was a slowish flash because a flight from London to Canada is at least six hours. Try this example then. When my wife returns home from an afternoon with her friends, she loses sight of her self-identity as a chic, social and attractive gal and becomes "mama" to our kids who are jumping up to greet her, complaining about how their siblings misbehaved and wiping grubby hands on her clothes. I don't think her self-identity fundamentally changes. She merely becomes more or less aware of certain aspects of it. That's more like a flash.

Similarly, physical changes can force a change in self-identity, as often happens when women undergo a mastectomy or when people dye their hair.[25] It'd be interesting to study how a woman's self-identity changes when she transitions into a blonde, given the meanings associated with being a blonde, at least in Western culture. For what it's worth, in Pakistan, though, blonde doesn't mean stupid. Self-identity's fluidity can be quite complex. Note, for instance, when somebody who self-identifies as an individual then self-identifies as part of a group. You can start a train journey to a sports game as an individual, but by the time you're near the stadium, you reprioritise your individualism for a group identity, cheering away, "We're going to win," which sounds nonsensical because *we* aren't even playing.[26] Most of those in "we" are often simply too unfit to play in a professional competitive game.

Self-identities can also change over decades or centuries and needn't be event-driven. The Caucasian face was America's self-identity in the nineteenth century but is less prominent now. Obama, Winfrey and Michael Jordan are just some of the many faces that have gradually become part of America's self-identity.[iv] Such headline-grabbing changes of self-identity contrast with more nuanced changes. Psychologist Lisa Diamond, for example, suggested that some lesbian women ("fluid lesbians") migrate between lesbian and nonlesbian self-identities over decades.[27] Ten years ago, I didn't see myself as a father and now I do. Ten years ago, I didn't see myself as a fluid lesbian. As it happens, I still don't see myself as a fluid lesbian. One day, maybe, one day.

Organisational self-identity, which I once thought was relatively stable, is probably not. Management academics Dennis Gioia, Majken Schultz and Kevin Corley argued that in an era of instant global connectivity, even an organisation's skeletal identity labels might remain stable while the identity's meanings can rapidly change. As an example, Lehmann Brothers underwent significant changes in the meaning of its self-identity in a very brief timeframe, being just a few days in 2008. Interestingly, Gioia, et al., suggested that this fluidity of self-identity actually potentially *helps* organisations navigate the unexpected twists and turns which are part of any organisational journey.[28] It allows organisations to change their own *meaning* without having to change name, logo or structure.

Besides its fluidity, self-identity is also multidimensional. One reason that self-identity isn't singular may be that the mind is too complex for such simplicity. Irrespective of which of the two main schools of identity thinking in social psychology one subscribes to (a linear hierarchy of identities or several concentric rings with a nuclear identity at the core), our self-identities have many dimensions, which can conflict with each other.[29] I can simultaneously see myself as a graduate and as a big kid. I don't see these as separate self-identities

---

iv   I was going to mention Michael Jackson, but that would have really compli-cated things because I've no idea how to identify him, and his own self-identity never seemed clear to me.

despite the meaning of a graduate and of a big kid conflicting with each other. I doubt any person organisation or country can say they have only a single self-identity which always dominates them. Let me correct that: they can say what they want, but I might then think that they haven't really thought through their statement.

At any given moment, Mohandas Gandhi saw himself as a Gujarati, Indian, man, father, liberator, lawyer and defender of the Untouchables—amongst many other aspects of his self-identity.[30] British Petroleum sees itself as an employer, a provider of shareholder value, an oil and gas giant, a British business and maybe even as a *victim* of the 2010 Deepwater Horizon oil spill.[31] Depending on context, Pakistan's officials see the country as an Islamic state; a secular state; a bastion against Islamic, Hindu and Stalinist extremisms; and a victim of American-Zionist conspiracies.[32] That Pakistan struggles to identify itself in a positive manner in relation to its own people may help explain why the country is a cow's mess and almost anybody (especially its top politicians and army officers) who can has a nice secondary home in Dubai or London.[v]

In addition to being fluid and having multiple dimensions, self-identity can come from a wide range of sources: parents, gender, race, ethnicity, religion, age, employment, interests, friendships and even a celebrity—all of them can be a source of self-identity. In 2003, for example, a television documentary covered a group of women who socialised every morning during their commute on the 8:15 Staten Island Ferry, in New York. Over the years, these women developed a strong self-identity as the "8:15 Staten Island Ferry women," and it meant a lot to them.[33] Something as simple as a regular boat commute generated a strong group self-identity for these women. That should

---

v   The fact that cholera and diarrhoeal diseases alone kill more Pakistani children per year (typically an incredible 230,000) than have all foreign countries killed Pakistanis since 1971 has not affected the state's self-identity.

give a flavour as to the range of sources which identity can draw upon.

Saddam Hussein identified himself as the successor to two specific leaders from Iraq's past—King Nebuchadnezzar II of the sixth century BCE and Saladin of the twelfth century, the only leaders in Iraq's history to have captured Jerusalem. That neither was Arab didn't matter. Perversely, Saladin was a Kurd, the same people upon which Saddam inflicted genocide in the Al Anfal campaign in the late 1980s. He killed more than a million Kurds, some with American, German and other chemical weapons, and destroyed 4,500 Kurdish villages. Yet, Saddam stressed being born in Saladin's birth town (Tikrit) and referred to himself as "the noble and heroic Arab fighter Saladin II Saddam Hussein" or "Saladin II."[34] Saddam's self-identity partly, therefore, originated from a champion of the very nation whose people he butchered. Now that is really messed up!

With that nasty irony, it's easy to see how an organisation's self-identity can come from a founder, vision, relationship, transaction, branding exercise, media article, strength, successful strategy, etc. . . . The list does, indeed, go on. Likewise, a state's self-identity can come from a war, founding father (note: rarely a mother) or the myths surrounding that father. It can also come from the country's borders, the polemics of a neighbouring country, a resource, a religion, esteemed artists, a lunatic fringe, even fiction . . . and so on. None of this feels specific. That's because it is not. In fact, trying to understand how organisations and countries get their self-identities, given the fuzzy notions of mind, experience, personality, culture and society, is a merciless exercise. It's another one of those things that I doubt we will ever be able to meaningfully detail.

In 2011, Newt Gingrich argued that Palestinians don't deserve a state. He sneeringly referred to the Palestinians as an "invented" people because "there was no Palestine as a state" during the Ottoman Empire. He was partly accurate.[35] National identities are *invented* figments of our imagination. But so what? All national identities are invented ... there are no exceptions. The Palestinian identity is thus no different from the American identity. It doesn't take a genius to work out that America didn't exist for most of the Ottoman Empire (which began in the thirteenth century). Indeed, Gore Vidal, a political commentator, wrote a book on America's origins precisely titled *Inventing a Nation: Washington, Adams, Jefferson.*[36] The American identity is a recent *invention*, pre-dated by thousands of years by other national identities. The idea that an invented nation doesn't deserve statehood is pretty ridiculous given that all nations are invented.

The question of how self-identity takes shape and is developed is challenging. Overall, so many factors combine with and are filtered through our experiences, mind and personality that I would think that it's impossible to articulate a single coherent theory of the origins and development of self-identity. In fact, and Anderson became famous for stressing this in an ethnic and national context, the formation of any group is foremost an act of *imagination.*[37] One must first imagine an identity before it can come into being and be adopted. And with that I just can't see how we'll develop a robust theory for our imagination! It's probably one of the least likely concepts that we can develop a sensible framework for. The imagination seems not to have very many obvious boundaries.

That said, one possible anchor to understand where self-identity comes from is in dominant identity *categories*, which have an immense impact on who we think we are. The buckets which we use to self-identify can thus be very revealing. In the West, gender, race and religion are seen as essentialised identities—they are the base categories which people use to identify and explain themselves.[38] That's just a reflection of historical coincidence. In other societies, other categories are as important. India has a caste system in which half of all Indians are divided into four categories (each with thousands of subcategories) known as *varnas* (complexions) which determine what jobs they can do and who they can marry.[39] With 170 million *Dalits* (Untouchables) falling outside the varnas and living in apartheid-like conditions, such categorisations despite Gandhi's heroic efforts make a difference.

Religious sects are another example of an identity category unfamiliar to some in the West, but which have a big impact in other parts of the world. Ask any Ahmadi in Pakistan what it feels like to be harassed by the state on the basis of their sect, a practice legalised by the Oxford and Berkeley-educated prime minister Zulfiqar Bhutto. It just goes to show that having a top university degree doesn't mean you're educated.[40] Just ask any Shia in today's Pakistan what it feels like to be under the murderous attacks by the dominant Sunni sect's lunatic fringe, a fringe that was nurtured by the state which, ironically, was founded by a Shia! Both will tell you that sects as a category of identity really do matter. Their lives and those of their family members often depend on it.

In addition to fluctuating from one society to another, the available identity categories can change over time. This, of course, in turn affects how people see themselves. In the late fifteenth century, French villages treated *cagots* as second-class citizens. Depending on which story one buys, cagots had light skin, dark skin or lacked earlobes. Today, the cagot identity has been relegated to the history books and those who were placed in it have been moved into other boxes.[41] You simply won't find anybody self-identifying today as a cagot. Let's hope that somebody out there isn't now inspired to adopt this contrarian identity. Likewise, the *paekchong* used to be outcasts in Korea and were comparable to today's dalits. The paekchong category today no longer exists.[42] Many categories that we use to self-identify, to quote Culture Club's 1983 hit "Karma Chameleon," one of my favourite childhood songs, simply "come and go."

The idea that the categories of identity are transient has become quite vogue in academic circles. According to an increasingly influential school of thought in social theory, even the most fundamental identity categories are temporary and socially manufactured. Denise Buell, a religious studies scholar who looks like a younger version of tennis legend Martina Navratilova, noted:

> . . . Ethnicity/race and religion are discursively produced as well as socially and historically contingent. That is, instead of assuming that religion and race are either filled with some essential transhistorical content (otherwise known as a primordialist view) or are reducible to self-preserving political tools (otherwise known as an instrumentalist view), I treat religion and race/ethnicity as concepts that are formulated, maintained and revised through argument as well as through social practices and institutions.[43]

A more nuanced point is made by James Morris; he underwent a slow-motion sex change to become Jan Morris:

> Gender is not physical at all, but is altogether insubstantial. It is soul, perhaps, it is talent, it is taste, it is environment, it is how one feels, it is light and shade, it is inner music, it is a spring in one's step or an exchange of glances, it is more truly life and love than any combination of genitals, ovaries and hormones. It is the essentialness of oneself, the psyche, the fragment of unity. Male and female are sex, masculine and feminine are gender.[44]

I only partly agree with Buell and Morris. If I were drinking with them, my glass would be half full…providing the glass had no alcohol, in which case it would actually not be my glass because I don't drink alcohol. The categories which they refer to do involve some manufacturing, so there is the agreement, that's the half-full part. A definition of "man" and "woman" does at some point involve subjective choices. These choices are manufactured. These choices are created. Who selects the exhaustive list of what constitutes a "man" or "woman" and on what authority? Further, much of the meaning or narrative of both sex and gender is socially constructed. In other words, at some level, we create what it means to be male or female and masculine or feminine. We define what women are about just as much as we define what men are about.

That said, I just don't buy that all categories, including that of gender, are created *only* through social or cultural manufacturing. While many categories of self-identity are entirely the product of social context and thus the imagination, some have tangible, physical dimensions even if we have a (manufactured) choice in determining which dimensions we consider to be important or not. There are physical differences between men and women, as there are between toddlers and the elderly. It feels like a stretch to suggest that male and female self-identity categories are entirely socially or culturally manufactured. There's something over and above the imagination at play in crafting at least some categories of self-identity.

Almost as an aside, I want to flag the possible link between one's inner self and self-identity. I'm open to the idea that aligning one's self-identity with one's inner self may yield some kind of harmony. It may very well be that aligning one's self-identity with McGraw's "authentic" life leads to a higher state of existence. My principal hesitation to this entire idea is, though, that I doubt that we have the capacity to stabilise and identify our self-identity or the inner self, for that matter. Both are fluid and fungible and it might well be impossible to get a strong handle on either. That said, I intuitively feel that psychotherapists are on to something when they suggest that the more closely our lives reflect what we're about or what we think we're about and not just a set of identities which we project externally, the happier we're likelier to be. The idea just sits well in the gut.

The alternative to some kind of alignment between one's life and self-identity is to live out an alien identity or even multiple, conflicting alien identities. It's worth reflecting on Jan Morris's position that while living as a man but self-identifying as a woman, she felt trapped like a "silent prisoner."[45] Especially in countries where homosexuality is either taboo or illegal, homosexual folk are similarly confronted by the challenge of living out alien identities. Many decide that it's easier to live the imprisoned and disingenuous life of a heterosexual person than to share their sexual identity with their family, friends and the wider community. With between 2 and 5 percent of the world's population being homosexual and most of the world being hostile to homosexuality, this is a serious issue that causes considerable stress and anxiety to many millions of people.

Similarly, living with multiple, conflicting, strong alien self-identities can create havoc. Palestinian Mosab Hassan Yousef, the son of Sheikh Hassan Yousef, one of Hamas's co-founders and a junior leader in his own right, as well as an undercover agent for Israel, embraced multiple self-identities. Each came with its own story, with its own daily behavioural and operational implications:

> I was exhausted. I was tired of playing so many dangerous roles at once, tired of having to change my personality and appearance to fit the current company I was keeping. When I was with my father and other Hamas leaders, I had to play the part of a dedicated member of Hamas. When I was with the Shin Bet, I had to play the part of an Israeli collaborator. When I was at home, I often played the part of father and protector of my siblings.[46]

The situation eventually became too much for Yousef to navigate. Overwhelmed, he quit everything and left war-torn Palestine. In his post-Palestinian life he successfully sought political asylum in America. Given the chance to start a life on his own terms and truer to himself, he became an evangelical Christian and enjoyed life amongst California's fine wines. You really have to hand it to him—it was a pretty cool lifestyle upgrade. I'd be really curious to know whether the really courteous security officers at American airports "randomly" select him for further screening. After all, they know that he was once a Hamas fella. If you find out and are inclined to let me know, a quick e-mail through my blog at www.saqib.co would be highly appreciated.

One final dimension to self-identities that I want to surface is the role of narrative and stories in bringing identities to life. Narratives and stories help arrange events into patterns that may or may not mirror reality, but nevertheless help make sense of reality's many components. They're critical for self-identity because they flesh it out and give it meaning. A self-identity's meaning comes through its narrative, without which a self-identity is mere colourless bones. And this is why narratives are important to strategy, because to be ruthlessly pedantic, it is the narrative of a self-identity, *the story* or *meaning* of how a person, organisation or country sees themselves, that influences cognition. It is thus that meaning or the story of an identity that influences all three steps of the strategic process.

Allow me to illustrate. I know you have little choice, but let's not dwell on that. Trying to explain what an identity means is really tough without some kind of story or narrative. One historian dedicated fourteen pages to explaining an American: "He loves humour and a good joke . . . He likes a good time and to be a good fellow and to have all around him enjoy themselves."[47] Descriptions such as these of a people are useless. What a waste of fourteen pages multiplied by the number of copies published, not to mention the hours wasted by readers who tried to understand an American. The author may as well have been writing about any community on the planet. Even my German friends love a good joke! To understand an American or for that matter any other people, one has to turn to that people's narratives and stories, because it is those stories that help make sense of things, that add colour, texture and flavour.

Since narratives give meaning to identity, narrative preservation is important to self-identity. Given our self-identities need to stack up in our own eyes, our narratives cannot be wholly fictitious. They must continually integrate events and sort them into the ongoing story about the self.[48] In short, if one's self-identity is to be maintained, the narrative of the self must be preserved against life's flux and change. The narrative must continue for the identity to continue. It'd be too much for a student to see himself as a math genius if he failed his every math test. The self-identity wouldn't hold for long. Likewise, a country can't see itself as a superpower if several of its neighbours repeatedly thrash it (I say this without specifying Lebanon because I do like Lebanese food, which is the same food that the Lebanese army eat…just saying).

Inevitably, conflict occurs when one holds closely to identities with conflicting narratives, as in the earlier case of Yousef's multiple conflicting self-identities. Note also, for instance, Nazi Germany's armed forces employed up to 150,000 people of Jewish descent.[49] Let me rewrite that: the Nazi armed forces employed 150,000 people who were either Jews or of Jewish descent. Some of those employed were classified as Jews while others were classified as *mischlinge* (partial-Jews). Research by Bryan Rigg, a military historian, former Israeli army volunteer and former US Marine Corps officer (odd that he was in the armed forces of two countries), reveals that many Nazi soldiers actually identified themselves as Jews.[50] There's food for thought. These soldiers, some of whom were even senior officers, had to deal with one heck of a serious narrative clash.

So where does that leave self-identity? Ultimately, what I like about self-identity's characteristics is that they're flexible enough to work for everybody. Self-identity is a category that works across cultures, geographies and eras, while also providing a modicum of structure that we can then work with. Self-identity is a concept that merely asks individuals and groups who *they* think *they* are, on *their* own terms. That is flexible, as is evident in the range of sources of self-identity. The seemingly infinite range of sources that our identities can come from includes practically anything that we can imagine. The same flexibility is evident in self-identity's fluidity. Our self-identities are able to change instantaneously or over decades and in the case of countries, over centuries. We can even transition from self-identifying principally as an individual to then as group and vice versa, almost as fast as I can inhale a pack of French fries. Just to get it out there, that might be less than ten seconds for even a large pack. I've never tried it though.

On the other hand, self-identity provides structure. Extracting from people how they see themselves is precisely that, it's a structure. Self-identity's structure is one that allows for people to speak for themselves, albeit from the range of identity categories in their culture or society's arcade, however open or restricted those might be. This indigenous and authentic structure, which McGraw would surely applause, is something very real. It's how individuals, organisations and countries see themselves without any foreign consultant telling them that something is wrong or needs fixing while whacking on a hefty invoice and incidentals costs. It's not an exogenous, neoimperial imposition from Boston, Chicago or Los Angeles by somebody who has practically no living experience or insight of the sociocultural landscapes which 95 percent of the planet lives in and through.

And within our indigenous individual or group self-identity, we all have a core set of self-identities which we don't easily lose sight of. Those typically change slowly, and they gravitate our sense of self and thus our cognition beyond the self. These are precisely the self-identities that influence cognition and strategy. These are the self-identities that often matter to us, and we hold them close to ourselves. In contrast, we have other self-identities that can rapidly, even instantly, change, be strapped on or jettisoned. You can walk into a room packed with redheads and, unless you're amongst the 2 percent of the world that is redheaded and will soon become extinct, you can suddenly self-identify as the brown, black or blonde haired one. Some self-identities lack gravitas. We're not really very attached to them; thus they don't have that same influence on cognition as our core self-identities.

The argument made by those who subscribe to essentialist notions of self-identity—those who claim that we each have a true, stable and singular self-identity in line with Plato's notions of essentialist identity—is wishy-washy.[51] I don't think self-identity is a mysterious inner essence, nor do I think it is singular. I think it is a multidimensional work in progress. Self-identity *categories* are not only subject to change, but our self-identities within those categories can and do also change.[52] That's two distinct levels of change. If I simultaneously self-identify as both male and British, how then does it make sense to have a true singular self-identity? How does it make sense to speak of a static self-identity if I lose sight of my British self-identity when I am in the UK? Little wonder then that existentialist thinkers have cut into Plato's notions of essentialist identity for at least a century.

At the start of this chapter, I summarised the influence of self-identity in each step of the strategic process: It helps make sense of the world as-is, it feeds our future vision and, finally, it influences how we get from today to the future. I also touched upon the relationship between self-identity and cognition. The framework for identifying the self must be identical or at least similar to the framework for identifying everything beyond the self. It's a simple tautology. That so, making sense of today and the future vision, which are the start and end points of the strategic journey, must ultimately reflect how we self-identify. Finally, in the latter half of this chapter, I touched upon some of self-identity's properties. I did so to develop a greater awareness of this central concept to my treatment of strategy by explaining what self-identity is not and by outlining some of its characteristics.

In the next chapter, I'll conclude the focus on self-identity by discussing its power *irrespective of* its specific influence on cognition and strategy. Self-identity is a potent stimulus of human behaviour that can and does take us to the extremes of war and death. Self-identity might not sound like much. Many people might think that it's irrelevant when compared to other human stimuli such as economic benefit, power acquisition or enacting God's will. However, self-identity is a really sizeable factor in individual, organizational and national behaviour. Aside from being a piece that influences strategy, it happens to be quite powerful. What illustrates that power? What generates that punch? Where does the energy come from? These are the questions that I will touch upon in the first part of the next chapter.

That next chapter's latter half will then drill into the relationship between strategy and self-identity with more crunchy, detailed and tangible material than the cursory overview in this chapter. In other words, having explained self-identity in this chapter and its power in the early part of the next chapter, I then get stuck in with greater depth into my core argument: how one sees oneself has a huge influence on a person's, organisation's and country's foreign policy strategy. Specifically, self-identity impacts how each sees the world that they live in, feeds into the vision which they set out for themselves and influences the steps which they take to get between the two points. From this, it should become increasingly manifest that strategy isn't only about an external world. It's as much that as it is about how we see ourselves.

1   W Isaacson, *Einstein: His Life and Universe*, Simon & Schuster, New York, 2007

2   FA Gerges, *The New Middle East*, Cambridge University Press, New York, 2014

3   *The Social Network*, Relativity Media, West Hollywood and Trigger Street Productions, California, 2010

4   S Palin quoted from CBS with Katie Couric, 24 September 2008

5   D Campbell, *Writing Security: United States Foreign Policy and the Politics of Identity*, University of Minnesota Press, Minneapolis, 1998

6   Z Brzezinski, *Out of Control*, MacMillan Publishing, New York, 1993; SP Huntington, *Who Are We? America's Great Debate*, Simon & Schuster, London, 2005

7   L Freedman and E Karsh, *The Gulf Conflict: 1990–1991*, Princeton University Press, Princeton, 1995

8   "Not Qualified: Exposing the Deception Behind America's Top 25 Pseudo Experts on Islam," Muslim Public Affairs Council, Washington, DC, 2011

9   M Whitebrook, *Identity, Narrative and Politics*, Routledge, London, 2001

10   JD Fearon, *What Is Identity (As We Now Use the Word)?*, Stanford University, California, 1999

11   *Chambers English Dictionary*, Chambers, Edinburgh, 1990

12   *Ibid.*

13   M Hogg and D Abrams, *Social Identifications: A Social Psychology of Intergroup Relations and Group Processes*, Routledge, London, 1988

14   E Goffman, *The Presentation of Self in Everyday Life*, Anchor, New York, 1959

15   PV Ham, "The Rise of the Brand State," *Foreign Affairs*, New York, 2001

16   JMT Balmer, H Stuart and SA Greyser, "Aligning Identity and Strategy," *California Management Review*, Albany, 2009

17   F Halliday, *Rethinking International Relations*, Palgrave Macmillan, London, 1994; E Geller, *Nations and Nationalism*, Blackwell Publishing, Oxford, 2006; B Anderson, *Imagined Communities*, Verso, London, 1983

18   JMT Balmer and SA Greyser, *Revealing the Corporation*, Routledge, London, 2003

19   http://www.iep.utm.edu/ricoeur/

20   H Markus and Z Kunda, "Stability and Malleability of the Self-Concept," *Journal of Personality and Social Psychology*, Washington, DC, American Psychological Association, 1986

21   http://www.census.gov/population/socdemo/hh-fam/tabST-F1-2000.pdf *also* http://www.humanesociety.org/issues/pet_overpopulation/facts/pet_ownership_statistics.html

22   http://www.msnbc.msn.com/id/14738358/ns/health-pet_health

23   B McLean and P Elkind, *The Smartest Guys in the Room*, Penguin Books, London, 2003

24   G Hunter, *Spain: The Inside Story of La Roja's Historic Treble*, BackPage Press, London, 2013

25   JC Quint, "The Impact of Mastectomy," *The American Journal of Nursing*, New York, 1963

26   D Berreby, *Us and Them*, Hutchinson, London, 2006

27   LM Diamond, "A New View of Lesbian Subtypes," *Psychology of Women Quarterly*, Blackwell Publishing, 2005

28   D Gioia, M Schultz and K Corley, "Organisational Identity, Image and Adaptive Instability," *Academy of Management Review*, 2000

29   S Stryker, "Identity Theory: Developments and Extensions" in K Yardley and T Honess, *Self and Identity: Psychosocial Perspectives*, Wiley, New York, 1987; GT McCall and JT Simmons, *Identities and Interaction*, Free Press, New York, 1978

30   MK Gandhi, *An Autobiography: The Story of My Experiments with Truth*, Beacon Press, Boston, 1993

31   http://www.bbc.com/news/business-24378861

32   OB Jones, *Pakistan: Eye of the Storm*, Yale University Press, New Haven, 2009

33   D Berreby, *Us and Them*, Hutchinson, London, 2006

34   E Karsh and I Rautsi, *Saddam Hussein: A Political Biography*, Perseus, London, 2002

35 http://www.bbc.co.uk/news/world-us-canada-16138129

36 ELG Vidal, *Inventing a Nation: Washington, Adams, Jefferson*, Yale University Press, New Haven, 2004

37 B Anderson, *Imagined Communities*, Verso, London, 1983

38 MR Somers and GD Gibson, "Reclaiming the Epistemological 'Other'" in C Calhoun, *Social Theory and the Politics of Identity*, Blackwell, Oxford, 1994

39 G Pandey, *A History of Difference: Race, Caste and Difference in India and the United States*, Cambridge University Press, New York, 2013

40 OB Jones, *Pakistan: Eye of the Storm*, Yale University Press, New Haven, 2009

41 D Berreby, *Us and Them*, Hutchinson, London, 2006

42 *Ibid.*

43 D K Buell, "Race and Universalism in Early Christianity," *Journal of Early Christian Studies*, The Johns Hopkins University Press, Baltimore, Volume 10, Number 4, Winter 2002

44 J Morris, *Conundrum*, Faber and Faber, London, 2001

45 *Ibid.*

46 MH Yousef, *Son of Hamas*, Tyndale House, New York, 2009

47 JT Adams, *The Epic of America*, Routledge, London, 1938

48 A Giddens, *Modernity and Self-Identity*, Stanford University Press, Stanford, 1991

49 BM Rigg, *The Untold Story of Nazi Racial Laws and Men of Jewish Descent in the German Military*, University Press of Kansas, Sacramento, 2004

50 *Ibid.*

51 C Calhoun, "Social Theory and the Politics of Identity" in C Calhoun, *Social Theory and the Politics of Identity*, Blackwell, Oxford, 1994

52 LM Alcoff and SP Mohanty, "Reconsidering Identity Politics" in LM Alcoff, MH Garcia, SP Mohanty and PML Moya, *Identity Politics Reconsidered*, Palgrave Macmillan, Basingstoke, 2006

CHAPTER 5

———————

WHO YOU THINK YOU ARE
AND YOUR STRATEGY

McGraw hit the nail on the head when he wrote, "This stuff about identity, about who you are, matters, it really matters."[1] I only nuance this by noting that it's not who you are but who you *think* you are or your self-identity that matters. Self-identity influences cognition, including each step of the strategic process. However, putting the impact on cognition aside, self-identity is itself a charged space. Some people even see it as a basic human need. That's right, "need" and not mere "want." In its own right, it's got a V8 engine, and recognising this makes it easier to appreciate self-identity's influence on strategy. Self-identity is a powerful and unrecognised source of behaviour, which is the focus of the first part of this chapter. In the second part of this chapter, I will flesh out in a bit more detail the relationship between self-identity and strategy.[2]

Self-identity can be very sensitive. The wrong prefix to a name, an incorrect description of a firm or even keeping one's hat on during a national anthem can send those who think they've been messed around with right up the wall.[3] Self-identity excites and energises. It motivates, often inadvertently, a good chunk of human behaviour. Again, don't ask me for percentages. And we are now developing, amongst several academic disciplines, a growing appreciation for self-identity. For example, in religion, several experts such as Eileen Barker, a sociologist, have documented the growing prominence of individual identity.[4] Organisational self-identity, unheard of in the 1960s, emerged in the 1970s and has since blossomed.[5] And leading foreign policy practitioners increasingly discuss the search for national identity or the preservation of the old self-identity.[6]

The Power of Self-Identity

One way to gauge the potential power of self-identity at the level of individual is by its impact on depression and suicide, as extreme and powerful a behaviour or action as we are capable of. As an illustration of just how extreme an act that is, we are not aware of any living creature other than mankind that commits suicide. We humans are the only species that are able to, and tragically sometimes do, take our own lives. Many factors cause clinical depression, one of the key factors to suicide; these include familial and environmental influences. It's very hard to pin down a single person's depression to any one of these or many other causes, let alone identify the root of all human depression. Hard and complete generalisations about the causes of depression are difficult, further complicated by factors varying with age, gender and culture.

One approach, the bio-psychosocial model, suggests that biological, psychological and social factors collectively play a role in causing depression. Sometimes a poor childhood will combine with a genetic predisposition to tilt somebody into depression. Another approach, the diathesis-stress model, suggests that depression is caused when a pre-existing vulnerability is triggered.[7] For example, bad news about a close family member might trigger depression.[8] For others, that bad news might be yet another drone missile landing amongst innocent passersby who were simply in the wrong place at the wrong time without mentioning US missiles and Pakistani civilians. That those civilians might have been terrorised in the process does not, of course, make the instigators of the attack to be terrorists without mentioning the US's armed forces. After all, terrorizing innocent people doesn't make you a terrorist. Welcome to the world of George Orwell's *1984*.

Despite the uncertainty of depression's origins, psychologists and social theorists stress the importance of a positive self-identity to avoid depression.[9] Depression is less likely to occur and faster to dispel amongst those with strong social or religious self-identities, which tend to be associated with narratives of self-worth and optimistic outcomes. A strong, reassured and optimistic set of narratives and self-identity guards against depression—a point that has been repeatedly demonstrated in academic studies. One such study was of students in 1991 by psychologists Ronald Koteskey, Michelle Little and Michelle Matthews, who concluded that those with a stronger community, family or religious self-identity were less vulnerable to depression than those without.[10]

Some experts go further by suggesting that positive identity narratives can actually *help* those who are suffering specific challenges to overcome depression-related issues, such as drug and alcohol abuse.[11] In fact, psychologists James McIntosh and Neil McKeganey suggested that formal treatments to addiction such as prescribed medication may be *less* effective than progressive identity narratives in helping drug and alcohol addicts overcome their abuse problems. In other words, narrative therapy and reconstruction might be better at overcoming addictions than are medicines. I suspect that this isn't exactly welcome news for the world's largest pharmaceutical firms who have done really well out of the depression business, especially in America.[12] It's a bit like what our latest research on sugar is doing for sugary soft drink sales.

In contrast, there's a strong correlation between on the one hand, negative self-identity and on the other hand, depression and also suicidal tendencies. Aaron Beck developed the cognitive model of depression in the 1960s and has pioneered much of our understanding of depression despite having had his application to the American Psychoanalytic Institute rejected. He was amongst the first to emphasise the relationship between one's negative self-identity and depression.[13] Cohorts of psychologists and psychoanalysts have since built on Beck's work. One such is Albert Bandura, a psychologist, who is amongst many other psychologists and social psychologists who have noted that depressed people often have both a negative self-identity and an assumption that they cannot change themselves.[14] That isn't hard to understand. It's not counterintuitive.

Extending the point, people who feel suicidal often complain that their life has lost meaning. Put differently, their life has lost its narrative, a fuzzy and fractured story of where it came from and where it's going. Quite literally, they've lost the plot. In similar vein, psychologists recognise that major depressive disorder (MDD) is often accompanied by a poor self-identity, culminating in a lack of self-esteem and an inadequate sense of self-worth.[15] This is a serious issue given that about 3 to 4 percent of the MDD population in America go on to commit suicide. That same poor self-identity and its subsequent self-destruction can easily transmit from individuals to larger social groups or even nations, as is evident in the fractured African–American narrative:

> The sense of self or lack of, that forms an open wound from which most of the major ills affecting the black community ooze forth. . . . At the crux of the matter is a lack of self-esteem among black youths.[16]

Going beyond both the individual and the organisation, we can also gauge the impact of self-identity on countries. Some of the world's most difficult and painful political problems relate to issues of identity even if most political scientists and historians have ignored or relegated self-identity, an important factor in behaviour, in understanding and explaining events. Countries don't just act in defence of their economic, military and political interests—it would be something if they even did that.[i] They also make sense of and act in defence of or to impose their identities, and you'll see examples of this in chapter 8. Issues of self-identity are powerful enough to drive those same countries to self-destruction. Hundreds of millions of people have been murdered over many centuries because they didn't sufficiently embrace or even share the identities of their killers. This is why Hamas doesn't care too much if Jewish Israeli children are killed by its rockets just as much as why the government of Benjamin Netanyahu doesn't care too much if Muslim Palestinian children are killed by its rockets. As long as the kids are from the other identity, the other group, such killing is at best "regrettable." It is, however, never "unacceptable". It is never "criminal". This pivotal fulcrum of the interface of international relations and self-identity was crisply articulated by Ringmar:

> A war will protect our selves and our way of life and as long as we identify ourselves with our community, it may be worth fighting for it regardless of the costs involved.[17]

Don Podestra, an international relations academic who studied political conflicts and analysed twenty-five countries in ethnic and religious conflict concluded that the "conflicts (are) rooted in the

---

i   There is considerable literature by international relations scholars which demonstrates that foreign policy is not a function of national interests. In fact, the old realist school which emphasises foreign policy as a function of national inter-est has more holes in it than a sponge. A good initial book to read on this is Jim George's *Discourses of Global Politics*.

most basic forms of human identity" reflecting "the need to assert group identity."[18] He went on to argue that in most of the analysed conflicts, economic or political issues were only *manifestations* of other underlying problems. The conflicts nearly all gravitated around people fearing extinction of their *identity*. I'm a little surprised by the extent to which Podestra reduced all conflict to identity, and I suspect that could be a bit too reductivist. So though I might be inclined to discount his conclusions a touch, I do like his raising self-identity's profile in the context of war and suspect that his assessment will be all too familiar to many communities which are fighting for the right to form a state, to be recognised and legitimised.

In a more ambitious study, Ruth Sivard, an economist and military analyst, analysed the apparently 471 wars with casualties of more than 1,000 across the world between 1700 and 1987. The summation of these incidentally generated an astonishing 101.5 million deaths (of which 61 million were in World War I and II). Her conclusions were that most wars were about territory or independence. She then demonstrated that these could be roughly translated as proxies for self-esteem and self-identity.[19] Again, even though I have some concerns with her method (no doubt heightened given my self-confessed bias of any data-gathering or analysis by an economic or military mind), I do like her conclusion—that self-identity lies at the heart of war. Note this summary by Bubba, aka Bill Clinton:

> We're working, trying to bring an end to the Northern Ireland peace process now. We're trying to keep the Middle East peace process going. All of this stuff, it's rooted in whether people believe that their primary identity is as a member of the human race, that they share with others who are different from them; or if they believe their primary identity is as a result of their superiority over people who may share the same village, the same neighbourhood and the same high-rise apartment but they don't belong to the same ethnic

group or racial group or religious group, so if they have to be killed, it's just fine.[20]

Bubba's point was simple—how nations, communities and people choose to self-identify can be the difference between peace and war. I agree with that because people who self-identify *first* as a member of the human race see the world differently and subsequently behave differently from those who self-identify first as members of an ethnic, racial or religious group. It's fine to simultaneously have self-identities as a human being and as a member of an ethnic, racial or religious group. I have no problem with that. The two obviously aren't inherently diametrically opposed, unless there's something seriously wrong with the assumptions and prejudices of the latter group and that's obviously very, very possible.

However, at some point, on big and small issues, choices must be made to prioritise one lens, one perspective, one framework over the other. Either the human being lens trumps the ethnic, racial or religious lens or vice versa. And from that choice of seeing the world, there will be fewer choices to engage that world. In which case, some of us may de-prioritise our common human identity for whatever ethnic, racial or religious identity we have. As a consequence, issues of self-identity, of ethnicity, race or religion are integral to some of the most challenging and entrenched international conflicts of our time. For those who are unlucky enough to have experienced war, the issue of self-identity will be sharp and real. It might have brought about the destruction of their family, homes and livelihoods. It's no coincidence that most Jews *always* support Israel's interpretation of events and analysis when conflict breaks out in Palestine while most Arabs *always* support the Palestinian version.

With this in mind, if Professor Charles Xavier, of the X-Men from Marvel Comics, were able to wipe away from our minds the identities of Palestinian, Israeli, Jew and Muslim, he'd achieve instant peace in the Middle East. Let me be clear, lest some clown accuse me of advocating the massacre of a couple of billion people. I don't mean killing all Palestinian, Israeli, Jewish and Muslim people to achieve peace. That would be out of character for him—and me too, lest you had any doubts. I'm asking you to imagine a world where those *identities* cease to exist, a bit like the ending of France's cagots and Korea's paekchong identities.[ii] I think we'd achieve peace in the Middle East faster than I can make a Nescafé coffee. Nobody would know which group they have to love, support, tolerate or hate. Nobody would know which group to discriminate for or against. It's quite possible that the folk who live near some of the world's holiest places, engrossed as they are with their religious identities, have forgotten that we are first and foremost human beings.

The theme of peace was never far from the British pop group The Beatles, who were successful partly because the lyrics of many of their songs were quite moving. During his solo years, John Lennon, who was at the heart of The Beatles's songwriting, wrote in *Imagine* something quite profound in the context of war and identity, lending as it does to my earlier Xavier argument. Lennon encouraged us to imagine a world without countries, one in which there'd be "nothing to kill or die for."[21] Implicit was the idea that we have war because we have countries. I don't necessarily agree with that absolutist position because war isn't exclusively a state act. Religious groups go to war, as do ethnic ones. However, I do think that immersing ourselves in national identities can encourage us to overlook what unites us against foreign people. It filters our understanding of events. In this sense, it's obvious that countries have been responsible for more than their fair share of human suffering, misery and killing.

---

ii   That said, I fully expect some obtuse journalist to accuse me of encouraging or instigating the greatest genocide in history. Everybody else … look out for the obtuse journalist!

Another way of measuring the power of self-identity is in the various drives towards national statehood, a process which is seldom only about economic or political self-interest. Over the twentieth century alone, millions of people have offered extraordinary levels of sacrifice to achieving statehood, to have their self-identity legitimated and recognised in the world community. In decolonised countries across the world, precisely those millions abandoned their homes, belongings and communities and even fought with weapons to have their own country. My own grandfather left a sensible lifestyle in India to migrate to Lahore's slums. The same commitment to national statehood is evident in other people who have strived and shed blood for but not achieved statehood, including the Palestinians, Kashmiris, Balochis, Basques, Assamese and Tibetans. Struggles for national self-determination in the twentieth century alone have exacted a huge human and other cost.

I don't see the sacrifices from millions of people as outputs or by-products of calculations of interest or power. Individuals, families and nations rarely performed a detailed cost-benefit analysis of their migration. They didn't calmly analyse whether to support or reject the demands for statehood made by some leaders in *their* group. At the heart of nearly every national self-determination movement, meaning the emotional fuel that drives the movement, lies the desire for identity recognition.[22] Each people wanted their own country, they want others to recognise them, to accept their existence, irrespective of whether it was better or worse for them. So entrenched is the need for identity recognition that Erik Ringmar, an international relations academic, described the failure to recognise another people as a "crime against identity."[23] That could be pushing it a bit because it's hard to measure such a crime, especially given self-identity's fluidity. And though I can't see anybody being charged for this offence in my lifetime, his statement does nevertheless give a flavour of the importance of self-identity in creating new countries.

It's not difficult to bring home the reality of self-identity's value by comparing it to economic self-interest as an influence on human behaviour. Self-identity can and sometimes does trump economic considerations in driving human behaviour. The American people will never allow China to legally take over America, even if 99 percent of Americans could be guaranteed a better quality of material, economic life. Such a takeover would have nothing to do with American consumers buying so much from China...while the American government borrows billions from China. No amount of money is going to hoist the Chinese flag over Congress or the White House. It's not happening for any quantum of capital. Likewise, Israeli Jews will never accept the liquidation of their state, even if the Arab world gave each Israeli Jew a nice, tidy, hydrocarbon-backed payout. Israeli Jews want Israel *irrespective* of their net economic or political benefit. Israelis want Israel because it is now integral to their self-identity, their sense of who they are.

Given the impact and importance of self-identity to human behaviour, the absence of self-identity from the strategy literature is both surprising and not. That sounds like something from an economist. An accountant would first ask you if you wanted the statement to surprise you or not and then oblige. It's surprising because self-identity has a big impact on strategy, but it's hardly ever spoken of. None of the key strategy texts revolve around self-identity. In fact, most of them ignore self-identity altogether. Jack Covert and Todd Sattersten's *The 100 Best Business Books of All Time*, a book I personally thought shallow even by business academia's standards, explores eight strategy books, none of which revolve around self-identity.[24] Interestingly, I think some of those strategy books aren't even about strategy while Porter's *Competitive Strategy*, despite its titanic following, isn't even listed.

At the same time, it's not surprising that self-identity barely features in the strategy literature. For a start, self-identity is a difficult concept to get to grips with, probing an awareness of multiple intellectual disciplines. Its relationship with strategy isn't obvious. It requires a bit of thinking, reflection and breathing space. Today, too many (though not all) strategists lack the intellectual and conceptual horsepower to embrace novel concepts from outside of their cookie-cutter frameworks. In modern organisations, where the thinking person can easily be labelled as the daydreaming person, it's hard to really ruminate and break boundaries. Strategists need to venture beyond the plod, working plod hours in plod organisational machines. They need to embrace more thought, curiosity, doubt and learning into their working lives.

Another reason why self-identity isn't featured in the strategy literature is the pressure to conform. During my first project as a management consultant, I was introduced to the firm's hypothesis-led approach. This basically involved developing a hypothesis and finding data to prove or disprove it. I spent my entire first day arguing against this approach because it had a mega-bias in favour of the selected hypothesis. It could, for instance, easily be used to demonstrate that Elvis was still alive or the 1969 trip to the moon was fabricated. On the warning of a colleague to get over my problem or be left behind, I swallowed my objection and moved on. It's simply often easier to just get on with the way things have been done as opposed to re-think stuff. This problem is perhaps more so in the late modern world, characterised with its increased time sensitivity and impatience. We not only now communicate at the speed of light, we increasingly expect action at that pace too.

A final reason that might explain self-identity's absence from the strategy literature is the assumption made by strategists that man is capable of objectivity. In other words, there's nothing about self-identity in the strategy literature because strategists assume that people aren't influenced by nonlogical factors such as self-identity. Such strategists see the world through objectivity and truths—idols which have been challenged and long found wanting. You'll recall that I've demonstrated in earlier chapters that the world is not self-evident. No aspect of reality jumps up and down shouting its identity, and if you think it does, you've probably had a wee bit to drink. And I wasn't thinking of nonalcoholic beverages. Self-identity gets almost no recognition in the strategy literature because self-identity leans on a socially constructed and nonrational world. It is a world that most strategists are completely unfamiliar with.

One rare strategy book which I briefly touch upon and relish because it embraces self-identity and, as it happens, does so really intelligently, is by David Campbell, a culture and politics academic who once taught in Newcastle, an extraordinarily dull place. I briefly mentioned him earlier. I've no idea why a man from Australia's sunny beaches chose to live in one of Britain's most miserable towns, except that I ardently recognise that each person is entitled to choose where they live. *Writing Security: United States Foreign Policy and the Politics of Identity* reconstituted foreign policy strategy by defining "foreign" not as in foreign country but as foreign *identities*.[25] Campbell suggested that "foreign" policy is about the defence and promotion of a set of self-identities, simultaneously in and outside of a country's borders. He didn't see "foreign" as something outside of a Lego-like political border.

Campbell thus saw the Cold War not as a competition of interests with the USSR but as a competition of identities. America identified itself as a white, capitalist protector of freedom and mankind's last great hope. America also identified communist USSR as its embodied antithesis.[26] Meanwhile, American "foreign" policy *within* its borders disrupted movements that supported socialism, homosexuality and racial equality—identities that violated the then understanding of what it meant to be American. The FBI's COINTELPRO programme went after American homosexuals and American civil rights activists in the same way the FBI has since 2001 gone after American Muslims. Despite most members of those groups all having American passports, the FBI treated them as if they were *foreign* groups.[27] And as a result, the FBI hunted all of them not for criminal conduct but for violating popular understandings of what an American meant.

Even to this day, some half a century after Martin Luther King's famous speech at the steps of the Lincoln Memorial, the lessons of America's civil rights movement have not fully been learned. America's Muslims remain foreigners in their own country. While the New York Police Department's euphemistically named "Demographics Unit" spied exclusively on American Muslims for more than a decade without being stopped by the judiciary, the US president got pummelled for being associated with an Arab name. Barack Obama's middle name, Hussein, a common Arab and Muslim name, became an issue in his first presidential campaign as somehow being un-American. Several Republican Party stalwarts made a song and dance about it in February 2008. It took Colin Powell, a former secretary of state, national security advisor and chairman of the joint chiefs of staff, to punch through all that:

> Well, the correct answer is, he is not a Muslim, he's a Christian. He's always been a Christian. But the really right answer is, what if he is? Is there something wrong with being a Muslim in this country? The answer's no, that's not America. Is there something wrong with some seven-year-old Muslim–American kid believing that he or she could be president?[28]

What Makes Self-Identity So Powerful?

Having demonstrated the power of self-identity while briefly touching upon self-identity's absence from the strategy literature, I now want to explore that power a bit more. Why is self-identity such a powerful force and sway of human behaviour? What are the raw ingredients of self-identity's rocket fuel? I think there are, surprise, surprise, three key pieces which help give some insight. The first possible piece is that people don't like unpleasant information about themselves. They don't like doubts or negative information floating around about themselves, about their self-identity. It doesn't make them feel good about who they are and what they're worth. People like to have a positive self-identity and they suppress or fight against negative self-identity issues. Some experts even go on to suggest that the self *needs* to maintain its identity, as a primary human need, and enhance its esteem.

HSBC Bank staff doesn't brag about the bank being fined a whopping US $1.9 billion in 2012 for its role in laundering drug cartel funds from Mexico. It's not a smart thing to do. Nor do the London School of Economics alumni publicise that Muammar Qaddafi's son, Saif, graduated from Houghton Street in a cloud of plagiarised controversy. McKinsey consultants don't advertise that Rajat Gupta, who was imprisoned after being convicted in 2012 for conspiracy and securities fraud (at the time of writing subject to appeal), was elected the firm's chief executive, not once but three times. In fact, people regularly try to hide or rationalize any negative information that tarnishes their sense of who they are, that makes them look and feel bad.[29] Positive self-esteem, in fact, implies a self-identity which one can feel good about, which is probably why Ringmar defined friends as those people who "affirmed the identity of the self."[30]

To illustrate the desire to have a positive self-identity, I turn to Disney's *Toy Story*, a production that took animation to whole new levels. Woody and Buzz Lightyear's relationship gets off to a bad start. Their owner, Andy, throws Woody off the bed to make way for Buzz, his exciting new toy. The toys awaken when Andy runs out of the room:

> *Woody*: Look, we're all very impressed with Andy's new toy.
> *Buzz*: Toy?
> *Woody*: T-O-Y . . . Toy!
> *Buzz*: Excuse me, I . . . I think the word you're searching for is "Space Ranger."
> *Woody*: The word I'm searching for . . . I can't say because there's pre-school toys present.[31]

There are two interesting things about this dialogue. First, it immediately follows one of my favourite scenes in the movie. This is when Buzz reveals his identity in a supremely matter of fact, nonchalant way: "I am Buzz Lightyear, Space Ranger, Universal Protection Unit."[32] He rolls it off as if it's the most natural thing in the world, with delectable body language and facial expression. The way I've described it is a bit flat and does no justice to the scene, so you have to see the movie to appreciate my point. Disney and Pixar, in particular, can now thank me for the deluge of people who I'm sure will be clamouring to get their hands on a copy just so they can see that five second clip. As a quid pro quo, perhaps they can have my book stocked for sale at the long lines for the rides in their multiple theme parks? That'll be a sure way for me to get the book in front of some potential customers.

The second interesting thing about the dialogue is that it reveals the importance of having an identity that one is happy with. When Woody suggested that Buzz is "just a toy," Buzz responded that he's a Space Ranger, a member of an elite corps charged with protecting the universe, a role with a wow factor about it. Woody was tempted to hit back with an identity way inferior but refrained, maybe because the movie might have got a more restrictive film classification. You might think that whether Buzz was identified as a toy or as a space ranger was irrelevant. But it was relevant and important enough for the pair to have their first spat over. Woody tried to assign Buzz an identity which has a mediocre narrative. Buzz wanted nothing to do with it, claiming an identity that made him feel good about himself.

A second possible explanation of self-identity's power comes from ethno-methodologists who probably don't have much time for Woody and Buzz. They suggest that when people's realities or worldviews are threatened, they themselves feel threatened.[33] And there's little more—personal, influential or central—to somebody's reality than their own self-identity, its stories and narratives. Take, for example, Islam's main sects, the Sunni and Shia. The latter argue that the Muslim community's political and spiritual authority should have transferred from the prophet Mohammed (upon his death) to his cousin and son-in-law, Ali ibn Ali Talib. They reject the Sunni belief that political authority was correctly transferred to Mohammed's close friend and father-in-law, Abu Bakr. Nor do they accept the Sunni claim that spiritual authority died with Mohammed, the last of Islam's prophets.

Today, while most Sunni and Shia live well together, a few do not. Massacres between the groups aren't unheard of, especially in pre-modern communities. In 2010 alone, more than five hundred people were murdered in Shia–Sunni violence in Pakistan, including eighty worshippers in an attack in a Lahore mosque in May 2010.[34] It says something quite powerful if members of one group can kill eighty members of another almost identical group in a place of worship. This sectarian conflict has recently taken on a much darker turn in Iraq and Syria. Such violence, I think, doesn't emanate from diametrically contrasting views, as between Black African and pro-apartheid African. The two Muslim sects agree on most big-ticket items. They agree on God, righteousness, the Qur'an, Mohammed and Islam's Five Pillars of faith. In any case, most Sunnis and Shias are in no position to evaluate the merits of either sect's claim to the truth. The illiteracy rate in both groups is amongst the highest of any religious groups in the world.

The sectarian tension's epicentre, I think—the emotional root of the prejudices and violence—lies in each sect's threatened identity and narratives. Each sect implicitly challenges the other's story and in doing so, the self-identities of its followers. The niggling away of a person's most sensitive understandings, being their self-identity, something that they have grown up with since their younger days and that permeates into so much of their everyday life, can touch a raw nerve. And there are unfortunately enough nutcases out there who lose the plot when that happens. I don't, therefore, see this sectarian clash as intellectual or cerebral buttings of theological minds. Nor do I see it as a spiritual disconnection. I see the clashes as powerful emotional clashes and protections of self-identity and their immersing stories.

A final rationalisation of the power of self-identity is the multiple connections associated with a particular identity that in turn can set off fireworks. An attack on a group can become an attack on each individual and vice versa. There's something to a phrase I once heard in Dubai: "Hit a gay guy in Saudi, hit a gay guy everywhere." Indians in Indiana get stressed when Indians in Australia are racially abused. Lesbians in London are irked when a lesbian is arrested in or thrown out of a Gulf country for practicing her sexuality. Muslims in Malaysia don't for one bit like Muslims being incarcerated in Gitmo's legal balderdash. That the Indian in Indiana, lesbian in London and Muslim in Malaysia are thousands of miles away from their identity-compatriots, who they've got no other tangible relationship with, is immaterial. The common identities alone are enough to connect geographically removed strangers together.

I wasn't quite old enough to appreciate the comments in 1984 by "Beefy," aka Ian Botham, the cricketer, that "Pakistan is the sort of place every man should send his mother-in-law to, for a month, all expenses paid."[35] Yet I know my mother has begrudged him ever since. Never mind that Beefy was a brilliant cricketer who delivered a sporting miracle against Australia at Headingley in July 1981. Never mind that he walked up and down England to raise millions of pounds for cancer research.[36] Never mind that Pakistan was a difficult place in 1984 and is today well below levels suitable for mothers-in-law.[iii] Never mind that my mother embraces England, with its high tea, Wimbledon summers and lousy weather, as her home. All of that is irrelevant for my mother.

My mother's focus was very different. Beefy, a non-Pakistani, insulted Pakistan. Almost every person who self-identified as Pakistani, irrespective of where they lived, how they saw Pakistan or what they felt about Beefy, hated what he said and begrudged him for it. It's for good reason that seven million Pakistanis live outside of Pakistan and tens of millions of Pakistanis would give their right arm to join them. But Beefy, and not the millions of Pakistanis who have fled the country by hook or by crook, remains the pariah because he poked at something which is sensitive, volatile and primary: a people's core self-identity. It wasn't then surprising that when Wasim Akram had Beefy dismissed cheaply (and possibly erroneously) into the gloves of Moin Khan in the 1992 cricket world cup final, we saw dancing in the streets of Lahore, we saw *jalaybee* flowing in Karachi.[iv]

---

iii   In case you're curious, my relationship with my mother-in-law is pretty good. I wouldn't dream of "sending" her to Pakistan. In any case, if I did, my wife would throw a grenade at me. That might adversely affect her own relationship with her own mother-in-law, which is also pretty good.

iv   If you're looking for an explanation for *jalaybee*, try it in a Pakistani or Indian restaurant. And if you can't fine one, it's a really tasty, sticky orange-coloured sweet made by frying a wheat-flour batter with sugar syrup. I had to look that up because I'd no idea what it was made of. I typically don't see it being prepared. I'm just very good at wolfing it down.

And that cheerful note, against the background of streams of my favourite South Asian sweet, concludes my survey of self-identity's power and the possible explanations of that power. Putting aside self-identity's relationship with strategy, I hope that I've established that self-identity itself is an authoritative stimulus of human behaviour. It's something that we should be able to acknowledge because some us are prepared to die for it. Something that can motivate people to suicide and countries to war evidently influences human behaviour and is inevitably going to impact strategy. Self-identity motivates us, as do other things in life such as power, sex and money, but unlike those drivers, self-identity seldom hits the tabloids. It doesn't even feature in the serious newsprint's assessment of individual, organisational or foreign policy stories. So in demonstrating self-identity's gravitas, I hope it will be easier to appreciate the scale of its influence on strategy.

Deep Diving into Self Identity's Impact on Strategy

I've thus far given a taster of self-identity's relationship with strategy. I've also clarified the concept of self-identity in the previous chapter. Now, in this chapter, I have placed self-identity as a permanent member of the behavioural security council by demonstrating self-identity's intrinsic power and impact on human behaviour. Self-identity is neither some magic panacea for all human behaviour nor for strategy. Our using it will not solve global warming, poverty or the failure of the Toronto Maple Leafs to win a trophy since 1967. It will not even have a material impact on the seemingly odd fan loyalty amongst Torontonians who regularly pay some of the ice hockey league's highest ticket prices to watch one of the league's worst teams. Self-identity is, however, an important and underplayed source of our behaviour. With that, I now want to detail self-identity's influence on each of the three steps of the strategic process.

This is something of the finale in the book's journey. This began by creating the space to allow for the role of cognition in the strategic process. It now ends with detailing self-identity's influence on our making sense of the world as-is, on our vision for the future and the strategy to bridge the two. I now want to drill into self-identity's relationship with strategy in more detail than I have thus far, before sharing practical examples elucidating aspects of the relationship in the next three chapters. In this drilling and then in the subsequent illustrative chapters, it should become more apparent that our strategies are not simply dependent exclusively on an external world that we objectively know. Our strategies reflect how we see ourselves as much as they reflect an external world that we're engaging.

Self-Identity's Impact on Strategy: The World of Today

> When you identify yourself as a single chess piece—and by analogy, as an individual in a particular role—you can only react to, complain about or resist the moves that interrupted your plans. But if you name yourself as the board itself you can turn all of your attention to what you want to see happen.[37]

The first significant impact that self-identity and the stories and narratives it comes with has on strategy is in helping shape the starting point, in making sense of the world and our position in it. Self-identity shapes the starting point of strategy. Self-identity gives structure and meaning to things today, "identity affects the way actors understand the world."[38] It is not innately obvious but self-identity helps sense-making by acting as a "grid of intelligibility."[39] Self-identity, who you think you are and what you think it means, is an important component to making sense of that starting point partly because self-identity taps into something powerful, deep-seated and intrinsic. In doing so, self-identity impacts the selection of issues that are legitimate, acting as a cognitive anchor that is inherent to each of us.[40]

Don't get me wrong, there's more to making sense of a starting point than self-identity alone. For instance, a person's debts may not be an integral part of how he sees himself but may be a vital part of how he sees his starting point on a journey. I can't see how my self-identity helps me see a knife as opposed to a collection of iron, carbon and potentially manganese, chromium and vanadium atoms. I don't want to sound like an Israeli defence spokesperson when making the case for self-identity. In fact, it'd be a huge mistake to think that self-identity was the be-all and end-all of human cognition, because it's not. But because it's not the entire solar system doesn't mean it is insignificant either. Self-identity is a powerful and underrecognised influencer of how we see the world.

I've briefly made the argument that self-identity and the stories that flesh out self-identity dominate how a person, organisation or country sees themselves. That, to me anyway, sounds like a tautology. It's not a huge extension to suggest that the framework we use to see ourselves, to self-identify, is also the framework that we use to identify generally, to see and make sense of everything beyond the self. Those with simplistic self-identifications will have simplistic identifications of the world around them. In much the same way that the distinction between domestic and foreign policy is more cosmetic than we'd like to think, the distinction between how we think of ourselves and how we think of the world around us is equally thin because it's difficult to structurally segregate the "how we think of" element:

> An organization's identity or what organizational members believe to be its central, enduring and distinctive character, filters and moulds an organization's interpretation of and action on an issue.[41]

While I do have doubts as to whether we must as a matter of necessity first self-identify before we can make sense of the world around us, I think that having a tight self-identity does definitely help. Those people who have a stronger self-identity, a sharper sense of who they are and are not, also tend to have a more certain perspective of what the world is and where they're going in it. This, of course, simplifies decision-making and action. It also develops a reinforcing cycle and eliminates noise. The same is as applicable to organisations and countries as it is to individuals, which is why outperforming businesses often have a specific, narrow self-identity that corresponds to an equally specific, narrow set of goods or services that they offer or customers who they service. Senior business executives at high-performance firms will often define their firm's self-identity, including what business they are in and, as importantly, not in.

Making sense from the vantage of a particular identity invokes a worldview or narratives and stories which immerse and give life to the identity. In a crude hypothetical example, take somebody who strongly self-identifies as an Englishman. His universe may strongly focus on the Scots, Welsh and Irish and even Europe and the Commonwealth. He may be sensitive to the Queen and monarchy, Britain's historical traditions, Shakespeare, Beckham's goal against Greece and the spirit of his home being his castle. He might also see race as a strong cognitive filter, Germany or France as the other and America as a big brother. In short, much of his worldview will emanate substantially from that self-identity. That is a simplistic example, so let's not overread into it.

In contrast, somebody whose identity narratives are suddenly hit by AIDS has a different starting point because nothing of the present, of the world around the individual, seems to make sense any more. The narratives are blown apart because the future is dramatically liquidated. With the future lost, the past and present become meaningless. The impact of AIDS isn't simply a biological one. It has a powerful and hidden impact on the mind. AIDS often shreds and bulldozes a previous identity and narrative or more likely many, which had helped the individual understand the world around him and his place in it:

> Absolutely everything, everything that you have in life just breaks
> down, becomes dust, powder, you know and you become completely
> naked and utterly lost.[42]

The point worth stressing is that self-identity extensively influences our identification and cognition of other people. And with that, self-identity influences our understanding of the world as-is, which is hardly surprising because human beings typically dominate our respective worlds. Self-identity's influence on our cognition of others has been demonstrated by several studies of in-group bias, including by psychologist Harvey Hornstein, who has demonstrated since the 1970s that people are more likely to help people of the same identity than people of other identities.[43] Similarly, Henri Tajfel, a social psychologist, is amongst others who have demonstrated that people overwhelmingly empathise with and favour folk from their own "group."[44] In one frightening study, Miles Hewstone, another social psychologist, asked Hindu and Muslim students in America to imagine situations where they'd been helped and situations where they'd been ignored by a member of their own faith and then a member of the other faith. The results startled me a little.

Both sets of participants consistently said that any help they'd received from a member of their own religious group reflected the helper's good nature and that they'd expect their fellow co-religionist to help again. In contrast, when helped by a member of the other religious group, participants consistently said that the helper had little choice and probably wouldn't repeat it. Likewise, when participants were ignored by a member of their own group, they regularly interpreted the incident as an isolated example. In other words, they excused any intransigence from a member of their own group. However, the participant interpreted the response as normal when he or she was ignored by a member of the other group. Amazingly, this wasn't even heat of the moment, actual reality stuff. This was a test in a modern American city in which participants had to *imagine* their perceptions while in an *emotionally detached state.*[45]

It's thus no surprise that I disagree with Rughase, who wrote, "Identity appears to act as a mental constraint during the evaluation of external opportunities."[46] For one, this implies that opportunities can be assessed independently of mental constraints, a mistake evident throughout much of his work. For another, he missed the point that self-identity is itself a key prism through which the world and its opportunities are seen and understood. Our favouring of people from our own religious, ethnic or racial groups, a central identity issue, is not a new phenomenon. It's been around for millennia when people of one country, tribe or religion discriminated for (or in the name of) fellow members. Like I've mentioned before, it's no coincidence that most Jews support Israel when it's in conflict with Palestinians, and most Muslims and Arabs support whatever Palestinian polity is in conflict with Israel. The underlying rights or wrongs have practically no impact in influencing the two communities.

Rughase's mistake was one that has also been made since the earliest organisational strategists, including even those who were relatively generous to the role of identity. Andrews, one of the earlier organisational strategy academics and somebody who we touched upon in earlier in this book, believed that value-laden identity-related filters entered corporate decision-making only *after* an objective analysis of a situation had been completed.[47] Step 1: Objective analysis complete. Step 2: Identity influences decision-making. Self-identity is value-laden and yes, it does affect decision-making after an analysis is complete. That said, no, it does not come into play only *after* an analysis is complete. It actually helps *form* the cognition and analysis, neither of which in any case can ever be objective or pure.

Europe's exploration of foreign lands centuries ago illustrates the role of self-identity in understanding the world as-is. It demonstrates how Europeans saw and gave meaning to others through Europe's own self-identity and the stories that Europeans used to explain themselves. The Venetian explorer Marco Polo arrived in Java in the thirteenth century and described natives with "heads like dogs and teeth and eyes like dogs."[48] Sir John Mandeville, the fourteenth-century English Sinologist, described the same people as having lips . . .

> So big that when they sleep in the sun they cover all their faces with it. In another there are people of small stature, like dwarfs, a little bigger than pygmies. They have no mouth, but instead a little hole and so, when they must eat they suck their food through a reed or pipe.[49]

I can't imagine that the inhabitants of the world's most populous island would be too happy to learn that early Europeans thought the ancestors to modern Javans were akin to something out of a Steven Spielberg science fiction movie.

On the Western front, Sir Walter Raleigh, who popularised tobacco in England and thus has millions of cancer-related deaths to answer for, described Native Americans in 1596 as "a nation of people, whose heads appear not aboue their shoulders" with "eyes in their shoulders and their mouths in the middle of their breasts."[50] WTF! If it's not especially obvious, he was describing Native American Indians. Imagine that, he described them as having mouths in their chests! Again, that's hardly something that the indigenous population would today celebrate. Mind you, given that genocide of Native American Indians in the eighteenth and nineteenth centuries, I am not entirely sure that they care much for Raleigh's claimed observations. It's hardly going to get them restitution.

None of these explorers was sent to the dungeon or burned at the stake. They weren't considered mad or sick. No knighthoods were withdrawn. And despite their outlandish, crazy and sensationalist claims, they are still venerated. How do we then explain what they did? My argument is that their observations merely reflected dominant ways of how Europe saw itself with European self-identities invoking colourful and flamboyant stories, myths and fables about what it meant to be European and, as importantly, what it meant to be non-European. Europe's self-identity and its associated narratives positioned superior human Europeans in sharp contrast to barbaric, chaotic, subhuman non-Europeans. Fellow Europeans never doubted the explorers who, in turn, were celebrated for reaffirming the collective European identity. By seeing such strange, alien and inferior inhabitants in distant worlds, the explorers were simply reinforcing and reconfirming European self-identities.

Self-Identity's Impact on Strategy: The Vision of Tomorrow

Beyond its impact on making sense of where we are today, self-identity also influences the vision or objectives we set for ourselves. In other words, it influences the strategic journey's end point. Before anybody misinterprets what I mean by that end point, I want to stress that individuals, organisations and countries are rarely definite or purposeful about what they want to achieve or where they're going in the medium or long-term. In practice, objectives and vision have in most instances only a malleable and possibly even esoteric feel about them. More often than not, individuals, organisations and countries kind of, sort of, somewhat vaguely know where they want to be in one, five, ten or whatever number of years. They can often neither numerate most of that destination nor crystallise it, though it still definitely resides somewhere in their imaginations.

Part of the fuzziness of our vision and distant objectives reflects the reality of day-to-day living which aggressively vies for time and focus against bigger-picture and longer-term issues. In fact, the today often comprehensively outcompetes the strategic end destination for our mind share. Dealing with tactical and operational realities takes a huge part of a typical day. Part of the uncertainty surrounding our respective visions also reflects the diversity of mankind, since not everybody is driven, which is another way of saying some people are merely satisfied or even don't care. There are exceptions, as there always are. The emirate of Dubai (specifically in its ruler) is a good example, as is Singapore, of a state that has a taut sense of vision, a definite place where it wants to go. In most cases, however, the sense of where I (as a person) or we (as an organisation or country) want to be after a decade or two is seldom clinical or exact.

And don't be taken in by those verbose pseudo-visions that are crystalised into fancy, detailed words on a PowerPoint slide or a shiny plaque at a business's headquarters. I treat them sceptically because the vision as communicated is rarely the vision as embraced. This applies as much to individuals as it does to organisations. In fact, most vision statements are no more than public relations communication exercises, which carry no weight with either staff or management; in most cases, neither constituency is able to remotely articulate the vision they're supposed to be energised by and achieve! A real vision, even if it's vague or unspecified, is way more useful than a detailed one that is fake. Now that I'm on this, a fake vision probably hurts the organisation's internal and external credibility. It's worse to have a bogus vision than to have no vision at all.

Within these parameters, the obvious point to make is that given self-identity has a strong impact on our understanding of ourselves and the world around us today, it's almost inevitable that the same self-identity will impact a person's direction and vision. This isn't to suggest that today's self-identity will be the self-identity of tomorrow. It is to suggest that today's self-identity influences the vision we have of where we would like to be, what we aspire to or what we want to achieve. What we think of ourselves or how we self-identify shapes what we want to do. That's not difficult to grasp, I hope. America's seeing itself as a country that should (or does) redeem mankind obviously influences the vision that America aspires to: a mankind redeemed by America!

Exploring that in a bit more detail, the framework that feeds into today's self-identity includes and reflects a mental and intellectual infrastructure. That is as applicable to individuals as it is to organisations and countries. And it is that infrastructure which then not only feeds into the vision ahead but acts as its skeletal backbone. If race formed an integral and powerful part of one's self-identity today, as it might for a white supremacist, chances are that race will form an integral part of the vision for the future. Why? Part of the answer is that the mind, which hosts one's self-identity, is already sensitised to race. It's that same sensitised mind which then projects a vision ahead. And even if that white supremacist mind later reacts against racism, going, for example, as far as marrying a nonwhite woman and supporting all sorts of racial equality efforts, the reaction as such will probably still gravitate around race.

Charles Taylor was one of the earliest philosophers who noted the relationship between self-identity and one's future direction, even if I disagree with his sequencing:

> My identity is defined by the commitments and identifications which provide the frame or horizon within which I can try to determine from case to case what is good or valuable or what ought to be done or what I endorse or oppose.[51]

Deciphering the academic encryption, Taylor suggested that a person's responsibilities dictate his identity and direction. I respect that Taylor's own self-identity can be a function of whatever he wants it to be—I really do. As I've noted before, one's self-identities can come from many different and unusual sources. My push back is I doubt self-identity—of most people, organisations and countries—comes exclusively from commitments. I think that self-identity typically comes from so much more than that, again which I've already explained. To his credit, at least Taylor (not to be confused with the Liberian lunatic politician with the same name) made the connection between self-identity and a journey's end.

In the context of a vision or direction for the future, self-identity has a significant impact on individuals, organisations and countries. Self-identity influences what we aspire to do, our vision and our objectives. Rughase suggested that it is, in fact, *desired identity* that determines where one wants to go.[52] My problem with this is that desired self-identity is merely a function, a reflection of as-is self-identity. Furthermore, desired self-identity sounds itself very much like a vision or goal, in which case Rughase's position is a mere tautology. In other words, the identity that we desire for ourselves in the future determines where we want to go. That so, it is still self-identity as it is and not how we would want it to be that gravitates one's future vision and goals.

At the level of the individual, somebody who self-identifies as intellectually capable and intelligent will strive for cerebral success. In fact, it's no coincidence that universities are littered with people who self-identify as being smart. In contrast, somebody who thinks of himself or herself as an idiot simply won't aspire for an intellectually demanding career *irrespective* of what their intellectual capability is. Over the years, I've come across one too many a person who has been told enough times at a young enough age that they're stupid and incapable. This, in turn, has had tragic impacts on their sense of what they can or should do with their lives. Not only are their objectives and range of possibilities sharply curtailed, but their confidence in achieving simply those diluted possibilities takes a knock too.

Recently, Miles Kimball, an economist, and Noah Smith, a

finance academic, referred to several psychology studies which demonstrated that mathematical performance amongst children significantly depended on the child's self-belief and self-identity as somebody capable of doing well in maths. Kimball and Smith also focused on other studies that went beyond maths and into other academic disciplines and drew similar conclusions—that a child's self-identity is critical to his or her willingness to excel in learning.[53] It's no surprise that child psychologists advise that children should be strongly encouraged to believe in their abilities, and that their accomplishments should be celebrated to reinforce their self-identity as individuals who can accomplish, who can try and then succeed.[54]

Self-identity need not only directly influence our visions. Self-identity can indirectly influence our visions through third parties. In a study of young Muslim women in Norway, researchers concluded that the religious self-identity of the select sample of women influenced their aspiration or, more precisely, lack of it, to participate in sport.[55] The meaning of the Muslim female identity in that particular community excluded sport, which was seen as a male activity. In fact, across the Muslim world men dominate the sporting culture. At best, women can watch, and even then that's not guaranteed. That said, Muslim women are increasingly prominent in international sports, with one powerful example that comes to mind being the ruler of Dubai's daughter, Sheikha Maitha Bint Mohammad Bin Rashid Al Maktoum, who competed in karate in the 2008 Olympics. Who'd have thought that an Arab princess was an Olympian in a martial art?

Given the meaning associated with the Muslim female identity in this Norwegian community, most women in this particular study who flirted early on with participating in sports had to later abandon their desire to participate. Their aspiration was blocked by the meanings given to their Muslim female identity by their community, meanings which they were no doubt aware of. The few women who broke the trend and insisted on playing, the rebels if you will, continued to be discouraged by the community's identity guardians.[56] How perversely coincidental that despite such pervasive discrimination in the Muslim world, and gender discrimination is only one amongst many, Islam has historically led so much female emancipation.[57]

In the case of countries, Samuel Huntington, famous for his *Clash of Civilisations* (a book with a title as catchy as I thought its core content was wanting), was also sensitive to the impact of national identities on national visions and objectives. As an aside, one of the book's key foci is around Muslim antagonism to America. He suggested this comes from "envy of American wealth" or "fear of American power."[58] What didn't occur to him, sitting four thousand miles away from the nearest Muslim country without ever having lived in the Muslim world, is that many Muslims already have extreme wealth and significant regional power. At times, they have so much wealth that they don't know what to do with it, as is evidenced in some of them shipping over incredibly expensive cars to London for the duration of their summer retreats. Despite this, they're all still exasperated with America.

Huntington couldn't grasp that most Muslims resent America because of its policy to Israel and Palestine (even if Muslims are shockingly quite tolerant of intra-Muslim genocide). The same Muslims also dislike America for propping up crap dictators to miserably govern Muslim populations.[59] And if the cake needs icing, Muslims begrudge America for loudly lecturing them on justice, freedom and human rights while denying habeas corpus at Gitmo for more than a decade and prejudicially painting every Muslim with the "terrorist" brush of 9-11.[v] That all of this might be fuelled by the

---

v   Habeas corpus is a legal action which requires that somebody who is detained should be brought before a judge. It forces the detaining authorities to present reasons why the detention should continue.

Muslim world's own deep-seated racism and xenophobia as well as the lingering threat to its Islamic self-identity didn't register one iota with Huntington. How can somebody who rehashed Bernard Lewis's use of the term portray a clash of civilisations between the Muslim and non-Muslim worlds and fail to then understand the underlying animosities held by Muslims of the leading non-Muslim country?

In spite of Huntington's pale insight into the Muslim world, the political scientist understood the importance of America's self-identity to its foreign policy future: "How Americans define themselves determines their role in the world."[60] Bingo, bingo, bingo! You might argue that it's no surprise since Huntington lived practically his entire life in the United States. A country without a self-identity will tend to struggle to know how to anchor its decisions today or what its end game is about. In contrast, a country with a strong self-identity, with entrenched narratives and stories of where it came from and what it stands for, will tend to know where it is going and what it must do and have a crisper decision-making basis for future actions. It was for good reason that Huntington insightfully concluded:

> National interests derive from national identity. We have to know who we are before we know what our interests are.[61]

He and several American foreign policy folk have raised concerns over the years about different "definitions of national identity generat(ing) different national interests and policy priorities."[62] Zbigniew Brzezinski, a former National Security Advisor, and Gingrich have both moaned about America's old, Euro-centric identity being diluted by new answers (and some not even in English) to, What is an American?[63] They're not drawing attention to this as a means to resurrecting their public careers. They're not making a song and dance for nothing. Many of them don't need jobs and aren't looking for consulting contracts. If America's self-identity changes significantly, it will deeply impact America's foreign objectives and vision and the speed and efficacy of its government's foreign policy operations.

Self-Identity's Impact on Strategy: Getting from Today to Tomorrow

Finally, the impact of self-identity on how we get from where we are today to where we want to get to in the future, in other words the strategy itself, is felt at two levels. The first is that self-identity influences the two critical parts of the strategic process. As we've seen, self-identity helps define and make sense of where we are and where we want to get to. It informs the two poles which strategy then tries to bridge. As I've stressed before, once you work out where you stand today and where you want to get to, there are in many instances not much space left to think about how you'll get there. Often there aren't many sensible options to *how* one gets from today to the end result. Therein alone, self-identity straightjackets and thus influences strategy.

Once the start and end points of a journey are stabilised, the strategy itself becomes tightly constrained. Defining the strategy, I think, is way easier than stabilizing the strategic journey's start and end points.[vi] For instance, if I decide to start a journey in northwest London's Stanmore to get to Elstree (two miles away), I would have immediately restricted my strategic options by virtue of stabilising start and end points. I wouldn't fly, swim or take a train which would take me first into central London. Four options get thrown out instantly, leaving only five more options to consider: travel by car,

---

vi   I don't even want to explore another problem, which is ensuring the folk who craft the strategy also execute it, thereby including everyday learnings and changes of circumstances into the implementation of the strategy.

bus, motorbike, bicycle or foot.[vii]

Likewise, if I'm at college and want to become a physician, how many realistic routes do I have available? You can probably count them on one hand. A firm with a UK-only presence that wants to expand to China similarly has only a handful of options available. It won't hire a boatload of Spanish-speaking immigrants illegally entering the US from Mexico for this purpose. It might buy or partner with a local firm, or hire local talent. Those are three of the most obvious options. I will go on for one last time . . . a country with inept armed forces (and let's not mention Lebanon again because it's a bit unfair to keep singling it out, especially when I have a soft spot for its culinary expertise) isn't going to relax tariffs on banana imports as a strategy to strengthen those armed forces. It might instead recruit more soldiers, bring in foreign trainers or buy more or better military equipment. Bananas will do very little for its armed forces.

The second and more direct influence of self-identity on strategy is through behaviour. Sociologists and psychologists have developed something called "role theory" (or "identity theory"). This is an increasingly popular framework that focuses on the impact of self-identity on behaviour. Role theory basically says that just like actors on a stage have their roles defined for them, identities also have their roles scripted for them. The concept reminds me of Shakespeare's *As You Like It* and the cynical Melancholy Jaques's famous quote, "All the world's a stage and all the men and women merely players".[64] It is the expectations surrounding an identity that then generate and influence human behaviour.[65] Role theory's earliest proponents include the philosopher and sociologist Georg Simmel; the philosopher, social

---

vii Riding a horse or camel would not be practical since I don't have access to horses and there are no camels in northwest London. Even if there were camels, I wouldn't know how to ride one. And don't say that I should know just because I lived in Dubai for a few years.

psychologist and sociologist George Mead; and the anthropologist Ralph Linton. And, the bombshell surprise is that they all used the concept slightly differently.[66]

There is divergence within role theory (there's divergence in any theory, so excuse me if that feels like a cheap space filler). Mead stressed individuals are responsible for and craft their own roles.[67] In contrast, others have stressed that the social and cultural environment plays a bigger part in crafting the role. The latter camp is incidentally where I light my bonfire, but not zealously. I think we have a limited pool of socially generated identity categories to choose from, and their associated meanings are also highly influenced by society and culture. In either case, enacting the identity's role is integrated into daily life, which in turn reaffirms the self, a process described by one psychologist as "living to the label."[68] Identities come with roles; roles generate expectations; and expectations generate behaviour.[69] I'm simplifying but it gets the point across. This helps explain how our behaviour often becomes more or less consistent with the expectations flowing from the identities that we adopt.

The implication for strategy from role theory isn't that a self-identity defines a strategy, which would be obtuse even by my standards. It's that the role and meaning of a self-identity is performed and enacted during the journey from the strategic start to strategic end. In the process of effecting and implementing strategy, we live the role that we come to expect of an identity. Behaviour thus tilts towards *becoming* the identity and its narrative, a tilt that is especially evident in strong self-identities. You could argue that role theory suggests that self-identity *interferes* in the journey from start to finish, that it deviates us from the clinical path between strategic present to strategic future. Another way, though, to see self-identity is that those who implement strategy internalise their identity's story and meaning into their behaviour. This, in turn, influences their decisions, big or small: "How we see ourselves—who we think we are—has a great deal to do with how we act."[70]

Research by social psychologists Jane Piliavin, Pete Callero and Hong-Wen Charng suggested that such impact of self-identity on behaviour is irrespective of any attitudes associated with the individual. In other words, that any such behaviour typically draws upon broader identity narratives and stories over and above any personal stances or beliefs.[71] Commitment to an identity is demonstrated by a commitment to behave in a way consistent with that identity or to perform that identity for oneself and for others. One personal life coach who characteristically lacked any of the ivory tower vestiges of pseudo-objectivity and fact-worship captured the essence of role theory rather well:

> At the heart of the matter is what we call our "identity" . . . The internal memory you have about who you are and how you are supposed to behave will dictate your future behaviour. Your identity will lead you to all of your actions.[72]

Irrespective of any theological religiosity, my earlier fictitious Jewish example vaguely knows what's expected of him as a Jew. He knows what's expected from the big-ticket items to daily bits and pieces. He can deviate from those expectations, as did one of my non-fiction Jewish friends. Quite possibly a bigger rabble-rouser than I am, my friend happily ate pork hot dogs snugly nestled in regular buns during Passover. He did this while in Israel. When he mentioned it to me, I was fleetingly surprised that pork products were available in Israel but then realised there's a sizable Christian population there. For the most part, people who self-identify as Jewish keep to expectations of what it means to be Jewish, and within those expectations are certain dietary practices (including eating only unleavened bread during Passover and avoiding pork). That many Jewish people keep to those expectations selectively and even inconsistently is perhaps only human, even if openly flouting the expectations isn't quite so normal.

Research by Margaret Shih, an expert in organisations, demonstrated that when Asian women identified themselves as women, their maths test results were worse than those of men. In contrast, when they identified themselves as Asian, their results were better than those of men.[73] It's precisely this relationship between identity and behaviour which influences human behaviour and, therefore, also strategy, such that "your label will become a self-fulfilling prophecy."[74] For the record, I'm not suggesting that women are inferior at maths or that Asian people are superior at it. I do, though, suspect that many women and Asian people might see themselves as such. This has them lending towards, if not wholeheartedly, living the label. In a similar vein, note the point made by Jan Morris (who had a sex change):

> The more I was treated as a woman, the more woman I became. I adapted willy-nilly. If I was assumed to be incompetent at reversing cars or opening bottles, oddly incompetent I found myself becoming. If a case was thought too heavy for me, inexplicably I found it so myself.[75]

Jeff Stone, a psychologist, observed that when golf was presented to American black players as an athletic game, they outperformed their white counterparts (not that black or white accurately reflect the skin tones in question). However, when golf was presented as a strategic game, black players underperformed their white counterparts.[76] This, of course, suggests that black Americans think of themselves as better athletes but worse strategists than white Americans—or at least that the select sample did in 1999, in the early days of the Tiger Woods era. Again, this is an example of self-identity and its associated meaning impacting behaviour. And yet again, I don't want to engage a topic that I've opened the door of whether there is deeper substance to these self-identities and meanings. I will leave others to explore that one.

In 1971, Philip Zimbardo, a psychologist who, by the by, looks a bit like the image I have of a mafia don, and his colleagues divided a group of male university students into guards and prisoners in a simulated jail environment. The psychologists then observed the students. Sounds like fun. The men in white coats were shocked because in less than a week both guards and prisoners had changed their behaviour to align with their new self-identities with what they thought it meant to be a guard or a prisoner. Prisoners regularly sank into rage and despair while the guards looked down upon prisoners, were hostile towards them and in some cases even abused them—completely out of personal character.[77] Both groups rapidly adopted the behaviour that they associated with their allocated group's identity. They became their adopted identities.

The impact of self-identity on how we behave and implement strategy extends also to organisations. The commitment to results and performance at any firm that sees itself as the best differs from those at competitors. For years, McKinsey & Co has self-identified itself as "the best" (whatever that means) management consulting firm. That's not just some subtle external brand management because it's as much in effect internally as it's outside the blue-chip consulting firm's offices. McKinsey consultants aren't force-fed their employer's subtle hint at being the world's best consulting firm. That's simply a well-managed part of the firm's identity, which, as it happens, its clients seem to regularly reinforce. I'm sure there's some smart aleck out there who wants me to open a conversation on whether the brand accurately reflects the end product, but I move on.

What's important to my point is that the fulfilling of that self-identity is a strong motivator when McKinsey consultants work the sixty or seventy hours per week that they often do. If I can try to crystallise the emotion, "We're the world's best consulting firm, we only deliver the best work and we'll make a huge effort to deliver against those expectations, even if sometimes we lose money in the process." Sometimes, it doesn't work out that way. Not only are most junior management consultants commercially inexperienced and naïve, but also other factors such as a poorly scoped study or weak client team can blend to produce a poor result. Even then, my experience was that McKinsey took the fulfilling of its "best in class" self-identity quite seriously. It forms part of a virtuous cycle which, as Manchester United fans in the post Alex Ferguson era might testify, is hard to reestablish once broken.

During the closing stages of World War II, Japan's kamikaze (means "divine wind") pilots too lived and enacted an identity. They volunteered on suicide missions, embracing the meaning and story of the identity of a divine wind that supposedly protected Japan from China's Mongolian invaders in the late thirteenth century. Aged between seventeen and twenty-three, about 2,500 young pilots crashed their explosive-laden aircraft into enemy targets, sinking between thirty-four and fifty-four ships from October 1944 to August 1945.[78] Young pilots took the opportunity to *become* the legendary divine wind, to enact the myth. It's an extraordinary thing for thousands of young men in their prime to have done and can't possibly be explained by any sensible calculation of self-interest:

> So eager were many minimally trained pilots to take part in suicide missions that when their sorties were delayed or aborted, the pilots became deeply despondent. Many of those who were selected for a bodycrashing mission were described as being extraordinarily blissful immediately before their final sortie.[79]

In contrast, though Berlin had its own suicide pilots, the Leonidas Squadron, they were rarely used because there simply weren't enough German pilots who were clamouring for suicide runs.[viii] The squadron's relative redundancy retrospectively wasn't surprising, since Germany didn't assemble a comparable inspiring narrative to envelop such adventures. It didn't have a comparable identity and narrative to Japan's mythical wind. You need something awfully convincing to get young men in glamorous careers at the end of a war to fly suicide missions for a war which their country is about to lose. It takes a lot, and the Germans didn't have that narrative, they didn't have that story to inspire, energise and give meaning to its pilots.[80]

In the next three chapters, I'll explore some individual, organisational and country examples in more detail to illustrate self-identity's influence on each of the three steps of the strategic process, thereby underlining the importance of our own identities in the strategy process. I was tempted to explore as an example *Toy Story*'s Buzz and Woody, who are all too real to my youngest son, but thought it best not to.[81] A three-year-old may not represent the average reader of this book. Buzz and Woody used to be real to my elder sons but not anymore. I want to bring to the fore in the next three chapters various aspects of self-identity and its relationship with strategy, all of which I've touched upon already. Within that, I will cover the power and sensitivity of our self-identities. It's important to demonstrate that we are highly sensitive to any offence to our identities, which we subsequently powerfully defend.

For now though, let's briefly recap where we've got with this chapter. We've explored the power of self-identity, including touching upon the magnitude of that power and its source of energy. We've also given a flavour of self-identity's impact upon individuals, organisations and countries. This should serve to reinforce self-

---

viii Thirty-five German pilots conducted suicide missions against Russian targets in April 1945.

identity's overall gravitas as a concept that we should eagerly do business with. Self-identity is not an airy-fairy party trick or a pretty pink cupcake or even a dozen. It's an important albeit fluid part of human existence, serious enough for a lot of people to slay a lot of people for. Its influence, if only on that basis, in the strategic process shouldn't, therefore, be a whopping revelation. We never give it the attention of sex, power or money but we have our heads buried in the sand when we fail to recognise its impact on daily human behaviour.

The second important point in this chapter is the essence of this book, and it's an opportune moment to hammer the message home because the next three chapters will elucidate that argument through my analysis of actual individual, organisation and country examples. Self-identity has a powerful influence on all three steps of the strategic process: it influences how we make sense of our world today, including our own position in it; self-identity goes into generating a vision of the future, however blurred or vague that might be; finally, self-identity affects how we go about getting from where we are today to what our vision for the future is. In this, self-identity influences not only the start and end of a strategic process but it also directly influences the strategy. Self-identity isn't just a static filter to land the today and the future. Self-identity reacts, changes and influences our behaviour, and that is why it is so pivotal in our strategic thinking—or at least, should be.

1   PC McGraw, *Self Matters*, Simon & Schuster, New York, 2001

2   RJ Fisher, "Needs Theory, Social Identity and an Eclectic Model of Conflict" in J Burton, *Conflict: Human Needs Theory*, MacMillan Press, London, 1990

3   http://www.emporiagazette.com/news/2011/mar/29/and-home-brave

4   E Barker, "Rights and Wrongs of New Forms of Religiosity in Europe," *Temenos*, Helsinki, 2002

5   OG Rughase, *Identity and Strategy*, Edward Elgar, Cheltenham, 2006

6   SP Huntington, *Who Are We?*, Simon & Schuster, New York, 2004

7   AT Beck, AJ Rush, BF Shaw and G Emery, *Cognitive Theory of Depression*, Guilford Press, New York, 1997

8   *Ibid.*

9   P Sites, "Needs as Analogues of Emotions," J Burton, *Conflict: Human Needs Theory*, MacMillan Press, London, 1990

10   MV Matthews, MD Little and RL Koteskey, "Adolescent Identity and Depression," *Journal of Psychology and Christianity*, Batavia, 1991

11   D Waldorf and P Biernacki, "Natural Recovery from Heroin Addiction: a Review of the Incidence Literature," *Journal of Drug Issues*, Tallahassee, 1979

12   J McIntosh and M McKeganey, "Addicts' Narratives of Recovery from Drug Use," *Social Science and Medicine*, Paragon, 2000

13   AT Beck, AJ Rush, BF Shaw and G Emery, *Cognitive Theory of Depression*, Guilford Press, New York, 1997

14   A Bandura, "Regulation of Cognitive Processes through Perceived Self-Efficacy," *Developmental Psychology*, Washington, DC, 1989

15   DH Barlow, *Abnormal Psychology: An Integrative Approach*, Thomson Wadsworth, Belmont, 2005

16   F Harris and R Wilkins cited in DJD Sandole, "The Biological Basis of Needs," J Burton, *Conflict: Human Needs Theory*, MacMillan Press, London, 1990

17   E Ringmar, *Identity, Interest and Action*, Cambridge University Press, Cambridge, 1996

18   D Podestra cited in J Burton, *Conflict: Human Needs Theory*, MacMillan Press, London, 1990

[19]   RL Sivard, *World Military and Social Expenditure, 1987–88*, World Priorities, Washington, DC, 1987

[20]   WJ Clinton Interview with D Rather on 31 March 1999 in "Public Papers of the Presidents of the United States—Administration of William J Clinton 1999," National Archives and Records Administration, Office of the Federal Register, Washington, DC, 2000

[21]   JWO Lennon, *Imagine,* Ascot Sound Studios, Ascot, 1971

[22]   L Collins and D Lapierre, *Freedom at Midnight*, HarperCollins, London, 1997; W Laquer and B Rubin, *The Arab–Israeli Reader*, Penguin, London, 2008; C Rogel, *The Breakup of Yugoslavia and Its Aftermath*, Greenwood, Westport, 2004

[23]   E Ringmar, *Identity, Interest and Action*, Cambridge University Press, Cambridge, 1996

[24]   J Covert and T Sattersten, *The 100 Best Business Books of All Time*, Portfolio, New York, 2009

[25]   D Campbell, *Writing Security: United States Foreign Policy and the Politics of Identity*, University of Minnesota Press, Minneapolis, 1998

[26]   *Ibid.*

[27]   N Blackstock, *COINTELPRO: The FBI's War on Political Freedom*, Pathfinder Books, London, 2000

[28]   http://www.nbcnews.com/id/27266223

[29]   A Greenwald, "Self Knowledge and Self Deception" in JS Lockard and DL Paulhaus, *Self Deception: An Adaptive Mechanism*, Prentice-Hall, Englewood Cliffs, 1988

[30]   E Ringmar, *Identity, Interest and Action*, Cambridge University Press, Cambridge, 1996

[31]   *Toy Story*, Pixar Animation Studios, Emeryville, 1995

[32]   *Ibid.*

[33]   H Garfinkle, *Studies in Ethnomethodology*, Prentice-Hall, Garden City, 1967

[34]   http://www.satp.org/satporgtp/countries/pakistan/database/sect-killing.htm

[35]   http://www.cricketworldcupinfo.co.uk/funny-sir-ian-botham-quotes.htm

[36]   http://news.sky.com/skynews/Home/UK-News/Sir-Ian-Botham-Charity-Walk-From-John-OGroats-To-Lands-End-Celebrates-25th-Year/Article/201004215598289?f=rss

[37]   RS Zander and B Zander, *The Art of Possibility*, Harvard University Press, Cambridge, 2001

[38]   R Abdelal, YM Herrera, AI Johnston and T Martin, "Treating Identity as a Variable," Paper prepared for presentation at APSA, 30 Aug–2 Sept 2001, San Francisco

[39]   S Qureshi, "US Foreign Policy to Pakistan, 1947–1960: Re-Constructing Strategy," London School of Economics PhD thesis, London, 2001

[40]   JE Dutton and WD Penner, "The Importance of Organizational Identity for Strategic Agenda Building" in J Hendry, G Johnson and J Newton, *Strategic Thinking: Leadership and the Management of Change*, John Wiley & Sons, Chichester, 1993

[41]   JE Dutton and JM Dukerich, "Keeping an Eye on the Mirror," *Academy of Management Journal*, Briarcliff Manor, 1991

[42]   ML Davies, "Shattered Assumptions: Time and the Experience of Longterm HIV Positivity," *Social Science and Medicine*, 1997

[43]   HA Hornstein, "Promotive Tension and Prosocial Behaviour," *Journal of Social Issues*, 1972; DM Wegner and WD Crano, "Racial Factors in Helping Behaviour," *Journal of Personality and Social Psychology*, 1975

[44]   K Dutton, *Flipnosis: The Art of Split-Second Decision Making*, Arrow, London, 2011

[45]   *Ibid.*

[46]   OG Rughase, *Identity and Strategy*, Edward Elgar, Cheltenham, 2006

[47]   KR Andrews, *The Concept of Corporate Strategy*, Irwin, Homewood, 1987

[48]   P Mason, *Deconstructing America*, Routledge, London, 1990

[49]   *Ibid.*

[50]   *Ibid.*

[51]   C Taylor *The Sources of the Self: The Making of the Modern Identity*, Cambridge, Harvard University Press, 1989

[52]   OG Rughase, *Identity and Strategy*, Edward Elgar, Cheltenham, 2006

[53]   M Kimball and N Smith, "There's One Key Difference Between Kids Who Excel at Math and Those Who Don't," http://qz.com/139453/theres-one-key-difference-between-kids-who-excel-at-math-and-those-who-dont/, 27 October 2013

54   M Donaldson, *Children's Minds*, Harper Collins, London, 1986

55   K Walseth, *Young Muslim Women and Sport*, Routledge, Abingdon, 2006

56   *Ibid.*

57   M Yamani, *Feminism and Islam: Legal and Literary Perspectives*, New York University Press, New York, 1996

58   SP Huntington, *Who Are We?*, Simon & Schuster, New York, 2004

59   F Halliday, *Islam and The Myth of Confrontation*, IB Taurus, London, 2003

60   S P Huntington, *Who Are We?*, Simon & Schuster, New York, 2004

61   *Ibid.*

62   *Ibid.*

63   NL Gingrich, *A Nation Like No Other*, Regnery Publishing, Washington, DC, 2011; ZK Brzezinski, *Out of Control*, Touchstone, New York, 1993

64   W Shakespeare, *As You Like It*, Wordsworth Editions, Ware, 2005

65   R Biddle, "Recent Development in Role Theory," *Annual Review of Sociology*, Palo Alto, 1986

66   *Ibid.*

67   GH Mead, *Mind, Self and Society*, University of Chicago Press, Chicago, 1934

68   PC McGraw, *Self Matters*, Simon & Schuster, London, 2001

69   C Gordon and P Gordon, "Changing Roles, Goals and Self-Conceptions" in W Ickes and ES Knowles, *Personality, Roles and Social Behaviour*, Springer-Verlag, New York, 1982

70   SM Farmer, P Tierney and K Kung-McIntyre, "Employee Creativity in Taiwan," *Academy of Management Journal*, 2003

71   H-W Charng, JA Piliavin and PL Callero, "Role Identity and Reasoned Action in the Prediction of Repeated Behaviour," *Social Psychology Quarterly*, Washington, DC, 1988

72   R Thomas, *The Power of Your Identity*, AuthorHouse, Milton Keynes, 2006

73   K Dutton, *Flipnosis: The Art of Split-Second Decision Making*, Arrow, London, 2011

74   PC McGraw, *Self Matters*, Simon & Schuster, London, 2001

75 J Morris, *Conundrum*, Faber and Faber, London, 2001

76 K Dutton, *Flipnosis: The Art of Split-Second Decision Making*, Arrow, London, 2011

77 D Berreby, *Us and Them*, Hutchinson, London, 2006

78 RP Hallion, "Precision Weapons, Power Projection and the Revolution in Military Affairs," US Air Force Historical Studies Office, Washington, DC, 1999; PW Denis, *The Sacred Warriors: Japan's Suicide Legions*, Avon Books, New York, 1984

79 A Axell and K Hideaki, *Kamikaze: Japan's Suicide Gods*, Longman, New York, 2002

80 A Weir, *The Last Flight of the Luftwaffe*, Cassell Military Paperbacks, London, 2000

81 *Toy Story*, Pixar Animation Studios, Emeryville, 1995

CHAPTER 6

CAN I FOCUS ON ONE?

One way to surface the influence of self-identity in strategy is by exploring actual examples. Some people prefer theories to be served that way. Since at the outset of this book I chose to cover three contrasting levels of the individual, organisation and country, I'll explore three illustrative examples for each of those levels rather than focus on a single deep-dive case study for each. This approach allows me to cover a broader range of examples touching on a wider range of my arguments, albeit at the cost of dieting on detail and richness. Given where self-identity is in the context of the strategic literature and the strategy industry, which is almost nowhere, I think it's better to float out more illustrations than thoroughly investigate a single example. I am hoping that it might give more material for later researchers and thinkers to reflect upon.

I also reissue a couple of cautions. First, given my epistemological arguments earlier, I don't claim to know too much. This isn't a conducive thing to admit when encouraging readership. I'm not exactly sure how it feels to read something written by somebody who doesn't *know* much, even if I am wrestling that word's implications perhaps more than most folk do. Nevertheless, we tend not to see much epistemological humility out there. The world seems to be overpopulated with too many know-it-alls. I get we all want to *know*, and certainty is important to do things and influence people. Such self-certainty is a two-edged sword that has moored human suffering and often closed our minds. The slippery slope from "I know" to "I know what you should do" to "I will make sure you do it" has many, many, many bodies piled up.

So repeat reminders about our intellectual limitations is no bad thing, especially given that our intellects are indeed limited, even if I may be in a position to illuminate some bits and pieces, such as the relationship between self-identity and strategy. This isn't the same as saying that "I know." I don't claim to occupy the Mount Sinai of truth. It's one thing to share thoughts and insights and quite another to sermonise on a platform of truth or objectivity, while ignoring the continuously shifting sands of our understanding of human beings. And in any case, I do expect somebody to soon rethink elements of my perspective and analysis to see finer insights with greater clarity around the relationship between self-identity and strategy. I do expect the process that I have begun to be improved or even reconstituted by other people.

My second qualification, again which I've made earlier, is that it's important to not reduce human behaviour, including cognition and strategy, to self-identity. Mind you, it's equally dim to reduce human behaviour to any power, class or anything else for that matter. That, of course, doesn't stop some experts and their audiences from doing precisely that. Simpletons so love such reductivism. Reducing reality to single, big-ticket themes helps sell because it simplifies and enables followership. Reductivism also enables action, which thrives on simplicity and withers with complexity. I'm *not* the blinkered Israeli defence spokesperson's equivalent for self-identity. Self-identity is not the great Archimedean point that will redeem mankind. We shouldn't start sacrificing innocent lambs on its alter. It's a powerful and neglected influence on human behaviour and strategy, and that's why I'm writing about it.

Jan Morris

A great example to demonstrate the importance of self-identity in making sense of the world today, crafting one's vision ahead and the strategy to bridge the two, the three pieces of the strategic process, comes from Jan Morris. She sort of looks a bit like Rose Nyland from *The Golden Girls* (played by Betty White Ludden), but that doesn't do much to demonstrate my argument.[1] Morris has many striking credentials. She's a fellow at Oxford University's Christ Church, famous for its academic traditions and more so as the set for scenes from the *Harry Potter* film series.[2] Morris also served in the 9th Queen's Royal Lancers in World War II, before becoming a writer and journalist for *The Guardian* and *The Times*, for whom she wrote the first ever report of Edmund Hillary and Tenzing Norgay's climbing of Mount Everest in 1953.[3]

While at *The Guardian* and in the midst of the Suez crisis, she provided evidence of the Franco–Israeli collusion against Egypt in 1956. She interviewed French pilots who confirmed they were *supporting* Israeli troops, thereby puncturing the official Anglo–French position that France was merely trying to *separate* Israeli and Egyptian troops.[4] Arabs loved her for that. You would have thought, given the conspiracy, the French would have told their pilots to shut the hell up and especially not share military secrets with journalists, but they didn't. Morris also covered the trials of Francis Gary Powers in Moscow and Adolf Eichmann in Jerusalem.[5] Little wonder then that she was probably the most famous journalist in England in the 1950s.[6] Besides that, Jan has written on British history, published a couple of dozen travel books, has been described as amongst the most successful British writers since 1945 and was awarded a CBE. Couch potato, Jan Morris is most definitely not.

However, what I found most interesting about Morris, and no disrespect to Ms Ludden's aesthetics (or Morris's), was that she was born a boy. Jan Morris, who now lives in "the top left hand corner of Wales," was born in England in 1926 as James Humphry Morris.[7] Over eighteen years, starting in 1954, Morris took 12,000 pills to effect hormonal changes in a "slow-motion Jekyll and Hyde" process before finally having multiple sex reassignment surgeries.[8] And what's more, she had the courage to write about it in an insightful book titled *Conundrum* in 1974, during an era that was far less accepting than the one she lives in now. To illustrate just how nasty things got for her in Britain's 1970s, shortly after the book was published, Robin Day, the BBC television interviewer, had the audacity to ask her on TV if she was then having a "full sex life."[9]

All this sex change revelation stuff might dilute the Arab enthusiasm for her. I know, that's irrelevant since I'm not exploring social attitudes to gender change in the Arab world, which is struggling with gender issues way more basic. In contrast, James's wife, Elizabeth, not only remained supportive of her spouse's sex change but also remained married to Jan.[10] Elizabeth's enthusiasm and love for her spouse never changed. In fact, Elizabeth knew of her husband's gender challenges even before she married him.[11] Let me go on, for after Morris's first surgery, Elizabeth behaved as if absolutely nothing had changed or had happened.[12] The couple, who produced no less than five children, have (at the time of my writing) been married impressively for more than sixty years.[13] That's quite something, especially if you acknowledge the context.

I see Morris's gender journey in three parts. The consultant in me tediously strikes yet again. Maybe I should just stop trying to quit that bad habit, because my pathetic efforts clearly aren't succeeding. Anyhow, that journey starts with Morris's confusion about his self-identity and ends ultimately with her acceptance and embracing of *her* own self-identity. It is this journey that I want to explore in this mini-case study. I think that the central theme to Morris's personal life journey is the definition of his or her self-identity. Given the impact of self-identity on cognition and future vision, we should expect a confused self-identity to generate a confused understanding of the world as it is as well as one's own vision ahead. Likewise, a defined, strong and clear self-identity should effect an equally defined and clear understanding of where things stand and one's vision going forwards. Those are evident in this case study.

Morris's first phase, being that of a confused self-identity, was true to form. In fact, it not only muddled how he saw things, but also confused him on where he was going in life and how he was going to get there. Put differently, because he couldn't figure out his real gender, because he couldn't self-identify at a very base level, Morris struggled to make sense of the world and what he was to do in it. From an early age, he was aware that something wasn't right with his self-identity. He actually suggests that from the age of four he knew that he should have been a girl. I'm a little sceptical that he could have known something as profound as that at such a young age, but the point is that even when he was young, something felt wrong. He lived his younger years with a deeply ingrained confused sense of self, torn between a male exterior and a female interior: "In possessing these two landscapes of my childhood, I had felt myself to belong to neither."[14]

This uncertainty in gender, one of the most important dimensions of self-identity in the society that he lived in, in turn impacted his understanding of what his world was about and what he would do in it in the future. Unable to create cognitive certainty about the world around him with which he could then engage, Morris instead chose to simply disengage. To be more specific and to this effect, he noticed that these "inner conflicts, only half formulated, made me more solitary."[15] On the few instances when he got over the solitude and paralysis, as when playing at school, "It seemed to me perfectly natural to me to play the girl's role in these transient and generally light-hearted romances."[16] But for the most part, he couldn't give meaning to his world or to his future vision or goals:

> Everything seemed more determinate for those people down the hill . . . Mine was more like a glider's movement, airy and delightful perhaps, but lacking direction.[17]

That sense of dislocation and confusion marked this, the first phase of Morris's life. As an aside, I'm just thinking how this kind of problem might be treated today in the premodern world, such as in Afghanistan or the Congo . . . probably by a good hard beating by the communal elders. It's actually not so easy engaging with someone who feels that they're born with the wrong gender. On my first interaction with one person who had already had a sex change, I confess that I found the experience a bit unsettling. It somehow didn't feel natural or right. That said, you've got to respect an individual's decision to change their gender if that's what they want. Fortunately for Morris, he didn't have to deal with his problem anywhere like Kabul or Mogadishu. He dealt with it in a modern metropolis. And even then, he dealt with it privately.

Morris's ambiguity about his self-identity and his inability to make sense of the present or project a future continued into his early adulthood. How could it not, given his trials with his self-identity didn't get easier? If anything, those trials gradually got worse in this first phase, because on top of the intense stuff he was kneading, he began also dealing with a sexual dimension that had been absent in childhood. I don't want to get too involved in Freud's take on children and sexuality right now; suffice to say that I don't think sexuality features prominently in the consciousness of young children.[18] I don't buy the argument, therefore, that the impact of Morris's sexual desires on his self-identity had been there since he was four years old. You can get something of a flavour of what was going through Morris's mind in this revealing quote:

> My body often yearned to give, to yield, to open itself, the machine was wrong. It was made for another function and I felt myself to be wrongly equipped.[19]

It's pretty powerful stuff! Even as he entered the 9th Queen's Royal Lancers in the World War II as a young man, he carried an acute sense of being trapped. His autobiography reveals a sense of living outside of himself, without any obvious path to a solution:

> I invite my women readers to imagine how they would themselves have felt if, successfully disguised as a young man, they had been admitted to this closed and idiosyncratic male society in their late teens. For this is how I conceived my condition.[20]

During this first phase of his gender journey and despite his graduating from childhood to adulthood, Morris could only maintain a trend that had begun in his very early years. He continued to withdraw from daily life: "I was for the time being a kind of non-human, a sprite or monster, as you wish."[21] Morris was unable to self-identify on something that he, reflecting the society he was immersed in, considered critical. He was thus incapable of grounding where things stood or thinking ahead about what he wanted to do and where he wanted to go. He lacked the intuitive, almost reflexive, set of matrices which we each have and that help us make everyday decisions:

> I myself did not quite know what I wanted or what I might allow myself to want, beyond the touch of the hand or lip.[22]

In fact, so pronounced was Morris's withdrawal during his early adulthood that one observer made the point that Morris was "so unobtrusive that one hardly knows he is there at all."[23] Making himself inconspicuous thus became the outward hallmark of his first phase. Morris wasn't going to take control until he could first nail down who he was: "If I could not be myself, my subconscious seemed to be saying, then I would not be."[24] Without a stable self-identity, Morris simply refused to exist.

It was only, I think, with greater maturity and self-awareness that Morris began the second phase of his identity journey. This brief phase, in the late 1940s and early 1950s, was different not because Morris reengaged the world or understood how to make sense of things; how could he, given his self-identity was still confused? This phase was different because it was marked by a serious effort on his part to make some sense of his self-identity, which in turn would then stabilise his world and help generate a vision. Morris didn't emerge from hiding in the shadows. Nor did his daily problems disappear with some pixie dust. In fact, it's possible that his problems became worse even still because by exploring how to come to terms with his gender self-identity. As is often the case with any attempt to overcome or reconcile an emotional challenge, he would have been vulnerable to frustration, heartache and failure.

The point to stress, though, is that Morris in this second phase took it upon himself to get to the heart of who he thought he was. He looked for a solution to help him make sense of his gender confusion: "Could it be that I was merely a symptom of the times, a forerunner perhaps of a race in which the sexes would be blended amoeba-like into one?" A big chunk of his effort in this phase went into finding a legitimate space beyond traditional notions of male and female. There was no better place to start this type of journey than Manhattan's then emerging army of sexologists and psychiatrists. While American society has made visiting a shrink into a fashion statement, almost a prerequisite to fame and fortune, in fact, it's worth remembering that in around the 1950s it wasn't quite as easy as ordering a Quarter Pounder (without cheese). Let's ignore the inconvenient point that this burger was only introduced to the McDonald's menu in 1971.

In these early explorations, Morris turned to historical and exotic precedents to resolve his problem. Even though he had felt for decades that he should have been a female, that he was authentically a woman, such was his frustration and confusion that he was prepared to look at other gender categories. Having had the benefit of hindsight, I think Morris's explorations in this second phase were half-measures and temporary plasters. He was desperate for some kind of resolution, and transforming into a woman was not then on the radar. I think that it's possible that his mere act of searching for solutions may have provided relief for the stress and uncertainty that his self-identity was causing him. I nonetheless accept that at the time his explorations might have seemed to him like a real search for a comprehensive solution.

One potential precedent that Morris came across was the Phyrgians, a group who lived in modern day Turkey about three millennia ago.[25] They castrated men who thought themselves female. That's painful, especially given this was centuries before the discovery of the most basic anaesthetics. Think about that for a moment. It really can't have been a happy experience for any poor dude who advertised his true inner female. Another precedent that Morris learned about came through Hippocrates, a key thinker in early medicine who reported the existence of "un-men" among the ancient Scythians, a Persian nomadic people.[26] These un-men (unrelated to the twentieth-century American "Un-Men" comic characters) lived and worked as women. Local folklore had it that the gods had feminized them. Morris wasn't passionately excited by either precedent. Neither gripped him.

Morris's education didn't end there. The existence of people who don't self-identify as female or male isn't a modern Western problem, contrary to what I've heard from some religious traditionalists who love to blame the West for all sorts of social, economic and moral ills. Eunuchs and other unconventionally gendered folk have been around for at least four millennia in the sexually-liberal Arab world, of all places.[27] Ancient Vedic culture also recognised a third gender, *tritiya-prakrti* (third nature); although, that has yet to inspire Bollywood to offer a third-gendered movie hero. Indeed, no Bollywood blockbuster has ever anchored around even a gay movie hero let alone a third-gendered one. Still, there's time for Amitabh Bachchan, the one-time angry young man of Bollywood and now something of its honorary chairman, to perhaps one day take it up as a professional challenge.

A final example that Morris touched upon in his search for solutions came from ancient Israel, which accommodated no less than six genders: *zachar* (male), *nekeveh* (female) *androgynos* (both female and male), *tumtum* (without gender), *ay'lonit* (female to male transsexuals) and *saris* (male to female transsexuals).[28] The ancient Israelis clearly knew how to meet a wide range of consumer gender demand, though I'm not sure if today's Haredi Jews would be so proud of this aspect of their ancestral heritage. After all, and putting aside the behaviour associated with being a sari or ay'lonit, acts of homosexuality are subject to capital punishment under Halakha (Jewish law).[29] How exactly that sits with our current understanding that at least a hundred million people in the world today are naturally gay or lesbian is a bit above my intellectual pay scale.

It wasn't, if you haven't already guessed it, any religious doctrine that triggered Morris's emancipation, the characteristic of what I see as the third stage of his gender journey. Organised religion is to human emancipation what a hurricane is to a golf match—bad, bad news. My interpretation is that this final and emancipatory phase was triggered by Morris's realising that he could, in fact, achieve the self-identity that he had long wanted, a spark inspired by two events. The first event emanated from Morris's gender probes in his second phase.

He drew immense hope when he learned not only that his personal gender confusion wasn't unique but that somebody else had almost resolved it. Morris's reading an account of an attempted sex change which almost succeeded in 1931 changed his life.

Even though the patient eventually died from the gender change, Morris still took heart from Einar Wegener's book, *Man Into Woman: An Authentic Record of a Change of Sex*.[30] Specifically, Morris was thrilled that two decades before his coming across the account, medical technology had succeeded in four key procedures of a gender change operation.[31] The patient, a 48-year-old Danish painter named Lili Elbe, only died in Germany during the uterus transplantation, the fifth and final sex change procedure.[32] Elbe paid the ultimate price for insisting on becoming a mother.[33] I suspect Morris reasoned that if twenty years ago physicians could deliver four out of the five stages of a sex change, they could then achieve a successful sex change in the 1950s.

The second event that inspired Morris was his encounter with an avant-garde physician, Dr Harry Benjamin, in New York.[34] Benjamin was one of the early pioneers of sex change and transsexual issues and by many accounts, a really nice guy.[35] I suppose in premodern societies, there'd be nothing avant-garde about him, because he'd be seen as so ahead of the curve that he'd be considered a bloody heretic or a madman for encouraging somebody to change their gender. I've been to parts of the world where the local folk would have absolutely no idea how to deal with such a physician, leave aside the patient, irrespective of his being a nice guy, except to throw him off a cliff or into the ocean. Anyway, so deep was the impression that the physician left with Morris that he recalled every word of the physician's advice:

> If we cannot alter the conviction to fit the body, should we not, in certain circumstances, alter the body to fit the conviction?

It was the combination of learning about an almost successful sex change and the physician's confidence with respect to a sex change procedure that allowed Morris to embrace his deep inner self-identity, to grasp something that he'd long felt as part of his self but dare not hold. No longer would Morris have to entertain tensions about who he was. No longer would he struggle to see and make sense of the world around him. And no longer would he have to live without a sense of where he wanted to be in the future.[36] Once he embraced his self-identity as a woman, a eureka moment, everything made a lot more sense. This sort of reminds me of one of the final scenes in *The Matrix* where Neo, played by Keanu Reeves, stops the bullets in the hallway by seeing them (and everything else, for that matter) as computer coding.[37] Nothing changed but everything changed.

As Morris abandoned searching for an identity and embraced womanhood, she quickly established where she wanted her life to go, what her vision for herself was. Initially this was the fulfilment of womanhood, "to make a whole of me!" Despite being married with children, it was no surprise that Morris pounced on the opportunity to accept and live her self-identity. In doing so, in a matter of speaking, it was the opportunity to become alive and have the ability to make sense of the world and develop a direction within it. That helps explain why the decision to have sex-change surgery was so easy. It allowed Morris to celebrate an end to "those years of uncertainty." And this uncertainty had been total—not knowing who she was, how to make sense of her world and not knowing where she was going in that world.[38] "I should have been terrified, but I wasn't. . . . It was inevitable—I'd been heading there mentally all my life."[39]

Not wanting to be one of those who lived their lives in the wrong gender, ruining their lives, careers and children, Morris downed that sea of pills from 1954 to 1972. He then had sex-change surgery, which interestingly enough about six hundred people had already had before him. That is about the same number of people who now have a sex change per year. It's interesting that the surgery was conducted in the Arab world, in Casablanca, hardly what you'd expect from one of the world's more conservative communities.[40] Morris's British surgeon didn't want to facilitate a lesbian marriage. Pompous little twerp. He thus refused to conduct the surgery unless Morris first got a divorce, a quirk that the Moroccans, in contrast, couldn't care for.[41] The anonymous Moroccan physician "Mr B" had few hesitations in helping Morris to become a complete woman, minus a womb, though.[42]

Morris's vision, her Promised Land, a function of her self-identity, constituted the sort of things that were expected for women in the society and culture that she lived in. That vision included being embraced by a man, becoming a mother and running a home. Her vision was simply to be a normal, conventional and customary woman. Her female self-identity, supressed for decades, indeed retorted to dominate her vision. Given what Morris had experienced in living in a foreign gender and also what he had gone through to become a woman, it was no surprise that she was more aware of and sensitive to her self-identity as a woman than are other women. That helps shed some insight on why "when people took me to be unquestionably a woman, a sense of rightness calmed and satisfied me."[43]

With this self-identity, she took on the daily role and behaviours associated with being a woman, for in doing so she was also effecting that very vision, a point which nods to role theory. In short, her becoming a woman (in more than a biological or physiological sense) not only anchored her vision but also became her strategy. How was she to become a normal woman? By effecting whatever it meant to be a normal woman. She therefore very happily conformed to societal expectations. She behaved like women were supposed to in the society and era in which she lived: by becoming less forceful, friendlier, more emotional, more likely to cry and more vulnerable to flattery and sadness:

> If I was assumed to be incompetent at reversing cars or opening bottles, oddly incompetent I found myself becoming. If a case was thought too heavy for me, inexplicably I found it so myself.[44]

Extending this vein, Morris adopted behaviours from the portfolio of what was expected of womanhood. She developed a "simpler vision" which could "more easily see things for the first time."[45] In contrast to before her sex change, Morris described that she, "looked less for the grand sweep than for the telling detail. The emphasis changed in my writing, from places to people."[46] Such behaviour echoed the end goal of becoming a woman. Such behaviour also became the means of getting there, which again speaks to my earlier point on role theory. I'm sure somebody will accuse me of sexism for my caricaturing the behaviours of womanhood. The point is that Morris had a certain interpretation of what it meant to be a woman, which was partly a function of the society in which she lived. Morris merely conformed to it. I'm not suggesting that women are biologically or physiologically inclined to being less forceful. I've got no idea if they or are not!

To conclude this mini-case study, Morris's gender challenge demonstrates the importance of self-identity in making sense of the world as-is, in informing one's vision ahead, as well as influencing how one gets from today to that vision. The case highlights the importance of having a meaningful self-identity in getting things done, achieving and making a presence felt. A confused, weak or meaningless self-identity, as in Morris's childhood and early adulthood, holds back the individual from clearly seeing their world. Clarity of where things stand is a prerequisite to effective action or developing a direction or vision. People who don't feel confident about their self-identity or what they are struggle to assert themselves. In Morris's case, he did exactly that, he did whatever he possibly could to hide and barely exist.

In contrast, a strong or meaningful self-identity, as in Morris's later adulthood, helps to make sense of the journey's start and end points. It enables more pronounced and determinate action and achievement, while also encouraging gravitas and presence. Having a clear sense of who you are, irrespective of how accurate or true that sense actually is, reflects and reinforces an equally clear sense of the world around you and what you want to do in it or what your vision is. This is why people who have clear, strong self-identities are often those who also equally think they know both how things stand in the world around them and where they want to be. Certainty of self-identity generates cognitive certainty beyond the self. And that combination gives confidence to people to get on, get things done and achieve.

Ed Husain

Once upon a time there was a man called Mohammed Mahbub Husain. One day, presumably a drizzly one given he was in London, he shortened his name to Ed, which from a branding perspective in the post 9-11 world, didn't hurt one bit. For Ed is no ordinary Ed; our Ed is a smart Ed. In New York, where he occasionally works, the reception of an Ed differs sharply from that given to a Mohammed. An Ed can practise his faith freely. He can build his place of worship wherever he wants, subject to local planning and regulations. In contrast, a Mohammed's religious freedoms are sharply curtailed. He can't pray for peace, justice and mutual understanding or worship God near Ground Zero without a national firestorm. It's of course irrelevant that Ed and Mohammed pray to the same God. Ed isn't restricted. Mohammed is.

And having Mahbub, which means "Beloved" in many Asian languages, as his middle name wasn't going to dissipate the firestorm or make it easier for a Mohammed to pray to God in New York! No sir, you can be beloved all you want, but a Mohammed doesn't get an easy ticket to pray to God in the Big Apple. So, Ed was smart to change his name to sort of disentangle himself from a faith which Americans now distrust and which has done a class job of positioning itself as the world's leading terrorist religion. Let's face it—the Muslim world is partly responsible for that self-inflicted branding, as are xenophobic elements of the West's media and political class. Ed, of course, now has immunity from this fiasco. If he wanted to pray during a Manhattan meeting, nobody would be calling the FBI, there would be no *random* body pat search at JFK Airport . . . after all, he's only Ed.

Ed as a case study provides an excellent illustration of the potentially pervasive impact of self-identity in making sense of the world today, one's vision ahead and the strategy (to bridge between today and the future.) I bet he never ever thought that he'd be a case study in a book written on self-identity and strategy, but there you go, shit happens. His case illustrates the potential self-destruction in adopting the wrong self-identity. Born in 1974 in London to Bengali parents, Ed now writes on Islamic extremism and is also a founder of The Quillium Foundation, which works with the British government to counter Islamist terrorism.[47] I think that's admirable, because not enough Muslims are prepared to take on their religion's lunatic fringes. And it's very important that the Muslim silent majority stop letting the lunatic God Squaders speaking for the faithful. That said, given the bulk of that lunatic problem is in Muslim countries, London is an odd location from which to pursue that goal. Mind you, if the World Bank can be headquartered in Washington, DC, thousands of miles from its main work in Asia and Africa, so can Quillium, I still think both situations are odd.

Ed is a rare breed, and not because he is smart or that he was born on Christmas Day. And the name Mahbub has bugger all to do with the rarity of his breed. As a fellow at the Council for Foreign Relations, he's rare in America for being a Middle East expert who actually gets the Middle East. He actually has some vague insight and understanding of what is going on out there. Just as important, unlike most of his peers, he has lived in the region and can speak basic Arabic. This, of course, disqualifies him from appearing in large sections of the American media as a Middle East expert—a space dominated by folk who are regionally illiterate, don't know the first thing about the regional religions, can't speak the region's languages and have lived in the region for all of . . . three days at a swanky five star Dubai hotel.

The Islamist is a super read about Ed's migration first into and then out of his self-identity as an Islamist, a term which needs explanation because it confuses a lot of folk. What is an Islamist? I'd like to define an Islamist as having three characteristics. First, he is somebody who proactively seeks to reestablish a supposed social, political and economic system of the Muslim community of 1,400 years ago. Going back in time is thus critical to the Islamist mind set. Second, he believes that the Qur'an, Hadith (sayings of Mohammed) and Sunnah (traditions of Mohammed) all apply today and none of those is in any shape outdated. The idea that the context has changed doesn't mean very much here. Third, he emphasises a political dimension above spiritual, human and other dimensions to problems and their solutions. I don't think all Islamists are necessarily hostile to non-Muslims or the West (which many Muslims are an integral part of) but most might be.

Within this, there are two things that I've never understood about Islamists. First is their insistence that Islam demands an Islamic state, all the more controversial given the lunatics who now form the so-called Islamic State in parts of Iraq and Syria. Second is that Muslims must relive the era of the *Khulafa al Rashidun* (the Rightly

Guided Caliphs), an Abbasid concept which refers to Islam's first four caliphs (rulers after Mohammed's death in 632). I'll explore each insistence briefly. On the first, as Ed's father pointed out, the Qur'an isn't a political document.[48] It actually offers practically nothing on government or statehood. Even the Medina Compact, Mohammed's rules of governance in Medina and his clearest articulation on government, are not in the Qur'an and weren't later extended to Mohammed's governance of Mecca.[49] Islam's supposed governance rules materialised a century after the Qur'an states that its final verse had completed Islam.

Islam's silence on the rules of political succession, a critical piece of a political system, aptly illustrates its silence on government. The Qur'an and Islam's other key sources offer "no clear word or even contested word, on the succession."[50] This vacuum is apparent in the ascension of each of the first four caliphs. Abu Bakr became caliph by something of a fluke. He gate-crashed a meeting of random Muslim tribal leaders while Mohammed was dying. In that meeting and to his credit, Abu Bakr argued that the community's next leader should be Abu Ubayda or Umar. They instead endorsed and pledged allegiance to Abu Bakr—and there the matter ended.[51] That was the entire process of the first political succession in the Muslim world. Mohammed's father-in-law and confidant thus became the Muslim world's first caliph.

That random process set the tone for political succession in the nascent Muslim community, which might also go some way to explain the generally disastrous state of political succession in the Muslim world today. Abu Bakr picked his successor, Umar, after consulting a couple of close friends. Umar thus become the second caliph. Later and when it was time to consider succession after Umar, he in turn decided to appoint a six-person council to choose his successor. That council chose Uthman. This particular selection was the genesis of Islam's Shia sect, a group which felt Mohammed's nephew and son-in-law, Ali, should in fact have been chosen as the *first* caliph. When Uthman was killed, Ali then became caliph . . . without any apparent process whatsoever.[52] That there sums up Islam's approach to political succession. In a word: random.

The second thing that I don't get is why Islamists want to revert to the *Khulafa al Rashidun*, because parts of that era don't feel warm and fuzzy at all. Neither Ali nor Fatima, Mohammed's daughter, accepted the caliphate of Abu Bakr despite his occasionally having led even Mohammed (when he was alive) in prayer. Leading a prophet in prayer is no joke. In response, some of Abu Bakr's enthusiasts attacked Fatima's house and possibly even knocked her down in the process. The prophet's daughter lived only for another six months but would never again talk with Abu Bakr.[53] Umar, the second caliph, often got into fistfights, hardly the stuff of leadership material.[54] When he was killed, his son killed the assassin, which seems defensible within the legal custom of the community, but then also killed the assassin's daughter and a tribal elder who were completely innocent.[55]

Uthman, the third caliph, then failed to punish Umar's son for the murders. In other words, he let a murderer completely off the hook. Uthman then took a pasting for starting Islam's first de facto monarchy and for his economic and political corruption. While he may have merely intensified a trend begun by Umar, records suggest Mohammed's companions were pretty irate with Uthman's dishonesty.[56] Few were more irritated than Ali, by now a resentful figure who felt Uthman's selection as caliph had been "a deception."[57] When Uthman was murdered in a revolt, which Ali may or may not have influenced depending on which side of the fence you want to sit on, Ali refused to prosecute the murderer, letting another murderer off the hook. All of this hardly feels "rightly guided."[58]

And we can go on. And we will. There was the war between Ali and Mohammed's favourite wife, Ayesha. While Mohammed was alive, Ali had accused Ayesha of adultery and wanted Mohammed to divorce her. So, there was this bad blood in the family. When Ali became caliph, Ayesha blamed him for Uthman's death and, aided by two of Mohammed's friends, fought a battle against Ali in 656 in which more than 3,000 people died. It goes on still. Ali's followers often defied him after the Battle of al Nahrawan, which speaks to his lack of leadership.[59] His inability to retain the loyalty of his troops led to defections, allowing the army of Mu'awiya, Mohammed's brother-in-law, to regularly strike Ali's forces.[60] And after Ali died, the fifth caliph, Hassan, was audacious enough to trade his caliphate for a mere pension with Mu'awiya. In an act of petty self-degradation, Mu'awiya then initiated the cursing of Ali to the annual Hajj pilgrimage.[61]

I could make sense of all this if it was relayed by some of the Islamophobic media in the US or France, which has a habit of making stuff up about the Muslim world. However, these accounts come through respected Islamic academics who used the doctrine of *Adalat al Sahaba* (Probity of the Companions) to *downplay* negative accounts of Mohammed's companions' actions.[62] Despite this airbrushing, we still have these blotches which don't feel like anything to brag about . . . and even then, most Islamists still beckon to this "utopia." I really struggle to understand why they would want to effect that environment today. If that's not enough to fuel the Islamophobes, I don't know what is.

Anyhow, before immersing himself as an Islamist, clearly oblivious to even the most basic reading of Islamic history, Ed's self-identity and world were similar to those of other young London kids. I was going to say "regular kids" but realised that more than 600 million children worldwide live in absolute or extreme poverty.[63] London's Mile End district, with its tapestry and tradition of ethnic, religious and cultural diversity, gave to Ed an early cosmopolitan edge in life:

> My father used to buy us fresh cakes from a Jewish baker in Brick Lane . . . My mother would take us to see Santa Claus every year

after the school Christmas party. We made a snowman in our garden, lending it my mother's scarf. . . . School was the centre of my life. Our days were filled with painting, drawing, reading, writing, practice, physical exercise, mathematics, setting the tables for lunch, playing.[64]

In his own young, unreflective mind, Ed saw himself as what so many youngsters think of themselves—as just a kid. Within Ed's basic, intuitive understanding of what it meant to be a kid, he did the things that we expect young Western kids to do. He had fun, stayed up late . . . and didn't go to work to pay for his toys. Given this lifestyle, his portrayal of his childhood was, indeed, a happy one.

Ed's self-identity began to change in his teens, a vulnerable time, since it is during our teens that we try to carve out and refine our self-identities during our passage to adulthood. It was Islam, venerated by his parents and his wider Bengali community, which anchored Ed's teenage self-identity. For Ed, his choice of identities may indeed have been somewhat restricted since he didn't fit in at school, a fertile space for new identities. At Stepney Green School, described then by some British newspaper tabloids as one of Britain's worst schools, he was called "Glass Man" and "Boffin."[65] My inner Sherlock Holmes deduces Ed wore wall-thick spectacles. His first year there was amongst the worst of his life: "I could not relate to the boys and they knew I did not fit in."[66]

Boffin's initial sense of Muslim self-identity came from an elderly theologian, Grandpa, alias Sheikh Abdul Latif Chowdhury, under whose gentle guidance Ed learned to be an "erudite" Muslim.[67] I had to look up the word "erudite" because I've never ever used it and I had absolutely no idea what it meant. It apparently means somebody who shows extensive scholarship. I've also got no idea if Ed used "erudite" in his teens or picked it up a bit later. Or maybe his editor introduced it? Even for a boffin, it's an impressive word to deploy.

Anyhow, despite living in Bangladesh, Grandpa was a prominent member of the British Bengali community and was warmly received on his visits to the colonial motherland. Ed travelled across Britain with Grandpa and learned about Islam by observing Grandpa interact with the several pockets of Britain's Muslims, travels which gave Ed more ground than did his school to develop his self-identity.[68]

After Grandpa left for Bangladesh in 1990, the sixteen-year-old Ed stumbled into Islamist groups. Without Grandpa's moderating hand, Ed rapidly went from erudite Muslim to Islamist as he sought to "assert a new identity: we were young, Muslim, studious and London born."[69] Islamism provided not only a tighter framework for Ed to distinguish himself than did Grandpa's softer approach (which governed Ed's parents' community) but also a tighter framework to understand the world and set his vision ahead.[70] In other words, Ed was attracted by the simplicity and clarity that being an Islamist gave to his cognition of his world today and his future vision. More so, being an Islamist had religious credentials which were invincible in the community, unlike "foreign" identities which the community could sneer at.

The first Islamist group that Ed embraced was the Young Muslims Organisation (YMO), linked to the *Jamaat e Islami* (Islamic Party; or JI). It's a Saudi-backed South Asian sociopolitical movement that sees Islam as something of an ideology. Founded in 1941, JI calls for an Islamic state based on a Sharia-democracy hybrid.[71] It's sort of similar to Egypt's Muslim Brotherhood in that it's a right-of-centre, socially conservative Islamic revivalist political movement whose members are allergic to a lot of Western social and political concepts. This is somewhat ironic since it was in a hospital in New York, one of the West's modern great cradles, that JI's founder was medically treated and eventually died. Unlike the Brotherhood, JI has never had the chance to screw up in government and *Insha'Allah* (God willing), it never will.

The second Islamist organisation that Ed joined was *Hizb-ut Tahrir* (Party of Liberation; or HT). These clowns, for let's call a spade what it is, burst onto the British national scene when they called for the assassination of John Major, Britain's prime minister during the Gulf War in 1991.[72] The media, out for a story, picked the bait and amplified HT's homophobic and anti-Jewish enthusiasm. That having been noted, the charge that HT was anti-Semitic is misleading since most HT members were themselves Semites! HT organised confrontational debates, loud protests and distributions of inflammatory pamphlets. In fact, in the early 1990s, HT was one of the most active and abusive religious groups in Britain, an oxymoron if there ever was one.

Ed's choice of Islamist organisations had much in common because both YMO and HT "were as bad and cool as the other street gangs. Just without the drugs, drinking and womanising."[73] Both were organised expressions of zealous Islamist identity led by young, typically science graduates. I called them the "God Squad," complete with speed-dial access to God.[74] They shared Dubya's "with us or against us" syndrome, but unlike the right wing of the GOP, they had "several members in prison," "defied the police" and "were renowned for mid-game (football) interruptions to perform prayers."[75] As with other gangs, their main pull was neither intellectual nor spiritual. Many of these dudes and dudettes had never ever read a book on Islam. YMO and HT gave identity, meaning and purpose to teenagers who were caught in the chaos of nascent adulthood.[76]

The biggest difference between the two organisations was that HT was way more confrontational and hostile, which Ed liked. HT absolutely loved to hate. They hated Jews, Hindus, Christians, Shias, agnostics, atheists, Americans, Israelis, Britons, Saudis, Egyptians, Iranians, Russians, gays, secularists, communists, socialists, democrats, capitalists . . . as part of their "Never defend, always offend" approach.[77] They claimed that they wanted to be the "flame whose heat would transform the society to a boiling point and then to a dynamic force."[78] In short, they wanted to wind up everybody so much that the status quo changed. That HT deny that Ed was ever a member is somewhat meaningless, because from my own experience everybody who I ever knew at HT always seemed to deny his or her membership.[79] That oddly enough includes its one-time head honcho, Omar Bakri (OB) Mohammed, who was once affectionately known as Obi-Wan.

It was the Islamist identity's narrative that gave to Ed a sense of where things stood and where he had to go: "As an Islamist, I saw everyone along religious lines."[80] In just a few months of being introduced to the YMO, Ed's Islamist self-identity had wholly hijacked his understanding of the world. It wasn't just the speed of the cognitive commandeer but its all-pervasive nature which was so striking. Ed's self-identity as an Islamist quickly dominated how he saw and made sense of everybody and everything around him. It quickly became the overwhelming prism which he used to make sense of the world as-is. The big picture starting point that he immersed himself with was that the *Ummah* (Muslim community) was a mess. Foreigners were occupying Muslim lands (as if land has a religious belief) or conspiring against Muslims. Naïve or corrupt Muslims often aided the treachery. These themes are incidentally common to many Islamists.[81]

Exploring in more detail his Islamist-induced understanding of the world around him and especially its people, first there was the distinction between Muslim and *Kaffir* (nonbeliever), who was hell-bound. Those who didn't believe in God and Mohammed's prophethood were damned regardless of conduct or behaviour. Mother Theresa is unfortunately amongst those who Ed would have considered on the wrong side of the fence. Another distinction was between "partial" and "real" Muslim. Partial Muslims "confined religion to prayer, rosary beads, remembrance of God's name, piety and dress," as did Grandpa.[82] They were a bunch of wet fish. Secular and meek, they weren't much better than Kaffirs, because in co-existing with Kaffirs and the *Jahiliya* (ignorant), partial Muslims became de facto Kaffirs.[83] In contrast, the "real" Muslim was different:

> an altogether superior sort of Muslim. It was we who called for the resumption of Islamism as a way of life rather than a mere religion.[84]

Real Muslims, meaning Ed and his posse, saw that there was a war between Islam on the one hand and America, Britain, Israel, India, Russia and . . . every *Muslim* country on the planet! In fact, according to his worldview, every country was corrupt and trying to destroy Islam. They were all in cahoots in this spectacular conspiracy. From Ed's perspective, the past and present were both a "clash between good and evil. We represented the former, the West the latter."[85] This worldview wasn't unique to HT since it's also common to many Islamist organisations.[86] The insincerity of living in, contributing to (at least by way of taxes) and benefitting from a country that you're at war with didn't occur to Ed the Islamist as remotely problematic. Nor did he attempt to migrate to a geography where Islam supposedly wasn't at war . . . perhaps on an unclaimed desert island.

Ed's self-identity as an Islamist also profoundly and swiftly influenced his vision ahead: "Islamism provided us with a purpose."[87] Ed's newfound purpose was to help the *Ummah* achieve global dominance by rejuvenating religiosity amongst Muslims, enacting God's laws (or more poignantly his personal interpretation thereof) and appointing a *khalifa* (vice-regent) to lead them . . . all possibly a tad easier said than done. Ed drew inspiration from the narrative's historicity: "The unfinished business of Vienna in 1683, when the Ottomans tried and failed to conquer Europe, had to be completed."[88] Put differently, the centrepiece of Ed's vision, again derived from his

Islamist self-identity, was:

> to change the Muslims, to make them live Islam as a complete code of life, not as a mere religion. Islam is more than a religion. We want to see Islamic government.[89]

Ed & Bros, true to the narrative, wanted to reestablish the era of the *Khulafa al Rashidun*. Ed's goal or objective became to "create God's government on God's earth."[90] (We don't need to open the earlier point that God's government wasn't the same thing as what we saw during the *Khulafa al Rashidun*.) In just a few months, Ed had migrated from being somebody who mildly identified himself as an erudite Muslim, living melodiously with a cross section of British society, to somebody who saw himself as a real Muslim or what we call an Islamist. In those months, teenage Ed became Islamist Ed with a revised cognitive framework. This transformation put him at war with all partial Muslims, all non-Muslims, his home country, many non-Muslim countries and all Muslim countries . . . basically the entire human population.[91] The same framework had him pursue a tight politico-military agenda that demanded the subjugation of most of mankind. He may as well have plastered a self-destruct button on his forehead.[92]

Ed's Islamist self-identity not only dominated his framework to understand the world as-is and informed his vision for a world in the future, but it also influenced his strategy to bridge the two. In other words, it influenced the strategy itself. Ed immersed himself into playing the role of the Islamist, fulfilling the role expectations and wholeheartedly enacting the part of an Islamist. Besides dedicating time at the mosque and in prayer as any devout Muslim might, he went way beyond:

> My daily life was dedicated to activism: recruiting new activists organizing events, distributing leaflets, arguing and debating with those who opposed us.[93]

Ed fervently participated in *Da'wah* (inviting people, who I presume he was ironically at war with, to Islam) and embarrassed partial Muslims at his college for going to nightclubs, so much so that after enough sessions of his proselytising, parts of his college looked "like a scene from Tehran."[94] I've no idea if he'd ever been there to draw the comparison. His peers, as you might expect, "wondered at my transformation from school misfit to powerful student leader."[95] I doubt his wall-thick glasses came off as part of his transformation, but lest you want to benchmark his physical transformation, I don't think that he started wearing a red cape, thick gold belt or red underwear above skintight blue pants. He certainly couldn't compete with Superman in terms of visual impact. For a start, he didn't have the classic superman physique.

In the race to enact Islamism, Ed & Co were sometimes outdone by the Wahabi *Jam'iat Ihyaa Minhaaj al Sunnah* (JIMAS), such as when Ed's crew failed to connect their heels during prayer (as if God actually cares about these things). More vexing was his being outdone by "the ninja sisters," who not only hid themselves from head to toe but also in their drive to piety avoided communicating with Muslim guys (though strangely enough they were quite comfortable in communicating with non-Muslim guys).[96] When one sister insisted that Ed speak to her from behind a screen, he lost it: "Do I have a contagious disease of some sort? Or do you think I am going to rape you?"[97] If I'd been there at that time, I'd have had no qualms about intervening at the risk of being accused of not minding my own business by telling Ed, "No Ed, she's just a female version of you. She's just a religious nutcase." But I wasn't there at that time, so we all missed out on that opportunity.

In enacting the Islamist self-identity and as a great illustration of the self-destruction that came about from Ed's new identity, he neglected the things outside of the Islamist narrative. He did so because he interpreted such things as classified of "this world" and thus of little value, as opposed to other things which apparently affected one's entry into and place in the hereafter, which had far greater value. Ed's life beyond his Islamist story crumbled. For a start, he deprioritized his education.[98] His school grades crashed with the implications for his career and livelihood. This obviously suggests that his boffin status would have looked a bit suspect. After all, what kind of boffin crashes their grades? There's a living absurdity if there ever was one.

His relationships with loved ones disintegrated too. Ed was barely on talking terms with his parents, wider family or his non-Muslim childhood friends. He also gave less attention to his parents, a relationship that the Qur'an repeatedly weights and Muslim culture has traditionally cherished—and the prophet Mohammed himself is known to have repeatedly stressed. In fact, Muslims often quote a saying of the prophet that each person's heaven lies beneath their mother's feet.[99] All of that, though, didn't fit the Islamist worldview. So concerned was Ed's father about losing his son to the Islamist identity that he warned him, "If you want to stay under my roof, then you will be a normal Muslim, none of the politics in the name of religion."[100] Bad boy Ed, the former boffin and now effectively a gang leader, simply walked out of the family home, another very taboo thing in his community's culture. Silly, silly boy.

The worldview, the narrative that emanated from his Islamist identity, was getting him nowhere and costing him everything. It was little wonder that the teenager was bit dazed: "Now I had to wonder whether Islam had anything at all to offer."[101] Ed's disillusionment as an Islamist didn't spark from doubts about scripture or the efficacy of his preaching. It began with something much more fundamental:

> On a personal level, my relationship with God had deteriorated. If we were working to establish God's rule on earth, as we claimed, then Hizb-ut-Tahrir activists were the most unlikely candidates

God could have chosen . . . as I had become more active in the Hizb, my inner consciousness of God had hit an all-time low.[102]

Ed's disenchantment with his Islamist identity began ironically with the realisation of his collapsing relationship with God, which is as good a reason to reconsider a religious direction as I've come across. Not only did his spirituality crumble, Ed grew disenchanted with other Islamists. They were abusive, obsessive liars, used fake documents and focused more on Islamist-authored books than they did the Qur'an.[103] In fact, many Islamists hadn't even read the Qur'an. There was also the issue of the personal conduct of Islamists, such as smoking despite Islam strongly discouraging it.[104] Ed's tipping point seems to have been when he witnessed a petty argument about a snooker table between some HT members and a non-Muslim. The argument disintegrated with HT declaring jihad on the young Ayotunde Obunabi and an HT member putting a knife into his heart, just outside Newham library.[105] It didn't take a genius to work out that, in short, "There was nothing Muslim about our conduct."[106]

Ed's Islamist self-identity had so extensively saturated his life and so destructive were the narratives that it brought to bear, that everything that mattered to him—including his relationships with his parents, family and friends; sense of spirituality; and future career and livelihood—had all ground to a halt. In fact, these three important dimensions of human existence were all going in reverse. As a human being, he had taken several steps backwards since Grandpa returned to Bangladesh. If he needed a cherry on top, he was practically at war with the vast majority of living souls on the planet.[107] The wrong self-identity had gotten Ed totally up the creek, because that self-identity influenced both how he saw the world and his vision in it. By implication, it's not hard to see that if Ed had embraced the right self-identity, meaning one with wholesome narratives, he'd be in an equally positive space.

Eventually it took the support of his non-Islamist girlfriend and his teachers to help Ed unravel the disillusionment. They gave to him the intellectual tools and emotional support to unlock the Islamist narrative by, for instance, demonstrating how Islamists weren't offering a divinely-ordained political framework at all but little more than "European political ideals wrapped in the language of the Koran," specifically a Hegelian structure.[108] Ed had been through a tough journey and required considerable support from people who cared for and could connect with him to unshackle the grip of a self-destructive self-identity. It was then, only when he relinquished his Islamist self-identity, that Ed could appreciate the world that he had drifted from:

> We, however, failed to understand that the secular liberal ideals that allowed Muslims to congregate at college in Britain were the very same ideals that tolerated homosexuality.[109]

It's worth just briefly reflecting on Ed's case before we move to the final case study in this chapter. A young man adopts over the course of just a few months a new primary self-identity as an Islamist, albeit related to a previous self-identity as an erudite Muslim. In doing so he changes, he changes his entire life journey. That change was anything but mild. In those few months, Ed's new self-identity transformed him. He was once a person who had a spiritual existence, enjoyed loving or warm relationships with his parents and friends, and had a straight connection with Britain's heterogeneous society. With the change of self-identity, he became a person who tore up each of those facets to his life while declaring war left, right and centre. That transformation speaks to the power of self-identity. In going through this change, Ed's case illustrates the potentially destructive effects of adopting a corrosive self-identity. In doing so, it reinforces that how we see ourselves, how we self-identify, has a profound impact on how we live our lives.

New Fathers

A final demonstration of self-identity's impact on the individual is through fatherhood. The speed with which a new self-identity can deeply influence our strategy doesn't simply hold for the self-identities of religious nutcases but also holds in more prosaic situations. Embracing fatherhood, in other words, self-identifying as a father, tends to quickly change how men see the world, their future vision and the strategy that they take to get from the start to end points. Interestingly, the effect of the fatherhood self-identity is felt not in months but typically in just weeks, which in itself is a bit counter-intuitive. You'd think that most fathers have about six months lead time to make the adjustment. That's not, though, how fatherhood percolates the male psyche, so it seems.

Fatherhood isn't simply about producing a baby. One can be a father without biologically contributing to the baby, and adoptions are a good example of this. Likewise, one can biologically contribute to a child yet not be a father, as was Darth Vader (except for the last moments of his life when he did become Luke's father). Lest you're comparing, Jor-El did embrace his role as Superman's father from the get-go. After all, he protected his son from Krypton's collapse and also prepared a very cool system to advise and educate Superman as a young adult on earth. To more contemporary and real examples, Steve Jobs made the point bluntly in the context of his first child: "I didn't want to be a father, so I wasn't."[110] It's unlikely that Apple will be using that particular quote for the foreseeable future in any of its promotional materials.

I don't know if the distinction between producing a child and being a father underlies a deeper dynamic in modern societies—do women view the act of parenting more as a duty while men view it more as an option? It's possible. More than a quarter of children in America are raised without living with their biological father, which is more than three times the proportion of children raised living without their mother.[111] Indeed, the assumption that mothers are more responsible with respect to their families than are fathers has played an important part in Grameen Bank's extraordinary microfinancing success. Instead of lending to men, which remains the conventional commercial wisdom across Asia, the bank began life in Bangladesh by lending to women who desperately needed to economically succeed if only to support their families.[112]

The distinction between producing a child and being a father could also reflect the physical realities of pregnancy in that men don't carry a baby in a womb for nine months. Men might, though, contend with the oscillating hormones of their partners during the nine months, but they definitely do not carry a baby in a womb. That door was opened. And now it's being shut. In fact, impending fatherhood tends to typically sink in amongst men during the 25th and 30th weeks of their partners' pregnancy, in stark contrast to impending motherhood, which typically sinks in very early.[113] This interestingly ties to the observation that fathers tend to gain weight in their partners' third trimester of pregnancy.[114] My own wife had been kicked several times by our not-yet-born first child well before fatherhood's penny sank in my solitary brain cell. Most fathers, myself overwhelmingly included, in fact underestimate the life-changing impact on them of the first baby until it arrives.[115]

Most identities generate or have some kind of meaning or narrative, even if it's faint. In many cases, there's a dominant narrative around which other narratives emerge from or react against. Fatherhood is no different in that it also has dominant meanings. The role of the father extensively emerges from the meanings that societies attach to what it means to be a father. However, critical in all of this is the role that fathers see for themselves, because a father's understanding of what it means to be a father has a profound impact on delivering fatherhood.[116] That understanding of fatherhood or what a father should or should not do can and almost definitely will change as father and child both grow older, even if it will almost inevitably continue to gravitate to or react against the dominant societal meanings of fatherhood.

The dominant meaning of fatherhood has changed over the centuries even in the tight confines of Western Europe. Nursing researchers have noted that fatherhood's meaning in ancient Rome shocked even the battle-hardened Greeks.[117] A Roman father practically owned the lives of his sons and unmarried daughters.[118] Newborns gained citizenship *only* if the father approved, since "a citizen of Rome did not 'have' a child, but 'took' a child."[119] Fathers who didn't want their infants left them on the roadside or in the fields to die. The Romans thought the Jews were nuts for raising *all* of their children.[120] The tables have indeed now reversed. I wonder how many Jews think that modern Romans are nuts for having elected Silvio Berlusconi as prime minister of Italy three times? The dude currently stands convicted of tax fraud (subject to appeal) and has a litany of racial and gender controversies to his name.

Skipping almost two millennia of history, by the nineteenth century the meaning of fatherhood in Western Europe had softened to embrace delivering a religious framework, directing the family and leading prayers.[121] The father also became the wage earner and possibly his son's vocational teacher.[122] The mother assumed the role of main parent, especially since the father's job in the industrial revolution often took him to travel and distant geographies.[123] During the early twentieth century, fatherhood in Western Europe became even more involved with fathers expected increasingly to be at home, lest any son be mothered, an activity which would supposedly turn the son into a homosexual.[124] Fathers were expected to teach their kids, take them out and bond with them.

Interestingly, the "natural" desire in the West of fathers to be close to their children only actually emerged in the twentieth century.[125] It's actually a fairly novel social twist.

By the end of the twentieth century, fatherhood mutated yet again to what we have today. The "nurturing father" now co-parents his kids irrespective of their gender.[126] He's very hands-on, in a way which is practically unprecedented in the history of the West. That point made and lest it isn't obvious, not every father adopts this meaning of fatherhood. Some fathers, such as those succumbing to the rat race, still see their kids only on weekends, if that. Nevertheless, fatherhood has changed with fathers typically spending more time with their kids than they did in the nineteenth century.[127] Today's father still leans on his traditional economic role, but now has responsibilities which were once associated with traditional motherhood.[128] This trend, of course, partly reflects the growth of female employment and the development of the feminist movement in its broader sense.[129] The early modern father was barely there while the late modern father is very much there.[130]

The embracing as a self-identity of fatherhood, and especially its dominant meanings, impacts a man's cognition of the world as it is, his vision for the future and his behaviour in effecting the strategy to take him from how he sees his starting point to where he wants to get to. Fatherhood is a big change, "It opens up a whole new world."[131] It's one of the most significant changes that a man goes through. The interesting point is not that the change is dramatic and life shifting, which it is, but that it takes place typically within only twelve to fifteen weeks of adopting fatherhood as a self-identity. This is an extraordinarily short period given the magnitude of the changes that the role of fatherhood triggers. As we go through those changes below, it's worth bearing that in mind.

Adopting the identity of a father impacts how a man sees the world around him. Fatherhood impacts, in multiple ways, how a man sees his life journey's strategic starting point. For one, those who embrace fatherhood see more risk than they had seen before. They become more aware of the risks to their well-being and the subsequent consequences to their family if something should happen to them. It's not just life-threatening or economic risk which begins to weigh in on their cognition. Basic health risks become more prominent in a way which many parents will be all too familiar with. Hands are washed more frequently, tables are sanitised more thoroughly and the home is continuously assessed and reassessed through the lens of baby safety.[132] The focus on and sensitivity to risk extends beyond the immediate baby with fathers typically becoming more sensitised to risks associated with each of the family's other members too.

Family forms an important dimension to a further change in how a man sees and makes sense of the world as it is. New fathers typically become more aware of their own parents. With that, the new father sees himself over the course of less than a hundred days as a bit older. He no longer sees himself as part of the youngest generation. Fatherhood replenishes or for some people even creates a generation axis.[133] In fact, there's often a pronounced shift in the father's relationship with his own parents, characterised by stronger communication and understanding.[134] Suddenly, those who embrace fatherhood become more involved with and interested in their own parents. One father who hadn't talked with his parents for seven years suddenly resumed phone contact with them as soon as he learned he was becoming a father.[135]

Another change is that fatherhood often crowds out other self-identities to become the dominant self-identity and thus the dominant cognitive framework. In interviewing 208 fathers in America, child and family studies academics Greer Fox and Carol Bruce noted the fatherhood identity became for many a master identity that governed their focus, even while at employment.[136] Within this shift, fathers become less aware of their identity as an employee, spouse or partner, self-identities which they resultantly focused less on. Psychologists Rachelle Strauss and Wendy Goldberg assessed more than a hundred first-time fathers in America and noted that a father's self-identity as a spouse declined in the run-up to birth, only to be typically replaced by a stronger fatherhood self-identity.[137] This, of course, can cause colourful reactions:

> One of the wives became angered because her husband seemed to ignore her on his visits to the hospital, spending all of his time looking at the child.[138]

For a minority, fatherhood can crowd out other self-identities so much so that they can't embrace the identity and the roles that come with it. Fathers having less family and societal support than do mothers in early parenthood does not help this burden.[139] While most fathers are happier for their role as a father, the burden of what it means to be a father is simply too much for some.[140] As early as 1966, William Wainwright, a psychologist, suggested that the responsibilities of fatherhood can lead to psychoneurotic illnesses.[141] Teenage fathers, already struggling with their hormones going barmy and fraught in trying to stabilise their adult identities, have an especially tough time taking on the added role of fatherhood.[142] Some find it so much easier to simply walk away, which in turn can have a devastating impact on children. One study led by Bruce Ellis, a psychologist, concluded that women who grow up without fathers are more likely to suffer from depression, drop out of college and suffer from behavioural problems.[143]

Fatherhood not only impacts how a man sees the world as it is but it also impacts the vision which he has for the future, again typically taking effect within twelve to fifteen weeks of embracing the identity. A new father's vision undergoes a few big changes in this space. First, new fathers extensively replace their own personal vision for that of one for their child. There's ample research that suggests that on embracing fatherhood, a man's vision ahead becomes less self-centred.[144] Personal goals and objectives are often compromised, if not jettisoned, with fatherhood. In fact, that selflessness is a key distinction between fathers (being men who embrace fatherhood) from mere biological sperm-suppliers. I can still remember feeling lucky for simply getting thirty minutes of self-time a day when our kids were all infants, because so much of what was on my plate was dominated by my kids. In case you need to know, that self-time was typically in the gym.

There's also a stronger focus on the future at the expense of the past and present by those who embrace fatherhood. A father's vision becomes more important than it had before embracing fatherhood. Men pay more attention to the years ahead, initially with specific focus on the new baby's health and well-being. It's one of the reasons why blood-cord banking firms do such a roaring trade in maternity wings. Such firms can see that the father, often the family's main financial decision-maker, has very suddenly become sensitive to a long-term perspective in a way that before fatherhood he wouldn't have given two hoots to. It wasn't the case before fatherhood, but now decisions are being made for eventualities that may or may not occur in twenty years or even later.[145] And cheques are being written and credit card swiped with a wild abandon.

With that focus on the future, there's also an emphasis on fixing that future. When Larry, a teacher who was interviewed for research on fatherhood, revealingly said, "The day my baby was born, I said, 'I gotta find a better life,'" he wasn't looking to upgrade his car or buy a new watch.[146] He could have spoken for generations of modern fathers who want to raise their game and aim a touch higher only for the children. The replacing of personal wants, even if it's something as replacing a want to be a remote-control-holding couch potato with wanting to do something for a child's future, is a significant change. Just reflect upon how hard it sometimes is to change even our most minuscule human behaviour. It took me months to get into the routine of parking my shoes on the shoe rack when I entered our home after I'd become accustomed to merely flippantly flicking them to the side.

Drawing on my personal experience, when I became a father I still remember that sense of accommodation, thinking less about myself and what I wanted. Instead, I was more aware of my shift towards what was good for my child and his future. Several jobs that I might have considered before fatherhood were abruptly removed from my radar, because they'd leave me no time to contribute to the future development of my son or any subsequent children I might later have. My revised vision influenced my future places to live, in terms of country, city and neighbourhood. Even the car I had wanted to buy had to be shelved. And then of course there was a bit of financial planning around the kids' educations, if possible—all of which demanded a strong focus on my vision for them at the expense of me and myself now.

In some ways fatherhood demands a more dramatic act of selflessness than what takes place in marriage, where there's scope for dialogue and compromise. It's not surprising that some fathers actually feel that they're losing control of their lives given just how much of their previous envisaged future they suddenly either drop or dilute. This in itself creates complications with new fathers being especially vulnerable to depression.[147] Not a lot of people know that fathers suffer from postpartum depression. I didn't know that until I came across it in researching this book. It isn't a female monopoly. In abandoning what they wanted for themselves now or even for themselves in the future, fathers can feel a heavy toll. In fact, one study suggested that fathers are *more likely* to get postpartum depression that are mothers.[148] Comrade fathers, be guests of mine, don't hold back, preach the gospel and share that with your partners.

Fatherhood also has a big impact on a father's vision's texture. It's not just that the vision becomes more important. It's that the vision's flavour itself changes. Before fatherhood, men's goals and aspirations tend to be dominated by personal targets, numbers and accomplishments. These are often measurable or immediate—a job promotion, a new car or even a new model railway kit that goes around and around the basement . . . whatever tickles his fancy. In embracing fatherhood, there's a shift towards nonmeasurable aspirations, specifically in creating an environment at home. The father's vision ahead now envelops the creation of a sanctuary, of a space where the child can develop and thrive, where there is stability and security in a way which hadn't mattered till the man embraced fatherhood.[149]

Besides the impact of fatherhood on the (cognition or construction of the) journey's start and end points, there's also the vigorous impact of fatherhood on the effecting of strategy itself. Those who self-identify as fathers, who embrace fatherhood, also do the things that are expected of a father. In other words, in getting from their understanding of the world around them to whatever vague Promised Land they have of the future, a father's strategy is influenced, as role theory suggests, by what the individual, his family and society think a father does or should do. This obviously can be a challenge for fathers who aren't living with their kids, because the fulfilling of "fatherhood" partly needs for kids to be around.[150] One cannot easily effect the full role of fatherhood if the kids simply aren't there. And fathers who don't live with their kids feel partial and incomplete for precisely this reason.

Day in and day out, fathers make substantial daily behavioural changes to fulfil their fatherhood, doing the things that are simply expected of a father. I personally had to make those changes and some of them weren't fun, no sir. The meaning of fatherhood in today's modern societies unfortunately includes diaper changes, even the messy number twos, which I absolutely detested—dreaded them—yet I did them because that's what I understood good fathers do; and like millions of other fathers, I held my breath. I definitely didn't cheerily smile like my wife was able to do when she was changing even the messiest number twos. How she did that, I have no idea. If I'd been a father in nineteenth-century Western Europe, that entire diaper-change stuff would have been no-go territory. One single father with limited economic means and far more serious issues than diaper changes effected his fatherhood and took his son out of foster care:

> I feel I'm doing it because that's what I am supposed to do. Parents are supposed to take care of their children.[151]

Responsibility, the flip side of risk aversion, is another essential behavioural trait to fatherhood and influences how a father bridges the world he sees with his vision for the future. As we've already noted and as evidenced in the academic literature on fatherhood, a father becomes more sensitive to risk when seeing and making sense of the world.[152] However, new fathers also play out the role of fatherhood by reducing risky behaviours. Risk aversion and responsibility feed into the behaviour of the father, as poignantly revealed by one new father in New Zealand:

> I went down to the store the other night and I thought, shit, I didn't have my seatbelt on and I thought, hell, if I was to go through the window . . . that's your father gone; that kid would grow up without a father.[153]

The story that we have of fatherhood is that of influencing behaviour to become less risky. So in *Downton Abbey,* when Matthew

Crawley hurtled down the village road in his fancy olive-coloured AC sports car after seeing his son for the first time, it flew in the face of what we've understood about late modern fathers.[154] New fathers don't become risk blind and recklessly drive their cars into a death ditch. The scriptwriter portrayed Crawley as either having a screw loose or not being a late modern Western father. Since the 1920s wasn't a late modern period, the latter seems a sensible possibility, which means my choice of illustrative example was my bad. But don't deny it— you still get the point I am trying to make, even though my choice of example spectacularly backfired.

Few groups are as sensitised to the issue of responsible parental behaviour today as are African–American fathers. At least since the 1950s, they've suffered from the stigma of the "invisible father," a complex legacy perhaps of their ancestors' slavery.[155] Today, research suggests that though many African–American fathers aren't married, they're still very proactive fathers.[156] It's possible that today's African–American fathers have indeed reacted against the stigma and embrace fatherhood's responsibility more than is normal in American society.[157] The issue of race in America is like mixing fire and petrol, so having touched some of the latest research and since the point is slightly anecdotal to my argument, it's best to move on. But true to form, at least I pushed the door of this incendiary subject open a touch, and then walked on, minding my own business.

Another impact of fatherhood on a new father's strategy is in behaving *to be part of the better (social) environment* for children. New fathers tend to quickly appreciate that the qualities needed at work contrast with those needed at home. Specifically, evidence suggests that they develop a greater awareness of the need to replace the self-serving impatience with a willingness to care more about others, especially their children, and demonstrate greater patience with them.[158] In any case, being peed upon either through a diaper leak or possibly even more directly extends the tolerance frontier quite a bit. The first time that men are typically ever peed upon is by their infant children. The point that I want to stress is that a father's own behaviour reflects the qualities that he wants for the environment of his child. The father becomes part of the change.

As part of becoming that better environment, fathers who do live with their children tend to have far greater civic and religious engagement than do other fathers.[159] Fathers who live with their children often become active neighbours who are more protective of their communities. They have a better understanding of their neighbours and what's going on in the street. Again going back to my own experience, I'm *more* active in the affairs of my local community since becoming a father than I was before, despite now having a lot *less* time on my hands than I did when I didn't have any kids. In fact, all the men who I know to be active in my own neighbourhood, who lead local cleanups, come up with neighbourhood watch schemes and badger the local government on anything which needs fixing have kids, while the men without kids are nowhere to be seen and relatively inactive in the community.

It's interesting that research on the biological impact of fatherhood suggests that becoming a father dramatically reduces levels of testosterone, a steroid hormone linked to aggression and antisocial behaviour.[160] It's the sort of stuff that does the civic environment no good. It's also not especially useful for interacting with young children. More so, staying involved as a father, maintaining one's self-identity as a father which isn't the same thing as biologically reproducing, reduces testosterone levels even further. I thought it curious at least that embracing fatherhood as a self-identity and the roles associated with it, according to some research, actually has the physiological impact of making men calmer and more social. It's as if the physiological changes are aligned with the sociocultural ones. I don't know if that's a mere coincidence but it's interesting.

This is a good point at which to remind all and sundry that a father's behavioural changes are a result of adopting the fatherhood identity and the perspectives and roles that come with it. A father who doesn't see himself as a father will not bother making the types of behavioural changes that we've touched upon. Darth Vader and Steve Jobs never made those changes when their first kids were born. (I'm sure there's some Microsoft geek out there who is having a chuckle that I've bucketed Jobs with the evil Sith Lord. Eat this then—I am very much an Apple person.) And that Vader and Jobs didn't make those changes shouldn't be surprising. They simply didn't embrace fatherhood as a self-identity. Without being compelled by fatherhood, its meanings and narratives, they didn't see and give meaning to their starting strategic points and visions ahead through the lens of fatherhood. Nor did they influence their daily behaviour with what fatherhood expected of them.

It's obvious that in most cases, mothers sacrifice way more in their pregnancy, post-delivery and early nursing stages than do fathers. Even so, the changes that a father willingly makes speak to the power of what it means to be a father. Embracing fatherhood in today's modern society is one of the most powerful drivers of rapid, large-scale male behavioural change. It ranks up there with marriage and the death of loved ones in its ability to quickly alter a man's cognition of the world and his direction in it, as well as his behaviour. There's not a lot else out there that can make a man become less risky, transform him from being a society isolationist to active participant and force him to change smelly number two diapers, as does his embracing of fatherhood.

And that fine scent concludes my bringing colour to self-identity's impact on the life strategy of individuals. We can now move to repeating the exercise but in the context of organisations. Before ending the chapter, I do want to capture some of the key take-aways of this chapter. The Morris case brought home the importance of having a robust sense of who you are, a clear self-identity, in order to make sense of the world and one's future vision in it. The Morris who failed to establish a robust core self-identity suffered from a weak ability to both see and make sense of the world and also to develop some kind of vision ahead. That was a very different person to the Morris who embraced a female self-identity. The Morris who saw himself as a woman could see things clearly. She had a clearer sense of where she was going. And she was more confident about asserting herself.

Ed's case demonstrated a couple of quite different aspects of self-identity. Specifically, his case showed the speed with which we can embrace new self-identities. Unlike Morris, Ed adopted a new primary self-identity within months, which was also the same period he needed to get rid of that self-identity. His case also brought to the fore the potentially destructive impact of some self-identities. Buying into a destructive self-identity and all that came with it obliterated Ed's spirituality, relationships and economic future. How often do we link self-identity with such transformation? How often do we make explicit the impact that our self-identity has on all the things that matter to us? I don't often see that relationship explicitly defined. But as a result of changes in Ed's self-identity, our man was in a state of war with practically everything that inhaled oxygen.

Conversely, fatherhood also demonstrated the speed with which self-identity can influence an individual's strategic journey in a more fruitful way. A father in the modern West typically alters how he sees his life's strategic start and end points in just a few weeks, undergoing the sort of change that few stimuli can compete with. He views the world as-is with a greater focus on risk, he pushes out other self-identities and develops a generational axis by recognising not only the next generation but also the previous one. On embracing fatherhood, a man's sense of the future or his vision ahead becomes less self-centred and also more pronounced. The future becomes more important. There's also within that vision a more qualitative focus on the human environment, a change that doubles up to become simultaneously both the destination and the strategy.

The impact of self-identity is all well and good when you, as the individual, have a higher degree of control over your self-identity. It's all about me, myself and I. However, what about when we try to apply this framework of self-identity and strategy on a group of people in the shape of an organisation? Does self-identity have a similar impact on the strategy of organisations? The self-identity of an organisation does throw some different curve balls to the self-identity of an individual. That said, the core relationship is still binding. That should become evident in the next chapter, which explores precisely the impact of self-identity on the strategy of organisations through three mini-case studies.

1   *The Golden Girls*, Touchstone Television Production, Burbank, 1985–1992

2   *Harry Potter* film series, Warner Brothers Pictures, Burbank, 2001–2011

3   http://en.wikipedia.org/wiki/Jan_Morris

4   A Rusbridger, "Courage under Fire," *The Guardian*, London, 2006

5   http://articles.latimes.com/1989-10-20/news/vw-210_1_james-morris

6   http://www.independent.co.uk/news/uk/this-britain/love-story-jan-morris-
    -divorce-the-death-of-a-child-and-a-sex-change-but-still-together-839602.
    html

7   http://www.faber.co.uk/catalog/author/jan-morris

8   J Morris, *Conundrum*, Faber and Faber, London, 2001

9   http://www.telegraph.co.uk/comment/personal-view/3559244/After-a-life-of-
    travel-Jan-Morris-is-back-where-he-started.html

10 http://www.independent.co.uk/news/uk/this-britain/love-story-jan-morris-
    -divorce-the-death-of-a-child-and-a-sex-change-but-still-together-839602.
    html

11 http://www.nytimes.com/books/97/11/23/home/morris-interview.html

12 http://www.standard.co.uk/showbiz/the-moving-love-story-between-
    writer-jan-morris-and-her-exwife-who-she-remarried-after-her-sex-
    change-6889930.html

13 http://www.independent.co.uk/news/people/profiles/jan-morris-were-on-the-
    brink-of-colossal-cataclysmic-change-2240989.html

14 J Morris, *Conundrum*, Faber and Faber, London, 2001

15 *Ibid.*

16 *Ibid.*

17 *Ibid.*

18 SS Freud, *Three Essays on the Theory of Sexuality*, Martino Fine Books,
    Eastford, 2011

19 J Morris, *Conundrum*, Faber and Faber, London, 2001

20 *Ibid.*

21 *Ibid.*

22 *Ibid.*

23 *Ibid.*

24 *Ibid.*

25 *Ibid.*

26 *Ibid.*

27 *Ibid.*

28 http://www.transtorah.org/PDFs/Classical_Jewish_Terms_for_Gender_Diversity.pdf

29 MJ Wright, *Studying Judaism: The Critical Issues*, Continuum International, London, 2012

30 E Wegener, *Man into Woman: An Authentic Record of a Change of Sex*, The Beacon Library, New York, 1937

31 J Morris, *Conundrum*, Faber and Faber, London, 2001

32 http://www.lgbthistorymonth.org.uk/history/lilielbe.htm

33 http://en.wikipedia.org/wiki/Lili_Elbe#cite_note-etrans-10

34 http://www.nytimes.com/books/97/11/23/home/morris-interview.html

35 http://www.sexarchive.info/GESUND/ARCHIV/COLLBEN.HTM

36 J Morris, *Conundrum*, Faber and Faber, London, 2001

37 *The Matrix*, Warner Brothers, Silver Pictures and Village Roadshow Pictures, Burbank and Sydney, 1999

38 J Morris, *Conundrum*, Faber and Faber, London, 2001

39 http://www.nytimes.com/books/97/11/23/home/morris-interview.html

40 *Ibid.*

41 J Morris, *Conundrum*, Faber and Faber, London, 2001

42 http://www.nytimes.com/books/97/11/23/home/morris-interview.html

43 J Morris, *Conundrum*, Faber and Faber, London, 2001

44   *Ibid.*

45   *Ibid.*

46   *Ibid.*

47   http://www.aawsat.net/2010/10/article55249028

48   E Husain, *The Islamist*, Penguin, London, 2007

49   T Fatah, *Chasing a Mirage*, John Wiley & Sons Canada, Mississauga, 2008

50   T El Hibri, *Parable and Politics in Early Islamic History*, Columbia University Press, New York, 2010

51   *Ibid.*

52   *Ibid.*

53   *Ibid.*

54   *Ibid.*

55   T Fatah, *Chasing a Mirage*, John Wiley & Sons Canada, Mississauga, 2008

56   T El Hibri, *Parable and Politics in Early Islamic History*, Columbia University Press, New York, 2010

57   *Ibid.*

58   *Ibid.*

59   *Ibid.*

60   T El Hibri, *Parable and Politics in Early Islamic History*, Columbia University Press, New York, 2010

61   T Fatah, *Chasing a Mirage*, John Wiley & Sons Canada, Mississauga, 2008

62   T El Hibri, *Parable and Politics in Early Islamic History*, Columbia University Press, New York, 2010

63   http://www.childhoodpoverty.org/

64   E Husain, *The Islamist*, Penguin, London, 2007

65   *Ibid.*

66   *Ibid.*

[67]   http://www.thesundaytimes.co.uk/sto/news/world_news/article63360.ece;

[68]   E Husain, *The Islamist*, Penguin, London, 2007

[69]   *Ibid.*

[70]   *Ibid.*

[71]   http://www.newstatesman.com/religion/2010/02/british-muslim-islam-britain

[72]   http://en.wikipedia.org/wiki/Jamaat-e-Islami_Pakistan

[73]   H Ahmed, *Hizb ut-Tahrir: Ideology and Strategy*, The Center for Social Cohesion, London, 2009

[74]   E Husain, *The Islamist*, Penguin, London, 2007

[75]   H Ahmed, *Hizb ut-Tahrir: Ideology and Strategy*, The Center for Social Cohesion, London, 2009

[76]   E Husain, *The Islamist*, Penguin, London, 2007

[77]   http://www.newstatesman.com/religion/2010/02/british-muslim-islam-britain

[78]   E Husain, *The Islamist*, Penguin, London, 2007

[79]   *Ibid.*

[80]   http://edition.cnn.com/TRANSCRIPTS/0705/04/cnr.02.html

[81]   E Husain, *The Islamist*, Penguin, London, 2007

[82]   F Halliday, *Islam and The Myth of Confrontation*, IB Taurus, London, 2003

[83]   E Husain, *The Islamist*, Penguin, London, 2007

[84]   *Ibid.*

[85]   *Ibid.*

[86]   *Ibid.*

[87]   F Halliday, *Islam and The Myth of Confrontation*, IB Taurus, London, 2003

[88]   E Husain, *The Islamist*, Penguin, London, 2007

[89]   *Ibid.*

90   *Ibid.*

91   *Ibid.*

92   *Ibid.*7

93   F Halliday, *Islam and The Myth of Confrontation*, IB Taurus, London, 2003

94   E Husain, *The Islamist*, Penguin, London, 2007

95   *Ibid.*

96   *Ibid.*

97   *Ibid.*

98   *Ibid.*

99   *Ibid.*

100   http://islam.about.com/od/elderly/a/mothers.htm

101   E Husain, *The Islamist*, Penguin, London, 2007

102   *Ibid.*

103   *Ibid.*

104   *Ibid.*

105   http://islam.about.com/od/health/tp/smoking_health.htm

106   http://www.dailymail.co.uk/debate/article-1212114/ED-HUSAIN-I-Islamic-extremist-feel-given-fanatics.html

107   E Husain, *The Islamist*, Penguin, London, 2007

108   http://www.nytimes.com/2011/12/02/opinion/magazine-global-agenda-radical-changes.html?pagewanted=all&_r=0

109   E Husain, *The Islamist*, Penguin, London, 2007

110   *Ibid.*

111   W Isaacson, *Steve Jobs*, Simon & Schuster, New York, 2011

112   http://www.pewsocialtrends.org/2011/06/15/a-tale-of-two-fathers/

113   D Bornstein, *The Price of a Dream: The Story of the Grameen Bank*, Oxford University Press, Oxford, 2005

114 KA May, "Three Phases of Father Involvement in Pregnancy," *Nursing Research*, University of North Carolina, Chapel Hill, 1982

115 T Tripp-Reimer and SE Wilson, "Cross-Cultural Perspectives on Fatherhood" in FW Bozett and SMH Hanson, *Fatherhood and Families in Cultural Context*, Springer Publishing, New York, 1991

116 M Greenberg and N Morris, "Engrossment: The Newborn's Impact upon the Father," *American Journal of Orthopsychiatry*, Greenville, 1974

117 GL Fox and C Bruce, "Conditional Fatherhood: Identity Theory and Parental Investment Theory as Alternative Source of Explanation of Fathering," *Journal of Marriage and Family*, 2001

118 T Tripp-Reimer and SE Wilson, "Cross-Cultural Perspectives on Fatherhood" in FW Bozett and SMH Hanson, *Fatherhood and Families in Cultural Context*, Springer Publishing, New York, 1991

119 *Ibid.*

120 *Ibid.*

121 *Ibid.*

122 EH Pleck and JH Pleck, "Fatherhood Ideals in the United States" in ME Lamb, *The Role of the Father in Child Development*, John Wiley & Sons, New York, 1997

123 *Ibid.*

124 *Ibid.*

125 *Ibid.*

126 ME Lamb, "Fathers and Child Development" in ME Lamb, *The Role of the Father in Child Development*, John Wiley & Sons, New York, 1997

127 *Ibid.*

128 http://www.pewsocialtrends.org/2011/06/15/a-tale-of-two-fathers

129 ME Lamb, "Fathers and Child Development" in ME Lamb, *The Role of the Father in Child Development*, John Wiley & Sons, New York, 1997

130 EH Pleck and JH Pleck, "Fatherhood Ideals in the United States" in ME Lamb, *The Role of the Father in Child Development*, John Wiley & Sons, New York, 1997

[131] L Barclay and D Lupton, "The Experiences of New Fatherhood," *Journal of Advanced Nursing*, 1999

[132] PA Cowan, "Becoming a Father" in P Bronstein and CP Cowan, *Fatherhood Today: Men's Changing Role in the Family*, John Wiley & Sons, New York, 1988

[133] M Munroe, *The Fatherhood Principle*, Whitaker House, New Kensington, 2008

[134] JD Gage and R Kirk, "First-Time Fathers," *Canadian Journal of Nursing Research*, 2002

[135] DJ Eggebeen and C Knoester, "Does Fatherhood Matter for Men," *Journal of Marriage and Family*, 2001

[136] PA Cowan, "Becoming a Father" in P Bronstein and CP Cowan, *Fatherhood Today: Men's Changing Role in the Family*, John Wiley & Sons, New York, 1988

[137] GL Fox and C Bruce, "Conditional Fatherhood: Identity Theory and Parental Investment Theory as Alternative Source of Explanation of Fathering," *Journal of Marriage and Family*, 2001

[138] R Strauss and WA Goldberg, "Self and Possible Selves During the Transition to Fatherhood," *Journal of Family Psychology*, 1999

[139] M Greenberg and N Morris, "Engrossment: The Newborn's Impact upon the Father," *American Journal of Orthopsychiatry*, Greenville, 1974

[140] LR Cronenwett and W Kunst-Wilson, "Stress, Social Support and the Transition to Fatherhood," *Nursing Research*, 1981

[141] DJ Eggebeen and C Knoester, "Does Fatherhood Matter for Men," *Journal of Marriage and Family*, 2001

[142] WH Wright, "Fatherhood as a Precipitant of Mental Illness," *American Journal of Psychiatry*, 1966

[143] RL Coles, "Black Single Fathers: Choosing to Father Full Time," *Journal of Contemporary Ethnography*, 2002

[144] http://www.newscientist.com/article/dn3724-absent-fathers-linked-to-teenage-pregnancies.html#.U3ESvF4k_1o

[145] DH Heath, "What Meaning and Effects Does Fatherhood Have for the Maturing of Professional Men," *Merrill-Palmer Quarterly*, 1978

[146] R Inbar, "Is Commercial Blood-Cord Banking Ethical?" Amazon Media, Seattle, 2011

147 RL Coles, "Black Single Fathers: Choosing to Father Full Time," *Journal of Contemporary Ethnography*, 2002

148 KA May, "Three Phases of Father Involvement in Pregnancy," *Nursing Research*, University of North Carolina, Chapel Hill, 1982

149 JF Paulson, "Focusing on Depression on Expectant and New Fathers," *Psychiatry Times*, 2010

150 JD Gage and R Kirk, "First-Time Fathers," *Canadian Journal of Nursing Research*, 2002

151 JA Seltzer, "Relationships between Fathers and Children Who Live Apart," *Journal of Marriage and Family*, 1991

152 RL Coles, "Black Single Fathers: Choosing to Father Full Time," Journal of Contemporary Ethnography, 2002

153 JD Gage and R Kirk, "First-Time Fathers," *Canadian Journal of Nursing Research*, 2002

154 *Ibid.*

155 *Downton Abbey*, Carnival Films, London, 2012

156 EF Frazier, *The Negro in the United States*, Macmillan, New York, 1949

157 RL Coles, "Black Single Fathers," *Journal of Contemporary Ethnography*, 2002

158 JE Daniel, "A Definition of Fatherhood as Expressed by Black Fathers," University of Pittsburgh PhD thesis, Pittsburgh, 1975; JL McAdoo, "Changing Perspectives on the Role of the Black Father" in P Bronstein and CP Cowan, *Fatherhood Today: Men's Changing Role in the Family*, Wiley, New York, 1988

159 PA Cowan, "Becoming a Father" in P Bronstein and CP Cowan, *Fatherhood Today: Men's Changing Role in the Family*, John Wiley & Sons, New York, 1988

160 DJ Eggebeen and C Knoester, "Does Fatherhood Matter for Men," *Journal of Marriage and Family*, 2001

161 http://www.huffingtonpost.com/david-valdes-greenwood/5-more-shocking-sideeffec_b_962902.html

CHAPTER 7

———❦———

GROUPING THE MANY

The impact of self-identity on the strategy of organisations is no less pronounced than it is on individuals, a point made almost two decades ago by management academic Yolanda Sarason, who has written quite a bit on identity and organisations.[1] And why shouldn't it be given that organisations are merely collections of individuals? I'm treating "organisation" in its simplest sense—a group of individuals who work together within some kind of processes and systems, such as BP, Honda . . . and Al Qaeda. I also could have referred to other organisations such as Rashtriya Swayamsevak Sangh, Hinduism's lunatics and the American Christian Klu Klux Klan. I can't imagine BP or Honda celebrating my bucketing them with mankind's nastiest organisations, but still, life goes on . . . as long as they're all organisations in the broader sense of the term.

It might well be harder to nail down an organisation's self-identity than an individual's because a group has many people, each with their own self-identity. Still, I do think organisations have self-identities. Employees will share elements of their employer's self-identity, even if with variable intensity.[2] Hundreds of millions of people who work in organisations across the world will relate to a sense of who *we* are and what *we* do. In 2011, I asked a dozen staff at one of Germany's largest international banks if the bank was part of their individual self-identity. Nearly all said it was. Managers identified more closely while junior staff tended to be less attached. One memorable respondent in the investment banking division struggled to come to terms working for a bank that "couldn't give a flying fart about what was good for our clients as long as we made our cut." Welcome to investment banking.

To illustrate the impact of self-identity on organisations, I've enlisted examples to give aroma and colour to different aspects of self-identity's relationship with strategy. It's sort of like what I did for individuals in the previous chapter. The examples elucidate self-identity's influence on an organisation's making sense of its world and its vision ahead and finally how the organisation gets from its starting point to its end point. Once an organisation understands where it is today and where it wants to go in the future, its journey is straightjacketed. As I've said before, I think it's easier to craft strategy than it is to stabilise and crystallise the strategic start and end points. The psychological and emotive forces that drive our understanding and finalising of those journey points are hard simply because they emerge from the human personality. And in the context of organisations, that's not very easy to assemble.

And finally, I want to repeat two cautions from previous chapters, even at the risk of sounding like a particularly irritating parrot. I remind everybody that my take is no more than that. It's not the objective truth. I don't have the keys to objectivity and I don't suggest that my analysis overcomes the ontological, epistemological and methodological challenges that I've mentioned in earlier chapters. My take is just my plain, simple perspective. The second caveat is that self-identity doesn't explain everything. It's not a life-governing everywhere-particle which synthesises all great theories. I really don't have much time for grand, all-explanatory theories anyway. I've focused on self-identity at the expense of other factors only to illustrate its impact. Do not try to reduce the universe to self-identity. I'm sure some numbnut will ignore my caveats and blast me, so I guess I can only suggest that we let the numbnut be.

The Port Authority of New York and New Jersey (PANYNJ)

My first example in PANYNJ illustrates the organisational angst caused when an organisation's core self-identity is challenged and how an organisation then defends that self-identity. Organisations don't just prioritise economics, customer service or operational effectiveness in their daily or long-term objectives. They also seek to defend their core self-identities, which isn't the same thing as defending a brand. And my exploration of PANYNJ demonstrates precisely that. When an organisation's important self-identities are challenged, enough organisations will deploy resources, including time and money, to defend those self-identities *irrespective* of their economic or operational impact. The business sometimes values its self-identity more than its economic bottom line. That is not classic business or economic theory.

PANYNJ is responsible for most transport infrastructure within twenty-five miles of the Statue of Liberty in New York. The transport authority, America's first multiproject public authority, was founded in 1921 to protect transportation from local corruption, especially to cocoon the region's long-term infrastructure planning from short-term politics and scandals. Today most New Yorkers will know of PANYNJ, though perhaps they may not know of its vast mandate. PANYNJ runs the key harbours, ports, bridges, the World Trade Centre and airports of LaGuardia, Newark and John F Kennedy.[3] It doesn't run New York's subway or taxis, but it's far and away the big cheese in New York's transportation infrastructure, with more than 7,000 staff.

My example starts in 1981, a good year. Ronald Reagan won the

American presidency to fix the economy, Indiana Jones cracked his whip searching for the lost ark and the Spurs won the FA Cup with *that* Ricky Villa goal. Before going too far into the case, I do want to stress that I'm indebted to organisation academics Jane Dutton and Janet Dukerich for their primary research on PANYNJ, without which I'd not have been able to flesh out the subsequent analysis in my case.[4] Business academics are probably the most intellectually stale and stagnant of the lot, but Dutton and Dukerich did a great job in conceiving and then researching a relationship between an organisation's decisions and its self-identity. This is a relationship that most business academics haven't given even a thought to, but *Keeping an Eye on the Mirror*, which was published in 1991, brought that primary research out really well.

In 1981, PANYNJ's core self-identity was that of a top professional organisation with cutting-edge, technical transportation skills. That was how the organisation saw itself over and beyond any cosmetic branding campaign. This was the bedrock of PANYNJ's self-identity. It was partly built upon PANYNJ's impressive breadth of expertise (road, air, sea and rail) and its infrastructure assets. John F Kennedy Airport was the busiest air gateway into America with more Concorde flights than any other airport in the world. Port Newark-Elizabeth Marine Terminal handled the largest amount of shipping in America. And the George Washington Bridge was one of the world's busiest vehicle bridges and also a popular place, unfortunately, for suicides.[5] I don't think, though, the suicides piece featured front and centre in the organisation's self-identity. That aside, few transportation organisations in the world could boast such impressive feathers in the cap.

Another part of PANYNJ's core self-identity was that it was scandal-free, with one worker even describing it as "altruistic."[6] PANYNJ didn't suffer from the scale of embarrassment that hit many other public bodies.[i] Even to this day, PANYNJ distinguishes itself by sharing on its corporate website a detailed breakup of annual compensation for each and every single employee. I have never ever seen any organisation share its employees' compensation like that. Such organisations must exist. But I've never come across anything like this, that's all. In contrast, take the Environmental Protection Agency (EPA), which during 1981–1983 replaced its own staff with staff from firms that the EPA was regulating.[7] If that wasn't enough, Congress charged the EPA with mismanaging a $1.6 billion fund and then demanded records.[8] The cake's icing was the EPA director's response. She refused to comply and thus became the first agency director to be cited by Congress for contempt.[9] The director, a law graduate, resigned, to become a lawyer, which in turn gave the entire saga a Monty Python feel.[10]

Another part of PANYNJ's core self-identity was that it saw itself as a proactive, problem-solving organisation.[11] One manager at La Guardia airport who I talked with explained with a donut in his mouth:

> Nobody here wants to be the f***ing problem . . . . we are f***ing problem-solvers, not f***ing problems. Do you have any f***ing idea what would happen to the bridges, planes . . . to the entire f***ing city of New York if we sat there like f***ing donuts waiting for the next problem and then . . . ? We don't f*** around—we find a problem and we f***ing attack it. It's what we are—f***ing problem attackers.

Personally, I thought he swore a lot. Was he having a bad day? Perhaps. And I also thought that it was poetic that he referred to

---

i   PANYNJ wasn't perfect even if its self-identity reflected it as so. In 1977, a journalist discovered a pattern of fraudulent expense claims, including pointless expensive international travel by senior management.

"donuts" with his mouth stuffed with one. I daren't then point it out to him because it would have been, even by my standards, a really juvenile thing to do. Furthermore, given I was a Muslim in New York, he could have flagged me as terrorist and have me shipped out to Gitmo without any legal requirement to charge me. That would then leave me with several other incarcerated people who the US government knows to be totally innocent at Gitmo but can't quite figure out what to do with. This is all somewhat complicated, because if you detain somebody who you know to be innocent, that detainee could at some stage begin to hate you. And the reason it becomes complicated is that the US government might well have tortured several innocuous people into hardcore US-haters. Very smart.

Beyond its core self-identity, a less prominent part of PANYNJ's self-identity was that it was committed to the region.[12] That was evidenced in PANYNJ's motto alone, "To Keep The Region Moving."[13] The region was front and centre in the organisation's sense of self. Further, more than a third of the PANYNJ staff interviewed by Dutton and Dukerich cited regional commitment as part of PANYNJ's identity, and that, too, without being prompted. This identity was re-enforced by what staff could sense on the ground. Without an effective PANYNJ, the region would judder to a halt. In fact, the region's reliance then and today on PANYNJ's assets is quite something. It is the anchor transportation infrastructure to America's most important city, being one of the most important cities in the world.

Between 1982 and 1984, change was in the air. Change is always in the air. Air is never static, which sounds like another purposeless statement by me. I haven't shelled many of them out so cut me some slack. What I mean is that there were some important relevant changes. Let's not go down the route of what is or is not relevant. First, PANYNJ's bus terminal at 8th Avenue and 42nd Street, America's largest bus station, completed a $226 million renovation in 1982. The terminal expanded by almost half and gleamed in contrast to the adjacent dump of a neighbourhood.[14] Interestingly, while the terminal was praised in 1982, in 2008 it was ranked as the world's fifth ugliest building, a list headed by Boston City Hall.[15] Don't ask me how these lists are created. That said, the important point to make note of is that in 1982 PANYNJ's main bus terminal was groovier and bigger than ever.

A second change was the closure of several local low-income, single-room hotels in the vicinity of the bus station and for that matter across New York. In the first half of 1982, the US economy contracted by 4.2 percent p.a. followed by a 1.3 percent p.a. contraction in the second half.[16] In contrast, in 1983 the economy grew sharply at 4.5 percent p.a. Prime interest rates fell from 21.5 percent in 1981 to 11.5 percent in 1982. As often happens, entrepreneurs smelled the shoots of recovery. And with this instinct and appetite to profit, they snapped up local hotels in 1982 and 1983 to convert into apartments without thinking about where the underprivileged hotel residents would go. Naturally, these once-welcome residents got shoved out. In short, more poor people ended up homeless on the local streets.

The consulting universe has this wretched ability to clench its Luis Suárez teeth deep into you. This lists of three bad habit isn't one for kicking, so I am now officially going to cease trying. The third change was that unemployment in America led to even more homeless people. In November 1982, the unemployment rate hit 10.8 percent. As a comparison, even after the worst financial crisis in the US since 1929, unemployment in 2009 peaked at 10.0 percent.[17] Economists suggest that unemployment typically rises up to a year after an economy's recovery.[18] They often get paid a lot to get lots of things wrong, evidenced in their forecasts, and this example also falls in that bucket.[ii] American unemployment actually peaked during the recession and well before the economy recovered. The point remains that in 1982 and 1983, America had a lot more unemployed people, which led to an increase in the numbers of homeless folk in the vicinity of the bus station.

These changes triggered a decade-long struggle for PANYNJ and its self-identity. Quite suddenly, in 1983 many homeless people began living at the Authority's terrific and enlarged new bus terminal. And it didn't just end there, for with the homeless came illegal drugs, and with those drugs came drugs-related crime. The brand new pride of place in the PANYNJ portfolio was looking worse for wear faster than it ought to have.[19] So despite the euphoria of a brand spanking new bus facility, 1983 wasn't a time for a celebratory party for PANYNJ. Lest you're wondering, cricketers Javed Miandad and Mudassar Nazar's 451 runs stand against India in that year counted for bugger all at PANYNJ. There's nothing like having a brand new, state-of-the-art building flooded by smelly, drugged-out criminals. In fact, it's quite distressing to see something that you've invested so much time and emotion in to become so messed up so quickly.

However, what made this issue really moving and sensitive for PANYNY wasn't the unpleasant contrast between building and its "residents." Nor was it any economic or operational diminution, because the homeless did little to affect either. This is an important point to stress. It was that homelessness, narcotics and crime challenged PANYNJ's core self-identity as a top professional organisation. Top organisations do not have homeless junky crooks squatting in flagship premises. It's not part of who they, top

---

ii   In October 2008, the IMF's economic growth forecasts for 2009 were 0.1 percent for America, 0.2 percent for the Euro zone and 2.6 percent for the whole world. The actual growth rates turned out at -3.5, -4.2 and -2.6 percent respectively. I take the position that a monkey would have given more accurate forecasts.

organisations, are. I've never seen them in a McKinsey office. I've never seen them at the *Financial Times*. And if they were at HSBC Investment Bank, they were hiding rather well. The squatting homeless do not fit with the story of a top organisation. PANYNJ's anxiety and unease, which was considerable, came about because the effects of local homelessness hit PANYNJ's self-identity. In doing so, local homelessness hit something that was raw, sensitive and powerful.

PANYNJ's initial reaction to the pain and anxiety was to protect its core self-identity with rash simplicity. That knee-jerk reaction worsened the problem, which is sort of how some people suggest America manages its foreign policy problems in the Middle East. In 1984, at PANYNJ's request, cops used new laws to evict the homeless from the terminal. The initial response was thus to just kick the homeless out, albeit quietly.[20] That didn't mean that cops tiptoed around the station in their socks. Apparently, the cops were trained to evict without causing a scene, though who knows if they internalised what was taught. And thus began a daily cycle of musical chairs with homeless people camping on premises, being evicted temporarily and then returning, albeit to a different spot. In what feels like something from a Samuel Beckett play, it must have got a bit tiring for all people involved, because nothing really changed at the site.

In some respects, things actually got worse for PANYNJ. It implemented a solution, being soft eviction, to a problem, being the garrison of homeless at one of its important sites, and then got stuck with a garrison of homeless at nearly every site! Homeless people began squatting at other flagship facilities, including John F Kennedy and La Guardia airports. This failure of the initial defence was profoundly illuminated as the problem went from a single site issue to a multisite issue by 1985. The soft eviction approach wasn't working. The world's travellers were arriving in America into the welcoming arms of New York's homeless:

It wasn't until homeless people started to show up at the World Trade Center . . . and the image of the World Trade Center as being a place where homeless people were began to raise its head, that people started to say, "Wait, geez, this is a problem . . ." Then, ultimately, one or two people at the international arrivals building at Kennedy Airport and at LaGuardia Airport, then it began to touch upon the heart and soul of the organization.[21]

Even now this problem still significantly had practically no economic or operational impact on PANYNJ or its customers.[22] Management responded to the widening homelessness problem by stepping up the eviction effort. In other words, they continued to fail, but only fail harder. Clearly, the receiver was off the hook at PANYNJ's head office. The newly appointed director, in line with PANYNJ's core self-identity, steadfastly remained against "getting into the social service business."[23] After all, why should PANJNY get involved in something which it itself is not? That is, after all, what many organisations regularly refer to when assessing new opportunities: "What business are we in?" With PANYNJ encouragement, more police were trained and deployed to keep PANYNJ facilities homeless-free, even though PANYNJ remained disengaged from the underlying homelessness issue.

The "let's throw the homeless out faster" approach attracted the media's attention in late 1987.[24] Journalists, always hunting for a story, hammered PANYNJ for its social callousness. Shoving the homeless onto the streets, in turn, had consequences for PANYNJ's scandal-free self-identity:

"In its last board meeting before Christmas, the Port Authority of New York and New Jersey played Scrooge to Jersey City's poor by outlawing begging and sleeping at the Journal Square PATH Transportation Centre."[25]

Apparently, none of the newspapers or TV stations embraced the

Christmas spirit by offering their own premises to homeless beggars. Nor did a single journalist offer his own pad to the destitute. Strange, you might think—not. It sounds like, without being too cynical, just another piece of classic American media sensationalism.

And if reading the morning newspapers didn't help PANYNJ's management digest their bacon and eggs, taking note of the escalating homelessness problems sure would have. For a start, several years after the problem first surfaced, homelessness surreptitiously and slowly crept into PANYNJ's operations.[26] It actually began to be felt on the conventional operational radar. Cash, albeit in small amounts, was being sucked into homeless issues as PANYNJ was being shoved onto a slippery slope to becoming something besides a top technical transport organisation. One senior manager noted:

> The board is very unhappy and I think rightly so. They feel that we're spending money, which we are, which is money that is desperately needed for other things in terms of our mandate.[27]

I want to stress that sensitivity to cash in the context of homelessness at PANYNJ only surfaced in late 1987, which was four years *after* the homelessness issue hit the organisation. A second challenge cropped up in 1987, which certainly helped wipe any happy smiling faces amongst the board members. The City's anti-loitering legislation was repealed, thereby making it harder to kick the homeless out.[28] As a result, the number of homeless people at PANYNJ facilities increased yet still to a thousand, scented of course with drugs and crime. That, of course, wasn't the only type of scent filling the buildings. Not to put too fine a point to it, but the homeless don't have access to many basic hygiene facilities. If there was ever a time for PANYNJ's management to hold back the bubbly, it was now.

As PANYNJ's public image eroded, its self-identity and organisational morale took a hit. Staff were well aware that, "the homelessness issue is something that obviously affects the perceptions of us."[29] Having become accustomed to seeing themselves as part of a top transport organisation that fixed problems, employees didn't like that identity being challenged. One worker complained that when people found out where he worked, they gave him a paralysing response: "How can you stand that bus terminal?"[30] Other staff grumbled that passengers now saw PANYNJ facilities as dirty and dangerous. PANYNJ's core self-identity was threatened, which brought with it organisation-wide stress and anxiety:

> The Port Authority is—and part of our self-image as I put my fingers on it—is that we do things a little bit better than other public agencies. There's a whole psyche that goes with that. That is why, when there's time like now (referring to the severity of the homelessness issue), when times are tough, people are nervous a little bit, because that goes to their self-image, which is that the Port Authority does things first class.[31]

With the worsening problem hurting PANYNJ's core self-identity, management decided to put the lights on back at head office. That's important—it was when PANYNJ's self-identity took a pasting that management began to think with sophistication about the problem. In late 1987, PANYNJ abandoned the "let's fail, but let's fail harder" approach, which was an obtuse tactic if I ever saw one. The homeless made very little difference to PANYNJ's operational responsibilities with respect to transporting people.[32] Nor did the homeless issue hurt the bottom line, not remotely enough at least to justify senior management time, let alone a strong organisational response. If the homelessness issue hadn't pinched PANYNJ's core self-identity, meaning its seeing itself as a quality transportation organisation, I don't think PANYNJ would have changed course. There would have been insufficient cause to rethink and reflect, especially since the organisation's economics and operations were not being significantly eroded. In other words, PANYNJ didn't change course for what we might consider classic organisational reasons.

What drove PANYNJ to abandon the "let's fail harder" approach was the increasing attack on its core self-identity as a quality transport organisation and the organisational realisation that to protect that self-identity required PANYNJ itself to act. This was an almost existential attack on the organisation. And nobody else seemed prepared or willing to resolve the attack's underlying problem, which was damaging PANYNJ's core self-identity. Neither the government of the City of New York nor the government of New York State were particularly interested in the homeless issue. The former offered only limited funding but no leadership. Beyond those two governmental tiers, Reagan's federal government was captivated by economic restructuring and beating the "evil empire," and not interested in encroaching beyond its traditional turf, even for the country's most important city.[33]

In fact, the homelessness issue forced PANYNJ to hold more than it had wanted to, by embracing a self-identity that resided within its own background portfolio of identities. Caring for the community was a subordinate part of PANYNJ's self-identity. However, despite historically somewhat embracing that self-identity, PANYNJ didn't want to wholeheartedly bury itself with that self-identity so that it became a social welfare organisation. The problem for PANYNJ was that organisations that faintly self-identify with a commitment to local welfare don't then ignore a homeless garrison in their own buildings. PANYNJ found itself in the odd position of having to protect its core self-identity as a professional transport organisation by becoming more of a social welfare organisation. In short, it was being pressed to elevate and act out an ancillary part of its self-identity to defend and protect its main self-identity:

> We are going to have to do some things which clearly stretch our mandate, which commit both dollars and cents beyond what

is appropriate and what is probably on some level defensible, because the agencies that have this responsibility are just not prepared to act.[34]

The first step in the new approach was to get a grip on the issues, normally a smart thing to do before taking action. I'm now thinking if only Dubya had done something like this before attacking Iraq and Afghanistan. But he didn't. And that screwed up things for millions of innocent Iraqis, Afghanis and even American servicemen. Anyhow, to its credit and in contrast to the later 43rd president of the US, PANYNJ collected some data and analysed the problem. It also interfaced with the foot soldiers—social workers, police and Volunteers of America—to learn about the homelessness problem's nuances and subtleties. Just as important, PANYNJ began communicating with everyday customers, thereby publicly accepting that the organisation owned the problem, however reluctantly, and that someone was doing something about it.[35]

From this new understanding emerged PANYNJ's first attempt to tackle the problem in a thoughtful and sustainable way. At the end of 1987, PANYNJ organised a Homeless Project Team that established "drop-in" zones where services were offered to the homeless. These included provision for food, medical care and advice to access government services. PANYNJ's self-identity as an organisation that cared for its community was coming to the fore. The first drop-in centre was opened in May 1998 near the bus terminal and a second later near the WTC.[36] It had taken four years of mounting anxiety around PANYNJ's core self-identity before management came around to making a genuine attempt to resolve the problem and thus protect the core organisational self-identity.

That doesn't mean PANYNJ liked what it was doing. PANYNJ folk were all steamed up by this reprioritisation of self-identities, as one staffer noted, "Yeah, we're two feet deep into the business of homelessness and we don't want to be."[37] Management wasn't celebrating either. Despite doing a good deed, they didn't want any credit for the success of the drop-in zones! It's not often you see an organisation becoming a leader in a do-good space and then wanting to disassociate from that. PANYNJ wasn't thus a "reluctant hero."[38] It was more accurately a "resigned hero," desperately avoiding praise from having succeeded in an identity and role that it didn't want on its forehead. It really didn't want to be known as a homeless management agency, because its primary self-identity was all about transport and doing that job really well.

On a final note, I'm reminded of the Morton Salt Company's marketing slogan of 1914. I'm not that old. I just read it recently on a blog. Prior to their adding magnesium carbonate to salt, damp weather made salt clumpy, and thus their slogan emphasised their superior product: "When it rains, it pours."[39] Though I don't know where I first learned of the Chicago firm's slogan, I do think that it captured PANYNJ's predicament nicely. Not only was it annoyed by being forced into social services, but it also got dumped with the full costs of the drop-in zones after the City of New York withdrew its funding for the project. The director's "Partnership for Homeless" speech of 1998, part of a ploy to drag in local stakeholders, failed to secure even New York's own government to take care of its own homeless.[40] Shame on you, City of New York, for deserting those who can least take care of themselves.

In wrapping up this mini-case study, I liked PANYNJ's five-year journey because it illustrated the anxiety and frustration of an organisation that had its core self-identity challenged while its economic and operational affairs were unscathed. Furthermore, I also liked the case because it demonstrated the defence mechanisms that the organisation then used to protect and secure that self-identity. Those mechanisms evolved from the primitive shoving out of people, to the more sustainable and complex. PANYNJ resolved the threat to its primary self-identity as a top tier transport organisation by reluctantly embracing a subordinate part of its self-identity. It increasingly became a social welfare organisation. The subsequent actions alleviated the anxiety around the principal self-identity, which both the organisation's grassroots and ivory tower had increasingly felt for some time. In effect, PANYNJ protected its self-identity as a top tier transport organisation by embracing its self-identity as an organisation which cared for its community, and thus by playing out a role which it didn't really want.

Disneyland

In Anaheim it's Disneyland; in Orlando it's the Magic Kingdom Park; near Paris it's Disneyland Park; while in Tokyo and Hong Kong it's Tokyo Disneyland and Hong Kong Disneyland, respectively. Whatever its name, Walt Disney's anchor theme park with the castle in the middle is now the Walt Disney Company's spiritual temple.[41] Opened in 1955, the smart investment bankers could neither intellectually comprehend it nor did they subsequently fund it.[42] Yet in its first seven weeks, more than a million guests strolled through the gates as a precursor to Disneyland becoming the most successful theme park business ever...by a long shot.[43] Disneyland is a terrific example of self-identity's pervasive impact across all three steps of an organisation's strategic process, in making sense of the world as-is, in feeding a vision for the future and in influencing the steps to get to that vision.

In 2012, 126 million people visited Disneyland theme parks, being an astonishing 61 percent of the attendance at the world's top twenty-five theme parks. This included 18 million visitors at the Magic Kingdom alone, the world's most visited theme park, 16 million at Disneyland, 11 million at Disneyland Park, 15 million at Tokyo

Disneyland and 7 million at Hong Kong Disneyland.[44] So popular are specifically these parks and so emotionally invested are its visitors, that Disneyland gets *daily* requests from executors of last wills who have been asked to scatter the ashes of their client testators in the park, in the shadows of the castles, one of the world's most photographed structures.[45] The parks do have subtle variations. Cinderella's castle in Orlando is fifty metres taller than Sleeping Beauty's in Anaheim. I suspect that must vex Beauty since hers was Walt's first major animation movie, rewrote the rules of animation and was also much more commercially successful than Cinderella's. That said, I will refer to all of these parks as "Disneyland", only for simplicity.[iii]

As any organisation, the Walt Disney Company, including its theme park division, has many self-identities. Its self-identity as a business tends to be underfocused in the academic literature. It is, however, drummed in across the Walt Disney Company's offices, starting from the training programmes for the youngest trainees, "Disney is a business. As a business we are accountable to our stockholders to produce a profit."[46] If management were to ignore this self-identity, their financial results could easily lead to shareholder disappointment and ultimately the removal of that very same management. This identity, as a business that must generate profits for shareholders, was one that Walt's elder brother and the company's first CEO, Roy, embraced more willingly than did Walt.[47]

At the park's inception, while sceptics got the theme park's self-identity as a business, they never got their heads around an equally important part of the theme park's self-identity. Consultants and bankers doubted Disneyland's viability because they identified it only

---

iii   Interestingly, Sleeping Beauty's Castle started conceptually as The Medieval Castle, before becoming Fantasyland Castle and then the Robin Hood Castle. Walt even once labelled it as Snow White's Castle. By launch day, it had settled to what we now know it as—Sleeping Beauty's Castle.

as an amusement park:

> Why would Walt go way out there in the middle of nowhere and
> fool around with an amusement park when such parks were dying
> all over the country?[48]

They never understood Disneyland's other main self-identity,
which emanated in large part from Walt's own self-identity: "My
business is making people, especially children, happy."[49] It was this
core self-identity, as a happiness provider, which brought clarity to
Walt's understanding of the world, one which he felt was short of the
good things in life. It was also this self-identity which he introduced to
Disneyland and which charted the vision for his organisation.[50] This
self-identity, which Walt breathed deep into the organisation, ensured
that his was never just an amusement park. Disneyland's self-identity
has never, in fact, been that of an amusement park, a point that Walt
repeatedly hit home.[51] Disneyland knew its product was very different
from anything out there in the market: "We're selling happiness."[52] It's
a very unusual product to sell, if you think about it.

It was in playing out this self-identity, with the passion and detail
that Walt brought to bear, that made Disneyland one of the world's
greatest providers of happiness. So drilled has Disneyland become
at this that today it "produces, packages and sells experiences and
memories as commodities."[53] Its core self-identity is in evidence today
in the many references to happiness on the Disney World website and
as explained to me by a Disney Parks senior manager:

> We're in the business of memory making, we want to provide happy
> moments . . . a lot of effort at our end has gone into that, in trying to
> understand what that means and what creates that.

While the emphasis of Disneyland's self-identity has oscillated
between provider of happiness and of happy memories, the self-
identity has been remarkably locked between the two poles. In any

case I think the two go hand in hand.

Walt's world, coming from his self-identity, was sensitised to the things that took happiness away. For him, this meant non-white immigration into America, congested and dirty urbanisation, polluting traffic jams, depersonalising systems and artistic chaos. These themes, albeit presented sometimes slightly differently, are all associated with late modernity.[54] Walt resented the daily robotic grind, the graffiti in uncontrolled urban sprawls, the threat to the orthodox family and the malls that were destroying Main Streets. This was Disneyland's strategic starting point, this was the world as-is which the organisation saw. That, of course, didn't stop his company from later taking large retail spaces in those very malls from which it then sold a lot of "Made in China" plastic.

Given this understanding of the world as it was, it's no coincidence that Walt and Disneyland were associated with the Republican political party, which has a more traditional and simplistic worldview of reality in comparison to the Democratic Party's heterogeneous shades of grey. Walt was a Republican and part of the shameful anti-"communist" hysteria in the 1950s despite his own father's socialist leanings. It was no surprise that a litany of leading Republicans aligned with Disneyland, including Ronald Reagan, who presented on television the inauguration of Disneyland, and Richard Nixon, who began his presidential campaign there in 1968. It's an odd place to start that kind of campaign. Mind you, Nixon was an odd person. As it happens, he also inaugurated the Disneyland monorail in 1959 and in a classic bit of *Alice in Wonderland* gave his "I am not a crook" speech at Disney World in 1973.

Disneyland emerged from Walt's self-identity as a provider of happiness. It began with a vision as a parallel microworld rebuttal to what Walt saw and didn't like. There were, of course, other motivations, including his wanting to recreate the organisational harmony of Walt Disney's film studio as it was during the production of *Snow White and the Seven Dwarves*, a sanctity which had been punctured by war and industrial unrest.[55] That point acknowledged and given its self-identity as a provider of happiness, Disneyland's vision for the future was then and remains today ambitious and esoteric, "seen through the eyes of my imagination, a place of warmth and nostalgia, of illusion and color and delight."[56] We'll ignore that they couldn't correctly spell "colour." The world that Disneyland sought to create anchored around a mythical happy place:

> To all who come to this happy place, welcome. This is your land. Here age relives fond memories of the past and youth may savor the challenge and promise of the future. Disneyland is dedicated to the ideals, dreams and the hard facts that have created America, with the hope that it will be a source of joy and inspiration to all the world. Thank you.[57]

This, you might think, is idealistic stuff, charged perhaps by the emotion of Disneyland's opening ceremonies. The problem is that Walt was saying similar things a year *before* the inauguration, while his boots were clogged with construction mud and his head sweltered in a hard hat under the California heat: "Disneyland is going to be a place where you can't get lost or tired unless you want to."[58] Disneyland's vision was a utopia, for some, which is why I referred to "utopia" with "a." I can't imagine a senior official of China's Communist Party getting excited by that vision but that's OK, because it takes all sorts to build a functioning world society. Hamas officials aren't going to get wobbly knees either, because there's no amusement ride in the park which accommodates the theme of destroying the Israeli state.

Escape from today's world, from the ills of late modernity, was always the nucleus of the plan and was stressed at Disneyland's opening: "Here you leave today and enter the world of yesterday, tomorrow and fantasy."[59] Walt stressed the same privately:

> Like Alice stepping through the Looking Glass, to step through the portals of Disneyland will be like entering another world.[60]

Disneyland continues to thrive as a partial antonym to and escape from late modernity's troubles. Michael Eisner, the company's controversial former CEO, took a leaf straight out of Walt's escapism when he described his own first visit to Disneyland:

> I stepped from the chill and gloom of an Eastern winter into the sunny glow of Main Street, a place so clean that it seemed we could eat right off the sidewalk, a place where our cares and concerns couldn't get past the gate.[61]

That said, Walt's interpretation of a happy America was pretty narrow, excluding nonwhite people, organised labour and homosexuals. Today, nonwhites, being most of mankind, unionised folk and homosexuals are no longer treated as bogeymen.[62] Maybe the Walt Disney Company will one day have a brown or black homosexual trade unionist as its lead character in a major animation production.

Disneyland's self-identity not only influences how it makes sense of its starting point and its vision for the future, but also how Disneyland will get from one to the other. In other words, its self-identity influences the strategy. And as in previous case studies, the influence of Disneyland's self-identity wasn't just in the start and end points, which the strategy had to then bridge. It was in influencing the bridge itself. What made this bridge unusual was that to be a happiness provider, sweeping visitors from modernity's mischiefs, Walt drilled into Disneyland an extraordinary attention to detail. If he was to convince guests that Disneyland was a parallel universe, the implementation had to be complete. The mind wouldn't otherwise be fooled into embracing the story. That explains why when Walt saw litter in the park, an inconsistency in the narrative, he'd pick it up.

And that's exactly what top management still does today, a practise that might well be unique to Disneyland.[63]

So embedded and faithful was Disneyland to this attention to detail that even on Walt's death in 1966, "No announcements were made. No flags were lowered to half-staff."[64] Nothing would pierce Disneyland's happiness, not even the death of its visionary founder, architect and soul, because "in the Magic Kingdom, happiness and magic were practically on tap," undiluted by sadness.[65] There simply would be no break in the strategy of transporting people from a world which Walt didn't want to a world which he did. To illustrate the contrast, when the equally enigmatic Steve Jobs died in 2011, Apple plastered his face on the main company website for two weeks, linked his obituary to their website, flew flags at half-mast and even closed some stores . . . Odd perhaps, you might think, for a public company which was answerable to thousands of profit-seeking shareholders.

Disneyland's self-identity as a provider of happiness influenced its strategy at three levels. The first was in the park's planning because unlike other parks, Disneyland was immersed in storytelling, a panacea, if you will, to modernity's deconstruction of traditional narratives. Herb Ryman's original map of Disneyland consisted of lands which resonated with and held meaning for Americans: Frontier Country (later Frontierland), True-Life Adventureland (later Adventureland), Main Street, Fantasy Land (later Fantasyland) and World of Tomorrow (later Tomorrowland).[66] At the heart of this planning was meaning, a gamble that paid off over the decades when late modernity increasingly eroded societal meaning, tradition and structure:

> In other words, narrative won out over simple physical thrills. . . . Iron parks and carnival rides alone no longer can compete in a narrative-laden entertainment world.[67]

One aspect of the Orlando park's planning which was introduced after the original Anaheim park had long been completed, reflected Walt's desire to more tightly immerse visitors than he'd been able to in California. He wanted to avoid the clutter of shabby non-Disney shops and hotels that are visible from parts of the Anaheim park. He wanted to protect the narrative. Walt also wanted to hide the park's messy operations, such as the garbage collection and transportation of supplies which were in full view of guests, and which do nothing to sustain the story.[68]

> I don't want the public to see the world they live in while they're in the Park. I want them to feel they're in another world.[69]

And from this aspiration emerged a modified and improved theme park in Orlando with enhanced planning. To reinforce the narrative and protect guests from the outside world, Disneyland developed the Berm, a wall along the path of the train that goes around the park. At some sections, the wall is as high as twenty feet. It acts as an excellent mechanism to hide the real world from the park.[70] That wasn't the only thing that Walt introduced to protect the narrative. The park in Orlando was actually *built above a ground floor* that hosts the entire park's operations.[71] Dressing rooms, cafes and garbage chutes that suck trash at an impressive 60 mph are all hidden *under* the park. The Orlando park is, in fact, built above an entire underground village![72]

Another aspect of the meticulous care that went into the park's planning and thus Disneyland's strategy was in the park's detailed design, immaculately assembled by teams of animators and architects. Disneyland's meaning and narrative were supported by its architecture. It was as if the park came straight out of an animated movie. Architecture, including street architecture, is an essential part of Disneyland's storytelling, allowing visitors the opportunity to step into the journey from today to Disneyland's envisaged future.[73] Mark

West, a children's literary scholar, who suggested that Disneyland's buildings are designed to entertain, gets only part of the picture.[74] The buildings are designed to do a lot more than that—they're there to *immerse* visitors deep into the story.

That immersion was critical to the park's planning, supported as it was by "the architecture of reassurance," an expression coined by John Hench, a Disneyland artist, to refer to Disneyland's idyllic, orderly and uniform architecture.[75] Take for instance Main Street, reclaimed from traffic and shopping malls and something of a home for visitors to Disneyland. Main Street was designed flawlessly to reassure and ensure happiness with its sense of order, community and values. Nothing is out of place in this, one of the busiest streets in the world. None of the stains associated with urban sprawl, such as cheap bars, graffiti or seedy joints, are to be found here. And it presents an ideal landing pad for all of Disneyland's visitors to experience Walt's world, in contrast to what they've just left behind.

The park's design, part of the strategy that bridges the world that Disneyland saw and its vision ahead, demonstrates an extraordinary level of sophistication and intricacy. Main Street's buildings are decorated with colours and patterns to resonate warmth. Resilient asphalt cushions the feet of pedestrian visitors while windows, low enough for children to peer inside, are clean and graced with fresh flowers. Smells of vanilla, coffee and pastries are deployed along the street as fire engines, horse-drawn streetcars (with a poop collector and sanitary cleaner close by) and horseless carriages shuttle guests up and down the 850-foot stretch.[76] The trash cans, at twenty-seven-foot intervals, look far too clean for the trash that they are supposed to collect.[77]

Even the transition from Main Street to other "lands" is tightly managed, building on Walt's observation that "You can get information about a changing environment through the soles of your feet."[78] Disneyland's Imagineers, the folk who design and develop Disneyland, later elaborated:

> A stroll from Main Street to Adventureland is a relatively short distance, but one experiences an enormous change in theme and story. For the transition to be a smooth one, there is a gradual blending of themed foliage, color, sound, music and architecture. Even the soles of your feet feel a change in the paving that explicitly tells you something new is on the horizon. Smell may also factor into a dimensional cross-dissolve. In a warm summer breeze, you may catch a whiff of sweet tropical flora and exotic spices as you enter Adventureland. Once all of these changes are experienced the cross-dissolve transition is complete.[79]

A second level at which Disneyland's self-identity as a provider of happiness influenced its strategy was in its human resources. Having uncompromisingly nailed its physical assets, it's no surprise that Disneyland also dotted the i's and crossed the t's for its human capital. Indeed, Disneyland so tightly trained its staff to provide happiness that guests continue to consistently rate its customer service as outstanding as its physical infrastructure. The cast members, the term used for Disneyland staff, are indeed repeatedly cited as a big attraction in themselves for returning guests.[80] There aren't many public attractions in the world which can boast that. That Disneyland doesn't have an organisational position akin to head of quality speaks to the organisation-wide adoption of "quality."[81]

The emphasis on delivering happiness through human capital was instilled from Disneyland's founding steps. In the first Disney University classes of 1955, students were taught that, "we create happiness."[82] You might sceptically think that was a mere slogan, something to make staff feel good, because it does sound sort of weird. It sounds like the sort of crap many big companies throw out there purely as a cheap marketing stunt. Unfortunately, such scepticism for

Disneyland is undeserved, because what's really interesting about this is that this purpose was actually translated to specific, measurable behaviours by Van France and Dick Nunis in 1955! Students thus graduated with a detailed action plan of how they would, quite literally, manufacture happiness.[83]

> To make customers feel welcome, merchants trained workers to treat them as "special people" and as "guests" . . . Salespeople were grilled everywhere in the formulas of proper decorum—to be "gracious" at all times and neat in appearance, unobtrusive but accessible, careful to "emphasise the value of the merchandise" and equipped with the right questions.[84]

The education continues to this day. All new staff are prepared with a course called Traditions, after which management expects that the new hires will emerge drinking the Disneyland Kool-Aid.[85] As part of Traditions, the human capital learns to support the physical capital in maintaining the illusion, meaning the overall narrative, as well as those narratives for specific lands. For instance, staff can only go into lands which they're themed for and they can never take guests backstage. In contrast, on my last visit to Universal Studios in Florida, I was actually invited *inside* a ticket booth to help fix the computer that wouldn't spit out my prepaid entrance ticket. While wanting to let the assistant know that not all South Asians are IT contractors from Bangalore, I remember thinking the experience was just surreal. I felt almost entitled to give her an invoice for my IT services.

The emphasis on delivering happiness through Disneyland's human capital goes some way in explaining the dominant culture amongst Disneyland's staff, as noted by a former Disneyland employee: "all the staff I'd encountered there (Disneyland Paris) had just looked so goddamn happy."[86] This is interesting because in my experience and judging by travel website reviews, Disneyland's Paris staff are the most abrasive of the Disney lot. Still, one waiter in Paris's

Disneyland Hotel explained to me that having worked in several Parisian hotels, staff tended to be much friendlier and happier at Disneyland's hotels than were hotel staff elsewhere in Paris. The point that I want to stress, though, is that the majority of literature points to a positive social environment amongst Disneyland staff.

The third and final impact of Disneyland's self-identity as a provider of happiness on its strategy is its operations. To enable the park to take its guests from the strategic starting point to the journey's end, from a place short of happiness to one that is abundant with happiness, a Herculean project if you consider what that entails, Disneyland developed and implemented an extraordinarily comprehensive and optimistic flavour to its operations. It wasn't just that the operations were efficient, which was in itself an achievement given Disneyland's size, it was that the operations were executed in a positive, cheerful manner (otherwise guests simply wouldn't believe the story). The Disney Institute even produced a book, *Be Our Guest: Perfecting the Art of Customer Service*, which illustrates that comprehensive and positive operational engine.[87] Take, for example, litter in the park today. There isn't any . . . or if there is, it doesn't stay for long.

> Disneyland is notable for what you don't see—wrappers, gum or spilled popcorn. I'm always amazed that thousands of people can walk down Disneyland's Main Street and yet it remains spotless. Custodians clean the streets at night so it's "show ready" the next morning. During the day custodians are also hard at work, constantly cleaning, sweeping and picking up.[88]

And how could there be any litter given a mere candy wrapper, empty bottle or crumpled receipt detracts from the park's self-identity as a provider of happiness? This litter-free dimension, a commitment to protecting the narrative that Walt himself began and his own wife thought couldn't be sustained in the long run, is executed with surprising cheer.[89] Guests aren't scolded or penalized for dropping litter, which is what you'd expect in any modern urban center. The litter patrol staff go about their work, simply executing their job in a manner that preserves the bliss of the daily tens of thousands of guests. It can't be easy for such staff to hold back when they do see people chuck their litter on the streets.

Similarly, there's also the distinctive "Welcome Home" greeting, beamed with a smile, to any visitor at the several Disneyland hotel-apartments that support Disneyland. Incoming guests at the Villas at the Grand Floridian or Bay Lake Tower are not only verbally greeted in a manner which is rare for its warmth, but while the adults are organising the check-in paperwork, Disneyland staff are busy sharing stickers and other small novelties with young ones, who are typically all too desperate to dive into Disneyland. Every hotel in the world has a check-in process, but Disneyland's is distinct. The influence of Disneyland's self-identity as a happiness provider is quite evident in Disneyland's execution of that otherwise well-established but mundane operational step.

One data point to Disneyland's operations that illustrates both its attention to detail and its joyful flavour was on show on our last visit to the Orlando park. One of my sons ate too much at breakfast and an hour or so later vomited while in the park (between City Hall and the Town Square, in case you're dying to know). I was flooded with multiple emotions, primarily concern for my son and his health, even though I quickly guessed that his eating for breakfast as much as he did was the root cause to his vomiting. I was also concerned in the back of my mind and a little embarrassed about the mess on the road given the large numbers of people floating around us. It was late morning in the middle of the spring break vacations so the place was pretty busy.

What stunned me, though, was Disneyland's response. Within no more than five seconds, cast member Ben from Naples had come over, put his arm around my shoulder, smiled and asked:

"Are you OK, sir?"

"Yes, though I'm not the one who . . ." I was about to complete my sentence and point to my son when I glanced at him to see that he was being attended by a paramedic. I looked for the mess, which by now had been swallowed by a small pile of sawdust and was being swept into a small dustpan. Seconds later, the site was sprayed with what I presume was a disinfectant before being scrubbed. I could only complete my sentence with a "Wow . . ." because still within a minute of the incident, another attendant with a smile as wide as a PANYNJ bridge swung by with a toy for not just my befuddled son, but his siblings too. No doubt by now, they were wishing that somebody else in the family might perform Act II. If that whirlwind wasn't enough and once the paramedic had cleared my son, we were whisked away to meet Mickey and Minnie to cheer our spirits. The photo from that meeting is now on our fridge, just to let you know.

Like I say, it wasn't just the detailed, efficient and comprehensive response that I noticed. It was also the nice, fuzzy feeling that went with it, the optimism and jollity in the staff's faces even during an unpleasant situation. Disneyland through its cast members had effected its self-identity as a provider of happiness into its operations. The staff were playing the part of and being the happiness provider. I can't think of any other theme park that I've been to, and I've been to a few, that delivered such a high standard of service while being as happy about it as do staff at Disneyland. And central to that performance is that Disneyland staff, for the most part, do their job in a way which effects their organisational self-identity as a happiness provider. Put another way, the cast members become their organisation's self-identity.

In demonstrating the strong impact of Disneyland's self-identity on all steps of the strategic process, I've praised Disneyland a bit. But this book wouldn't be *chatpatta* if I left it there. Self-identifying as a "happiness deliverer" isn't the same as delivering happiness to all, always. It's worth putting up a reminder that even if Disneyland's vision is something of a utopia, Disneyland isn't perfect. Nor is every moving atom in the park driven by delivering happiness. Given I don't want to reduce Disneyland to its main self-identity, let's puncture any illusions out there that Disneyland is a synonym for happiness deliverer. There's more to an organisation, including Disneyland, than its dominant self-identity. In any case, it'll spice things up if I bring Disneyland down to earth from its "Space Mountain."

Disneyland's opening on July 17, 1955 is a good place to start, somewhat counterintuitively not the happiest event which Disneyland has pulled off. Dubbed "Black Sunday" by Walt, some attractions stalled, Tomorrowland was half open, Fantasyland was closed altogether, while Adventureland and Frontierland were closed for part of the afternoon. Trees were being installed and the paint was literally still drying as the 33,000 guests entered. Many of them came with fake tickets, which overwhelmed the park, given it was expecting only 11,000 guests. The tarmac melted and, courtesy of the high-heeled guests who left quite an impression, took a real beating. If that wasn't enough, visitors to the jewel in Walt's crown lined up for hours just to drink a little water.[90] Nor was there enough food to go around, which is not good news for any public entertainment venue.[91] It's also a lost revenue opportunity, but let's not dwell on that aspect too much.

Even today, there's plenty to suck out the happiness from visitors and remind everybody that a dominant self-identity isn't an exclusive self-identity and doesn't dominate all actions or policies. Take the logistics, especially the commute and queues. Getting to the Magic Kingdom involves the following: drive to main car park, find parking and park, walk to and queue at tram station, take tram to monorail station, walk to and queue at monorail station, take monorail to second monorail station, walk to and queue at security, have bags checked, walk to and queue for tickets, buy tickets, queue to present tickets, present tickets . . . enter park! Once in, if guests queue in July at 1 pm for "Space Mountain," they can expect to wait a whole hour to experience the 155-second attraction, after having paid for the expensive ticket.[92] This is not happiness by any stretch of the definition.

Disneyland's own folk have also occasionally wallowed in unhappiness. Management wasn't exactly bathing in Tinkerbell's pixie dust when in 2004 a sizeable 43 percent of shareholders, including several Disney family members, refused to reelect CEO Eisner to the board. In the universe of listed corporate America, that's a pretty bloody nose to inflict on a CEO. James Stewart's exposé of the bitterness and intrigue at the Walt Disney Company under Eisner is enough material for a movie blockbuster, even if not a Disney script.[93] Meanwhile, the staff often complains that they're underpaid and stifled, with regulations extending even to their hair.[94] In fact, one study concludes, "Disney's control of its labor force is apparently near total."[95] That probably helps explain why in 1992 1,700 of Disney's Paris staff protested against working conditions without singing "Heigh-Ho" to work.

Despite these anomalies that help ricochet any reductivism of Disneyland, I still think that Disneyland's self-identity as a happiness provider has profoundly influenced all steps of its strategic process. Disneyland's senior management has seen its worlds of today through a happiness filter (which changed with shifting American values), and in doing so they've seen a world without toasted marshmallows. Disneyland's vision has too been derived from its self-identity, as an esoteric escape from today's ills. And then there's the effecting of self-identity in strategy in park planning, human resources and operations. Despite the sporadic warts, the influence of this self-identity has probably been the magic dust underlying Disneyland's position as the world's most financially lucrative theme park. That in itself should at least nudge glamorous financiers to think twice about ignoring self-identity when assessing other businesses.

The Dubai Development and Investment Authority (DDIA)

The final organisational example comes from my days in Dubai, a place with three big draws. First, tourists love it. Dubai, with less than two million residents, had almost ten million visitors in 2012. Every hairdresser who has cut my hair in the last decade seems to have "always" wanted to go there. It's an incredibly popular place given its size. A second appeal is the emirate's breakneck growth, led by its popular and entrepreneurial ruler, Sheikh Mohammed bin Rashid al Maktoum, and sustained by the wider region's shortage of quality retail, transport and more. In only a decade, Dubai went astonishingly from desert town to regional hub. Dubai's third presence on the radar comes from its societal fissures. I'm specifically referring to the cases of abused maids and unpaid construction workers, both sporadic but inexcusable. This nevertheless feeds anti-Semitic foreign sensationalist journalists who are all too keen to paint every wealthy Arab with an oppressive brush.

It was into this milieu that in 2005 I joined DDIA, a government department that conceived and developed projects to attract domestic and foreign investment. DDIA privatised in 2005 to Tatweer and became a subsidiary of Dubai Holding. That Dubai's ruler owned the state and 99.67 percent of Dubai Holding gave this privatisation an unusual spin—it didn't involve a change in ownership. For practical purposes, the privatisation didn't even change the organisation's culture or focus, which is why for simplicity I've used "DDIA" for both DDIA and Tatweer.[96] DDIA is another good example of self-identity's impact on all three steps of the strategic process, demonstrating the extent to which self-identity can affect an organisation, even one which is not Western.

One of the first things I noticed when I arrived at DDIA was just how manically the ruler's first tier stressed his "Vision for Dubai." Vision and Sheikh Mohammed were like salt and pepper. It became hard to separate the two. From there, each of the ruler's organisations, private or public, needed their own vision statement as much as a Big Mac needed beef. Countless mignons, myself included, crafted vision statements for several organisations late into our evenings. DDIA's vision statement, one that was crafted before I joined the organisation, had complications, though. The downside of vision by committee was quite evident to a new pair of discerning eyes:

> We will make Dubai the Region's economic hub of choice; through the developing and implementing of world-class policies, regulations and initiatives.

The first complication I noticed was that by the time the vision had been signed-off, Dubai had already become that "economic hub of choice." People certainly weren't using Cairo, Tehran or Riyadh as the hub. Dubai was then the region's centre, a position that it has since cemented. Another issue that I gradually learned was that DDIA had practically no interest in "policies, regulations and initiatives." The overwhelming focus of the organisation had nothing to do with policies and regulations. This related closely to the third complication, being that DDIA's self-identity wasn't that of a government entity, which is who the vision statement was for. A huge chunk of DDIA's self-identity, and part of the reason for its several successes, was really that of a private-sector entity, albeit under the veneer of a government scaffold, as one manager noted:

> We were always private sector, we behaved like one, we worked like

one, we sold land like one . . . were we government? No and deep down we never saw ourselves like that.

One thing that the ruler seemed especially good at was selecting folk to run his organisations. DDIA's director general and executive chairman was no exception, led as it was by a charismatic and principled Saeed al Muntafiq. He is probably one of the few Emirati business leaders who can lead a top global firm without the cushion of state patronage. In the context of DDIA's self-identity, Al Muntafiq observed:

> We never really saw ourselves as part of government. We were all private-sector types with private-sector instincts . . . DDIA effectively was a private-sector organisation.

As I learned quickly, the only folk who thought DDIA was part of the government were outside the office . . . and three cocooned mid-tier staff on the 24th floor of the glamorous and iconic Emirates Towers Offices. They were the government guys, the "Penfolds" from that popular but peculiar British animation production from the 1980s, *Dangermouse*, a solitary percent of DDIA's staff.[97] The remainder of the staff, energetic and ambitious, were spread across businesses, including Dubai Energy, Dubailand and Dubai Industrial City—all organisations that were broadly run as if they were from the private sector. Their staff were typically recruited from the private sector and nearly always eventually left for the private sector.

Interestingly and unlike other private-sector organisations, DDIA's own de facto self-identity didn't include an industry or role. There was no reference to energy, leisure or healthcare, or for that matter the role of developer, owner or operator. As a result, the organisation was spread across many sectors with highly divergent roles covering the full spectrum of value-addition opportunities. When McKinsey's then regional head, Kito de Boer, one of the outstanding consultants of his generation, attended a top management brainstorm session in 2007 and insightfully asked, "What kind of animal is your organisation?" the answers were not surprisingly muffled. One response was, "an explosion in the sky," which made me wonder if the respondent owned any pets and if so, how he treated them. For the record, I was mute, which is unusual because I'm normally quite vocal in meetings. I just couldn't think of an animal that fitted with DDIA!

Being a private-sector organisation was only half of DDIA's self-identity. The other half of DDIA's self-identity was as a Dubai organisation. This isn't obvious given that DDIA didn't see itself as a government agency, when it legally was. In any case, it's not unheard of for organisations to have in their names places that they no longer meaningfully identify with. One example is KFC, which doesn't self-identify with Kentucky. I suspect there's somebody out there who might even question whether KFC self-identifies with chicken given the campaign supported by Pamela Anderson, Paul McCartney and the Dalai Lama against how KFC breeds the world's most populous bird.[98] That, though, is a debate not for me to get involved in. Anyhow, unlike DDIA's private-sector self-identity, Dubai was stamped all over DDIA's forehead.

If a private-sector organisation meant profits, efficiency and results, influenced as the Gulf was by Anglo-American business philosophy, a Dubai organisation had its own meanings and narratives, all of which were instilled and pressed by the ruler. One was around superlatives and pushing boundaries. Tallest and biggest prefixed every second potential project. There was no "world's second" project. That would have made headlines for all the wrong reasons. On second thoughts, given Dubai's media is state-controlled, it wouldn't have made the headlines at all. And now that we are speculating, it might in fact have gotten the project's sponsor in a bit of trouble for diluting the meaning of Dubai.

The universe of DDIA wasn't one of regulations or policies except to promote a specific commercial project, which is exactly what you'd expect from any private-sector firm. Much of its daily canvas was occupied by revenues and with it, a cosmos of real estate developers, investors and blue-chip firms. It had meaningful relationships with banks, consultants, engineers and corporates, such as GE. Its daily challenges were private-sector ones, illustrated by the energy and late nights that the accounts team gave to resolve DDIA's cost of capital, which reflected neither the archetypal content nor culture of a typical government. That calculation incidentally wasn't a mere doddle, by the way, because the ruler effectively transferred the land to DDIA.

DDIA's Dubai self-identity also influenced how DDIA saw the world. For a start, it meant that DDIA didn't see much beyond Dubai except for the purposes of attracting talent and capital into Dubai . . . or to beat in a superlative race. Further, DDIA ignored financially profitable opportunities which it felt weren't good for Dubai. Property flipping, where off-plan properties were booked with a small deposit and then sold profitably days later, was highly lucrative in 2006, but DDIA consciously refrained from it. And finally, DDIA acutely focused on Dubai's citizens, demarcating between "local" and expat, a distinction ingrained in any indigenous Dubai organisation.[iv] In the hierarchy of UAE nationals, DDIA even subtly prioritised Dubai citizens above their compatriots, such as those from Sharjah or Al Ain.

Though DDIA's dual-sided self-identity helped DDIA make sense of the world around it, oddly enough and contradicting the grain of my wider argument, DDIA's self-identity did not translate into a vision. Indeed, the closest that DDIA got to a meaningful vision

---

iv   I recall an occasion outside of DDIA when an Emirati and a Lebanese executive returned to their Dubai organisation from their MBA ceremonies from the same school. The Emirati boss knew about both graduations and gathered the office to celebrate only the Emirati's success. Nobody objected.

was to be "world class," which is less vision and more slogan. DDIA struggled to paint a picture of what it wanted to be world class in let alone what world class looked like. In any case, firms first typically know what business they want to be or are in *before* they want to be world class in it. That's why DDIA felt as if it was a player wanting to be a champion before identifying his sport. Partly to help unlock this, DDIA drafted in McKinsey in 2007 to help set a vision and journey, but that didn't help. As with most indigenous Gulf organisations, DDIA lacked enough mid-tier strength needed to interface with the consulting world's big gorilla; and in any case, the credit crunch of 2008 pulled the funding for the entire consulting project.

It was interesting that while DDIA's self-identity clarified and helped to make sense of the world of today, it failed to clarify DDIA's vision. Why so? There's the argument that Dubai's rapid rate of change made it hard to entrench directions. Things changed so quickly in Dubai generally that DDIA struggled to think in the long term. There's another argument that DDIA focused more on the visions for each of its businesses than it did for itself. My view, though, is that DDIA failed to develop a meaningful vision because nobody dared to ground themselves in the vision space, one of the competencies that the ruler was revered for. Nobody wanted to generate a real vision because that was the ruler's prerogative. After all, he owned DDIA. Whatever the reason for not having a meaningful vision, DDIA sometimes felt rudderless, wanting to do everything, everywhere, simultaneously—and be world class at it.

Without a telling vision for itself, one that would have flowed out of its self-identity, DDIA instead did the next best thing. It strapped on the standardised, off-the-shelf, tried and tested objectives that emanated from the two pillars of its self-identity. Since it couldn't imagine the long-term in a self-expressive, soulful way from within, it just borrowed the objectives most often associated with its main self-identities. From the private sector, it objectified revenues and especially sustainable ones, as opposed to one-off land sales. DDIA also objectified developing talent, a fashionable appendage to the meaning of any private-sector firm that fancies itself. It was an adjunct that also tied nicely to Muntafiq's passion for mentorship that he pursued after his DDIA days.

From its self-identity as a Dubai organisation, DDIA objectified the enhancement and protection of Dubai's reputation, which is why landing the Universal Studios Dubai theme park in 2007 was such a big deal. DDIA never publicly advertised the project's economic benefits, because it saw them as secondary to Dubai's self-identity and reputation. The mere securing of one of the world's leading theme parks was enough of a self-evident coup for DDIA. Another Dubai-based objective was rejuvenating the Arab identity. DDIA overtly embraced the objective of pushing back against the dominant global narrative of the Arab. This was not an easy task given what Al Qaeda and, more accurately, those who it has inspired had been up to left, right and centre in that decade. It's still not an easy task now that ISIS seems intent on making Al Qaeda look like a bunch of Care Bears.

Closely related was the objective of developing Dubai's talent, as important an objective as generating revenues. It made me realise that DDIA was one of many massive training facilities for Dubai nationals. I sometimes think that this objective mattered more than any project's delivery or economics. Certainly some of DDIA's most consequential economic projects were headed up by Dubai citizens who were overwhelmingly not up to the task and who cost their shareholders quite a financial fortune. That said and to Dubai's credit, if most African and some Asian countries tried as hard to develop their most important resource, they'd probably eliminate poverty in a flash, but they don't . . . which is why so much of Africa and parts of Asia are tragically a social, political and economic dump.

This sidetracks me to the tension that runs to this day in Dubai's big firms between their private-sector and Dubai self-identities. The private-sector identity expects profits, revenues and returns. The Dubai identity prioritises Dubai's reputation, development and talent. In often promoting Dubai citizens to responsibilities which they aren't ready for, these firms frequently prioritise their Dubai identity over their private-sector one. This not only holds back private-sector performance but also contributed to the collapse of several Dubai firms during the credit crunch. If they had then adopted a clean meritocracy, I think they'd have had better management who'd have had better visibility of the crash and would have dealt with it with the benefit of greater expertise and experience.

Take for instance Emaar, one of Dubai's big property developers, which runs a human resources policy firmly tilted to Dubai citizens. Emaar hurt its investors when its share price fell from AED15.0 in 2008 to AED1.8 a year later. That's a whopping 88 percent reduction in price. Its creditors got smacked silly too. It's conjectural, but if Emaar hadn't embraced the role of delivering superlative assets and prioritising Dubai's talent, it's quite probable that its investors wouldn't have suffered so badly. Management would have better dealt with economic risks and the downturn by having the right talent and experience at key organisational tiers instead of prioritising Dubai talent. But then again, let's acknowledge the counter argument. It's equally probable that Emaar wouldn't have built the world's tallest building and Dubai's talent wouldn't have had the chance to get the experience and the training that it did.

Not only did DDIA's two main self-identities influence how it saw the world and what objectives and vision it set for itself, but those self-identities also influenced how DDIA was going to get there. Given its private-sector self-identity, the manner in which DDIA went about its work was with private-sector gusto. It wanted deals and results. It moved with an urgency which even most of its private-sector partners struggled to keep pace with. Its breakneck speed and fast decision-making complemented its performance management aspirations. Each business was judged on several KPIs, reflecting a performance intent. Meanwhile, talent from the private sector was recruited from top European businesses to develop sustainable revenues (even though the credit crunch killed many of those projects).

While it's true that staff were rarely fired (until the credit crunch), which was till recently a curious Gulf cultural nuance, DDIA's environs were still pretty high performance. Office hours energetically ran from 8 am to 5 pm (in contrast to the graveyard energy in the public sector's 7 am to 2 pm) and many staff worked regularly into the evening, for which they earned bonuses. In contrast, the three "Penfolds," who unluckily worked for a government department in massive self-denial, left like clockwork. The team's boss left at 5 pm sharp, followed by both reports at 5:02 pm. A DDIA marketing brochure to recruit foreign talent nodded to a culture which government generally hasn't got a hope in hell of offering:

> We hope that the scale and pace of our work, which may surprise some of you, will push and test your growth and development curve.[100]

That was an understatement. Muntafiq himself was aware that DDIA worked differently from the public sector:

> If DDIA had seen itself as more of a government department, it would have been less obsessive about tight timetables, wouldn't have aggressively engaged the war for top talent, [would have been] more focused on getting the teeth to craft government policy to invite FDI and had spent much more time on working with government departments.

I wasn't then surprised when after touring "other" government agencies, one West Indian government delegation was blown away by DDIA. As we finished the tour of DDIA and waited for the elevators from the 24th floor, the tour manager, a frail, elderly West Indian civil servant, asked me, "Has DDIA been outsourced to the private sector? Is that why you're different and faster than other government offices?" I was expecting her question as much as I was expecting her to break-dance to a Bob Marley remix and could only mutter some absolute nonsense about the decline of West Indian cricket. She nodded her understanding. I still don't know what was more embarrassing—my stupid response or her approval of it. It was just one of those teeth-clenching moments that I distinctly remember even if I can't explain it.

As part of the impact of DDIA's private sector self-identity, talent development was an important part of how DDIA sought to get from the world that it saw to the world that it wanted to get to. All staff were given training on stuff ranging from ethics to negotiations and managers were encouraged to mentor. There was also the High Performance Employee programme, which involved direct mentorship from Muntafiq himself, as well as the Dubai Global Internship Programme. This particular programme gave post-graduate students from some of the world's best universities an opportunity to spend two months with DDIA and its businesses. Many of these students went on to join DDIA, which spoke volumes about the culture and challenging work at the organisation.

It wasn't just DDIA's private-sector self-identity that influenced its strategy. DDIA's Dubai self-identity was equally important, with significant influence on its strategy. First, there was the celebration of the Arab identity. Some DDIA businesses had Arabic names such as Bawadi, while all business headquarters had a *majlis*, an intimate meeting room with comfy sofas, which is a better place to talk than the typical hard, confrontational Western boardroom. DDIA also supported the Young Arab Leaders, an initiative to encourage younger Arabs to aim higher. Then there were the several Dubailand theme parks that invoked Arab identity, including Freej Dubailand, an Arab version of The Simpsons; Desert Kingdom; and Islamic Culture and Science World. That none of them was built due to the credit crunch is irrelevant. DDIA's Dubai self-identity influenced DDIA's pursuit of these important Arab-resurrecting projects.

The same self-identity also influenced how Dubai citizens were prioritised. Talent sourcing, training, retaining and promotion were governed by this filter with Dubai citizens the first to be hired, last to be fired (if at all) and promoted in astounding leaps. Quite often they managed expats who were, bluntly put, much more able and qualified than they were. At least one CEO of a DDIA business struck me as suited for nothing more than a basic clerical job. To illustrate my point, he thought that the best use of a Johns Hopkins post-graduate intern with several years of work experience was to have him photocopy for two whole months. That being said, the idea that all Dubai talent was poor and all expat talent was good is complete nonsense. There were several capable and high performance Dubai citizens at DDIA who did well both there and in subsequent careers.

DDIA was not unique in favouring or biasing talent by nationality. In fact, most of the Gulf's indigenous organisations haven't a hope of abiding with the International Labour Organisation's rulings on workplace equality.[101] Most Gulf organisations favour for their citizens in ways that Western Europe and America haven't seen in decades. Now that the Gulf's organisations are expanding internationally, though seemingly less so in the litigious US, they will be scrutinised without the luxury of state patronage. It will be interesting to see how they manage themselves going forwards. They'll either have a human resources policy clash between head office and satellite; or head office will extend its human resources policies in violation of foreign equal opportunities laws. Let's see how that shapes out.

There's a desperately needed debate to be had in the Gulf on this. At one end, local Gulf citizens argue that without such partiality, which some call discrimination, their lot (especially in the UAE, where local citizens are a minority of the population) might become bystanders in their country's development, fail to develop skills for the future and lose economic control to foreigners—all of which has implications for politics and government. You don't need to be a rocket scientist to understand that. However, the counter arguments rarely get an airing in the Gulf. There are costs of partiality, discrimination, affirmative action or whatever else people call it. Some are economic, such as the impact of a diluted meritocracy and in having many people in the wrong jobs. Other costs are much deeper. Discrimination corrodes the human soul and any society that allows for it.

DDIA's Dubai self-identity also influenced DDIA's embracing of Dubai's superlative emphasis, a part of the meaning of a Dubai organisation. Staff, encouraged by Muntafiq, explored avant-garde projects and pushed boundaries with wild abandon. Few firms have, in fact, ever engaged the magnitude and range of projects that DDIA had on its roster. In 2007, not only was it rolling out several region-leading businesses but some of these were mind boggling in their ambition and magnitude, including a leisure destination which was more than *twice* the size of the entire Disney World complex in Orlando and a desert hotel-entertainment-retail strip which was *several* times the length of the Las Vegas strip. That is some very serious ambition.

Finally, the same Dubai self-identity influenced how DDIA protected Dubai's reputation. When a real estate developer in Dubailand withheld the salaries of construction workers for months, DDIA intervened by not only forcing payment but by ensuring the issue, sensitive with the foreign media, remained under wraps. In fact, DDIA's PR arm was always spinning stories to enhance Dubai's reputation whether by reminding everyone about the "Vision of Dubai" or drafting Dubai citizens into every photo op irrespective of their actual contribution. I'd often see photos in the state-controlled media of Dubai citizens being allocated credit for stuff that they simply didn't deserve, that they had practically no role in. To be honest, after a while, everybody got used to it and the mis-credits flew above everybody who was familiar with how things worked in Dubai.

In conclusion, this final example of self-identity's impact on an organisation's strategy illustrates my core argument using a non-Western organisation. The DDIA mini-case study demonstrates that self-identity's impact on strategy isn't confined to North America or Europe alone. The entire strategic process of DDIA, a Gulf organisation, including how it saw the world, what it wanted to achieve and how it would get there, was influenced by two anchor self-identities—one of which was unique to Dubai. That its two main self-identities sometimes clashed is perfectly normal. Most individuals, countries and organisations have self-identities with multiple dimensions. None of us has a single, solitary self-identity. At some stage, there is going to be a clash and a prioritisation . . . and the DDIA example was able to nicely illustrate that point.

If people and organisations pose different challenges with respect to self-identity and strategy, it's not incredibly difficult to see that countries might also have nuanced challenges. For a start, countries tend to be big. They have an average of some thirty-five million people on their terrain, a quantum that is well in excess of the world's largest employer. Just in case you are curious, in the private sector, that accolade belongs to Walmart, which employs a paltry two million people. And typically countries have way more resources, even those countries which are teetering on bankruptcy. Only a tiny, miniscule proportion of the world's businesses have anything like the resources which even small countries have. We can easily forget that the ICBCs, China Construction Banks and Agricultural Bank of Chinas, the world's biggest companies, are very, very few and far between.

My editor suggested another difference, which is that countries struggle to throw out citizens unlike businesses that can more easily fire staff. His point was that self-identity management was more challenging at the country foreign policy level than at the business level. I'm not so sure, because troublemakers who don't conform to the official national self-identities can easily be taken care of. Many countries, especially outside of Western Europe, are quite good at mysteriously liquidating people in their country. Western European countries stopped this wretched practice a few decades back. Clean, transparent countries are, though, few and far between. Even the US has its massive Gitmo black hole while Canada has practically ignored the murders of aboriginal women in the 1980s. Without further ado, let's move to the next chapter, in which I will conclude the last set of case studies by exploring the influence of self-identity on the foreign policy strategies of three countries.

[1] Y Sarason, "Identity and the Baby Bells," University of Colorado PhD thesis, Boulder, 1996

[2] L Lerpold, D Ravasi, JV Rekom and G Soenen, *Organisational Identity in Practice*, Routledge, Abindon, 2007

[3] http://en.wikipedia.org/wiki/PANYNJ

[4] JE Dutton and JM Dukerich, "Keeping an Eye on the Mirror," *Academy of Management Journal*, Briarcliff Manor, 1991

[5] *Ibid.*

[6] *Ibid.*

[7] "Anne Gorsuch Burford, 62, Dies; Reagan EPA Director," *The Washington Post*, Washington, DC, 22 July 2004

[8] "Burford Resigns as Administrator of Embattled EPA," *Toledo Blade*, Toledo, 10 March 1983

[9] *Ibid.*

[10] "Anne Gorsuch Burford, 62, Dies; Reagan EPA Director," *The Washington Post*, Washington, DC, 22 July 2004

[11] S Albert and D Whetten, "Organisational Identity" in LL Cummings and BM Staw, *Research in Organisational Behaviour*, JAI Press, Greenwich, 1985

[12] JW Doig, *Empire on the Hudson*, Columbia University Press, New York, 2001

[13] http://www.panynj.gov/about/

[14] JE Dutton and JM Dukerich, "Keeping an Eye on the Mirror," *Academy of Management Journal*, Briarcliff Manor, 1991

[15] http://www.reuters.com/article/2008/11/14/us-travel-picks-ugly-idUSTRE4AD2V720081114

[16] http://www.bea.gov/

[17] http://www.bls.gov/home.htm

[18] R Jackman, R Layard and SJ Nickell, "Combating Unemployment," Centre for Economic Performance, London School of Economics, 1996

[19] JE Dutton and JM Dukerich, "Keeping an Eye on the Mirror," *Academy of Management Journal*, Briarcliff Manor, 1991

20   *Ibid.*

21   *Ibid.*

22   *Ibid.*

23   *Ibid.*

24   *Ibid.*

25   *Ibid.*

26   *Ibid.*

27   *Ibid.*

28   *Ibid.*

29   *Ibid.*

30   *Ibid.*

31   *Ibid.*

32   *Ibid.*

33   *Ibid.*

34   *Ibid.*

35   *Ibid.*

36   *Ibid.*

37   *Ibid.*

38   J Campbell, *The Hero with a Thousand Faces*, New World Library, Novato, 2008

39   http://www.huffingtonpost.com/2012/03/14/when-it-rains-it-pours_n_1344667.html

40   JE Dutton and JM Dukerich, "Keeping an Eye on the Mirror," *Academy of Management Journal*, Briarcliff Manor, 1991

41   M Eisner quoted in B Dunlop, *Building a Dream: The Art of Disney Architecture*, Harry N Abrams, New York, 1996

42   LJ Le Mon, *The Disneyland Book of Secrets*, Amazon Digital Services, 2011

43   C Ridgeway, "Spinning Disney's World," *The Intrepid Traveller*, Branford, 2007

44   "Theme Index: The Global Attractions Attendance Report," Theme Entertainment Association, Burbank, 2012

45   LJ Le Mon, *The Disneyland Book of Secrets*, Amazon Digital Services, 2011

46   Disney World College Program cited in J Wasko, *Understanding Disney*, Polity Press, Cambridge, 2005

47   N Gabler, *Walt Disney: Triumph of the American Imagination*, Vintage Books, New York, 2007

48   C Ridgeway, "Spinning Disney's World," *The Intrepid Traveller*, Branford, 2007

49   *Ibid.*

50   Disney Institute, "Be Our Guest," Disney Editions, New York, 2001

51   C Ridgeway, "Spinning Disney's World," *The Intrepid Traveller*, Branford, 2007

52   B Thomas, *Walt Disney*, Pocket Books, New York, 1980

53   SM Fjellman, *Vinyl Leaves: Walt Disney World and America*, Basic Books, New York, 1992

54   L Mosley, *Disney's World*, First Scarborough House, Lanham, 1992

55   N Gabler, *Walt Disney: Triumph of the American Imagination*, Vintage Books, New York, 2007

56   WE Disney quoted in B Dunlop, *Building a Dream: The Art of Disney Architecture*, Harry N Abrams, New York, 1996

57   WE Disney quoted in LJ Le Mon, *The Disneyland Book of Secrets*, Amazon Digital Services, 2011

58   WE Disney quoted in B Dunlop, *Building a Dream: The Art of Disney Architecture*, Harry N Abrams, New York, 1996

59   Plaque at Disneyland, Anaheim, 17 July 1955

60   WE Disney quoted in B Dunlop, *Building a Dream: The Art of Disney Architecture*, Harry N Abrams, New York, 1996

61   M Eisner quoted in R Bright, *Disneyland: Inside Story*, Harry N Abrams, New York, 1987

[62] N Gabler, *Walt Disney: Triumph of the American Imagination*, Vintage Books, New York, 2007

[63] LJ Le Mon, *The Disneyland Book of Secrets*, Amazon Digital Services, 2011

[64] C Ridgeway, "Spinning Disney's World," *The Intrepid Traveller*, Branford, 2007

[65] CR Howard, *Mousetrapped: A Year and a Bit in Orlando, Florida*, Amazon Digital Services, 2011

[66] LJ Le Mon, *The Disneyland Book of Secrets*, Amazon Digital Services, 2011

[67] http://www.themeparkinsider.com/flume/201205/3060/

[68] RE Foglesong, *Married to the Mouse*, Yale University Press, London, 2001

[69] WE Disney quoted in http://disneyshawn.blogspot.ca/2010/07/traveling-berm.html

[70] LJ Le Mon, *The Disneyland Book of Secrets*, Amazon Digital Services, 2011

[71] Disney Institute, "Be Our Guest," Disney Editions, New York, 2001

[72] R Niles, "Stories from a Theme Park Insider," *Niles Online*, Pasadena, 2011

[73] C Scibelli, "Forget the Prozac, Give Me a Dose of Disney" in KM Jackson and MI West, *Disneyland and Culture*, McFarland and Company, London, 2011

[74] MI West, "Disney's Role in the Creation of Children's Architecture," KM Jackson and MI West, *Disneyland and Culture*, McFarland and Company, London, 2011

[75] LJ Le Mon, *The Disneyland Book of Secrets*, Amazon Digital Services, 2011

[76] K Yee, *Walt Disney World: Hidden History*, Ultimate Orlando Press, Orlando, 2011

[77] Disney Institute, "Be Our Guest," Disney Editions, New York, 2001

[78] *Ibid.*

[79] Imagineers, "Walt Disney Imagineering," New York, 1996

[80] Disney Institute, "Be Our Guest," Disney Editions, New York, 2001

[81] http://www.forbes.com/sites/carminegallo/2011/04/14/customer-service-the-disney-way

82 Disney Institute, "Be Our Guest," Disney Editions, New York, 2001

83 *Ibid.*

84 W Leach quoted in C Scibelli, "Forget the Prozac, Give Me a Dose of Disney" in KM Jackson and MI West, *Disneyland and Culture*, McFarland and Company, London, 2011

85 J Wasko, *Understanding Disney*, Polity Press, Cambridge, 2005

86 CR Howard, *Mousetrapped: A Year and a Bit in Orlando, Florida*, Amazon Digital Services, 2011

87 Disney Institute, "Be Our Guest," Disney Editions, New York, 2001

88 http://www.forbes.com/sites/carminegallo/2011/04/14/customer-service-the-disney-way

89 LJ Le Mon, *The Disneyland Book of Secrets*, Amazon Digital Services, 2011

90 L Mosley, *Disney's World*, First Scarborough House, Lanham, 1992

91 C Ridgeway, "Spinning Disney's World," *The Intrepid Traveler*, Branford, 2007

92 www.touringplans.com

93 JB Stewart, *Disney War*, Simon & Schuster, London, 2006

94 J Wasko, *Understanding Disney*, Polity Press, Cambridge, 2005

95 *Ibid.*

96 S Abdin, O Al-Madhi, W Ali, S Oknayan, and K Saiduddin, "Tatweer and the One Thing," MIT, Cambridge, 2007

97 *Dangermouse*, Cosgrove Hall Films, Manchester, 1981

98 http://www.kentuckyfriedcruelty.com

99 STS Al-Hassani, "1001 Inventions: The Enduring Legacy of Muslim Civilisations," *National Geographic*, Washington, DC, 2012

100 Dubai Global Internship Programme, Dubai Development and Investment Authority, Dubai, 2006

101 http://www.ilo.org/dyn/normlex/en/f?p=NORMLEXPUB:12100:0::NO::P12100_ILO_CODE:C111

Disneyland never saw itself as an amusement park. Its self-identity has always been as a provider of happiness.

Homelessness in the 1980s challenged the Port Authority of New York and New Jersey's self-identity.

Gulf-based businesses often embrace two self-identities, each with powerful meanings as a private-sector firm and as a Gulf organisation.

Nehru's rejection of America's self-identity was key to Truman's tilt to Pakistan.

The Israeli, British and French attack at Suez was a watershed in Britain's "great" self-identity.

Ayatollah Khomeini's view on Iran's true self-identity dramatically impacted Iranian foreign strategy.

CHAPTER 8

LET'S NOT FORGET
MY COUNTRY

There has been more work on self-identity's impact on countries in the context especially of foreign policy than on organisations, partly reflective of business academia's general intellectual mediocrity. You've got to remember business academia's close ties with the business community, a group which treats three data points as "proof," and upon which basis it then often makes billion-dollar decisions. In contrast, several disciplines that study countries and their relationships have embraced a wide breadth of learning from other subjects and with real rigour.[1] International relations academia, which isn't the same thing as the study of international politics, for example has thought across and incorporated a spectrum of academic disciplines. Anthropology, hermeneutics and law are legitimate lines of inquiry in ways which business academia simply couldn't even imagine.[2]

This intellectual curiosity has driven some to explore self-identity's impact on countries and their foreign policies. Michael Barnett, a political scientist, concluded that Israel's participation in the Oslo peace process between 1991 and 2001 came from a change in Israel's self-identity and not from any power calculations.[3] Thomas Banchoff, another political scientist, demonstrated that Germany's self-identity deeply impacted its post-Cold War policies.[4] Thomas Risse, an international relations academic, reduced to different self-identities the divergences amongst French, British and German foreign policies to EMU.[5] Another international relations academic, Peter Katzenstein, placed culture and identity at the heart of foreign policy making.[6] So unlike the landscape for businesses and organisations, there's plenty of material on self-identity's impact on foreign policy to dive into.

US Policy to Pakistan 1945–1960

My first example stems from my PhD, an ideal text for insomniacs.[7] My thesis explored how America's self-identity influenced its policy to Pakistan from 1945 to 1960. Specifically, it argued that America's self-identity impacted how it saw the world, including Pakistan, and where it wanted to go. The chief take-away from this case is that self-identity didn't just influence America's big-picture cognition of the world as-is as well as tomorrow's landscape vision, but that its self-identity influenced its strategy with respect to a specific country. That's interesting, I think. My thesis, however, gave it the full academic treatment with the sort misery-inducing language that'd infuriate the most placid vicar. So, my using this example, albeit in somewhat more readable form, is thus something of an act of redemption. Incidentally, that's a word which I oddly enough associate with Darth Vader.

As a first step, let's explore America's self-identity, because that's what influenced America's making sense of the world and its future. As I mentioned briefly in the last chapter, it quickly becomes apparent that engaging self-identity at the country level has subtleties which one does not have to deal with at the individual level. Defining American self-identity in the 1940s and 1950s isn't easy. Are we referring to all Americans or a few? What evidence do we have? Given that millions of Americans probably had conflicting interpretations of their American identity, which do we work with? Which do we neglect and why? These questions are pertinent to the study of any country's self-identity. I could easily get swallowed up in a deep dive on the methodology in understanding American self-identity or even the intensities of subscription to multiple facets of what it meant to be an American at that time.

Having studied the era in some detail, I feel confident enough, though, to assert that America's senior policymakers had a broadly common understanding of America's self-identity in the 1940s and 1950s.[8] I don't know it for sure, but it's something I am prepared to push forward. It's an impression that I have developed from a fair chunk of reading of that era. That understanding, shared across America's leaders of politics, industry, media and culture, has since diluted. The emergence of critical perspectives inspired by the Vietnam War, the strengthening of female, Latino and black voices, and the proliferation and fragmentation of mass media has challenged what was for many decades a dominant understanding of what America was. Back in the day, after World War II, America's self-identity was more stable and restrictive than it is today.

Despite this dilution, the main facets of America's self-identity from the 1940s and 1950s will still be familiar today. They include America as an anti-Socialist country of free enterprise; a Caucasian country, exemplified in slavery and segregation; an exceptional people, outside of history with a Manifest Destiny to redeem mankind. Finally, there was America as an anti-Communist country, an identity that dominated America's self-identity, perhaps acting as America's meta-identity and thus providing for America's main focus in the late twentieth century.[9] It was the latter two identities, America seeing itself as an exceptionalist country with a Manifest Destiny and America as an anti-Communist country, which I think became especially relevant to America's engaging of Pakistan. It's those that I want to focus on.

Many people claim to be exceptional. It sounds pretty stupid but there you go. The Japanese definitely claim to be through the *Hakko Ichiu*. Jews claim something similar in the '*Am Segula*. I suppose you can just as easily throw Hindus into that mix with their *Hindutva*. Lots of people like to think that they're exceptional and in an oxymoron sort of way, Americans are no different. Americans claimed exceptionalism with the early seventeenth-century colonies to establish God's creed.[i] John Winthrop compared the second and third Puritan missions to Moses's freeing of the Israelites, albeit without Charlton Heston. This comparison helps explain why the colonists named their towns Edenville, Freedom, New Hope, New Jerusalem and Paradise.[10] Exceptionalism has since ingrained itself into America's sense of self. Abraham Lincoln linked America's exceptionalism and mission with the "last, best hope of man," Woodrow Wilson with his Fourteen Points and Franklin Roosevelt with the Four Freedoms.[11] Irrespective of the window dressing, America has self-identified as an exceptional people, working on God's mission.

Writers and artists including Nathaniel Hawthorne, Walt Whitman, Ralph Waldo Emerson and Frederick Jackson Turner gave depth to exceptionalism and Manifest Destiny.[12] Herman Melville, author of *Moby Dick*, spoke for generations in proclaiming that "we Americans are the peculiar chosen people; the Israel of our time; we bear the ark of the liberties of the world."[13] Even some

---

i   It's worth noting some folk at Jamestown weren't exactly prime exceptionalist material. Jamestown's president in 1609–10 wrote that some of his community ate "dogs, cats, rice and mice." Others attacked Native Americans and "put the Children to death . . . by throwing them overboard and shooting out their brains in the water." If that wasn't enough, "One of our colony murdered his wife, ripped the child out of her womb and threw it into the river and have chopped the mother in pieces and salted her for his food."

foreigners drank the Kool-Aid. In 1835 Alexis De Tocqueville, a political sociologist, described America as "quite exceptional."[14] Before anybody gets the wrong idea, I'm not suggesting that America *is* exceptional. Many people who read this book will have serious concerns about associating the US with exceptionalism in its positive sense. I'm just suggesting that in the 1940s, Americans thought they were exceptional with a Manifest Destiny; and probably still do.

A second dimension to America's self-identity was anti-Communism, which very importantly pre-dated the Bolshevik revolution. Here I refer to America's hysteria when the Paris Commune briefly assumed Paris's government in 1871.[15] America's press was more vitriolic of the Commune than was any constituency from Europe, even though America was thousands of miles farther away from the Commune than was Western Europe. Interestingly, that fear cemented decades before Communism posed any kind of political, economic or military threat to Washington. America's fear of Communism had less to do with any Communist menace and more to do with the *meaning* of America, for it was thought that only Communism could "change our way of life so that we couldn't recognise it as American any longer."[16]

In fact, the obsession with Communism was rarely proportionate to its threat. An American threat-analysis on the eve of World War II dedicated 256 pages to Communism (despite Russia's foreign benignity) and an astonishing only eighteen on the combined threat from Nazism and fascism.[17] The paranoia about Communism continued into the early Cold War. In 1945 America owned two-thirds of the world's gold, half of its manufacturing capacity and all of its atomic bombs.[18] In contrast, Russia was totally devastated, having suffered twenty million deaths in the recent war.[19] American policymakers believed that Moscow's economic and military weakness and its resource and infrastructure deficiencies would take at least fifteen years to fix.[20] Even then, "The very existence of the Soviet Union constituted a nightmare."[21]

Anti-Communism was probably, in fact, America's meta-identity because it canvassed so much more than just Communism. Anti-Communism was also about defending a specific white, capitalist and male identity.[22] Nonwhites were painted Communist, with one sociologist describing Native Americans as the "primal communist of American history."[23] The FBI enforced that narrow "American" identity through "anti-communism" with "devastating effect upon the cause of blacks' civil rights and civil liberties," illegally surveying and infiltrating not just African-American movements but others who challenged a narrow view of American self-identity.[24] The FBI monitored, beat up and even assassinated outspoken or active homosexuals, socialists, trade unionists and feminists. Anybody who challenged the dominant identity and narrative of America was a threat.[25]

So how, then, did these two facets of American self-identity influence America's understanding of Pakistan and America's aims with respect to Pakistan? In 1945, while only a concept, Pakistan barely echoed in any of the narratives of America's self-identity. It had no place in the stories that constituted America. It had no meaning in America.[26] And thus, within the story of America, of how America saw itself, Pakistan had no role. The US couldn't make sense of Pakistan, and what it couldn't make sense of it was reluctant to work with. It's worth noting that one historian went so far as to suggest that in 1947 Harry Truman wouldn't have even been able to locate Pakistan on a map.[27] Then again, the former haberdasher and farmer was no intellectual giant, so let's not inflate the point.

Other factors also made it hard for America to make sense of Pakistan. For a start, Pakistan was created very quickly.[28] In 1945, it was a mere concept. In 1946, it became a bargaining chip. And in

February 1947, the British government announced that it would create Pakistan and India in August of that same year. That is very fast. Then there was Washington's distraction in balancing its own spending budget, generating employment and retrenching from a Europe and East Asia that were both trying to restabilise. These were regions that meant something in the story of America's past and future.[29] Had America been able to make heads or tails of Pakistan, it might have seriously looked at Pakistan. However, from 1945 to 1947 America gave scant attention to Pakistan, given it was barely featured in the stories that constituted America's self-identity.[30]

In contrast, America understood India. I say "understood," but it wasn't understanding India on India's terms. India had a role in the meaning of America, as a canvas upon which America would enact its vision to redeem mankind as part of America's Manifest Destiny. Indians themselves had no choice about this role, a point which would just a few years on create a fracture in American-Indian relations. While that painting's main landscape was China, India also featured in this westward emancipatory narrative. The unstated idea being that after America redeemed China, as civilisation moved westward, America would then gallantly go on to redeem India. Sounds like a pile of nonsense, but Americans believed it. Between 1892 and 1922, 2,085 American religious, social and educational missions sprung up in India. That is an astonishing one per week during an era when international travel was extraordinarily harder than it is today.[31] America's "understanding" of India strengthened with Gandhi, whose resistance of the British Goliath, captured poignantly in his Salt March of 1930, evoked America's past and the Boston Tea Party. It didn't matter one bit that the narrative was a far cry from *satyagraha,* which is how Gandhi viewed his protest.[32] It was thus that America encouraged India's independence and discouraged Pakistan's creation until it became a reality.

Unable to locate Pakistan in America's self-identity and pressed with priorities elsewhere, what did Washington do after Pakistan's independence in August 1947? The US lumped India and Pakistan together and practically forgot about them. The CIA's appraisal of Pakistan in 1948, as every US appraisal of Pakistan at that time, bound it to India.[33] Further, Secretary of State George Marshall instructed strict impartiality between the two given that America still couldn't make out Pakistan.[34] As for ignoring Pakistan, none of America's major plans cited Pakistan.[35] In 1947, the CIA ranked Pakistan in the lowest priority group while Washington failed to send an ambassador there for two years when Paul Alling returned sick in 1948 after a four-month stint. Even as late as 1951, the US embassies in India and Pakistan (combined population 380 million) had fewer staff than in Greece (population 8 million).[36] US officials knew:

> Secretaries of State and Defense attached no high priority to the location and exploitation of opportunities for a major American role in Pakistan.[37]

The only faint meaning that America gave to Pakistan in those early years was through anti-Communism, America's meta-identity. This meaning-making mechanism, this framework to make sense of reality, encouraged Washington to ask London to proactively manage India's independence and prevent conflicts, which Washington thought Communism thrived on.[38] More specifically, America encouraged Britain, Pakistan and India to resolve their disputes, especially on Kashmir to "immunise" the region from the Commies.[39] If it wasn't for its anti-Communism, America had absolutely no business at that time with Pakistan, because America's entire early focus in Pakistan, however faint, revolved around conflict resolution to supposedly prevent the spread of the Communist disease.

Washington indeed supported every effort by the UN Commission for India and Pakistan (UNCIP, established in 1948 principally to resolve the Kashmir dispute), paid for almost two-thirds of its costs and loaned it an aircraft. London, partly but not wholly responsible for the Kashmir mess, might have shouldered more of the costs, but Britain was on its economic knees. Interestingly, despite paying UNCIP's costs, America offered not a single proposal on Kashmir in UNCIP's first two years. In other words, the American position was something like, "we need you to resolve your differences, we'll pay for most of the negotiation costs but we've got no idea on a solution and we're not getting involved."[40] That actually pretty much summed up the early American engagement of Pakistan.

Given this barge-pole approach to Pakistan, how then by 1952 did America suddenly understand and embrace Pakistan with economic and military aid? Why did it sign a mutual security programme with Pakistan? And in doing so, how was it willing to upset India, the world's biggest democracy, and the setting of America's westward journey?[41] What changed between 1949 and 1952 to enable America to make sense of and then engage Pakistan? Until 1949, America maintained its arm's-length posture with Pakistan. Three years later, it cuddled Pakistan with an aid commitment in February 1952 through the Point Four Program and by including Pakistan in the Middle East Defence Organisation (MEDO).[42] With no change in Pakistan's, America's or India's political direction, the million-dollar question is, Why did *Amreekah* hug Pakistan?[ii]

First, America's anti-Communist cognitive lens tightened, which in turn sharpened America's sense-making of the world. With Europe's Iron Wall firming, Russia tested an atomic bomb in 1949 that shocked the US. Weeks later, Communist Chairman Mao won the Chinese civil war. This was another shock to America because of China's pivotal role in America's self-identity as the landscape

---

ii   The Pakistani pronunciation of "America."

of its westward mission and Manifest Destiny.[43] America reacted hysterically, as you might expect with an existential threat, with accusations flying around of "losing" China, as if it was theirs to lose! If that wasn't enough, Communist North Korea, lunatic from the get-go, invaded South Korea in 1950 and a month later China began supporting the communist Viet Minh.[44] By late 1950, America felt its anti-Communist identity and story being severely challenged.

Second, America got fed up with Nehru rejecting the role that America had given to India. It didn't really matter that nobody in India was consulted about the role. That never crossed the minds of American policymakers who had assumed that Nehru would be only too delighted to fulfil India's supposed obligations. Decades later and in a parallel context, Henry Kissinger, Nixon's foreign policy sidekick, noted that Egypt's Anwar Sadat:

> handled four American presidents with consummate psychological skill. He treated Nixon as a great statesman, Ford as a living manifestation of good will, Carter as a missionary almost too decent for the world and Reagan as the benevolent leader of a popular revolution, subtly *appealing to each man's conception of himself* and gaining the confidence of each.[45] [Italics added]

Taking the same principle and adapting it to a different context, Nehru simply refused to reassure America's leaders of their conception of America. He refused to recognise America in the way that American policymakers needed him to. He refused to support America's anti-Communist identity and its self-identity as mankind's redeemer with a Manifest Destiny, which in turn engendered disappointment, distress and anxiety in the US.[46] In fact, one enlightened American foreign policy official suspected that Nehru thought:

> the US was an overgrown, blundering, uncultured and somewhat crass nation and that Americans in general were ill-manned and

immature people, more interested in such toys as could be produced by modern technique and in satisfaction of their creature comforts than in endeavouring to gain an understanding of the great moral and social trends of the age.[47]

In this, our official was surprisingly insightful. Hard confirmation of Nehru's rejection of America's self-identity came in October 1949:

> Nehru's visit jolted Americans into the realization that India would resist playing the Cold War role that the United States had hoped to assign it.[48]

He warned Truman and Acheson, neither of whom he liked, of India's independence in the Cold War. Weeks later, his warning crystallised into nuts and bolts when India became the first non-Communist country to recognise Communist China and support Mao's application at the UN Security Council. Nehru then provocatively described North Korea's attack on the South as a pre-emptive strike against a US invasion, which didn't align with America's perception of attack. No, let me correct that, it didn't just not align with—it outright publicly contradicted it. On Indo-China, he turned a blind eye to China's supporting the Vietcong; while on Kashmir, he was content with the status quo without a resolution, which translated in the US as an invitation to Communism, given how Washington interpreted the causal relationship between conflict and Communism.[49]

America's intelligent international press, so often an oxymoron during times of war or international tension, slammed Nehru for failing to fulfil India's role. *The Washington Post* complained, "Never has Mr Nehru's neutralism shown such a bias, a bias in the Russian direction."[50] *The Chicago Tribune*, a fanatical supporter of South Korea's KMT, spoke of "Nehru, Battling for Stalin."[51] Mind you, it wasn't just the press that was in a tizzy. Truman, the last US president to not have got a college degree, even told his new ambassador to India, "The first thing you've got to do is to find out if Nehru is a communist, he talked just like a communist."[52] It's amazing what supposedly qualified people are capable of saying and doing.

The third change between 1949 and 1952 was that Pakistan's support of America's self-identity began to stand out. While "the Indians spat in America's eye," Pakistanis "compared with the wishy-washy neutralist Indians, were a breath of fresh air."[53] Right from the start, Karachi understood that to get badly needed American aid, it had to reassure America about its self-identity. It needed to make the US feel good about itself. And Pakistani policymakers provided that reassurance by stressing their supposedly strong anti-Communist credentials.[54] Thus began a very clever façade that Pakistan's elite worked hard to repeatedly concoct for decades to come. They may have been amongst the worst practitioners of public policy in the twentieth century, but Pakistan's politicians sure knew how to play Uncle Sam.

The pretence began early enough and came from the top. In 1947, Mohammed Ali Jinnah, Pakistan's founder, alerted American officials of Communist agents in Kalat and Gilgit.[55] There is no evidence of there being any Communist agents in Kalat and Gilgit. In that same year, Malik Feroz Khan, who later became prime minister, repeatedly portrayed Pakistan to US officials as an anti-Communist pillar.[56] On his trip to the US in 1950, Prime Minister Liaquat Ali Khan, a "Penfold" lookalike, also impressed upon his hosts Pakistan's anti-Communist credentials.[57] Unlike India, Pakistan was willing to sell a chunk of itself to get an upper hand against its rival, which is why it was no shock for US officials when they noted Karachi "went firmly down the line for the American position on all important questions."[58]

Some, especially within the fold of political realism, will argue that America changed policy to Pakistan because of a change in

Washington's interests, perceived or otherwise. Theirs will be an argument stressing calculated and rational national interest and power politics. I don't, however, buy this explanation for a shift in American policy. While I agree that between 1949 and 1952 Communist countries made significant political gains in Asia and Europe, the national interest argument itself struggles to explain why America tied up with Pakistan. In fact, that argument is really quite easy to pick apart. For a start, London repeatedly warned Washington that any American help to Pakistan would be directed against India and not against Communist Russia. Helping Pakistan was never going to help deliver on American designs to contain Moscow. Pakistan was obsessed with its neighbour:

> The two countries seemed to be more preoccupied with the threat from each other than any from outside . . . there was no guarantee that the equipment we might furnish the subcontinent would be used for the ends we desire.[59]

Six decades on, with some of that aid nicely nestled in the Swiss bank accounts of Pakistan's politicians and military leaders or, for that matter, invested in their fancy homes in London's Knightsbridge or Mayfair, the India obsession is still evident today. Pakistan's government spends about the same amount in *one day* on its army, insanely infatuated as it is with India, as it does *annually* on the entire country's education.[60] If it's not blatantly obvious, Pakistan's army cannot survive without a perceived adequate threat from India. Rawalpindi needs the Indian threat. Interestingly, Pakistan's support for Kashmiri national self-determination, which would demand a succession from India, stands in sharp contrast to Pakistan's suppression and brutal clampdown of Balochi national self-determination, which doesn't damage India at all.

Besides Pakistan's single-minded focus on its bigger neighbour, there was also Karachi's very real weakness. Its politics was, as it is today, a cow's mess. Sorry if I cut to the chase. Political failure was endemic even before kickoff. In 1945, so enamoured was Jinnah with the scruples of Sindh's senior politicians that he claimed he could *buy* all of them for a touch more than his annual income as a barrister.[61] To phrase that differently, the country's founding father knew that a good chunk of the country's political elite were simple crooks. Part of London's concern in 1946, even if it was a small part, with caving into Jinnah's demand for Pakistan was precisely the corruption of key members of any future Pakistani political hierarchy.[62] What kind of Pakistan would Britain create if that new country's leadership was so frail?

Both Jinnah and Whitehall were spot on about Pakistan's political health. It didn't take long for elements of the American foreign policy establishment to cotton on, too. The US ambassador to Pakistan, who would ordinarily advocate his assigned country to his political masters, noted in 1950, "The statement that, 'Pakistan has demonstrated a high degree of internal stability and vitality' must be accepted with certain reservations."[63] This is something which he noted before 1951, which is when Liaquat Ali Khan, a rare clean guy in Pakistan's political elite, was murdered. Scotland Yard, who were invited to investigate the crime, then complained about Karachi's lack of cooperation. The Pakistani government actually resisted investigating the assassination of its first prime minister![64] And since then, there has been no serious effort to investigate the murder.

Beyond its focus on India and political corruption, there was also Pakistan's lack of physical resources. When Pakistan was created, ministers couldn't find homes, offices lacked desks and government lacked even the most basic administrative infrastructure. In 1948, even the ambulance with the dying founder of the country inside ran out of fuel in the desperate heat. Food shortages hit Pakistan almost every year until 1952.[65] In 1948, Pakistan had only thirteen tanks, each with about fifty hours of life.[66] And what's more, US officials knew of Pakistan's weakness, which is why in 1949 America felt that in every single Indo-Pakistan war scenario, Pakistan would collapse and disappear.[67] In 1951, the American intelligence community concluded the same:

> In a long war (with India) Pakistan would almost certainly lose East Pakistan (containing 60 percent of its population) and major Punjab areas and its economic and political stability—even its very existence—would be threatened.[68]

It's stuff like this which helps explain why as late as 1956, Pakistan's prime minister Huseyn Suhrawardy asked:

> The question is asked: Why don't we (the Muslim countries) get together rather than be tied to a big Power like the UK or America? My answer is that zero plus zero plus zero plus zero is after all equal to zero.[69]

It's not often that a country's chief calls his own country a "zero." It's actually quite a damning indictment. Even if Pakistan had the best will in the world to assist the US in its fight against Communism, it lacked the most basic resources to provide any kind of support. Given that milieu, it's so much easier to forgive Faiz Ahmed Faiz, a left-wing intellectual and poet, who mourned the bankruptcy of his new country on its independence:

> This scarred, marred brightness, this bitten-by-night dawn
> The one that we awaited, surely, this is not the morn[70]

America clearly didn't partner with Pakistan for its obsession against Communism. Karachi, the political capital, and Rawalpindi, the military headquarters, had a radar which was dominated almost entirely by India. Nor did America value Pakistan's strength for use against either Moscow or Beijing. Pakistan was militarily, politically and economically not just weak. It could barely hold itself together. So why then did Washington turn to Pakistan? At the heart of Washington's hugging of Pakistan was America's *identity insecurity*. When Communism's growth and India's snubbing of America's mission to redeem mankind threatened America's narratives, Pakistan reassured America about the same narratives that explained America. Pakistani policymakers soothed Truman and his senior brass about America's sense of self: "We believe you and we believe in your story." And it was for providing this comfort, this reassurance to America's self-identity and its trajectory ahead, that Pakistan was rewarded with an emerging alliance and some much-needed partisan aid.

That is a far more convincing argument than the conventional one, which is deployed by historians, political academics and journalists, and which stresses calculated national interest. It's on that point that I will begin concluding this case study, because I've now presented and elucidated my framework. What I like about this case is that it demonstrates that not only was America's understanding of the world and its vision deeply influenced by its self-identity, but that the same cognitive framework helped America to understand and engage a specific country. And that country, Pakistan, gained meaning only within the narratives of America's self-identity. Pakistan emerged on the America radar only as Americans made sense of it through America's self-identity.

By reaffirming America to Americans just when the identity and story of America were increasingly challenged, Pakistan was able to draft its way out of obscurity and land firmly onto America's sensors. Several factors helped that process. Mao's success in China and the Korean War struck at America's anti-Communist identity. Nehru's independence made a mockery of America's westward emancipatory mission. To rescue that came Pakistan's adulation of all America. Earlier I referred to Ringmar's suggestion, albeit in the context of individuals, that friends are those who reaffirm one's self-identity. America saw Pakistan precisely as that friend, as that endorser of what it meant to be America. And that's why, and not because of some rational national interest calculation, America embraced Pakistan.

The Shah and the Ayatollah

Fred Halliday, an international relations academic, saw revolutions as important as wars in shaping world affairs.[71] Few modern revolutions were heftier than Iran's in 1979, which replaced Mohammed Reza Pahlavi, the Shah, with Ayatollah Ruhollah Mostafavi Musavi Khomeini. The two protagonists differed acutely on Iran's true self-identity. That difference mattered because they were both unqualified dictators, which is why I've taken their perspectives on Iran's self-identity as proxies for Iran's own self-identities. While identity was at the revolution's heart, let me repeat an earlier caveat: self-identity didn't control either leader's each and every subatomic action. For instance, I struggle to link the Shah's use of pimps such as Madame Claude to help import prostitutes with Iranian self-identity.[72] So let's be clear yet again that it is problematic to reduce everything to self-identity.

Mohammed Reza, who ascended to Iran's throne in 1941, held to a pre-Islamic Persian identity for Iran with two distinctions. The first invoked Persia's superiority. The Shah thought that Iranians were a superior ethnic people, the Aryans. In stressing the superiority of Iran, a name which derived from *Aryanam* (the land of the Aryans), the Shah pointed to several great Persians including Cyrus, the ruler of southwest Asia; Ibn Sina (Avicenna), the father of medicine; Jalal ad-Din Muhammad Rumi, the poet and theologian; and the Mughal emperor, Jalal-ud-Din Muhammad Akbar (Akbar the Great). There were also the Persian-influenced Abbasids of Islam's Golden Age, an era when Islam's arts, sciences and *fiqh* (jurisprudence) flourished.[73]

341

That their Persian credentials were a tad stretched is typical of national narrative constructions. And that certainly didn't get in the way of the Shah's employment of their credentials.

A second distinction to Mohammed Reza's Iran was that it wasn't Arab or Islamic. The Persians, being *Mellat e Aryan* (Aryan Nation), were close to Europeans, but in a galaxy far away from the Arabs.[74] We are still in the pre-*Star Wars* era, by the way. In fact, Arabs and Islam were always the Shah's "other."[75] Like his father had, the Shah believed Iran "had to be purged, if not of Islam's core values, at least of its Arabisms."[76] The Shah actually linked Persia's downfall precisely to Arab Islamic invasions, blaming Arab culture for Iran's prevailing mediocrity. While this might be hard for Arabs and Muslims to digest, it should hardly be a surprise. The development of the arts, science or almost any substantial positive discipline in the past five centuries has had very little input by Arabs and Muslims. Pakistan's Pervez Musharraf recently sharply made a similar point while in his role as Pakistan's chief executive:

> Today we (the Muslims) are the poorest, the most illiterate, the most backward, the most unhealthy, the most un-enlightened, the most deprived and the weakest of all the human race.[77]

In contrast, the Shah's Iran spoke to two historical empires. One was Cyrus's, and in 1971 the Shah celebrated Cyrus's capture of Babylon in 540 BC as the Iranian monarchy's 2,500th birthday. If he'd done the maths, he'd have realised that he was eleven years late. No worries; a decade or so between friends is no biggie. Cyrus had built a huge empire and pioneered both human rights and military thinking. He wasn't a party animal, which, though, didn't stop the Shah from hosting a five-day, $100 million (US) party in which 25,000 bottles of wine were served to six hundred guests.[iii] I've seen videos of the event on YouTube and, to be honest, the event looked really cheesy.[78] Anyhow, the second empire was the Safavid from 1501 to 1722, famed for its government, arts and the merging of Iran's heterogeneous ethno-linguistic groups into a single national consciousness, similar to Britain's creation of India.

It was against this Iranian identity that the Shah saw and made sense of the world, the strategic starting point for Iran. Initially, he didn't see a lot that he could be happy about. In fact, this alumnus of the Institut le Rosey saw a weak Iran immersed in regressive Islamic and Arab culture and a shadow of its true self.[79] He felt that "Iranians had slept through much of the past."[80] During the Shah's early years of rule, Iran had little influence on the world stage. If Tehran had, for instance, requested a permanent Security Council seat, which might have aligned with the Shah's take on Iran's true self-identity, diplomats of the world would surely have burst into hysterics. They may even have been tempted to send the video recording of any such request over to *Candid Camera*, which began on TV in 1949. One British diplomat in 1951 captured Iran's weakness nicely:

> It appears that Persia will remain a backward, corrupt and inefficient agricultural state from which the most can be hoped is that it shall not totally disintegrate or disappear.[81]

As often seems to happen in corrupt societies, the gap between reality and ideal was explained by victimhood and conspiracy.[82] The Muslim world is a leader in this space, partly because the gap between where Muslims are and where they think they should or deserve to

---

iii   The maths suggests each guest drank an average of 8.33 bottles of wine per day. Given the VIP rank of invitees, this seems high, unless most bottles weren't emptied? Or perhaps each bottle was an airline-sized bottle? I suppose there's a third obvious possibility that bottles served isn't the same thing as bottles drunk.

be is so vast, and partly because local corruption in the Muslim world of various types is so endemic. The Shah does deserve kudos here for his originality, because his conspiracy was *domestically* led. He felt that Iran's enemies were fundamentally in the country. This was a contrast with the foreign-led conspiracy norm in the Muslim world, which is all too blissful about blaming failure or calamity on Zionists, Americans or a combination of them. Pakistanis of course blame India's main foreign intelligence agency, the Research and Analysis Wing (RAW). If nothing else, you gotta admire the Shah's originality.

That same self-identity of Iran as a superior, non-Arab and non-Islamic Persian also influenced the Shah's vision for Iran. After prime minister Mohammed Mossadeq's ousting in 1953, the Shah proclaimed "Iran would begin anew."[83] What that initially meant was anybody's guess, even if it was an early glimmer that things might change.[iv] The young Shah initially demonstrated little by way of early leadership or authority, thrust as he unexpectedly was by foreigners to assume the role that his father once had. If he had a vision, he kept it very hush. That wasn't exactly surprising. After all, not only did the Russians and British appoint Mohammed Reza after their invasion of Iran in 1941 but also, as if to underline their superior rank, Reza's father was sent as a British prisoner to South Africa, where he died. The country that had placed the ruler of Iran on his throne also denied him access to his father.

The Shah's vision for Iran nevertheless emerged with time, as his self-identity developed and personal confidence grew. His vision was for an Iran that was strong, free of Islamic and Arab culture, modern and the Indian Ocean's political leader.[84] There was even water

---

iv   The myth that the CIA and MI6 alone removed Mossadeq still persists to this day, fuelled by Muslims and Anglo-Americans for different reasons. They both ignore that the Shah, the army and ayatollahs were keen and active partici-pants in the coup.

cooler chat about becoming the next Japan.[85] His book *Toward the Great Civilisation*—published as the curtain to his rule was coming down in 1978—envisioned an Iran without poverty, ignorance, illiteracy or corruption, where he would be the "fifth most powerful person in the world," a peculiar career aspiration.[86] Not the fourth, not the sixth, but specifically fifth. Humbly proclaiming himself *Arya Mehr* (light of the Aryans), the Shah wanted Iran to reembrace its Manifest Destiny—different, of course, from America's manifest destiny, but manifest destiny all the same.[87] Given that Iran had geography before the US had history, the Shah could claim that Iran's manifest destiny was way more authentic or original than was America's. That is, if he wanted to have that kind of debate.

Mohammed Reza's interpretation of Iran's true self-identity not only influenced Iran's strategic starting point and vision, but it also drove how Iran would engage that strategic journey. We come back to the notion of role theory where the self-identity of an individual or group influences the behaviour of those people. In accordance with this, Iran enacted a role appropriate to its manifest destiny. The Shah pursued *Tamadon-e-Bozorg* (Revival of the Great Civilisation), a programme to effect Iran's apparently true self-identity by giving to Iran a role that aligned with and played out that identity.[88] Interestingly enough, some people have compared that programme to Franklin Roosevelt's New Deal between 1933 and 1936.[89] I'm not so sure about the comparison because the Shah's programme didn't focus just on economics or economic justice. It was far more encompassing.

Tamadon-e-Bozorg began before the Shah gave it a name. Domestically, the Shah had Iran enact its true Persian self-identity by banning turbans and the veil, dumping the Islamic calendar and relinquishing education from the clergy "charlatans."[90] Smack! In fact, as icing on the antagonistic cake, he conscripted the mullahs into

Iran's secular and Israeli-friendly armed forces for two years to sober them up. Smack, smack! The cherry on the provocative top was the introduction of liquor stores in Qom, famous for the Shia institution of temporary pleasure marriages and Shia scholarship.[91] Smack, smack, SMACK!!! Though the Qur'an doesn't explicitly prohibit the drinking of alcohol, it is a huge taboo in the Muslim world. The Shah may as well have built strip clubs under mosques and forced mullahs to dye their beards a proud LGBT pink. As it happens, he didn't go that far, but he certainly was smacking vestiges of Islam and Arabia.

From one angle, His Imperial Majesty was undoing historical abuses, because despite Islam's egalitarianism, Muslim rule after Mohammed was often quite ethnically discriminatory. For instance, Umar, the second caliph, forbade Arab Muslim women from marrying Persian Muslim men.[92] Arabism defined Umar's state, which is why he was relatively disinclined to convert non-Arabs or conquer their lands.[93] Meanwhile, the Umayyads, who ruled from 661 to 750, relegated non-Arab Muslims to cattle-class status as part of *sabiqa* (the idea that early converts to Islam should be prioritised over later converts, who more often than not included non-Arabs).[94] The Umayyads even humiliatingly barred non-Arabs from leading prayers and taxed non-Arab Muslims with *jizya* (a tax supposedly for non-Muslims).[95]

Another part of Iran's strategy was to become more European by investing in archetypal Western modern themes such as industry, education, gender equality, urban development and infrastructure, including dams (which as it happens turned out to be quite useless). The Shah had some success with an annual average economic growth of 7 percent between 1954 and 1969.[96] From 1963 to 1978, GDP per capita rose astonishingly from $195 to $2,400 (though oil's share of GDP more than doubled in the 1970s). Intriguingly, that's a level it would return to in 2003. After the Shah's rule, the Iranian economy collapsed courtesy of mullah economics.[97] The White Revolution in

1963 privatised industry, enfranchised women and allowed them to run for elected office and become judges. The Revolution sharply increased the numbers of children in primary and secondary education.[98] Iran, actually a brain-gainer in 1975, was even showcased by development agencies.[99]

Within the Shah's strategy for Iran to become more European, not only did Iran's system have to be modern, but Iranians had to look the part too. Modern Western dress codes were made mandatory, with men encouraged to wear European Pahlavi hats. If you've not seen them, they look a lot like an upside down round cake tin with a small cosmetic visor attached . Actually, they also look a bit like the French kepi hats. In the 1970s, Tehran was full of women wearing miniskirts, mingling in the nightclubs and the Chattanooga restaurant. While The Black Cats, founded at Crouchini's nightclub, jived the music, Western icons danced across daily urban life. Fifty thousand Americans in cocooned, superior-than-thou compounds integrated with elite urban Iranians to sustain a wide range of American products ranging from Coke to Ford.[100]

The carrying out of Iran's non-Islamic and non-Arab identity was very evident in Iran's dealings with Israel. The Shah gave de facto recognition to Israel in 1950 by granting both an Israeli mission in Iran and landing rights to Israel's airline. The Shah's Iran also sold oil to Israel and shared with it intelligence about Arab Muslims, which really couldn't have gone down well in the region's capitals.[101] Iran formally recognised Israel in 1960, an act which pierced Muslim and Arab hearts and earned him no friends in the region. Let's not forget that Israel had humiliated Arab Muslims in 1948 with its mere creation and the subsequent war, attacked the Arab nationalist Nasser in 1956 and drove out some seven hundred thousand Palestinians from their homes. Iran's recognition wasn't trivial—it drove the entire Muslim world up the wall.

As a *chatpatta* aside, if the Shah was alive today and if I met him (big ifs, I admit, but it's good to have a healthy imagination), I'd ask him how his Great Civilisation project was compatible with the subordination of Iran's culture to the West's. Jalal Al-e Ahmad, a thinker, coined the popular term *gharbzadegi* (aping the West) precisely to critique the Shah for copying the West.[102] Sexual promiscuity and booze crashed into Iran's traditional culture, with the indigenous distinctly demoted to the Western, a hierarchy which was laced by a litany of abuses. The American School admitted only American kids into its ranks while the American Hospital then had the audacity to ban the Persian language on its premises and even ban non-Americans from entering its canteen.[103] If that subtle apartheid wasn't a wallop across the face of a host community, I don't know what is.

If the Shah's guards hadn't pummelled me for that question, I'd probably ask him another: If he was so keen to ape the West, why then was he such a control freak? Did he miss Class 1.01: Western Political Philosophy, and with it the piece about liberal democracy? I get that the Shah felt Iran had a long journey ahead to become that Great Civilisation in the Shah's own lifetime. I get the urgency. Even then, his portfolio of controls was a bit nutty. One such control came through his military's half a million soldiers, the latest American equipment including F-14, F-4 and F-5 aircraft, the world's largest hovercraft fleet and one of the world's largest helicopter fleets. By 1978, Iran had the strongest armed forces in the region. Counterintuitively, this arsenal was domestically focused, much to one US senator's shock:

> Do you know what the head of the Iranian army told one of our people? He said the army was in good shape, thanks to US aid— it was now capable of coping with the civilian population. The army isn't going to fight the Russians. It's planning to fight the Iranian people.[104]

The Americans had this thing about arming partners in the hope that they'd fight the Communists, only to realise that their partners had different ideas.

Another control came in politics. In 1957, the Shah created two political parties, the *Melliyun* (National) and the *Mardom* (People's) parties. They were known as the "Yes Party" and the "Yes, Sir, Party," the sort of thing you might see in BBC TV's brilliant comedy sketch *Yes Minister*.[105] In 1975, in a classic third-world polemic, the Shah merged both parties into the *Rastakhiz* (Resurgence) party and then forced *every single Iranian* to join and pay fees to it. This sort of stuff would have been well beyond even the wildest imaginations of the scriptwriters of *Yes Minister*. The *Rastakhiz* party lasted only three years because Iranians, especially the trading classes, simply got fed up with the nonsense, and the Shah's political capital was rapidly diminishing in the months leading to his overthrow in 1979.

Then there was the social control brutally exercised through *Sāzemān-e Ettelāāt va Amniyat-e Keshvar* (SAVAK; the National Intelligence and Security Organization). With its unchecked powers, CIA support and up to 60,000 staff (though getting accurate numbers is a real struggle, with some estimates of full-time staff coming in as low as 4,000), SAVAK rigged elections, controlled the press and tortured to death the unruly, including even its own first director.[106] I can't imagine that his replacement completely ignored his predecessor's fate as he took on his new assignment. I really hope for his sake that he wasn't expecting a pension or golden handshake at the end of his term, because if he was, he clearly wasn't thinking straight. Amnesty International noted the Shah's Iran had the:

> Highest rate of death penalties in the world, no valid system of civilian courts and a history of torture which is beyond belief. No country in the world has a worse record in human rights than Iran.[107]

No prizes for guessing if the satirical magazine *Private Eye*'s description of the Shah as "the Shit of Persia" was a typo or reflected something more meaningful.[108] Since its humble beginnings in 1961, the magazine has repeatedly entertained millions of people with its intelligent humour, and this labelling of the Shah is a great example.

In contrast to the Shah's Iran, Khomeini held a different true self-identity for Iran. Now that I've introduced him, it's worth noting that he's a perilous topic. Despite the Qur'an's impressive commitment to freedom of thought, few communities stifle thinking as do Muslims (Americans do it too, as Chomsky has demonstrated).[109] Take the founders of Islam's five jurisprudence schools, central thinkers in Islam's early development. Ja'far al Sadiq was poisoned by Caliph Al Mansoor, who also tortured Abu Hanifa and flogged Malik ibn Anas. That's three of the founders of the schools of jurisprudence. Other caliphs imprisoned Al Shafi and tortured Ahmad ibn Hanbal, the other two founders. To this day, fatwas averse to dancing to the tune of "Staying Alive" are hurtled with remarkable ease. In 1989, Salman Rushdie got slapped with a death sentence fatwa and, as if he needed it, a reminder in 2012. Conclusion? Given the Muslim world's intellectual "tolerance," be careful what you say about Khomeini!

It was Islam or one of its many, many versions which gave to Khomeini's chosen identity for Iran what the Shah's identity for Iran lacked—simplicity. Whereas the Shah convulsed with two empires, Persian superiority and the tilt to the West, Khomeini only had to say, "Iran is an Islamic country."[110] All facets of his interpretation of Iran's true self-identity stemmed from this powerful statement. In contrast, when the Shah spoke of Cyrus and the Safavids, both of which had a significant historical impact on Iran, he failed to appreciate that they never enjoyed amongst Iranians the gravitas of Islam, Mohammed or his son-in-law, Ali. The empires were pretty abstract reference points, almost historical relics for typical Iranians.

Your typical Alireza and Fatemah neither related to the empires in their everyday lives nor cared much for them.

Unlike the Shah's remote references for Iran's self-identity, Khomeini's was scorched on every Shia heart and central to his understanding of Islam and identification of Iran. In 680, Mohammed's grandson, Hussain, refused allegiance to Caliph Yazid because Yazid inherited the caliphate. That Shias simultaneously demand the hereditary succession of Muslim leadership in Mohammed's family is mystifyingly unproblematic. Anyhow, Yazid's army killed Hussain at Karbala. It's a martyrdom that Shias to this day grieve for a whole month every lunar year. Muharram is a month of very real mourning in the Shia calendar and has no equivalent in the consumerist West. Karbala, narrated with tragedy and heroism, touches Iran's depths and the soul of every Shia Muslim in a way which Cyrus and the Safavids simply don't get close to.

Khomeini's Islamic identity for Iran, imbued with Karbala, permeated how he saw Iran's strategic starting point.[111] His understanding of the world as it was, including Iran, emanated from the Islamic self-identity which he wanted for Iran. His cognitive filter of the world as-is, derived from this self-identity, split society into the *mostazafin* (oppressed) and the *mostakberin* (oppressors); the *foqara* (poor) and the *sarvatmandan* (rich); the *mellat e mostazaf* (oppressed nation) and the *hokumat e shaytan* (devil's government).[112] Khomeini saw foreign status quo powers as oppressors; these included Iraq, Saudi, Israel and the *Shaytan-e-Bozorg* (the Great Satan), being America, which led the oppression.[v] Khomeini's take on Iran's true

---

v   Muslims get very upset when any non-Muslims commit mass crimes against Muslims, but don't fret about Muslim-upon-Muslim atrocities. The largest ever genocide against Muslims (the Islamic Republic of Pakistan's army killing of between 300,000 and 1,000,000 Bengalis in nine months of 1971) and the destruction of Muslim heritage (by Wahabi Muslims in Saudi Arabia) registers practically

self-identity structured his overarching framework of the world.

When the Shah marginalised Islam, Khomeini wasn't the happiest bunny around.[113] His take on Iran's true identity was such that he gave no currency to the Shah's Great Civilisation project.[114] Given Khomeini thought Iran without Islam simply could not be, it's no surprise that he thought that under the Shah, "Iran, as a nation, thus lay dormant" and "a vast cemetery."[115] It was from this cognition that Khomeini criticised all aspects of the Shah, including his policies, seeing most government initiatives as violating Iran's true identity.[116] For example, the Family Protection Law of 1967 gave women rights to divorce, granted them custody of young children and allowed them to block husbands from marrying a second wife. Khomeini, however, thought the law was passed "to destroy the Muslim family."[117] Likewise, on the monarchy's 2,500th celebratory party, and not because he wasn't invited, Khomeini was contemptuous:

> These festivities have nothing to do with the noble people of Iran and that those who organised and participated in them have committed treason against Islam and against the people of Iran.[118]

In his *Velayat e Faqih* (Guardianship of the Jurist) lectures in 1970, Khomeini called the monarchy a non-Islamic, non-Iranian institution, adopted by the Umayyads from the Romans and Sassanids.[119] He roasted the title of the Shah (short for *Shahenshah* or King of Kings), a title he argued which should be exclusive to God, and scathingly attacked the Shah:

> "The son of Reza Khan has embarked on the destruction of Islam in Iran . . . [a plan] perhaps drawn up by spies of the Jews and the Zionists."[120]

From their "hate at first sight" meeting, Khomeini thought

---

no pushbacks from Muslims.

the Shah was nothing less than Satanic.[121] In the Shah's final days, Khomeini drew upon Karbala, that same soul of Iran's self-identity, to label the Shah's old guard as *mufsed fil arz* (corrupter on earth) or *mohareb ba khoda* (warring against God) and the Shah and his immediate posse as *madhur ud dam* (persons to be murdered).[122] Those are pretty serious accusations if you ponder them for a moment. There's not much space for negotiation, conciliation or due process. The embracing of such detestation by religious folk for other human beings never ceases to amaze me. Again, we see a self-identity, in this case Khomeini's interpretation of Iran's self-identity, influencing how a person or people see and make sense of the world.

Not only did Khomeini's identity for Iran govern his cognition of the world as-is, but it also governed his vision for Iran. Before assuming power, Khomeini did not make clear his vision for Iran. In opposition, his vision was actually hazy enough to look remarkably like the Shah's—an Iran free of hunger, illiteracy and corruption.[123] Isn't that just a wonderful coincidence that the bitter adversaries apparently wanted the same things for Iran? Generations of mankind thank Ayatollah Morteza Motahheri, a Khomeini disciple and one of the key thinkers behind the new Islamic Iran, for clarifying that vision as democracy, human rights, equality, justice and reformation.[124] I don't know if he handpicked words from a list of the most opaque, fungible, meaningless and misused political expressions in the history of mankind. If he didn't, he did a good job of saying not very much.

In initially defining Iran's vision as a world without bad, Khomeini electrified Iranians who responded hysterically to their blank-canvas messiah. Marxists, democrats and mullahs rejoiced his return.[125] The former two groups would later get hammered, but in the early part of 1979, they venerated and adored Khomeini. While millions claimed to see on the moon's surface an image of Khomeini, whose first name *Ruhollah* means "soul of God," even America's envoy to the UN speculated that Khomeini might "be hailed as a saint."[126] I bet you he later regretted that, especially after some of his diplomatic colleagues (alongside some CIA agents who we shouldn't forget about) were held hostage for 444 days. The vociferously anti-Muslim journalist Oriana Fallaci was eating from Khomeini's hands (mere expression, not to be taken literally, so hold back the death sentences fatwas):

> The most handsome old man I had ever met in my life. He resembled the "Moses" sculpted by Michelangelo . . . not a puppet like Arafat or Qaddafi or the many other dictators I met in the Islamic world. He was a sort of Pope, a sort of king—a real leader.[127]

Close advisors, such as Sadeq Qotbzadeh, would later be wrong-footed by Khomeini's undisclosed vision, as was Foucault:

> By "Islamic government" nobody in Iran means a political regime in which the clergy would have a role of supervision or control.[128]

Retrospectively it sounds lazy and stupid, but until then, "No one in Iran or in the West took the trouble of reading what Khomeini had written."[129] Few registered Khomeini's self-appointment in 1977 as Imam, meaning the spiritual and *political* authority of the Muslim world, a title which no Shia had dared claim for himself in eight centuries.[130] That in itself should have sent a signal that there was something odd about the man from Khomeyn, that this wasn't a regular Ayatollah.

Khomeini's real vision for Iran's future, the one he either kept hidden or dare not crystallise until he took and consolidated power, was to re-create Karbala, but succeed where Hussain had failed. In other words, his vision going forwards was to turn the clock back twelve centuries. I don't know if you think that stunt, which is something you might see in a Michael J Fox *Back to the Future* sequel, sounds a bit odd, but I offer no comment. I suppose you can, though guess what I think of that. I am just bursting to say that going back twelve centuries doesn't sound like progress. But I won't. Arousing the decade-earlier warnings of the late Bijan Jazani, a leading social intellectual, that if the left didn't organise itself, the mullahs would take over, Khomeini tentatively publicised his vision only after his return from exile and as he assumed control of Iran:[131]

> This will be a government based on the Sharia. Opposing this government means opposing the Sharia of Islam . . . Revolt against God's government is a revolt against God.[132]

Khomeini's self-identity for Iran, as an Islamic state imbued with the events of Karbala, influenced his vision for Iran. Two initiatives were simultaneously part of that vision and also the strategy, nodding again as I am at role theory. First, there was revolution, which wasn't only a means to a destination or a vision. Revolution from Khomeini's vantage was a reliving of Karbala and was itself a part of the vision. Martyrdom, in Hussain's tradition, fuelled the "revolutionary sacrifice to overthrow a despotic political order."[133] Becoming part of the revolution thus became incumbent on every Iranian Shia, which helps explain why on *Ashura*, the climax of the mourning of Hussain's death, in December 1978, at least a million protestors marched in Tehran, reliving Karbala's revolution. Those who died protesting were called *shaheed* (martyr).[134]

After Khomeini took control of Iran by the summer of 1979, that revolution went beyond domestic borders: "The Iranian people's revolution was the starting point for the great revolution of the Islamic world."[135] *Sudur-e Enghelab* (Export of the Revolution) was central to Iran's leading a *universal* Iranian-inspired Islamic state.[136] Khomeini created the *Vahed Nehzat Ha* (Office of Liberation Movements) to support the oppressed.[137] His emissaries travelled extensively (unluckily for them before the region's airlines introduced air miles rewards) to encourage revolutions against imperialists, contrasting Iran's humility with Western materialist arrogance. Khomeini even rewrote Islamic history, recasting Mohammed as a humble shepherd and Ali as a poor water carrier to support the message, hardly accurate and perhaps not the sort of experience needed to manage a twentieth-century government.[138]

While the Great Satan was spared, bar the detention of its 52 citizens for 444 days, direct revolutionary forces from Iran by virtue of its geographic distance, most "oppressors" were in Iran's own vicinity. It was here that Iran got busy. In 1981, Khomeini helped a revolutionary plot to overthrow Bahrain's monarchy. It failed. In 1982, he encouraged a revolution in Saudi by having a hundred thousand Iranians serenade his picture and protest against America and Israel during the *Hajj* (pilgrimage). That too failed. In 1983, while Ayatollah Hussein Ali Montazeri called the Saudis unfit custodians of Islam's holy sites, Khomeini again encouraged pilgrims to revolt. No prizes if you guess correctly, that also failed. I don't want to bring up mullah economics at this stage, partly because I've touched upon it before and partly because there's no point in reminding everybody how it continued the vein of failure.

Iran probed revolutionary opportunities in the Philippines, Malaysia, Ivory Coast, Afghanistan, Eritrea, Palestine, Morocco and Lebanon—meaning the entire breadth of the Muslim world.[139] As Khomeini's son noted, it was, however, Lebanon that in 1982 gave to Khomeini "an opportunity to tell the world about the power of the revolution, the power of the Imam."[140] Iran really did roll up its sleeves in the country that was known in the 1960s and early 1970s as the Middle East's Switzerland. In fact, it was from Iran's Revolutionary Guards that Lebanon's *Hizb-Ullah* (Party of God) eventually emerged to defend against Israel's invasion, an invasion, which it should in fairness be pointed out, was partly aimed to arrest the guerrilla warfare attacks on Israel's border.

One unintended consequence of playing out revolution was war.[141]

In 1979, Khomeini encouraged a Shia revolution in Iraq. This stunned Saddam, who'd hitherto welcomed Khomeini as a replacement for the anti-Arab Shah. Despite Saddam's continued overtures, Khomeini didn't change course. He wanted a Karbala-inspired revolution in Baghdad.[142] In 1980, Saddam got fed up and retaliated by executing the Shia cleric, Mohammed al-Sadr, expelling 35,000 Shias and invading Iran, initiating a war which cost half a million lives and US$1,200 billion. It was the costliest war *ever* fought between two third-world countries.[143] The argument that Iran was a humble victim of an unprovoked Iraqi attack is drivel. Nobody asked Khomeini to repeatedly poke a lunatic in the eye, but he did. And those pokes and the hare-brained response resulted in hundreds of thousands of Iranians and Iraqis losing their lives and many more tragically suffering from the loss of loved ones.

A second aspect of Iran's identity that was both vision and strategy was *Velayat-e-Faqih*, a mechanism that both allowed Khomeini to govern and was part of his final form of Iranian government. For centuries, Shia leaders had refrained from government on the basis that politics was for state rulers and spirituality was for the clergy. With rare exception, the clergy maintained the distinction and discouraged political activism.[144] Instead, they preferred to wait for the Hidden Imam, who's been hiding since 941 and who will return, unite political and spiritual authority and save mankind one day. Incidentally, all Shias do believe that he will reappear. It's not just a fringe superstition within the sect. *Velayat-e-Faqih* thus traditionally referred to the clergy's interventions only in low-level social welfare, a stand that Khomeini initially accepted.[145]

However, in 1970 he performed theological acrobatics to allow imams direct political rule. I doubt that this is because he grew tired of waiting for the Hidden Imam, even if waiting for somebody to come out of hiding after more than a thousand years is a stretch.

Khomeini argued that Sharia was the law of the land and those who knew the Sharia, being the clergy, should therefore rule the land (even if they were inept at managing that same land).[146] His acrobatics were so odd that they were initially ignored. Iran's mullahs thought the idea was a bit nutty. In any case, the Shia clergy general distrusted him and didn't pay much attention to anything he said. But when Khomeini returned in 1979, such was the social frenzy around him, as well as the intimidation meted out by thugs, that the clerics simply bowed to his idiosyncratic version of *Velayat-e-Faqih*, which was both Khomeini's vision and strategy.

With starting point and destination set, Iran's new self-identity influenced other key strategic national initiatives. Iran's nuanced Islamic self-identity influenced the government's behaviour and policies. It influenced its strategy or how Iran was going to achieve its vision. Television was engulfed with religious content. All female presenters had to dress in a black *niqab* (mask) and *hijab* (veil) which made them look like shadowy ninjas.[147] They were the lucky ones, because thousands of other women across Iran were laid off. Men were allowed four wives, everybody was allowed temporary pleasure marriages and the minimum marital age for females was reduced to a shocking nine—yes, that's right, a year below ten! Symbols of Pahlavi's modernisation, ranging from banks to booze stores, were destroyed, while education was returned to the clergy.[148]

Khomeini overlearned from Shia narratives. Going back in history, Ali's soldiers sometimes disobeyed him, such as by threatening mutiny at the Battle of al Nahrawan in 659.[149] Khomeini, in contrast wouldn't let Ali's history repeat itself. Khomeini crushed dissent and banned political parties.[150] He took over the judiciary, the executive and the Revolutionary Guard.[151] Restrictive press laws closed news media across the country, including even *Ayandigan*, a leading leftish, fiercely anti-Shah newspaper.[152] Hundreds of *Komiteh*, initially groups to defend against the Shah's thugs, became a religious morality police who could imprison you or just as easily pay for your wedding.[153] At least one protestor smelled the coffee, albeit rather late in the day: "We are simply going to replace one dictator with another."[154]

Similarly, Khomeini was ruthless in a way that Hussain wasn't. During the revolution, while millions of Shias across the world celebrated his ascension to power and helped by the *Fadayan-e-Islam* (Devotees of Islam), Khomeini had tens of thousands of people killed without trial.[155] He even killed many supporters of his very own first president, Abulhassan Banisadr. That Yazid's polity some thirteen centuries ago had also killed innocent people in Hussain's group, the entire basis of *Ashura*, didn't strike Iran's Shias as at all problematic. The massacres continued. SAVAK, with its notorious Evin Prison, remained fully operational but was renamed as the Ministry of Intelligence and Security. When Ayatollah Sayid Kazem Shari'atmadari urged moderation from Khomeini, his own supporters weren't given ice cream sundaes with cherries on top. They were killed en masse and indiscriminately.[156]

It was on this basis, having overcome internal dissent, that Khomeini self-effacingly claimed his was the most successful Islamic revolution *ever*, an incongruously pompous thing to say given Islam's stress on modesty and humility.[157] From his perspective, he had actualised the true self-identity of Iran as an Islamic state that would both enforce Sharia and inject the revolution of Karbala in oppressed lands. That Iranian-sponsored foreign revolutions were a failure didn't hinder the selective interpretation. He had thus achieved in his eyes that which both Ali and Hussain had failed to do. And in this actualisation of self-identity, of an Iran that was Islamic and true to Karbala, he had also protected and then rejuvenated what the Shah, a far lesser mortal, had tried unsuccessfully to destroy.

Iran's revolution elucidates self-identity's influence on a country.

The rapid change between two dictators who held strong, specific and contrasting views of Iran's true self-identity deeply influenced how Iran saw the world, its vision ahead and its strategy. The events of 1979, some of the most dramatic of the twentieth century, demonstrated that changing Iran's self-identity impacted its everyday reality, its envisioned future and the strategy to bridge the two. Iran's supposed true self-identity had a significant impact on how Iran saw things, where it wanted to get to and how it was going to get there. Neither dictator saw many nice things at the start of their country's strategic journey, but each developed a vision for the country based upon what each thought was their country's true identity. And each effected a strategy that was influenced by precisely that self-identity.

Great Britain and Suez

My final example of self-identity's influence on a country's strategy is Britain's defence of its "Great" self-identity during the Suez crisis. I must say that I found this fascinating, partly because I'm British and partly because it invoked foreign conspiracy, which ties nicely to my Muslim self-identity. The crisis is a story about what happens when a key self-identity is challenged, that of British greatness, but can't fully recover because the identity lacks credibility. To manage the damage in this particular case, the identity was subtly reinvented so that it was neither out of step with reality nor too traumatic for the national consciousness. This case study illustrates self-identity's sensitivity to being challenged. It also demonstrates self-identity's real importance given the effort and energy that Britain's political leadership and wider population expended to keep the self-identity alive, albeit with nuanced changes.

Greatness has been and remains important to British self-identity, even if in recent decades it only feels like a sort of diet great. With its origins dating at least to Elizabeth's Golden Age in the sixteenth century, British greatness preceded any formal naming of Britain as "Great" by more than a century.[158] "Great" was only formally adopted by Britain after the Anglo-Scottish political union of 1707, in the Kingdom of Great Britain.[vi] In 1801, version 2.0 was released as the United Kingdom of Great Britain and Ireland and updated by version 2.1 when most of Ireland left the union in 1922, leaving us with the United Kingdom of Great Britain and Northern Ireland. In 2014, there was very nearly a version 2.2 when the Scots came close to walking out of the United Kingdom. That, though, didn't happen, despite the herculean attempts of the great Scot Sean Connery, who was ironically entitled to as much of a vote in the referendum as was Raja the male Komodo dragon in London Zoo.

Before 1945, Britain's "Great" self-identity had solidified upon many successes. For a start, Britain had never ever been invaded, which is a stark contrast to every other European country. Furthermore, it had been a key player in the defeat of several empires, including the French, Spanish and Mughal.[vii] While building an empire, it had lost wars in America (1775–1783), Afghanistan (1838–1842) and South Africa (1880–1881), but selective amnesia had kicked such bumps to the kerb. In any case, Britain exacted revenge on the Afghans and Boers. More recently, while Europe melted in World War II, Britain stood up against Germany . . . or at least that's how British leaders sold it, and the masses lapped it up. And then there were Britain's extraordinary alumni, including Shakespeare, Dickens, Newton, Darwin, Faraday, Keynes, Hobbes and Locke. Not a bad show.

---

vi   Between 1603 and 1707, Scotland and England had the same monarch but different parliaments.

vii   The last successful invasion of the territory that is now Great Britain was in 1066. However, at that time, there was no "Great Britain." The Normans (of current day France) merely conquered Anglo-Saxon England.

Britain's "Great" self-identity has for centuries influenced its strategic process, meaning how it saw the world, its vision ahead and the pathways to get to the Promised Land. The label was not some clever early modern marketing claptrap. "Great" is integral to the way Britain has made sense of things. Sir Oliver Franks, Britain's ambassador to the US between 1948 and 1952, succinctly captured at a high level in his Reith Lectures of 1954 the importance of "Great" to Britain's self-identity:

> We assume that our future will be of a piece with our past and that we shall continue as a Great Power. What is noteworthy is the way we take this for granted. It is not a policy arrived at after reflected by a conscious decision. It is part of the habit and furniture of our minds: a principle so much at one with our outlook and character that it determines the way we act without emerging itself into clear consciousness.[159]

Britain's "Great" self-identity influenced how Britain saw and made sense of the world it was in, the world of today. This was echoed in Britain's consistent focusing on the dominant issues and powers of the respective era, from the Portuguese in the sixteenth century, to the later empires of Holland, Spain, France, Austria, Prussia, Russia and Turkey.[160] Great Britain's cognitive focus never gravitated to Iceland, Luxembourg or Norway, even if each of those three countries is geographically nearer to Britain than is either Russia or Turkey. Borrowing from an earlier analogy, large French fries never played with kid-sized French fries. Greatness demanded focusing on great issues and other great countries. And conversely it demanded ignoring or snubbing smaller countries. No point in playing with the riffraff.

That cognitive focus extended to the post-war decade. Britain's radar was tuned to the things that you'd expect from being "Great." The consensus in Britain was that it sat at the table with the US and

USSR, in a way which France, Japan and Germany didn't. Indeed, most British governments since 1945 have expected to be consulted on every major problem in the world, as they have sought to be involved in those problems.[161] In the years after the war, nobody in Britain batted an eyelid when London demanded flying rights or air bases over or in Jordan, Cyprus and Ethiopia. Nor did anybody's other eyelid blink when the armed forces in 1954 wanted a hydrogen bomb so that they could "be on terms with the United States and Russia."[162] For some countries, engaging Britain was almost like dealing with an overly intrusive grandparent.

Similarly, Britain's "Great" self-identity has influenced its vision of where it wanted or expected to go. It has regularly sought and anticipated a great role for itself, meaning at the least a lead role amongst the world's known powers.[163] Britain has consistently held a vision for itself which aligns with its being "Great." Indeed, one culmination of aiming high, fuelled by greatness, was that at one point Britain had the largest empire in history (by land area), covering an extraordinary 23 percent of the world's land mass and a fifth of the world's population. It was as big as the (not "Great") French and (not "Great") Spanish empires *combined at their respective peaks.*[164] That's quite an achievement for such a small country with very few natural resources.

At the end of World War II, Britain's "Great" self-identity was intact.[165] "Great" still had some underlying legs, which is why in 1944 William Fox, a political scientist, coined the term "superpower" to include the US, USSR and UK.[166] Fox was American, lest you're wondering, born and bred. There was some justification for his including Britain in such a glamorous group. His Majesty's Government and the US had just signed Italy's surrender to the Allies and were now also demanding Germany's surrender and at Bretton Woods they designated Sterling as one of the world's two anchor currencies.[167] No other country could claim third place with Germany, Italy, Japan and China in ruins and France having surrendered only a pitiful forty-six days into the war. I'm not quite sure what their military budget was used for but it clearly didn't do them much good.

In any case, Britain was quite unwilling to expose potential issues with its "Great" self-identity. Its greatness would not be publicly questioned. When Prime Minister Clement Attlee hinted in 1946 at a reduced British role in the Gulf, Ernest Bevin, the foreign secretary and the chief of staff, practically overpowered him by threatening to resign.[168] There would be no diminution to Britain's "Great" self-identity or role. Victory, empire and an unwillingness to reassess the comfort of a key part of Britain's self-identity had left Britain with the impression that it was, and is indeed still, great. It was thus that Bevin argued in 1947:

> Not accept the view . . . that we have ceased to be a great Power . . . We regard ourselves as one of the Powers most vital to the peace of the world and we still have our historic part to play.[169]

Even though Britain continued to self-identify as "Great," Britain's influence had declined since as early as 1871 when Bismarck founded the German empire.[170] World War II accelerated a process which was decades in the making, costing as it did an extraordinary quarter of Britain's economic wealth.[171] London's external debts grew from £476 million in 1939 to £3.3 billion in 1945.[172] Bread, potatoes and sugar were rationed after the war in a way that great powers don't do, and Britain was struggling with its responsibilities in its colonies including the jewel of its crown, the Raj. Generations of South Asians curse Britain for the bullet-speed decolonisation that left India and Pakistan with the task of resolving tensions, especially in Kashmir. Lord Halifax, ambassador to America, and Field Marshall Smuts, intimately familiar with Britain's strength, both privately doubted that Britain was a superpower in anywhere near the league of the US or even the USSR.[173]

To maintain face after its economic and military losses, Britain instead banked its greatness on its relationships. Empire, especially for the Tories, anchored and confirmed British greatness, which is partly why Anthony Eden, prime minister during the Suez crisis, treated the empire as sacred.[174] Ordinary Britons had scant interest in the colonies themselves, except for the effect that they had in reassuring Britain's "Great" self-identity.[175] Churchill, the racist, chemical warfare champion and often described as the greatest ever Englishman, was hell bent against any post-war imperial dilution.[176] It's interesting how people select their heroes or villains. The imperial crutch to support British greatness helps explain Britain's sensitivity to any "interference" with its Commonwealth:

> His Majesty's Government feels competitive toward the USA in India and does not look with favor on American cooperation with the Government of India.[177]

Furthermore, Britain's media, way less independent then than it is now, plastered over the economic and military fractures to maintain the "Great" in Britain.[178] Everything and the kitchen sink were used to reaffirm Britain's greatness, including even the loss of the Raj![179] Britain was categorically *thrown out* of India. It didn't even have the resources to organise a clean separation of India and Pakistan. However, British media broadcasts presented the immaculately dressed last Viceroy being hailed by thousands of unclean, poor Indians on their independence. BBC Radio's Robert Stimpson, who'd later eyewitness Gandhi's assassination, practically wet himself, "All I know is that I've never felt happier or prouder to be an Englishman in India."[180] That was reassuring, of course, for greatness, but a far cry from how those Indians saw things.

The great cover-up of "Great" Britain was exposed in 1956 with the most serious challenge in the twentieth century to Britain's

"Great" identity, a challenge which in turn changed Britain's self-identity and its foreign policy strategy. Egypt's president, Gamal Abdel Nasser, announced on July 26 the nationalisation of the Suez Canal, a decision so popular in Egypt that even his enemies supported it.[181] While Brits were diverted by Jim Laker's haul of nineteen wickets against Australia's cricketers, Nasser's decision soon panicked Her Majesty's subjects and government, culminating in a joint Israeli, French and British attack in October on Egypt. Suez became a profound reference point for British self-identity, "a watershed. It did infinite harm to the look of Britain."[182] While others stress Britain's defeat in Singapore in 1942 or its exit from India in 1947, I think that no event in the past century hit Britain's self-identity as hard as did Suez.

The Suez Canal Company built the canal, which brought Asia and Africa closer to Europe, in 1869 with a 99-year lease from Egypt.[viii] In 1875, Britons bought 44 percent of the shares, only for London to take political control of Egypt in 1882. In 1936, a new Anglo-Egyptian treaty gave Britain control of the canal till 1956 on the condition that London had to remove its troops from Egypt except for those at Suez.[183] There matters rested until 1951, when Nasser unilaterally repudiated the 1936 treaty to renegotiate a treaty in 1954. In this treaty, Britain agreed to leave Egypt, withdraw its troops from Suez by 1956 and transfer the canal to Egypt in 1968. In the summer of 1956, Nasser then got embroiled in superpower politics that led to America and Britain withdrawing financing for Egypt's Aswan Dam, which then inspired him to nationalise the canal.[184]

Britain's reaction to the premature nationalisation by a mere dozen years wasn't just strong; it was apocalyptic. The retort was

---

viii The full name was *Compagnie universelle du canal maritime de Suez* (The Universal Suez Ship Canal Company). Names always seem to be longer in French than in English.

totally disproportionate to the economic or military impact of Nasser's move. The good colonel challenged Britain's greatness when it was already vulnerable, given Britain's declining economic means. Not-great countries, including "wogs," which is what Britons then called Egyptians, were expected to treat "Great" countries with extreme reverence. Nasser's jab thus struck at the heart of what it meant to be British, being "Great." This in turn had Britain hyperventilating, a somewhat OTT response which was fuelled further by Eden's personal anti-Semitism (a term I use to mean against Semite people).[185] Note the seemingly prepubescent hysteria of Alan Lennox-Boyd, Colonial Secretary:

> If Nasser wins or even appears to win, we might as well as a government (and indeed as a country) go out of business.[186]

While politicians reminded each other how Nasser had used poisonous gas (just like Churchill, the greatest ever Englishmen, had desperately wanted to), Alec Douglas-Home, commonwealth secretary, wrote to the foul-mouthed Eden that "we are finished if the Middle East goes."[187] The Foreign Office's top bureaucrat, upon learning that Eden was in a political fight with a few domestic peaceniks who didn't want a military response, wrote that "PM was the only man in England who wanted the nation to survive."[188] Britain's press, so often a fair reflection of British society, chimed in. *The Daily Mail* howled that "The time for appeasement is over. We must cry 'Halt!' to Nasser as we should have cried 'Halt' to Hitler."[189] A lot of people were clearly getting very stressed by Nasser's challenging "Great" Britain.

There was, of course, more than identity at play here, so let's not overly reduce things. Let's not be one of the know-it-all reductivists. The canal was a conduit for two-thirds of Western Europe's oil needs. Fifteen thousand ships per year, including a third of all British shipping, went through it. Further, the canal enabled Britain to efficiently fulfil its role in the Manila and Baghdad Pacts, at a time when efficiency was becoming more important to British public policy.[190] That said, Britain's hysteria reflected a powerful emotional undercurrent, which mere economics and politics really don't do justice to. My take is that the heart of the stress and anxiety was Britain's "Great" identity, which was threatened because Nasser challenged it against a backdrop of British economic weakness. That Nasser did eventually help clip Britain's greatness is captured poetically by the study by Chester Cooper, a historian, in his book on the crisis, *The Lion's Last Roar*.[191]

As with any existential threat, Nasser's challenge to British identity necessitated a robust response, preferably without waffly, pie in the sky, esoteric dialogue.[192] With America opposing any British or French military action because Dwight Eisenhower wanted the West to earn the support of the Third World in the Cold War and John Foster Dulles detesting both Eden and colonisation, Britain reasserted greatness by "a totally unexpected willingness to revert to the law of the jungle."[193] Viewed as an earlier than anticipated nationalisation event of a British asset in a foreign country, Britain's military attack makes very little sense. Viewed as a threat to Britain's core self-identity and an essential piece of what it meant to be British and part of the core framework which Britain had grown accustomed to in understanding the world, the same military attack makes a lot more sense.

The French-conceived plan was for Israel to attack Sinai and then for Anglo-French troops to separate the "belligerents," and keep control of Suez. Nobody bothered to ask why a country that had just been militarily crushed in forty-six days in World War II was now lead-planning this military venture, but stranger things have happened, I am sure. Neither Eisenhower nor MI6 knew of the conspiracy.[194] At this stage of his career, James Bond was operating only in book format since his first film, *Dr No*, came out later in 1962.[195] Thus began Operation Musketeer on October 29 with an Israeli attack two days later. Thirteen hours after an ultimatum to Israel and Egypt to stop fighting, Britain and France *bombed Cairo, and not Tel Aviv,* to separate the combatants.[196] That clearly makes a lot of sense. By November 5, British forces started taking the canal's mouth, which they almost secured when combat ended on November 7.[197] The entire military campaign really didn't last very long.

Over the twentieth century, France perfected the art of fighting wars that eventually lead to national humiliation, and the disaster at Suez was no exception.[ix] Though Britain and France achieved their military objectives, being primarily the control of the canal, their conspiracy was immediately exposed. During the attack, French pilots even told journalists, including our very own James Morris (he hadn't changed gender then), that they were assisting Israeli troops and not separating two combatants. Who didn't eat their morning croissant then? Further, Israel reached its preset destination before Anglo-French forces could "separate" it from Egypt. For a while, Israelis were just hanging about waiting for the Egyptians. And then there was the speed of the Anglo-French ultimatum and its nanosecond expiry. All in all, it was a rather pathetic show and unbefitting a country that saw itself as "Great."

The consequences of the attack were significant. Almost four thousand people were killed, the canal was blocked for months and 25,000 Jews were expelled from Egypt with little more than what they could each fit in a suitcase. The impact on Britain's "Great" self-identity was momentous. Britain was condemned at home and abroad and humiliated as its economy collapsed.[198] Domestic opinion

---

ix   Putting aside minor roles in wars and with the exception of the Franco–Turkish war of 1920–21, in the twentieth century the French took a pasting in Algeria, Suez, Indochina and of course both World Wars.

rapidly slammed the war with protests in London being accompanied by desertions in the armed forces. Louis Mountbatten, the head of the navy and a cousin of Prince Philip, told the Queen that her government compatriots were "behaving like lunatics."[199] Lady Violet Bonham Carter, a liberal politician, spoke for many: "Never in my lifetime has our name stood so low in the eyes of the world. Never have we stood so ingloriously alone."[200]

Abroad, Eisenhower was furious, especially given his strong personal relationships in the British political and military spheres.[201] The UN General Assembly condemned the attack by sixty-four votes to five.[202] Lester Pearson, later Canada's prime minister, seemed to speak on behalf of many colonised and commonwealth countries: "It was like hearing a beloved uncle had been had up for rape."[203] Not only did Canada abstain from the UN vote, but it also later symbolically dropped the British Union Jack from its own flag and replaced it with a maple leaf, the emblem of French Canadians in the seventeenth century. Pakistani protestors, unable or unwilling to articulate themselves sagaciously, burned the British High Commission in Karachi to the ground. The only Commonwealth country to support Britain was Australia, whose prime minister, Robert Menzies, might have been awake but whose lights were so definitely switched off.[204] Talk about towing the motherland's party line.

The attack on British greatness was intensified by the economic meltdown which brought Britain mortifyingly to its knees. Syria sabotaged the pipeline that brought oil from Iraq and Lebanon to Britain, while Saudi banned all oil sales to Britain, resulting in oil rationing in Her Majesty's "Great" kingdom. Britain's foreign exchange reserves collapsed, falling $279 million in November or 15 percent of Britain's entire gold and dollar reserves.[205] The country's reserves of $2 billion hovered just above the post-World War II low of $1.3 billion in September 1949.[206] Even the

US Treasury was shocked by Britain's economic plummet. George Humphrey, the US Treasury secretary, however offered no support (on Eisenhower's instructions) until Britain changed policy.[207] Just so that we're all on the same page here, Britain was on the verge of financial bankruptcy in the autumn of 1956.

After Britain eventually backed down by committing to withdraw its troops that year and after it got much needed emergency US funding, at one level some people might argue that nothing had dramatically changed. Britain's economic and military assets were broadly unscathed. It continued to be a member of many key organisations, including having a permanent seat at the UN Security Council and still had an empire. And Peter May had most importantly just led the cricket team to victory over Australia in the Ashes. However, all this misses the point. "Great" countries don't get slapped silly by small ones. Nor do they get brought to their hands and knees in just a few weeks. In doing so and almost by definition, they exit from the "Great" club. They don't get to call themselves "Great." The Suez crisis examined and left wanting precisely Britain's greatness and rapidly intensified a mounting questioning of the costs of "maintaining pseudo-great power status."[208]

In just a few weeks, a core part of Britain's self-identity had been ruptured, leaving a Britain that looked like "the Cheshire Cat whose grin had outlasted its material presence."[209] Britain, in its own eyes, was no longer the "Great" that it had been before the Suez crisis. The government didn't immediately say so, taking till 1969 in the "Duncan Report on British Overseas Representation" to accept that Britain was merely a "major power of the second order."[210] Nor did people protest and petition to officially detach "Great" from "Britain." There was no dramatic expression of this national cataclysmic event. Nevertheless, things had changed, subtly yet powerfully. At the very least, there was recognition in government, British society and the world theatre that

Britain no longer sat as an equal to either of the real superpowers.

As I've touched upon before, the underlying source of that diminution wasn't new. Britain's relative decline had been proceeding for some time and was evident even in Britain's recent relationship with America. Without being too blunt about it, the US had saved Britain in World War II. Even as late as in 1945, the mop-up phase of the war, the British Cabinet knew that without continued US aid, London would be insolvent.[211] When American goodwill eroded on Roosevelt's death and Congress's getting tough with London, Britain had to borrow from America in December 1945 on humbling terms.[212] If that cold shower was insufficient, two years later, Britain actually received American *aid*.[213] In short, well before the Suez crisis, the groundwork for Britain's relative decline was well entrenched.

That the diminution wasn't new is immaterial because Britain never embraced a *diluted* "Great" self-identity, at least until the Suez crisis. It never really accepted any dwindling of itself, and selective amnesia, patriotic reporting and classic storytelling masked any cracks to its national story. Prior to the Suez crisis, Britain was "Great," and any doubters were few and to be silenced or ignored. It took the crisis to shine the light through the gap between Britain's claim to being "Great" and the underlying weakness of its economic and military machine. And once that gap had been exposed and communicated in Britain and across the world, British greatness never really recovered. This had profound implications for the world which Britain saw, its vision ahead and its means of getting there. The gap between "Great" and British weakness fundamentally changed the national strategy.

An immediate spin-off from the Suez crisis and the puncturing of British greatness was that the captain who crashed the "Great" ship had to go. Eden, who shamefully lied in his last speech to the House of Commons that "there was not foreknowledge that Israel would attack Egypt," resigned in January 1957.[214] That made his tenure of twenty-one months as British prime minister deservedly the shortest since 1743, which is when Spencer Compton died in office after being prime minister for less than seventeen months. I'm sure Tony Blair would agree with me that if you're going to blatantly lie to a legislature with respect to war, you don't deserve a Starbucks Venti Frappuccino. Having suffered publicly earlier by supporting the appeasement of Hitler, it was ironic that Eden later self-destructed by firmly standing up against any appeasement of Nasser, notwithstanding the argument made by a few revisionist historians that Eden actually didn't want to attack Egypt.[215]

However, the big long-term effect of the crisis was to Britain's self-identity, and that's what I want to focus on. Unable to recover from the damage to British greatness, rather than letting the identity die, which might have caused more social and political anxiety, Britain instead developed a quite crafty way to sustain it. "Great" continued to resonate. Wendy Webster, a social historian, saw greatness as one of three dimensions of Britain's self-identity from before World War II to well into the 1960s (the others being the "people's empire" and "little England").[216] There would be no letting up on an identity that Britain had immersed itself with for centuries, that had wrapped the national social, culture and political landscape. Britain would remain "Great" even if the bloody Oxford English Dictionary had to reinvent the word.

That indeed is almost what happened. To keep Britain's "Great" self-identity in step with political realities, Britain as both state and people reinvented the meaning of "Great." Without any noise, fuss or fluster, "Great" henceforth really meant "diet Great." The "diet" part, though, was not pronounced. It was silent. It was not introduced to official documents. There was no national debate on this. It may in any case have been too stressful. There was no official press release.

Nor was there a hue and cry in the press or through street protests.[217] Soon after Suez, there simply emerged an acceptance that Britain was "Great," even if "Great" wasn't the "Great" it once was. The post-Suez "Great" was a diet version of the pre-Suez "Great," preceding Coke's diet drink by a couple of decades, another classic British invention that was not properly marketed. Britain's "Great" identity had been clipped, but nobody in the country dare speak to it.

What did this mean? If economic and political realities were going to remain for everybody to see and Britain was going to remain at least nominally "Great," what were the implications of changing the meaning of that regular "Great" to "diet Great"? What impact did this change in the meaning of "Great" have? For a start, "diet Great" maintained the facade of greatness through sustained, unrelenting reassertion of British greatness.[218] Macmillan, speaking on television, principally to a domestic audience just weeks after Suez's humiliation, asserted:

> Britain had been great, is great and will stay great, providing that we close our ranks and get on with the job.[219]

His defence of British greatness, while Alec Guinness and Jack Hawkins heroically triumphed despite being maltreated as prisoners of war in the desperate heat of the Japanese-controlled Burmese jungle in *The Bridge on the River Kwai* in 1957, would be continued by Macmillan's successors for years. Harold Wilson harped on about the same theme in 1964 with his assertion, "We are a world power and a world influence or we are nothing."[220] In 1982, Margaret Thatcher celebrated victory over (not "Great") Argentina during the Falklands War by reaffirming, "Great Britain is Great again."[221] And again in 2012, in the glow of the successful London Olympics, David Cameron avowed the same age-old self-identity: "the world will take a message that Britain is a great country with a great future."[222] Politicians have helped ensure that "Great" has remained to Britain what fries have been to burgers.

The impact of the revised self-identity on British foreign policy strategy was deep, changing Britain's cognitive focus of where it was and where it wanted to go. Before the Suez crisis, Britain saw itself as a superpower. Being "Great" that it apparently and so evidently was, Britain was cool on Europe because that was incompatible with Britain's world power status and vision, much to America and France's irritation.[223] Britain, therefore, shunned the European Defence Community in 1950, the European Coal and Steel Community in 1952, the Treaties of Rome in 1957 and the European Economic Community (EEC) in 1958. Had Britain joined, Herbert Morrison, a former deputy prime minister, feared "the end of a thousand years of history."[224] You do sometimes wonder whether some of these politicians should think about retiring to Hollywood given their propensity to dramatize and embellish.

In contrast, after the Suez crisis, Britain's "diet Great" self-identity drifted its focus of its situation as-is as well as its vision ahead away from the superpowers towards Western Europe's second-tier not "Great" club. In fact, Britain's shift to Europe was extensively driven by the events of Suez. With British senior politicians privately questioning its "Great" self-identity (having de facto come to terms with its new "diet Great" meaning), Britain became a founding member of the European Free Trade Area in 1960.[225] Despite resistance from the Commonwealth, which rightly felt betrayed, Britain even tried to join the EEC in 1961.[226] De Gaulle, who was hosted by Britain for almost the entire war because Germany chewed and spat out France's armed forces, rejected Britain's application—hardly surprising since he was one awfully pompous and irritating politician.[227]

A final important effect of diluted greatness was in how Britain would get from where it was to where it wanted to be, meaning the strategy itself. In short, Britain's strategy was undertaken with less confidence and gusto than it had before the crisis.[228] "Diet Great" Britain, without its "national swagger," would project greatness but in the final test, not enact it.[229] When Britain sent troops to Jordan in 1958, it did so only with America's blessing, an unprecedented British acquiescence of hierarchy.[230] London had never before needed a foreign country's permission to use force. When the Rhodesian Front government from the Dark Continent unilaterally declared independence from Britain in 1965, which was a far more serious challenge than Suez's premature nationalisation, Britain led sanctions against Rhodesia but didn't use force.[231]

With Britain's "Great" self-identity having been transformed into a zero calorie version, other countries were also emboldened to engage Britain. Rhodesia's independence was one of many occasions where Britain struggled to be heard in the way it used to be. US president Lyndon Johnson practically ignored Wilson's attempts in 1965 to broker a peace deal in Vietnam and wasn't even polite about it: "Why don't you run Malaysia and let me run Vietnam?"[232] Mind you, Johnson was ordinarily a crude and sometimes obtuse human being, so his ticking Wilson off wasn't as odd as it might seem.[233] Wilson had scant more success in India and Pakistan, swaying them in 1965 to a ceasefire…that collapsed after only three months. Even Iceland, hardly a titan country, had the guts to engage three "Cod Wars" with Britain between 1958 and 1976. All that wasn't helped by the name of the wars, which really feel unbefitting of a "Great" country.

As other countries saw Britain as "Diet Great," they in turn accelerated their decolonisation. After all, why should they be subjugated to a "Diet Great" country? In the decade before Suez, four countries became independent from Britain. In the decade after, twenty-seven became independent.[234] In seeing itself really as only

"Diet Great," Britain's willingness to fight against any independence movements in its empire, as might a "Great" country, had eroded. The Colonial Office did earn some generous consulting fees from the newly independent states that needed the advice and technical skills of their former colonial masters.[235] But Her Majesty's government would have preferred relinquishing the fees if it could keep the empire. Suez's impact thus extended globally, because it sent a signal to both Britain and its colonies. And the signal that was understood that "Great" was preceded by a silent "Diet" emboldened decolonisation. Without the revised meaning of British greatness, decolonisation would probably not have generated the momentum that it so powerfully did.

Decolonisation and its impact on British greatness made it important to develop a post-colonial framework. If "Great" Britain needed an empire to get to the Promised Land, "Diet Great" Britain needed a diet empire, the Commonwealth. This helps explain why Britain's decolonisation was better managed than France's, which had no illusions about its greatness given how Germany ate it for breakfast, twice.[236] You need an extraordinarily wild national imagination to think you're a great a country if your neighbour pulverises you twice in less than three decades. Dean Acheson, a former US secretary of state, entirely missed the point with his famous quote that, "Great Britain has lost an Empire and not yet found a role."[237] Britain's role didn't depend on its empire. Britain's role depended on its self-identity. Suez punctured that self-identity well before the loss of empire. Britain lost its self-identity, and thus its role and empire.

The Commonwealth, with its London headquarters and the Queen as its Head, reassured Britain that it was still the centre of something vaguely important:

> The transformation of Empire into Commonwealth both helped to allay their (Conservatives in the UK) resentment at the process and

appeared to hold out the prospect of the retention of channels of influence which would enable Britain to retain her role as a world power more effectively.[238]

And that, my fair ladies and gentlemen, concludes the final of my nine case studies of self-identity's influence on strategy. We did it! Let's re-cap. The first case from this chapter demonstrated how America's self-identity influenced its foreign policy to Pakistan. Initially, Pakistan was meaningless within how America saw itself, except to the extent that the US made meagre sense of Pakistan through American anti-Communism. That lens tightened as the Cold War became frosty. Meanwhile, India refused to recognise, let alone play the part assigned to it within the stories of America. Washington thus turned to Pakistan. Karachi's undiluted support of America's self-identity influenced the US to ally with Pakistan. It didn't click in DC that Pakistan was militarily, economically and politically a calamity, and whatever defence resources it had would be directed at India, which would be infuriated at any American tilt to Pakistan.

The second case focused on Iran's foreign policy strategy. Using the self-identities of Iran as crystallised by two contrasting dictators as proxies of the supposedly true self-identities of the Iranian state and people, the rapid and sudden replacement of the Shah by Khomeini in early 1979 allowed us a window to explore self-identity's impact on foreign policy. The Shah's interpretation of Iran's true self-identity spoke to a superior Persian people and excluded Arab and Islamic identities. And it was this lens that influenced how he saw the world that Iran was in, his vision for Iran's future and the steps that Iran would take to get from where it was to where it had to get to. When Khomeini abruptly took power, all that changed, because he had a different interpretation of Iran's true self-identity, one that revolved around Islam, Karbala and the Shia sect. Iran's foreign policy changed by virtue of the change in self-identity, which changed Tehran's understanding of the world and what Tehran aspired to.

The final case explored the damage done to a key British self-identity, that of "Great" Britain. Nasser's nationalisation of the Suez Canal generated an intense emotional response in London because it endangered British greatness, which had for centuries been intrinsic to British self-identity. This self-identity had influenced Britain to focus on great issues and have great visions. Britain's conspiracy and its being exposed in the Suez crisis led to its greatness being internationally condemned. It also brought Britain to its economic knees. Political connoisseurs were partly right when they talked about the end of "Great" Britain. Britain would emerge, but no longer as the "Great" it once was. However, so important was "Great" to British self-identity, that the country simply engineered "Great" to a stripped-down version, akin to "Diet Great." Britain was still "Great" just as long as you knew that the "Diet" was silent. As a result, Britain's focus, vision and tone changed to align with precisely that "Diet Great" self-identity.

The three case studies demonstrate that self-identity lies at the heart of significant foreign policy transformations. In the cases, some of those foreign policy changes were stressfully forced upon countries. Other changes were more effortlessly effected. It doesn't really matter to my core argument—foreign policy strategy depends extensively on self-identity. Mind you, without sounding like a broken record, I also said the same thing about self-identity's impact on individual and organisational strategy. Strategy extensively depends on self-identity. Self-identity doesn't create strategy. Nor is self-identity a synonym for strategy. However, self-identity has a huge impact on strategy. And that sounds like a terrific diving board to plunge into the concluding chapter: Where does our journey of the relationship between self-identity and strategy take us?

1   M Hoffman, "Critical Theory and the Inter-Paradigm Debate," *Millennium Journal of International Studies*, London, 1987

2   C Brown and K Ainley, *Understanding International Relations*, Palgrave Macmillan, Basingstoke, 2010

3   M Barnett, "Culture, Strategy and Foreign Policy Change," *European Journal of International Relations*, 1999

4   T Banchoff, "German Identity and European Integration," *European Journal of International Relations*, 1999

5   T Risse, D Engelmann-Martin, HJ Knope and K Roscher, "To Euro or Not to Euro," *European Journal of International Relations*, 1999

6   PJ Katzenstein, *The Culture of National Security*, Columbia University Press, New York, 1996

7   S Qureshi, "US Foreign Policy to Pakistan, 1947–1960: Re-Constructing Strategy," London School of Economics PhD thesis, London, 2001

8   CS Fischer, *Made in America*, University of Chicago Press, Chicago, 2010

9   S Qureshi, "US Foreign Policy to Pakistan, 1947–1960: Re-Constructing Strategy," London School of Economics PhD thesis, London, 2001

10 R Hine, *Community on the Frontier*, Oklahoma University Press, Norman, 1985

11 A Lincoln quoted in T Smith, *America's Mission*, Princeton University Press, Princeton, 1995

12 R Horsman, *Race and Manifest Destiny*, Harvard University Press, Cambridge, 1981

13 H Melville quoted in RS Levine, *The Cambridge Companion to Herman Melville*, Cambridge University Press, Cambridge, 1998

14 A de Tocqueville, *Democracy in America*, Fontana Press, London, 1994

15 MJ Heale, *American Anticommunism*, Johns Hopkins University Press, Baltimore, 1990

16 "Public Papers of the Presidents: Harry S Truman," US Government Printing Office, Washington, DC, 1961

17 S Qureshi, "US Foreign Policy to Pakistan, 1947–1960: Re-Constructing

Strategy," London School of Economics PhD thesis, London, 2001

[18] P Kennedy, *The Rise and Fall of Great Powers*, Fontana Press, London, 1989

[19] RH Ferrell, *The Eisenhower Diaries*, George J McLeod Limited, Toronto, 1981

[20] MA Evangelista, "Stalin's Postwar Army Reappraised," *International Security*, 1982/83

[21] MP Leffler, *A Preponderance of Power: National Security, the Truman Administration and the Cold War*, Stanford University Press, Stanford, 1992

[22] MJ Heale, *American Anti-Communism*, Johns Hopkins University Press, Baltimore, 1990

[23] *Ibid.*

[24] M Marable, *Race, Reform and Rebellion*, Pelgrave, London, 1991

[25] T Weiner, *Enemies of the FBI*, Random House, New York, 2012

[26] S Qureshi, "US Foreign Policy to Pakistan, 1947–1960: Re-Constructing Strategy," London School of Economics PhD thesis, London, 2001

[27] MS Venkataramani, *The American Role in Pakistan 1947–58*, Radiant, New Delhi, 1982

[28] J Singh, *Jinnah: India, Partition, Independence*, Oxford University Press, New York, 2010

[29] D McCullough, *Truman*, Simon & Schuster, New York, 1993

[30] MS Venkataramani, *The American Role in Pakistan 1947–58*, Radiant, New Delhi, 1982

[31] R Horsman, *Race and Manifest Destiny*, Harvard University Press, Cambridge, 1981

[32] GR Hess, *America Encounters India 1941–1947*, Johns Hopkins University Press, Baltimore, 1971

[33] CIA, "India–Pakistan" (Report SR-21), Harry Truman Papers, 19 May 1948

[34] GC Marshall to Consulate at Madras, 16 July 1947, *Foreign Relations of the United States*, 1947, Volume 3, Washington, DC

[35] S Qureshi, "US Foreign Policy to Pakistan, 1947–1960: Re-Constructing Strategy," London School of Economics PhD thesis, London, 2001

36   C Bowles, *Ambassador's Report*, Harper and Row, New York, 1954

37   MS Venkataramani, *The American Role in Pakistan 1947–58*, Radiant, New Delhi, 1982

38   DG Acheson to GR Merrell, 11 December 1946, *Foreign Relations of the United States*, Volume 5, Washington, DC, 1946

39   RJ McMahon, *The Cold War on the Periphery*, Columbia University Press, New York, 1994

40   S Qureshi, "US Foreign Policy to Pakistan, 1947–1960: Re-Constructing Strategy," London School of Economics PhD thesis, London, 2001

41   S Nawaz, *Crossed Swords: Pakistan, Its Army and the Wars Within*, Oxford University Press, New York, 2008

42   "A Report to the NSC by the Secretaries of State and Defense and the Director of Mutual Security on Reexamination of United States Programs for National Security," 19 January 1953, *Documents of the National Security Council*, University Publications of America, Washington, DC

43   D McCullough, *Truman*, Simon & Schuster, New York, 1993

44   *Ibid.*

45   H A Kissinger, "Sadat: A Man with Passion for Peace," *Time Magazine*, New York, 19 October 1981

46   R J McMahon, *The Cold War on the Periphery*, Columbia University Press, New York, 1994

47   LW Henderson quoted in S Qureshi, "US Foreign Policy to Pakistan, 1947–1960: Re-Constructing Strategy," London School of Economics PhD thesis, London, 2001

48   RJ McMahon, *The Cold War on the Periphery*, Columbia University Press, New York, 1994

49   S Tharoor, *Nehru: A Biography*, Arcade Publishing, New York, 2011

50   *The Washington Post*, 28 August 1951, Washington, DC

51   *The Chicago Tribune*, 1 September 1951, Chicago

52   HB Schaffer, *Chester Bowles: A New Dealer in the Cold War*, Harvard University Press, Cambridge, 1993

[53] AJ Rotter, "Class, Caste and Status in Indo–US Relations," CG Appy, *Cold War Constructions* University of Massachusetts Press, Amherst, 2000

[54] S Nawaz, *Crossed Swords: Pakistan, Its Army and the Wars Within*, Oxford University Press, New York, 2008

[55] Lewis to GC Marshall, 2 September 1948, Department of State Central Files in MS Venkataramani, "The American Role in Pakistan 1947–1958, Radiant, New Delhi, 1982

[56] S Qureshi, "US Foreign Policy to Pakistan, 1947–1960: Re-Constructing Strategy," London School of Economics PhD thesis, London, 2001

[57] *Danger Mouse*, Cosgrove Hall, Manchester, 1981

[58] Memo by RL Thurston of South Asian Affairs quoted in RJ McMahon, *The Cold War on the Periphery*, Columbia University Press, New York, 1994

[59] General Scoones quoted in "Record of Informal US–UK Discussion", 18 September 1950, *Foreign Relations of the United States*, Washington, DC, 1950

[60] http://ipl.edu.pk/document/Pakistan_Army.pdf

[61] I Talbot, *Pakistan: A Modern History*, St Martin's Press, New York, 1998

[62] L Collins and D Lapierre, *Freedom at Midnight*, HarperCollins, London, 1997

[63] AM Warren to DG Acheson, 17 May 1950, *Foreign Relations of the United States*, Washington, DC, 1950

[64] S Qureshi, "US Foreign Policy to Pakistan, 1947–1960: Re-Constructing Strategy," London School of Economics PhD thesis, London, 2001

[65] V Ahmad and R Amjad, *The Management of Pakistan's Economy 1947–1982*, Oxford University Press, Karachi, 1984

[66] MA Khan, *Friends, Not Masters*, Oxford University Press, London, 1967

[67] Appendix B, Report by SANAAC, "Appraisal of US National Security Interests in South Asia," 19 April 1949, *Foreign Relations of the United States*, Washington, DC, 1949

[68] Memorandum by the Central Intelligence Agency: National Intelligence Estimate, "Probable Developments in the Kashmir Dispute to the End of 1951," NIE 41, 14 September 1951, *Foreign Relations of the United States*, Washington, DC, 1951

69 SJ Burki, *Pakistan's Foreign Policy*, Oxford University Press, London, 1973

70 T Fatah, *Chasing a Mirage*, John Wiley & Sons Canada, Mississauga, 2008

71 F Halliday, *Rethinking International Relations*, Palgrave Macmillan, London, 1994

72 GR Afkhami, *The Life and Times of the Shah*, University of California Press, Berkeley, 2008

73 T Fatah, *Chasing a Mirage*, John Wiley & Sons Canada, Mississauga, 2008

74 AA Moghaddam, *Iran in World Politics*, Hurst and Company, London, 2007

75 JB Saad quoted in AA Moghaddam, *Iran in World Politics*, Hurst and Company, London, 2007

76 GR Afkhami, *The Life and Times of the Shah*, University of California Press, Berkeley, 2008

77 http://news.bbc.co.uk/2/hi/south_asia/1824455.stm

78 http://www.youtube.com/watch?v=0kL4bJCP3gA

79 A Milani, *The Shah*, Palgrave Macmillan, New York, 2011

80 GR Afkhami, *The Life and Times of the Shah*, University of California Press, Berkeley, 2008

81 *Ibid.*

82 GE Fuller, *The Center of the Universe: The Geopolitics of Iran*, Westview Press, Boulder, 1991

83 GR Afkhami, *The Life and Times of the Shah*, University of California Press, Berkeley, 2008

84 GE Fuller, *The Center of the Universe: The Geopolitics of Iran*, Westview Press, Boulder, 1991

85 F Halliday, *Iran: Dictatorship and Development*, Penguin, London, 1978

86 GE Fuller, *The Center of the Universe: The Geopolitics of Iran*, Westview Press, Boulder, 1991

87 GR Afkhami, *The Life and Times of the Shah*, University of California Press, Berkeley, 2008

88   GE Fuller, *The Center of the Universe: The Geopolitics of Iran*, Westview Press, Boulder, 1991

89   http://iranian.com/main/blog/darius-kadivar/new-deal-shah-explains-great-civilization-during-press-conference-1971-0.html

90   C Coughlin, *Khomeini's Ghost*, MacMillan, London, 2009

91   GR Afkhami, *The Life and Times of the Shah*, University of California Press, Berkeley, 2008

92   T Fatah, *Chasing a Mirage*, John Wiley & Sons Canada, Mississauga, 2008

93   T El Hibri, *Parable and Politics in Early Islamic History*, Columbia University Press, New York, 2010

94   LN Takim, *The Heirs of the Prophet*, State University of New York Press, 2007

95   T Fatah, *Chasing a Mirage*, John Wiley & Sons Canada, Mississauga, 2008

96   A Parsons, *The Pride and the Fall*, Jonathan Cape, London, 1984

97   GR Afkhami, *The Life and Times of the Shah*, University of California Press, Berkeley, 2008

98   M Axworthy, *Iran: Empire of the Mind*, Penguin, London, 2008

99   GR Afkhami, *The Life and Times of the Shah*, University of California Press, Berkeley, 2008

100   JA Bill, *The Eagle and the Lion: The Tragedy of American-Iranian Relations*, Yale University Press, New Haven, 1989

101   GR Afkhami, *The Life and Times of the Shah*, University of California Press, Berkeley, 2008

102   M Axworthy, *Iran: Empire of the Mind*, Penguin, London, 2008

103   M Downes, *Iran's Unresolved Revolution*, Ashgate, Farnham, 2002; M Axworthy, *Iran: Empire of the Mind*, Penguin, London, 2008

104   W Blum, *Killing Hope*, Black Rose Books, Montreal, 2000

105   E Abrahamian, *Iran Between Two Revolutions*, Princeton University Press, Princeton, 1982

106   C Coughlin, *Khomeini's Ghost*, MacMillan, London, 2009

[107]   W Blum, *Killing Hope*, Black Rose Books, Montreal, 2000

[108]   C Coughlin, *Khomeini's Ghost*, MacMillan, London, 2009

[109]   N Chomsky and ES Herman, *Manufacturing Consent: The Political Economy of the Mass Media*, Pantheon Books, New York, 1988

[110]   RMM Khomeini quoted in V Martin, *Creating an Islamic State: Khomeini and the Making of a New Iran*, IB Taurus, London, 2003

[111]   C Coughlin, *Khomeini's Ghost*, MacMillan, London, 2009

[112]   E Abrahamian, *Khomeinism*, IB Taurus, London, 1993

[113]   GR Afkhami, *The Life and Times of the Shah* University of California Press, Berkeley, 2008

[114]   C Coughlin, *Khomeini's Ghost*, MacMillan, London, 2009

[115]   RMM Khomeini quoted in C Coughlin, *Khomeini's Ghost*, MacMillan, London, 2009; M Ganji, *Defying the Iranian Revolution*, Praeger, Westport, 2002

[116]   R Alvandi, "Muhammed Reza Pahlavi and the Bahrain Question 1968–1970," *British Journal of Middle Eastern Studies*, London, 2010

[117]   GR Afkhami, *The Life and Times of the Shah*, University of California Press, Berkeley, 2008

[118]   *Ibid.*

[119]   E Abrahamian, *Khomeinism*, IB Taurus, London, 1993

[120]   RMM Khomeini quoted in C Coughlin, *Khomeini's Ghost*, MacMillan, London, 2009

[121]   GR Afkhami, *The Life and Times of the Shah*, University of California Press, Berkeley, 2008

[122]   C Coughlin, *Khomeini's Ghost*, MacMillan, London, 2009

[123]   E Abrahamian, *Khomeinism*, IB Taurus, London, 1993

[124]   M Motahheri, "Objectives of the Islamic Revolution," DH Albert, *Tell the American People: Perspectives on the Iranian Revolution*, Movement for a New Society, Philadelphia, 1980

[125]   N Alavi, *We Are Iran*, Portobello, London, 2004

126   *Ibid.*

127   AA Moghaddam, *Iran in World Politics*, Columbia University Press, New York, 2008

128   E Abrahamian, *Khomeinism*, IB Taurus, London, 1993; T Fatah, *Chasing a Mirage*, John Wiley & Sons Canada, Mississauga, 2008

129   GR Afkhami, *The Life and Times of the Shah*, University of California Press, Berkeley, 2008

130   M Axworthy, *Iran: Empire of the Mind*, Penguin, London, 2008

131   T Fatah, *Chasing a Mirage*, John Wiley & Sons Canada, Mississauga, 2008

132   C Coughlin, *Khomeini's Ghost*, MacMillan, London, 2009

133   E Abrahamian, *Khomeinism*, IB Taurus, London, 1993

134   *Ibid.*

135   RMM Khomeini quoted in GE Fuller, *The Center of the Universe: The Geopolitics of Iran*, Westview Press, Boulder, 1991

136   C Coughlin, *Khomeini's Ghost*, MacMillan, London, 2009

137   M Panah, *The Islamic Republic and the World*, Pluto Press, London, 2007

138   E Abrahamian, *Khomeinism*, IB Taurus, London, 1993

139   M Panah, *The Islamic Republic and the World*, Pluto Press, London, 2007

140   C Coughlin, *Khomeini's Ghost*, MacMillan, London, 2009

141   GE Fuller, *The Center of the Universe: The Geopolitics of Iran*, Westview Press, Boulder, 1991

142   C Coughlin, *Khomeini's Ghost*, MacMillan, London, 2009

143   http://en.wikipedia.org/wiki/Iran–Iraq_War

144   GR Afkhami, *The Life and Times of the Shah*, University of California Press, Berkeley, 2008

145   E Abrahamian, *Khomeinism*, IB Taurus, London, 1993

146   R Aslan, *No God But God*, Random House Trade Paperbacks, New York, 2011

147   M Ganji, *Defying the Iranian Revolution*, Praeger, Westport, 2002

[148] E Abrahamian, *Khomeinism*, IB Taurus, London, 1993

[149] T El Hibri, *Parable and Politics in Early Islamic History*, Columbia University Press, New York, 2010

[150] NR Keddie, *Modern Iran*, Yale University Press, New Haven, 2006

[151] C Coughlin, *Khomeini's Ghost*, MacMillan, London, 2009

[152] V Martin, *Creating an Islamic State: Khomeini and the Making of a New Iran*, IB Taurus, London, 2003

[153] N Alavi, *We Are Iran*, Portobello, London, 2004

[154] C Coughlin, *Khomeini's Ghost*, MacMillan, London, 2009

[155] M Axworthy, *Iran: Empire of the Mind*, Penguin, London, 2008

[156] *Ibid.*

[157] E Abrahamian, *Khomeinism*, IB Taurus, London, 1993

[158] AL Rowse, *The England of Elizabeth*, Palgrave Macmillan, Basingstoke, 2003

[159] OS Franks quoted in P Darby, *British Defence Policy East of Suez 1947–1968*, Oxford University Press, London, 1973

[160] EA Wasson, *A History of Modern Britain*, Wiley-Blackwell, Chichester, 2010

[161] PS Northedge, "Britain's Place in the Changing World," M Leifer, *Constraints and Adjustments in British Foreign Policy*, George Allen & Unwin, London, 1972

[162] R Self, *British Foreign and Defence Policy Since 1945*, Palgrave Macmillan, London, 2010

[163] PJ Marshall, *The Oxford History of the British Empire: Volume II*, Oxford University Press, Oxford, 2001

[164] N Ferguson, *Empire*, Penguin Books, London, 2002

[165] R Self, *British Foreign and Defence Policy Since 1945*, Palgrave Macmillan, London, 2010

[166] *Ibid.*

[167] JK Sowden, *The German Question 1945–1973*, Crosby Lockwood Staples, St. Albans, 1975

[168] R Pearce, *Attlee's Labour Governments, 1945–1951*, Routledge, London, 1993

[169] E Bevin quoted in R Self, *British Foreign and Defence Policy Since 1945*, Palgrave Macmillan, London, 2010

[170] FS Northedge, *British Foreign Policy*, George Allen and Unwin, London, 1962

[171] *Ibid.*

[172] *Ibid.*

[173] G Goodwin, "British Foreign Policy Since 1945" in M Leifer, *Constraints and Adjustments in British Foreign Policy*, George Allen & Unwin, London, 1972

[174] DR Thorpe, *Eden: The Life and Times of Anthony Eden, First Earl of Avon, 1897–1977*, Chatto and Windus, London, 2003

[175] GK Evans, *Public Opinion on Colonial Affairs*, HMSO, London, 1948

[176] FS Northedge, *British Foreign Policy*, George Allen and Unwin, London, 1962

[177] Memorandum of Conversation by JS Sparks, 26 December 1947, cited in S Qureshi, "US Foreign Policy to Pakistan, 1947–1960: Re-Constructing Strategy, London School of Economics PhD thesis, London, 2001

[178] W Webster, *Englishness and Empire*, Oxford University Press, Oxford, 2007

[179] *Ibid.*

[180] R Stimpson quoted in W Webster, *Englishness and Empire*, Oxford University Press, Oxford, 2007

[181] CL Cooper, *The Lion's Last Roar: Suez 1956*, Harper and Row, New York, 1978

[182] R Braddon, *Suez: Splitting of a Nation*, Collins, London, 1973

[183] FS Northedge, *British Foreign Policy*, George Allen and Unwin, London, 1962

[184] A Marr, *A History of Modern Britain*, Pan Macmillan, London, 2007

[185] *Ibid.*

[186] L Johnman, "Defending the Pound: The Economics of the Suez Crisis, 1956" in A Gorst, L Johnman and WS Lucas, *Post-War Britain, 1945–1964*, Pinter Publishers, London, 1989

[187] D Carlton, *Britain and the Suez Crisis*, Basil Blackwell, Oxford, 1988

[188] *Ibid.*

[189] CL Cooper, *The Lion's Last Roar: Suez 1956*, Harper and Row, New York, 1978

[190] http://en.wikipedia.org/wiki/Anthony_Eden#cite_note-historytoday1-30

[191] CL Cooper, *The Lion's Last Roar: Suez 1956*, Harper and Row, New York, 1978

[192] *Ibid.*

[193] R Braddon, *Suez: Splitting of a Nation*, Collins, London, 1973

[194] D Carlton, *Britain and the Suez Crisis*, Basil Blackwell, Oxford, 1988

[195] *Dr. No*, Eon Productions, London, 1962

[196] J Pearson, *Sir Anthony Eden and the Suez Crisis*, Palgrave Macmillan, London, 2003

[197] D Carlton, *Britain and the Suez Crisis*, Basil Blackwell, Oxford, 1988

[198] *Ibid.*

[199] A Marr, *A History of Modern Britain*, Pan Macmillan, London, 2007

[200] AN Wilson, *Our Times*, Hutchinson, London, 2008

[201] CJ Bartlett, *A History of Postwar Britain 1945–1974*, Longman, London, 1977

[202] A Nutting, *No End of a Lesson: The Story of Suez*, Constable, London, 1967

[203] LB Pearson quoted in R Hyam, "Winds of Change: the Empire and Commonwealth" in W Kaiser and G Staerck, *British Foreign Policy 1955–64: Contracting Options*, Palgrave Macmillan, London, 2000

[204] RG Menzies, *The Measure of the Years*, Littlehampton Book Services, London, 1970

[205] L Johnman, "Defending the Pound: The Economics of the Suez Crisis, 1956" in A Gorst, L Johnman and WS Lucas, *Post-War Britain, 1945–1964*, Pinter Publishers, London, 1989

[206] *Ibid.*

[207] *Ibid.*

[208] S Schama, *A History of Britain: The Fate of Empire*, BBC, London, 2002

[209] G Goodwin, "British Foreign Policy Since 1945" in M Leifer, *Constraints and Adjustments in British Foreign Policy*, George Allen & Unwin, London, 1972

210 *Ibid.*

211 CJ Bartlett, *A History of Postwar Britain 1945–1974*, Longman, London, 1977

212 FS Northedge, *British Foreign Policy*, George Allen and Unwin, London, 1962

213 CJ Bartlett, *A History of Postwar Britain 1945–1974*, Longman, London, 1977

214 DAL Owen, "The Effect of Prime Minister Anthony Eden's Illness on Decision-making During the Suez Crisis" in *International Journal of Medicine*, Oxford University Press, June 2005

215 J Pearson, *Sir Anthony Eden and the Suez Crisis*, Palgrave Macmillan, London, 2002

216 W Webster, *Englishness and Empire: 1939–1965*, Oxford University Press, Oxford, 2007

217 *Ibid.*

218 G Goodwin, "British Foreign Policy Since 1945" in M Leifer, *Constraints and Adjustments in British Foreign Policy*, George Allen & Unwin, London, 1972

219 R Self, *British Foreign and Defence Policy since 1945*, Palgrave Macmillan, London, 2010

220 JH Wilson quoted in G Goodwin, "British Foreign Policy Since 1945" in M Leifer, *Constraints and Adjustments in British Foreign Policy*, George Allen & Unwin, London, 1972

221 http://www.totalpolitics.com/quotes/?tag=Falklands+War&count=30

222 http://www.sbs.com.au/news/article/2012/08/14/what-made-london-success

223 G Goodwin, "British Foreign Policy Since 1945" in M Leifer, *Constraints and Adjustments in British Foreign Policy*, George Allen & Unwin, London, 1972

224 M Charlton, *The Price of Victory*, BBC, London, 1983

225 G Martel, "Decolonisation after Suez," *Australian Journal of Politics and History*, 2000

226 G Goodwin, "British Foreign Policy Since 1945" in M Leifer, *Constraints and Adjustments in British Foreign Policy*, George Allen & Unwin, London, 1972

227 http://en.wikiquote.org/wiki/Charles_de_Gaulle

228 S Schama, *A History of Britain: The Fate of Empire*, BBC, London, 2002

229 *Ibid.*

230 M Leifer, *Constraints and Adjustments in British Foreign Policy*, George Allen & Unwin, London, 1972

231 J Day, "A Failure of Foreign Policy: The Case of Rhodesia" in M Leifer, *Constraints and Adjustments in British Foreign Policy*, George Allen & Unwin, London, 1972

232 http://www.americansc.org.uk/Online/Wilsonjohnson.htm

233 DK Goodwin, *Lyndon Johnson and the American Dream*, St. Martin's Press, New York, 1991

234 R Hyam, "Winds of Change: the Empire and Commonwealth" in W Kaiser and G Staerck, *British Foreign Policy 1955–64: Contracting Options*, Palgrave Macmillan, London, 2000

235 G Martel, "Decolonisation after Suez," *Australian Journal of Politics and History*, 2000

236 R Hyam, "Winds of Change: the Empire and Commonwealth" in W Kaiser and G Staerck, *British Foreign Policy 1955–64: Contracting Options*, Palgrave Macmillan, London, 2000

237 DG Acheson quoted in W Wallace and C Phillips, "Reassessing the Special Relationship," *International Affairs*, London, 2009

238 G Goodwin, "British Foreign Policy Since 1945" in M Leifer, *Constraints and Adjustments in British Foreign Policy*, George Allen & Unwin, London, 1972

CHAPTER 9

CONCLUDING REMARKS

The journey through the forest of self-identity and strategy hasn't exactly been conventional. We've been on an unusual trek, at least for a study of strategy. Normally strategy expeditions take place along tapered, linear paths within a particular single cocooned branch of the social sciences. The business strategist stays glued to business academia and its methods. The source materials tend to be other business books or research papers. The ideas tend to be those that have currency only in a business academic surrounding. Foreign policy and personal strategists parallel the same itinerary in their respective hemispheres, keeping to the straight and narrow. Such conventional approaches also don't suffer from much diversion. Nor are they interrupted by cheap witticisms. This journey of strategy, the one in this book, is different, and not only for those reasons.

Having equipped ourselves with a definition of strategy, which was to be vital in later rethinking it, we started by understanding modern philosophy and its key epistemological assumptions. Now that was unusual. It's not often that you see a strategic dialogue emanating from epistemology. From there, we cut deep into modern philosophy, which underpins an extensive range of modern scholarship, including modern strategy. We didn't "shock and awe" modern philosophy because we're not pompous, self-righteous guardians of truth and justice. But we did hit modern philosophy quite hard. It was more than a mere jab. We challenged modern philosophy on its claims to objectivity, knowledge and the truth. We also confronted it on ignoring the subject's role in making sense of its object universe. Finally, we spotlighted modern philosophy's hubris. In doing so, we undermined and weakened the foundations of modern strategy.

To bring that challenge to life, we scrutinised the works of three of the most prominent modern strategists—one from each of three genres of strategy which we focused on, being foreign policy, organisation and life strategy. And lo and behold, all three were found guilty of the very same failures that we'd identified in modern philosophy. Messrs Morgenthau, Porter and McGraw all presumed and advocated mankind's ability to be objective and neutral, ignored the subject's role in seeing and giving meaning to his reality and their approaches suffered from modern philosophy's intellectual hubris. As a result, they ignored or did not engage decades, if not centuries, of learning and insights from many fields that explore the human being and his mind. The irony of this, given the centrality of the human being to all matters strategy, was not lost on us.

From there we developed our understanding of the role of self-identity in strategy and specifically the impact of self-identity on all three steps of the strategic process. Self-identity feeds into how we make sense of where things are today, it helps develop some kind of vision or objectives for the future, and it influences the steps that take us from today to where we want to get to. The underlying premise of this was that the cognitive framework to see or understand the self, being self-identity, must also be the same or at least very similar to the framework which helps makes sense of everything beyond the self. And lest the centrality of self-identity to strategic decision-making needed reenforcing, we explored the power of self-identity, a power that is strong enough that it frequently takes countries to war and individuals to suicide.

And finally, to illustrate the conceptual framework, we meandered through a total of nine real examples, spread evenly across the three genres of strategy. After all, there'd be something amiss if we left things hanging without practical examples to elucidate our points. Islamist Ed Husain, Disneyland and "Great" Britain were just some of the case studies that brought to life different aspects of self-identity and its influence on each of the three steps of the strategic process. Time and again—and without reducing strategy or human behaviour to self-identity as a means to simplify the message, generate book sales or encourage followership—we could see self-identity's powerful role. We could see that self-identity impacted our making sense of the strategic today, of our vision ahead and the steps to get from today to the future.

What Does It All Mean?

It, referring to the role of self-identity in strategy, of course in and of itself means both nothing and everything, since meaning is imposed and doesn't come from within the conceptual relationship. Having corrected myself, what meaning then do I give to the relationship between self-identity and strategy? What do I think is important about this? I guess one piece that I'll mention almost as an aside, not about the relationship per se but from the earlier chapters, is that modern disciplines, those based on modern philosophy, would benefit from greater intellectual humility. Not only do we as mankind not know half as much as we would like to think we do, but if some of these intellectual disciplines are to accelerate their learning from the mere incremental to leaps and bounds, then a healthy dose of humility will be no bad thing. In fact, lack of certainty might enable us to even become better human beings, forcing us to listen more carefully and act more sensitively. There is a depressing familiarity to the extreme certainty that has accompanied much of the world's most notorious mass butchery, elements of which can be traced to modern philosophy.

That point made, the first meaning that I impose on the relationship between self-identity and strategy is that our self-identities are quite important. Actually, they're very important. They're not something that one merely sprinkles on as an afterthought. They're not some high-definition gloss that is purely nice to look at or a tactical component to be sliced and diced by PR firms. They're not something that you fix with a new haircut or a trip to the manicurist. Self-identities make a difference to individuals, organisations and countries. And what's more, we generally have grossly underappreciated the difference that they can make. We've been blind to that impact. It's not just in the strategic space that we've ignored the impact of self-identity but in a broader, more holistic sense.

For a start, self-identities give us a sense of who we are and where we are going. In doing so, they and their associated narratives give us purpose and meaning. This point shouldn't be neglected given how many of us search for meaning and purpose in our daily living and working existence. If anything, self-identity's meaning-making function will become more appreciated in the future in societies that confront the onslaught of late modernity's fragmentation, chaos and fluidity. Social theorists have long talked about the impact of our growing reliance on systems, our increasing challenge of authority and the proliferation of information technology. The West, with its explosion of media diversity and bent-against-authority traits, will become especially sensitive to the importance of self-identity and narrative. Irrespective of where we live, we will all become more reliant on self-identity to stabilise us and give our lives meaning.

A second meaning that I want to apply is that defined and strong self-identities enable faster and cleaner decision-making. There are costs to delayed or protracted decision-making, and these are frequently unaccounted for and thus ignored. Clear and aligned self-identities enable individuals and groups to see the world more sharply, more consistently and with a clearer sense of where decisions have to take them in the future. This enables faster decision-making. It took the Dubai government a mere five years to conceive and build its first metro line in 2009. Millions of businesses and ordinary folk have benefitted from this and the subsequent forty-four train stations. Such decision-making reflects a defined self-identity, which Dubai has. Dubai, in fact, has a very powerful sense of itself and where it wants to get to in the future.

In contrast, Toronto's government had shifted little since 2007 beyond masses of paper on the Scarborough extension of the Toronto Transit Commission. Tonnes of paper have been printed, bound and shelved, again and again. There has been no progress on this or in managing the city's excruciating public transport issues. And now Toronto's average daily commute at thirty-two minutes is the longest of any of Canada's big cities.[1] Indeed, the rush hour leaving the city to the suburbs now typically starts before 3 pm, and that's on days without any snowfall! Slow decision-making, which is a product of a fractured and diluted government self-identity, has cost millions of people in Toronto both time and money. Underlying this is that the government of the City of Toronto simply has little sense of what it is about, its own self-identity, a problem which wasn't helped in 2013–2014 by the antics of its former mayor, Rob Ford.

My final point is that self-identities have a profound impact on where we end up. Ed Husain's was a terrific example of the impact of a bad self-identity. It impacted his today, tomorrow and strategy. And that impact was not only comprehensive, but it also was very rapid. Self-identity ultimately influences whether we succeed or fail, whether we end up in a good or bad place—hardly surprising given self-identity influences how one sees the world, one's vision ahead and also the means and tactics to getting from start to end. And I think it's important to stress that where we end up isn't simply a function of our vision or vague sense of what we're trying to be at some later date, but given the interconnectedness, also a function of how we see the start point and also the strategy which we deploy.

Taking the above thoughts, there are different, more nuanced takeaways which flow upon specifically the individual, organisation and country from self-identity's impact on strategy. Some themes are consistent to all three buckets, and it's worth laying them out a little before we touch upon material specific to each of the three genres. The first common consequence is that we as individuals, groups and countries need to actively manage our self-identity, as opposed to letting it passively meander. We do need to think about who we think we are. We need to play the idea around a bit. Given that self-identity is important and has a significant impact on the individual, organisation and country, it's no surprise that we should manage our self-identity and give the concept some thought.

Individuals, organisations and countries need to dedicate time, energy and resources to think about their self-identities and how they are manifested in their daily and long-term lives. The exact exercises to facilitate that thinking will, of course, vary amongst the three categories, since you can't expect a person to flesh out their self-identity in the same way that you might expect a country to do so. You can't expect the same resources or processes to effect changes in self-identity either. That said, the importance of self-identity doesn't waiver. And, in fact, merely being sensitive to the relationship between self-identity and strategy is in itself a significant step and possibly the most important, because the universe begins to look very differently with that sensitivity and self-awareness in place.

Managing self-identity poses challenges, as you'd expect, since the mind can't easily be hoodwinked into believing things about the self that are either not credible or completely unsubstantiated. This leads me to the second consequence, being the need for credible self-identities that can be sustained. That's not to say that we can't find incredible self-identities. Individuals, organisations and countries sometimes, or even frequently, genuinely believe stuff about themselves, about who they are, which is so misaligned with any sane perspective of the underlying reality that an outsider would struggle to understand. For example, apartheid South Africa frequently self-identified as a naturally "just" political system.[2] That's hard to get our heads around. But those self-identities are still, and this is the important point, credible to those who adopt them.

I don't know which type of entity has an easier task of managing a self-identity. Organisations and countries often have greater resources (money, time and staff) than do individuals and can take advantage of group-think vulnerabilities where influencing a few people can easily end up as influencing many more. That said, in effecting self-identity they may also find it harder to shy away from nice opportunities that aren't part of "who we are." In other words, businesses and governments are often exposed to more opportunities, which makes it harder to keep to the self-identity that they want to embrace. Either way, convincing the self, organisation or country of a specific self-identity, which is partly a figment of the imagination, requires thought, persistence and delicate management. It is, after all, a contest between convincing one's own mind against those of many. And that's hard, especially when future events inevitably throw curve balls and challenges that then need to be integrated into the existing narrative.

Think for a moment of the current Syrian civil war, which began in the spring of 2011 and has led to more than a hundred thousand deaths, about seven million people being displaced and the use of chemical weapons on several occasions in 2013.[3] I'm not suggesting that the right thing for the country that most fiercely self-identifies as the leader of the free world and redeemer of mankind is to lead a meaningful response to the bloodbath, but the crisis nevertheless does pose an acute challenge to the US. If Washington really is on a God-given mission to save the world and fight the bad guys, the question can be asked as to why it is doing little more than having seemingly pointless discussions at the UN? America's self-identity itself generates a pressure on its foreign policy which, at the time of my writing, it is forced to navigate against its wanting to avoid getting sucked into yet another Middle Eastern war.

A final common consequence to all three genres is aimed at those who want to help a country, organisation or person's self-identity. In short, there needs to be a relationship of intimate-level trust between those who are working on and helping with somebody's or some group's self-identity. I am referring to the relationship between consultants, therapists and experts and those whose self-identity is being worked upon. How we see ourselves is a sensitive space. It demands extreme care and delicate manoeuvring. That doesn't mean presenting everything with icing and chocolate sprinkles, though, because tough messages are sometimes necessary. But effective timing, content and delivery of those messages must coexist with trust, and that's a critical ingredient for those who want to help people better engage their self-identity.

Delving down a tier into some specific consequences for each of the three genres, at the level of the individual, there's a particular responsibility amongst parents, teachers and anybody else closely interacting with individual children to develop positive and productive self-identities. Our appreciation of the value of self-identity should influence the way we go about raising children if we want them to be happy and well-adjusted kids. Getting self-identities right at an early stage of human development can help prevent later misery and frustration. There's a lot that goes into this, including reminding children that they're loved, injecting in them the idea that they are human beings from which they and everybody else has innate worth and explaining that they can't be great at everything but they can be great at something.

There are also consequences when dealing with more mature individuals. Therapists, physicians and counsellors need to integrate self-identity into their daily work and specifically filter patient or client issues through the lens of self-identity. Recognising the power of self-identity on human behaviour will encourage the embracing of self-identity as a driver and filter. While we are gradually moving away from a world that reduces all illness to mere biochemical reactions, it's important that practitioners delve into self-identity as an important part of the world that we are moving towards.[4] Drug addiction, obesity and diabetes are amongst many illnesses that can be seen as outward manifestations of underlying issues of self-identity, which can in turn also be a source for their panaceas.

The same can be said of our approach to social or community welfare and prisons—integrating sensitivity towards the self-identity of individuals will go some way towards preventing people from committing criminal offences and offenders from repeating.[5] In its study of the London riots in 2011, the Economic and Social Research Council cited discrimination against the young, the intergenerational gap and a lack of control or influence felt by younger Britons as underlying causes of the riots. What it failed to do was to imagine the link between all that and any underlying issues of self-identity.[6] That blind spot needs to be challenged. I can't be the only person on the planet to intuitively link hooliganism and vandalism to a lack of self-worth and poor self-identity.

Amongst consequences for organisations, one is that senior

management needs to actively define an organisation's self-identity, including developing that self-identity, sharing it across management so that those in an executive role are on the same page, and then communicating it to rank and file. That organisations often dedicate extensive resources to branding and very few resources, if any, to self-identity despite the latter's impact suggests that organisations are ignoring a big opportunity to energise and focus their organisations. It's not without reason that many people who lead or think about organisations will have either heard or given the advice that an entrepreneur or business should have a targeted focus, to know what they are and what they are not about; in other words, to define their self-identity.

An organisation should get a handle on its self-identity because if it can't tightly self-identify, it will struggle to know what its universe is about, where it's going and how it will get there. This set of problems is becoming increasingly apparent in American politics and especially in Congress. Not only have cross-party human relationships taken a hammering in recent decades; America's traditional self-identity and its meanings are also gradually fracturing. Decision-makers share a less common understanding of America's world as-is or its future. Decisions become slower, with all the associated unrecorded costs of what might have been. Strategies, tactics and programmes then generate tensions and frustrations, because those decision-makers see different start and end points and practically talk past each other. Things do eventually get done—but more slowly, painfully and in diluted fashion than if everybody shared a common self-identity.

Any such defined organisational self-identity needs, of course, to be real. It needs to stand up in the face of consequential decisions. It can't be a mere cheap logo. If an organisation self-identifies as a people developer, it needs to dedicate significant resources to that or prioritise that against more traditional targets of revenues or earnings. If it sees itself as a lender to big firms, it needs to hesitate about profitable opportunities in trading gold. If it sees itself as an environmentally clean business, it has to potentially pay more for green materials, supplies or even infrastructure. The point is that effecting any meaningful self-identity, putting aside its potential benefits, has costs that typically involve dollars and cents, at least in the short term. Without such trade-off, any self-identity is vulnerable to a loss of credibility, which in turn engenders cynicism and does nothing for productivity.

In touching upon some of the consequences for a country, public policy makers, both focused on domestic and foreign issues, need to develop positive self-identities and narratives for their populations to embrace. A destructive and fragmented self-identity and narrative, one, for instance, which revolves around victimhood, will absolutely struggle to deliver success. I could mention Pakistan but what's the point in beating a dead horse? In contrast, a tight national self-identity that embraces hope and a can-do spirit with clearly defined narratives, which we today see in other countries in Asia, including especially the ministates of Singapore and Dubai, tilts the dice heavily in favour of a virtuous circle. I think these two ministates will do rather well in the twenty-first century because they have strong, positive self-identities.

In fact, one reason why the twenty-first century may well be Asian is that many Asian countries have that positive national self-identity and narrative, which the West increasingly seems to lack.[7] And with that self-identity, many Asian countries not only have a sharper handle of the present, of the way things are today, but they have a richer and more compelling vision. Indeed, it's hard to not notice the role of the future in much of Asia's developmental and political discussion today. The staggering development of places such as Dubai and Singapore has practically no comparable in the West. Britain's Milton Keynes simply doesn't cut it, nor does Canada's Oshawa. Yes,

abundant room to further research this foundation block. What, if any, are the differences between the internal and external application of that cognitive framework? When is the internal and external application of self-identity as a cognitive framework most aligned? And when does it most differ?

I do think we need to rethink strategy. I do think that we've shown up the modern strategy industry. And I do think that we've taken several strides in the right direction by laying out self-identity's influence on the strategic process, by positioning self-identity as the prime strategic directive. That said, the journey of strategy is not complete. I look forward to seeing how this book motivates and prompts others to rethink the strategy universe.

[1] http://www.thestar.com/news/city_hall/2012/10/10/antigridlock_campaign_how_would_you_spend_an_extra_32_minutes_a_day.html

[2] L Thompson, *A History of South Africa*, Yale Nota Bene, New Haven, 2000

[3] http://www.politico.com/story/2013/09/united-nations-7-million-syrians-displaced-by-civil-war-96150.html

[4] RJ Contrada and RD Ashmore, *Self, Social Identity and Physical Health*, Oxford University Press, New York, 1999

[5] AP Goldstein, *The Psychology of Vandalism*, Plenum Press, New York, 1996

[6] http://www.esrc.ac.uk/research/research-topics/security/conflict/what-led-to-the-riots.aspx

[7] SB MacDonald and J Lemco, *Asia's Rise in the 21st Century*, Praeger, Santa Barbara, 2011

[8] http://www.businessinsider.com/smartphone-and-tablet-penetration-2013-10

ILLUSTRATION CREDITS

Page 33- "The earliest strategic frameworks were religions, including Christianity." © Angelo Cavalli/Corbis, reprinted with permission.

Page 34- "Many people consider Rene Descartes's Discours de la méthode of 1637 the first text of modern philosophy." © adoc-photos/Corbis, reprinted with permission.

Page 130- "Immanuel Kant was one of the most important figures in Western philosophy, even if he thought that black people ,learned like parrots'." © The Print Collector/dpa/Corbis, reprinted with permission.

Page 131- "Ibn Sina was amongst many Islamic philosophers who shaped Western philosophy." © Bettmann/CORBIS, reprinted with permission.

Page 132- "Phil McGraw, probably the most influential life strategist of our time and a firm advocate of facts and objectivity." © Ted Soqui/Corbis, reprinted with permission.

Page 132- "Steve Jobs: "'I didn't want to be a father, so I wasn't.'" © ROBERT GALBRAITH/Reuters/Corbis, reprinted with permission.

Page 133- "Ed Husain was briefly attracted to Hizb ut Tahrir, who were amongst the most abusive and active religious groups in Britain in the 1990s." © Peter Marshall /Demotix/Demotix/Corbis, reprinted with permission.

Page 133- "Jan Morris had the courage to change her gender . . . and then later write about the transformation." © Colin McPherson/Corbis, reprinted with permission.

Page 322- "Disneyland never saw itself as an amusement park. Its self-identity has always been as a provider of happiness." © Bettmann/CORBIS, reprinted with permission.

Page 322- "Homelessness in the 1980s challenged the Port Authority of New York and New Jersey's self-identity." © Bettmann/CORBIS, reprinted with permission.

Page 323- "Gulf-based businesses often embrace two self-identities, each with powerful meanings as a private-sector firm and as a Gulf organization." © Shuli Hallak/Corbis, reprinted with permission.

Page 323- "Nehru's rejection of America's self-identity was key to Truman's tilt to Pakistan." © Bettmann/CORBIS, reprinted with permission.

Page 324- "The Israeli, British and French attack at Suez was a watershed in Britain's, great 'self-identity." © Hulton-Deutsch Collection/CORBIS, reprinted with permission.

Page 324- "Ayatollah Khomeini's view on Iran's true self-identity dramatically impacted Iranian foreign strategy." © Bettmann/CORBIS, reprinted with permission.

INDEX